Hollywood Remaking

The publisher and the University of California Press Foundation gratefully acknowledge the generous support of the Kenneth Turan and Patricia Williams Endowment Fund in American Film.

Hollywood Remaking

HOW FILM REMAKES, SEQUELS,
AND FRANCHISES SHAPE INDUSTRY
AND CULTURE

Kathleen Loock

UNIVERSITY OF CALIFORNIA PRESS

University of California Press
Oakland, California

© 2024 by Kathleen Loock

Library of Congress Cataloging-in-Publication Data

Names: Loock, Kathleen, 1981– author.
Title: Hollywood remaking : how film remakes, sequels, and franchises shape industry and culture / Kathleen Loock.
Description: Oakland, California : University of California Press, [2024] | Includes bibliographical references and index.
Identifiers: LCCN 2023038209 (print) | LCCN 2023038210 (ebook) | ISBN 9780520375765 (cloth) | ISBN 9780520375772 (paperback) | ISBN 9780520976221 (epub)
Subjects: LCSH: Film remakes—History and criticism. | Film sequels—History and criticism. | Motion picture audiences.
Classification: LCC PN1995.9.R45 L66 2024 (print) | LCC PN1995.9.R45 (ebook) | DDC 791.43/6—dc23/eng/20230909
LC record available at https://lccn.loc.gov/2023038209
LC ebook record available at https://lccn.loc.gov/2023038210

33 32 31 30 29 28 27 26 25 24
10 9 8 7 6 5 4 3 2 1

For Álvaro Ceballos Viro and our son Oscar

Contents

	List of Illustrations	ix
	List of Abbreviations	xi
	Acknowledgments	xiii
	Introduction	1
PART I	A THEORY OF HOLLYWOOD REMAKING	
1.	Making Sense of Repetition	31
2.	Hollywood's Usable Past	64
PART II	FILM REMAKES	
3.	Cinematic Pasts and Presents	101
4.	The Remake as Archive	135
PART III	SERIES, SEQUELS, AND FRANCHISES	
5.	Cinematic Seriality from "B" to "A"	161
6.	From Sequelitis to the Forever Franchise	186
	Conclusion: Rebooting the Past	221
	Notes	233
	Selected Bibliography	269
	Index	285

Illustrations

FIGURES

1. Hollywood Remaking and total US theatrical productions, 1927–2021. — 16
2. Hollywood Remaking—percentage of total US theatrical productions, 1927–2021. — 16
3. Production of remakes, series, and sequels, and other remaking formats, 1903–2021. — 17
4. Distribution of remakes, series, sequels, and other remaking formats, 1903–2021. — 18
5. The film poster for Van Sant's remake plays on the familiar narrative image of *Psycho* (1960). — 45
6. Kevin McCarthy's Miles Bennell in Don Siegel's *Invasion of the Body Snatchers* (left) reappears in Philip Kaufman's 1978 remake—still screaming "They're here! You're next!" (right). — 54
7. DVD sets assembling film remakes and other remaking forms promote repeat viewing, intertextual proficiency, and film-historical knowledge. — 57
8. "Who's Batman to you?"—Mac's (Seth Rogen) superhero talk with Teddy (Zac Efron) is not only about taste but also about time-bound media experiences and generational belonging. — 65
9. Judy, Peter, Alan, and Karen form an unlikely, all-white family in *Jumanji* (1995). The characters in *Jumanji: Welcome to the Jungle* (2017) are more diverse and appeal to younger, global audiences. — 74

x   LIST OF ILLUSTRATIONS

10. Erin (Kristen Wiig) visits Abby (Melissa McCarthy) and Holtzmann (Kate McKinnon) in the Paranormal Studies Lab and reads an online comment. With the joke, *Ghostbusters: Answer the Call* (2016) also calls out the hostile fan reactions surrounding the production of the movie.   79

11. MGM's promotional campaign for the talker remake of *Anna Christie* (1930) centered on the simple slogan "Garbo Talks!"   108

12. This contest in the fan magazine *Screenland*, emphasized Ramon Novarro's voice and musical talent. It asked readers to pick a movie Novarro should remake as a sound film.   110

13. Production of film remakes, 1928–1942.   115

14. For fan magazines, the release of talker remakes presented an opportunity to revisit the cinematic past.   126

15. Fan magazines advertised both the timelessness of a story and the timeliness of the talker remake.   130

16. Production of film remakes, 1940–2021.   138

17. "One more look" is a recurring line in the multiple versions of *A Star Is Born*.   142

18. Production of film remakes and series, 1930–1960.   168

19. The series' signature title card promises that James Bond will have a future.   180

20. Production of sequels, 1970–2021.   194

21. *Back to the Future Part II* (1989) mocks Hollywood's seemingly unlimited potential for self-renewal.   203

22. *Star Wars: The Force Awakens* (2015) is nostalgic about the franchise past.   210

23. *Blade Runner 2049* (2017) juxtaposes old and young, original and copy.   215

24. Production of crossovers, spin-offs, and prequels, 1998–2021.   225

TABLE

1. DVD titles released under the "Double Take: Original & Remake" label.   55

Abbreviations

AMPAS	Margaret Herrick Library, Academy of Motion Picture Arts and Sciences, Los Angeles
LOC	Library of Congress, Moving Image Section, Washington, D.C.
MHDL	Media History Digital Library (https://mediahistoryproject.org/)
NYPL	New York Public Library for the Performing Arts, New York

Acknowledgments

It is sometimes hard for me to believe that I managed to write this book. As one of the so-called "Wendekinder," the generation born between 1975 and 1985 in the GDR, I had a unique upbringing that spanned two very different political and cultural systems. Following German reunification in 1990, my life (like that of many other East Germans) was marked by radical changes that affected every aspect of society. However, it was not until I reached adulthood and had already spent time living abroad and settled in a West German university town that I realized that my cultural experiences were different from those of my West German friends or my friends from the United States, Spain, France, and the UK. I had not watched the movies that they all seemed to share as common points of reference and childhood memories. I embarked on a game of catch-up on American popular culture, binge-watching two *Star Wars* trilogies with a friend, who explained every detail to me, for instance. When I began to pursue an academic career, my East German biography influenced my research interests in the field of American studies. Specifically, I focused on immigrant experiences, cultural memory, and the role of popular culture in shaping generational identities. But it was not until I wrote this book that I began to understand how all of this was connected. *Hollywood Remaking* made me think in so many ways and it taught me a lot about myself. I want to thank everyone who was involved in making this book possible.

First and foremost, I need to thank the German Research Foundation (DFG) and the German Academic Exchange Service (DAAD), as well as the Dahlem Research School and the Graduate School of North American Studies at Freie Universität Berlin. Without their generous funding of my positions and research stays as well as my attendance and organization of conferences and workshops at different moments during this project, this book would not have seen the light of day. *Hollywood Remaking* would not exist without my research stays at the Margaret Herrick Library, the Library of Congress, and the New York Public Library. I owe thanks to the librarians and archivists for their invaluable assistance. And the publication of this book by the University of California Press would not have happened without Raina Polivka, who was convinced of this book's worth and helped make it a reality. It was a pleasure to work with her.

Most influential for this entire undertaking was the Popular Seriality Research Unit (2010–2016), of which I was a member, and which shaped my understanding of Hollywood remaking in terms of seriality. The research unit owes much of its success to the visionary leadership of Frank Kelleter, who served as its director and was instrumental in setting up its theoretical framework. His boundless intellect and expansive knowledge have profoundly influenced every aspect of this book, far beyond what I can express in this acknowledgment. I am deeply grateful for his unwavering enthusiasm about researching film remakes, sequels, and franchises together with me in the context of the research unit (2013–2016), and for his ongoing support of the project that finally took the shape of this book. His intellectual curiosity has been a constant source of inspiration and motivation for me, and I consider myself fortunate to have had the opportunity to work with and learn from him.

In addition, I want to extend my thanks to the members of the Popular Seriality Research Unit. Their collective efforts and expertise have provided a supportive and intellectually stimulating environment for me to develop my ideas and explore new avenues of inquiry. I am indebted to each and every member for their invaluable feedback. In particular, I want to mention Ilka Brasch, Felix Brinker, Shane Denson, Christine Hämmerling, Ruth Mayer, Christina Meyer, Bettina Soller, Daniel Stein, Andreas Sudmann, and Maria Sulimma, whose work I found extremely inspiring in ways that expanded and shaped my own thinking. Among the associated members of the Research Unit, this is also true for Jason Mittell, as well as Sean O'Sullivan, Robyn Warhol, and Jared Gardner from the Ohio State University's Project Narrative. I am grateful for this academic community and value the friendships that have come from it.

I have also found my people in the budding remake studies community. Their influence on my own work within the field shines through on every page of this book. Particularly, I want to thank Constantine Verevis for his gracious hospitality during my time as a visiting scholar at Monash University and for being a wonderful colleague and friend over all these years. His research on film remakes has been crucial for developing my own approach. I also learned from Iain Robert Smith, Agnieszka Rasmus, Jennifer Forrest, Daniel Herbert, and Eduard Cuelenaere, whose work has accompanied me during the process of writing this book and who provided important feedback and insightful conversations at a number of conferences and workshops. I am glad that we share the passion for studying film remakes, sequels, and franchises.

A significant chapter of this project and my academic career more generally was my stay at the Department of Communication Arts at the University of Wisconsin–Madison, from October 2016 through September 2017. During this period not only was my academic work enriched through inspiring conversations with Eric Hoyt and Derek Johnson, but I also benefitted greatly from spending time with the brilliant Jonathan Gray, who became a dear friend and whose comments on and suggestions for the manuscript of this book I value more than words can say. They have made this a better book than I could ever have hoped for.

Since I have presented my research on various occasions, I want to thank especially the following people, who have given me the opportunity to do so: Shane Denson at Stanford University, Sean O'Sullivan and Project Narrative at the Ohio State University, Rob King and Jane Gaines at Columbia University, and He Chengzhou at Nanjing University. The research colloquium at the University of Hannover, where I have recently taken up a position as professor of American studies and media studies, has not only welcomed me with open arms during the COVID-19 pandemic but has provided encouraging feedback on my work and valued me as a new colleague. I am thrilled to have found my place here with Ilka Brasch, Felix Brinker, Abigail Fagan, Florian Groß, Hanna Masslich, and

Anna-Lena Oldehus. I am also thankful for the help of my student assistants Lida Shams-Mostofi and Alissa Lienhard. Most of all, I want to thank Ruth Mayer, who has been an incredible mentor and role model.

Throughout all these years that I have worked on *Hollywood Remaking*, Julia Leyda and Maria Sulimma have been the best friends one could wish for. Time and again, they cheered me on when I was desperately working on the next grant proposal to be able to continue working on my book. But they also reminded me to take a break and have a cocktail. I miss hanging out and watching movies with them as we did in our Berlin days.

Finally, I want to thank my family. My parents, Hans-Joachim and Doris Loock, and my sister Ilka Nicken have been extremely supportive. I am a first-generation academic, and my precarious employment situation and endless deadlines have always seemed foreign to my family. But not only have my parents and sister been proud of my achievements and understanding of the demands of my academic career, they have also gone above and beyond to support me. They have been indispensable in helping me take care of my son, Oscar, who was born during the first lockdown of the COVID-19 pandemic. Their selflessness and generosity have made all the difference in my ability to navigate the challenges of motherhood and academic life, allowing me to focus on my work and make progress toward completing my book. I am incredibly lucky to have them in my corner. And then there is Álvaro Ceballos Viro, the love of my life. Admittedly, it is sometimes difficult to coax him to the cinema to watch the latest remake or sequel with me. I get it (especially after all those years). But he is always there for me, believes in me, gives me strength, and makes me laugh. Without him, none of this would have been possible. *Te quiero mucho, mi amor.*

Portions of chapter 2 were previously published in "Making Movie Generations: On the Cultural Work of Hollywood Remaking," in *What Film Is Good For: The Ethics of Spectatorship*, ed. Julian Hanich and Martin P. Rossouw (Berkeley: University of California Press, 2023), 249–60. An earlier version of chapter 3 appeared as "Sound Memories: 'Talker Remakes,' Paratexts, and the Cinematic Past," in *The Politics of Ephemeral Digital Media: Permanence and Obsolescence in Paratexts*, ed. Sara Pesce and Paolo Noto (New York, Routledge, 2016), 123–37. Portions of chapter 6 were previously published in "The Sequel Paradox: Repetition, Innovation and Hollywood's Hit Film Formula," *Film Studies* 17 (Autumn 2017): 92–110.

Introduction

HOLLYWOOD REMAKING

"There are three things we know about the movies," Hannah Ewens wrote on *VICE.com* in March 2016. "One: Hollywood will franchise anything if it made money. Two: Hollywood does not like new things. New is scary— new writers, female directors, black directors, scripts, ad infinitum. Three (and this is possibly the most important): Remakes and sequels are never very good."[1] Ewens's article "Why Hollywood's Obsession with Remakes and Sequels Needs to Die" directly responded to news that Hollywood was working on a sequel to Tim Burton's 1988 horror comedy *Beetlejuice*. For Ewens, this was reason to take a stand against the industry's practice (or, what she provocatively calls "Hollywood's hubris")[2] of creating follow-ups to cult classics. Her conviction was that Hollywood must change its business model if the undisturbed afterlife of "untouchable originals"[3] is to be ensured. The piece is representative of contemporary attitudes among popular film critics toward movies that repeat, continue, revise, and expand an already familiar story. Writing for the *Los Angeles Times*, Justin Chang similarly vented his discontent about the fact that most of 2016's summer movies were derived from preexisting material. While bashing blockbusters like *Independence Day: Resurgence* (Roland Emmerich, 2016), *Ben-Hur* (Timur Bekmambetov, 2016), and *Ghostbusters: Answer the Call* (Paul Feig, 2016), Chang, however, remained keenly aware that "the only thing more tedious and predictable than sequels, remakes and reboots is a critic who complains about sequels, remakes and reboots."[4]

Such witty displays of outrage, frustration, and disappointment have indeed become a cliché in popular film criticism, a performance in and of itself that pits Hollywood's industrial imperatives against concepts of art, creativity, and originality. In fact, critics frequently suggest that cinema as an art form—invariably associated with the singularity of supposedly original, self-contained films that make a pretense of transcending their commercial nature—is on the verge of falling victim to Hollywood's love affair with the franchise, to the market potential of sequel-izable tentpoles, and to an all-encompassing logic of remaking. Tropes of death and destruction often permeate such assessments in popular film criticism to illustrate the pernicious effects of twice-told tales on Hollywood's cinematic output, on audiences, and on the cultural legacy of classic movies. Some critics have predicted that Hollywood's preference for brands and reluctance to invest in new ideas will eventually cause "the death of the great American art form."[5] Chang worried in 2016 that "for the regular moviegoer, this season's steady IV drip of sequelitis and overall multiplex mediocrity seemed to usher in a kind of slow spiritual death."[6] And Ewens, who describes Hollywood remaking as "destructive regurgitation" that deliberately risks "bastardizing a legacy with a follow-up" in the name of box-office success, was anxious about protecting long-dead "originals."[7] She believed that since these classics were already "preserved . . . in our collective cultural history for the rest of time, on film studies syllabuses everywhere," there was no point in reviving them as soulless, zombie-like versions of their former formidable selves.[8]

Taken together, these examples encapsulate current concerns about Hollywood remaking in popular film criticism, but they also put the spotlight on much of what is fascinating about the practice: industry trends, discursive constructions, cinematic formats, and audience appeal as it relates to both cultural memory and generational attachments to popular culture texts. These intersecting topics are at the center of this book, which seeks to challenge the categorical dismissal of Hollywood remaking in popular film criticism and, to some extent, in academic film studies by examining it as a meaningful and meaning-making cultural and industrial activity. What are the political implications of an all-female team of paranormal exterminators in the 2016 *Ghostbusters* movie? What does it mean to bring back the chariot-racing Bible epic *Ben-Hur* as a spectacle-laden action picture, or to continue *Independence Day* with a follow-up that once more hinges on the premise of an alien invasion threatening to obliterate humanity? These new versions are surely movies of and for their times, and yet they can never exist in isolation from what has come before them. They always hint back at the past, deriving their own commercial value, cultural legitimacy, and audience appeal from the retrospective relations to their respective predecessors. That these recent films invoke the memory of past renditions and conjure their aura is, in fact, the selling point and cultural capital of the new *Ghostbusters*, *Ben-Hur*, and *Independence Day: Resurgence*.

But—and herein lies the bone of contention for popular film criticism—remaking is never "a one-way process: a movement from authenticity to imitation, from the superior self-identity of the original to the debased resemblance of the copy."[9] Remaking also transforms the meanings, pop-cultural afterlives, and legacies of earlier films; and this reciprocity, in turn, triggers nostalgia for an unchanged and unchangeable past, fomenting fears that the past might be rendered moot and superseded by the present. In this regard, remakes and sequels appear to threaten a broader sense of self that was once forged in relation to the movies' predecessors. For the vast majority of popular film critics, remaking seems to register as an unwelcome irritation because it flaunts the fundamental instability of narratives—including those of the self. The underlying paradox is, of course, that remaking enables such "recognitions" (to evoke Rita Felski's meaning of the term)[10] in the first place and that the perceived instability ultimately translates into an enduring repertoire of shared media texts that play a formative role in the shaping of selfhood as well as in the construction and maintenance of communal coherence.

The complexities of remaking are routinely being obscured by current debates about the film industry's waning creativity and commercial imperatives. Hollywood's long history of making and remaking films, however, hints at long-term meaning-making processes that affect how people understand (and remember) themselves and the world in which they live in relation to the popular culture products they have come to know and love. Past attitudes toward Hollywood's penchant for recycling its properties have little in common with the overwhelming discontent that radiates from today's film reviews and journalistic think pieces, and remaking certainly never had the "deadly" effects that Justin Chang and Hannah Ewens describe. On the contrary, the reliance on familiar formulas not only ensured many film studios' continued existence in times of crisis but was also instrumental in preserving stories; in creating cinema's formal, stylistic, and generic conventions; in shaping memories and lived experiences; and in encouraging cinephilia and enduring fandoms. Rather than ushering in death, remaking has proven to extend the lives of studios, narratives, and even film as an art form through a self-perpetuating combination of repetition and renewal.

With these ideas in mind, *Hollywood Remaking* is intended as an intervention into widespread popular and academic assumptions about remaking that echo Chang's and Ewens's sentiments. It offers a detailed account of remaking's persistent presence in Hollywood cinema that is undergirded with historical statistics, industry perspectives, and popular and academic perceptions of the practice, as well as discussions of intertextuality, cultural memory, and generation theory. The aim is not to endorse Hollywood remaking but to theorize it and to complicate our understanding of a constantly evolving commercial practice that intersects with creative processes of cultural production, shifting sets of cultural values, and complex negotiations of identity. Looking beyond the general sense of annoyance at ever more remakes and sequels coming out of Hollywood, then, this book critically examines what these films *do*.

"REMAKING" AND "HOLLYWOOD" IN HOLLYWOOD REMAKING

Remaking is used both as a concept and a shorthand in this book. As a concept, remaking stands for *a medium-specific process of innovative reproduction that creates new economic and cultural value from already existing properties and that is imagined, discursively constructed, and defined by stakeholders from production and reception contexts*. Remaking is a historically dynamic process with shifting operating principles, cultural meanings, and communicative functions. As a shorthand, *remaking* never exclusively refers to the production of film remakes in the more restricted sense of the term (i.e., movies based on previous movies). Instead, remaking, as conceptualized here, describes *a process that generates different cinematic formats by repeating, modifying, and continuing past renditions in the present.* These remaking formats include film remakes proper as well as series, sequels, prequels, spin-offs, and crossovers that rely on familiar source material and already established fictional worlds in order to sustain or reboot film franchises. This is crucial because cinema's preference for repetition with a difference, for telling familiar stories as new stories, for combining the comfort of the already-seen with the thrill of the unexpected has never been reduced to film remakes alone but constitutes a much more wide-ranging phenomenon. While not doing away with cinema's well- and lesser-known categories—after all, labels like *remake*, *sequel*, or *prequel* serve to group films with similar characteristics and to activate audience expectations—this approach draws attention to the fact that boundaries are fluid and that clear distinctions between remaking formats continue to dissolve in today's media environment. The focus on just one format would limit the epistemological scope of this book, whereas a broader understanding opens productive new pathways and offers a more comprehensive (and possibly more adequate) perspective for investigating remaking's historically evolving commercial, narrative, and cultural meanings.[11]

It seems important to stress that the focus is exclusively on Hollywood cinema; more precisely: this book only examines *Hollywood films based on Hollywood films*. Although the combination of "Hollywood" and "remaking" immediately conjures up ideas of globalization, transnational flows, and cultural imperialism, the emphasis here is expressly not on Hollywood remakes of foreign films. Such transnational film remakes are exciting objects of study in their own right and have long dominated the research that is undertaken in the field of remake studies.[12] However, the business of transnational film remakes generally depends on quickly producing culturally adapted and, in the case of Hollywood, often streamlined, globally marketable English-language versions, whereas remaking follows entirely different rules within the context of national cinemas (including the US cinema that Hollywood produces). I have therefore proposed the distinction between *diachronic remaking* and *synchronic remaking* in order to adequately engage with the social function of Hollywood remaking as a mode of timekeeping and catalyst for generational identification.[13] *Diachronic remaking* describes the repeated, regular recycling of the same popular storytelling material over many decades, usually within the same national context, and *synchronic remaking* refers to the production of another, usually foreign-language, version shortly after the release of a movie. Put simply, movies that are remade time and again in the same national context *already have a past* in that national context and therefore raise other issues than transnational film remakes. Hollywood remakes of world cinema—including the French comedy *Trois hommes et un couffin* (Coline Serreau, 1985) / *Three Men and a Baby* (Leonard Nimoy, 1987), the Dutch thriller *Spoorloos* (George Sluizer, 1988) / *The Vanishing* (George Sluizer, 1993), J-horror like *Ringu* (Hideo Nakata, 1998) / *The Ring* (2002, Gore Verbinsky), the Hong Kong thriller *Infernal Affairs* (Andrew Lau / Alan Mak, 2002) / *The Departed* (Martin Scorsese, 2006), and Nordic Noir like *Man som hatar kvinnor* (Michael Nyqvist, 2009) / *The Girl with the Dragon Tattoo* (David Fincher, 2011)—pose pertinent questions about processes of cultural translation and global power dynamics. By contrast, the movies that are at the center of *Hollywood Remaking* unfold their stories over time: on the diegetic level as well as on a more abstract level of imagined collectivization, where they come to form part of *cultural memory*.

The negotiation of memory in popular culture (and film in particular) is not dependent on more or less contested representations of national traumas or historical events. Rather, popular fictional stories and characters that are not explicitly tied to a national past can, through transgenerational repetition, become elements of collectively shared experiences and thus store, circulate, and transmit cultural memories that help maintain what Benedict Anderson has called the "imagined community" of the nation.[14] If, as Marita Sturken writes, "cultural memory is a field of cultural negotiation" in which a nation's "collective desires, needs, and self-definitions ... are simultaneously established, questioned, and refigured," remaking certainly partakes in such processes.[15] US cinema is, of course, both a national *and* a global force: Hollywood dominates the global media entertainment market, and its films are therefore bound to shape the memories and lived experiences not only of domestic viewers but of audiences living outside the United States as well. Questions concerning the global flow of cinematic texts and the underlying economic, aesthetic, cultural, and political implications that drive much of the scholarship on transnational film remakes are consequently, if not the main concern, nonetheless relevant for this book, and the theory that I develop around a broad, complex, and historically evolving concept of Hollywood remaking necessarily extends beyond the national framework of the United States.

Following Mette Hjort's idea of thematic "aboutness," Ulf Hedetoft has convincingly argued that Hollywood produces a national cinema "whose taken-for-granted assumptions and common sense understandings (and occasionally explicit ideological or philosophical loyalties) are of a US origin, no matter how strongly they might parade as global plots, themes or ideas, or how effectively 'American' problems are frequently given an all-human, universalistic spin."[16] At the same time, the global consumption of Hollywood movies challenges notions of a US national cinema that can be boiled down to a fixed set of attributes and instead reframes it as an ongoing process of cultural negotiation and meaning-making in different national and local contexts.[17] As Arjun Appadurai reminds us, the flow of Hollywood movies in a global cultural economy does not automatically transform them into a destabilizing force of Americanization and cultural homogenization, but offers "new resources and new disciplines for the construction of imagined selves and imagined worlds."[18] Accumulated, long-term memories as well as sentimental attachments to certain movies, characters, storyworlds, and stars are key components in the "work of the imagination" that Appadurai describes.[19] While my primary focus is on the production and reception of Hollywood remakes, series, sequels, and long-running film franchises within the United States and on how the movies' "aboutness" is managed in successive iterations, cultural memory is a crucial tool in order to probe how remaking operates both on the national stage and in a global mediascape.[20]

My central aim is to come to terms with Hollywood remaking, to take it seriously not despite but precisely because of its commercial impulses and undeniable success with audiences, to recognize its complexity and explore the cultural work it performs. When Iain Robert Smith and Constantine Verevis call out "the Hollywood-centrism of film remake scholarship," they have a point where transnational remakes are concerned.[21] Comparative analyses of Hollywood remakes based on foreign films overwhelmingly dominate the work that is being done in this field, often distracting from other trajectories and remaking traditions. It is, however, misleading to think that the "Hollywood-centrism" Smith and Verevis identify for the scholarly research on transnational film remakes translates into substantiated knowledge about Hollywood's long-standing practice of recycling its *own* properties. "Little has been written about film remakes," Michael B. Druxman remarked in 1975.[22] Almost fifty years later, his statement still rings true when it comes to comprehensive analyses of Hollywood remaking.

It seems odd that there should still be such a research gap. Among the relatively small number of monographs and articles that exclusively focus on Hollywood, only a few provide historical accounts, and, if they do, they are not necessarily examining the cultural work of different remaking formats, or they leave key questions unanswered.[23] How has remaking developed as a commercial practice? By what strategies and patterns has it been managed and institutionalized? How is the actual number of Hollywood's remaking output related to the evolving media-ecological conditions of the film industry? To what extent have historical production trends informed the discursive constructions of remaking in the cultural arena? Has remaking always been imagined to be the destructive force today's critics claim it to be? What kinds of negotiations does it entail when popular narratives unfold over time? What is the extent of remaking's critical potential? How does the practice engage in processing social, political, and cultural change? How are remakes and sequels shaped by cinema's shifting affordances? How do these movies convey film-historical knowledge? How do they become active in the formation of generations? How do they perform cultural remembrance work? This book theorizes Hollywood remaking as a unique (and uniquely overlooked) industrial practice of cultural reproduction that perpetually generates, sustains, and renews popular media texts, whose enduring economic and cultural relevance adds up to more than Hollywood's deeply ingrained profit principle. I argue that these movies actively shape how the film industry, cinema, and audiences imagine themselves as they constantly negotiate past and present, stability and change through a *serial* dynamic of repetition and variation.

HOLLYWOOD REMAKING AND SERIALITY

Without doubt, Hollywood remaking—broadly conceptualized as an industrially driven, yet creative and culturally relevant process of innovative reproduction based on tried-and-proven material from the popular storytelling repertoire—has been and continues to be first and foremost a commercial endeavor. This observation seems shockingly obvious and yet it hardly distinguishes remakes and sequels from any other form of commercial mass entertainment in capitalist market cultures. Unlike their ostensibly more original and artistic cinematic counterparts, though, remaking's derivative movies lead a highly conspicuous commercial existence in the cultural imagination. In contrast to standalone films that claim to miraculously escape their economic conditions, remakes and sequels unapologetically appear as *"undisguised commodities."*[24] Because remaking always creates "multiplicities," to borrow a productive term from Amanda Ann Klein and R. Barton Palmer,[25] it constantly challenges culturally valued ideas of closure and self-containment and draws attention to the profit-driven business model of the film industry, which is interested in the endless generation of more movies and, hence, more money. Remaking is diametrically opposed to any claims to textual singularity and instead serves as the motor of ongoing film production. For, despite the fact that films might have initially been produced as self-contained works of art in the traditional sense, their narrative closure can always be undone, their stories reactivated by a remake or a sequel. Hollywood remaking, then, is an inherently commercial practice that shapes the past, present, and future of individual movies, which, lined up in a decades-spanning remaking chain, eventually operate as *serialized* narratives.

If seriality depends on the dialectical tension between repetition and variation and involves the task of creating something new by reproducing something already familiar with a difference, as Umberto Eco suggests,[26] Hollywood remaking can certainly be considered a serial storytelling practice. To be sure, remaking follows a possibly more haphazard, definitely slower-paced, and generally longer-lived dynamics of repetition and variation than more explicitly serialized formats in other popular media.[27] However, even though they are not released on regular daily or weekly schedules like serial narratives in newspapers or on radio and television, remakes and sequels still exhibit similar serial strategies and storytelling techniques—from episodic structures and progressing story arcs to recurrent characters and delayed narrative closure. The long, drawn-out, much less predictable serial rhythm of such films, meanwhile, affects the cultural work that remaking performs (and may explain why it has been overlooked by popular film critics and scholars for so long). Instead of offering soothing everyday routines that can counterbalance the exhausting acceleration and fragmentation of modern life, as daily cartoons, soap operas, and even complex television series are bound to do, remaking formats operate on a larger temporal scale: they structure the passage of time over many years and decades by providing economic, aesthetic, and cultural reference points that are relevant for how the film business, the medium, and, indeed, people come to recognize and position themselves within a longer historical trajectory.[28]

Seriality opens up a long-term perspective on the cultural work of remakes, series, sequels, and film franchises. It helps to understand how movies are connected to each other and paves the way for productive inquiries into how Hollywood remaking impacts the industry, shapes cinematic codes and conventions, and how it encourages generational identification and imagined collectivization. The strong emphasis on *continuity* this entails does not only—and not even necessarily—play out on the level of plot, yet it always extends beyond the sustained storyworlds and narratives that unfold on-screen. Hollywood remaking hence fulfills an orienting function because it structures time outside the fictions it presents—in economic, aesthetic, and cultural terms. Economically speaking, cinematic iterations derived from one or more already existing movies mark historical production trends and the marketability associated with certain narratives, stars, and remaking formats at a specific moment in Hollywood history. In the course of the last century, uncertainties and crises in the film industry have often occasioned the studios' recourse to presold properties as a way to reduce production time and costs and because the familiarity of already-existing material promises built-in audiences for new releases. Preferences for the remake, the sequel, or other formats of recycling have never remained stable so that the films emerging from Hollywood's remaking trends become legible as historical records of the many shifts and changes cinema has undergone in a constantly evolving media environment. The aesthetic of these films, meanwhile, forms part of a similarly time-bound framework and structures the development of cinema's medium-specific affordances (and limitations) as well as its representational standards. By remaking popular films, Hollywood essentially supports an evolutionary view of cinema as it not only repeats, continues, expands, and revises familiar stories but also inscribes a larger narrative of technological and cultural progress into successive film versions.

It is in this sense that "remaking operates as a method of *cinematic self-historicization*"[29]: individual follow-ups in a remaking chain demarcate distinct periods in film history (such as the silent and sound film era) and draw attention to cinema's prevailing visual regimes and their related technological and cultural configurations. Frank Kelleter and I have suggested that "cinema writes its own history with remakes, sequels, or prequels . . . within the evolving network of expectations, recognitions, allusions, variations, and reinterpretations that makes these iterations possible and keeps them in circulation."[30] This process necessarily involves on-screen negotiations of accepted norms and values that are embedded in changing cultural, social, and political contexts. Over time, remaking underlines both the persistence and malleability of dominant ideologies and the recurrent urge to process them in familiar scenarios. But remaking is not only intricately linked to Hollywood's economic and aesthetic history. It is also always documenting ongoing cultural debates that are inevitably inscribed, erased, and overwritten in the already-seen. Repetition (of themes, plots, and successful formulas) provides the canvas for negotiating change while it simultaneously reinforces an overall sense of continuity that helps stabilize the imagined community; that is, remaking enables communicative practices that strengthen feelings of togetherness, of belonging to one and the same collective.[31]

Underlying my approach is an acknowledgment that *remaking produces serial texts*—regardless of whether they are called remakes or sequels, or any other name. These films are never unconnected; they are serialized—sometimes only retrospectively, but always at what Frank Kelleter and I have termed "a higher level of cinematic self-observation."[32] This has two important methodological consequences for the study of Hollywood remaking. First, the peculiar seriality remaking creates suggests that what

Kelleter writes about popular series also applies to the remaking formats at the center of *Hollywood Remaking*: they "are appropriately described as active cultural institutions that consist not just of the stories they tell but also of the manifold proceedings and forces that are gathered in their acts of storytelling."[33] These movies can be understood as self-observing systems with agency of their own.[34] More precisely, remakes and sequels are parts of larger actor-networks; they belong to assemblages of individuals, institutions, technologies, and objects that shape Hollywood remaking, even enable its existence as an industrial and cultural practice in the first place. The movies in question tend to display an acute awareness of their status as remaking formats and actively participate in their own discursive constructions. Consequently, to study Hollywood remaking as a larger historical phenomenon means to trace the processes that bring such assemblages into being. In order "to reconstruct how shifting positions of commercial 'production' and 'reception' are created, maintained, and complicated through historically specific (i.e., evolving) practices of pop-cultural self-description and self-performance,"[35] I examine a variety of different materials ranging from movies to paratexts, trade papers to fan magazines, popular film criticism to scholarly works.

The movies self-reflexively negotiate the formal and narrative possibilities of remaking, which, in turn, depend as much on the content, form, and cultural meanings of earlier renditions as they depend on cinema's technological affordances, media-ecological conditions, and the place of Hollywood remaking in the cultural imagination at a given moment in film history. Paratexts such as press kits, promotional material, trailers, and posters, as well as interviews with filmmakers, producers, and actors belonging to the production context suggest how these films want to be watched, thereby shaping their pop-cultural circulation and the ways in which remaking can be imagined. While trade papers like *Variety*, *Film Daily*, and *Hollywood Reporter* primarily engage in assessing the commercial value and strategic logic of Hollywood remaking, these industry publications also coin much of the vocabulary used to discuss remaking and, hence, partake in its discursive institutionalization. Fan magazines such as *Photoplay* or *Modern Screen* play an important part in providing cinemagoers with an interpretative framework for understanding the film industry and the products it creates as well as in cultivating audience responses to Hollywood remaking (e.g., in the form of fan letters). In their role as cultural gatekeepers and tastemakers, popular film critics publish film reviews and think pieces (in the *New York Times* or *Village Voice*) that contribute to how Hollywood remaking is imagined. On the one hand, these texts feed back into the production of remakes and sequels, and, on the other hand, they impact the reception of Hollywood remaking in academic circles. Scholarly works that analyze remaking (including my own) therefore constitute another piece of the puzzle, another part of the assemblage that this book sets out to examine.

Second, that Hollywood movies are serialized at "a higher level of cinematic self-observation"[36] distinguishes them from popular series in other media. More precisely, the kind of seriality that remaking produces operates both in terms of an "evolving, recursive, proliferating, and multi-agential mode of storytelling"[37] *and* at one remove from it. Frank Kelleter and I use the term *second-order seriality* to capture how remaking creates texts that are, above all, "ongoing narratives about (and through) ongoing narratives."[38] To think of Hollywood remaking in terms of seriality, then, does not only mean to approach remakes and sequels as "moving targets," whose "designs keep shifting in perpetual interaction with what they set in motion"[39] and to consider remaking as a practice that is itself constantly produced and reproduced by different forces at work in what can best be described and analyzed as actor-networks. In addition, the concept of second-order seriality introduces yet another layer of meaning that helps to understand the long-term cultural work that remaking performs through the repetition and unfolding of familiar narratives. The recognition that remaking showcases the temporalities by which we live (as a mode of timekeeping); a diffuse desire (or: compulsion) for narrative, economic, aesthetic, and cultural continuation; and, not least, Hollywood's own self-reflexive historicity comes in tow with new impulses for remake scholarship and, indeed, the necessity to take remakes and sequels seriously as temporal markers, stabilizing agents, and sites of film-historical memory and knowledge production.

With the concept of second-order seriality the study of Hollywood remaking reaches a threshold beyond which more complex questions become possible to ask and address—about the longevity of certain popular narratives and how their repeated retellings in changing social, political, and cultural contexts impact memory and identity. On the diegetic level, remakes and sequels *remember* earlier versions of themselves (through the restaging of iconic scenes, flashbacks, cameo appearances, etc.) and self-reflexively comment on the conditions of their own existence as follow-up to their respective predecessors. This *intertextual memory* serves to render the movies' own past visible (and relevant) for audiences and is often supported by paratexts, journalistic writing, and academic articles that draw attention to the movies' intertextual connections. But, more importantly, I contend that Hollywood remaking also mediates the past in a more abstract sense. To be sure, what I call *extratextual memory* is generally not related to the "memory-making fictions"[40] involving historical subject matter that Hollywood produces in cinematic renderings of World War II, as in *Saving Private Ryan* (Steven Spielberg, 1998), or of the civil rights movement in the United States, in films like *Selma* (Ava DuVernay, 2014). Nor am I concerned with movies like *Memento* (Christopher Nolan, 2000) that are about memory itself, in Hollywood's explicit fascination with its own past in works such as *Singin' in the Rain* (Stanley Donen and Gene Kelly, 1952), *The Last Picture Show* (Peter Bogdanovich, 1971), and *Pulp Fiction* (Quentin Tarantino, 1993), or in "genre memory" and the peculiar mode of pastiche that defines *American Graffiti* (George Lucas, 1973), *Star Wars* (George Lucas, 1977), and *Raiders of the Lost Ark* (Steven Spielberg, 1981).[41] Instead, extratextual memory describes how remaking always draws attention to cinema's shifting affordances and how any reworking of familiar fare carries meanings that reach beyond narrative, plot, and formal structures to a specific media-historical and cultural moment with which the film is henceforth associated and in which it is forever recalled. By triggering memories of previous movies and their particular production and reception contexts, remaking "encourages communities of knowledge and belonging"[42] and is bound up in the complex processes of individual, cultural, and national identity formation this book seeks to investigate. The point of departure is a statistical survey of Hollywood remaking that allows us to identify historical production trends for film remakes, series, and sequels in the twentieth and twenty-first centuries that can then be further explored and matched against the ways in which the practice has been discursively constructed, imagined, and defined over time.

HISTORICAL PRODUCTION TRENDS: HOLLYWOOD REMAKING BY THE NUMBERS

Hollywood remaking has been a staple of cinema since its inception. A number of scholars have already made this claim, often with the film remake in mind. It is meant as a corrective with regard to popular criticism that routinely treats remaking as characteristic of today's mediascape. At the same time, it serves to uncouple remaking from these negative popular discourses and position it as a legitimate object of study. Even so, these observations are seldom backed by empirical evidence, which is why we still know astonishingly little about the production of film remakes, series, and sequels and how it has evolved over time. My Hollywood Remaking dataset, while unlikely to be complete, lists more than 6,500 remakes, sequels, series films, prequels, spin-offs, and crossovers that were produced in the United States between 1896 and 2021. I have compiled the data using reference guides and various other sources.[43] And, while it will certainly not be the last word on the subject, the dataset constitutes a reasonably comprehensive basis for informed statistical observations about historical industry trends and provides an overall more accurate impression of how Hollywood's film production has developed over the past 125 years. Curating the dataset has revealed the challenge of distinguishing between different types of movies (film remake, series film, sequel, prequel, spin-off, and crossover), as the boundaries between them are frequently blurred. At the same time, it has confirmed the necessity to understand all of these categories as belonging to one and the same dynamic practice of cultural reproduction that I call Hollywood remaking.

By situating Hollywood remaking in the larger context of US film production, it is possible to observe that film remakes, sequels, series, and other movies based on already-existing movies have always been a regular feature on Hollywood's production slate. Between 1927 and 2021, there are remaking peaks in the 1930s and 1940s, followed by a significantly lower output since the 1950s. However, the overall remaking numbers vary much less over time than the total number of US productions (figure 1). According to the statistical breakdown, the percentage of film remakes, series, and sequels in relation to the total number of US productions is as high as 30 percent in 1940 and as low as 3 percent in 1928 and in the

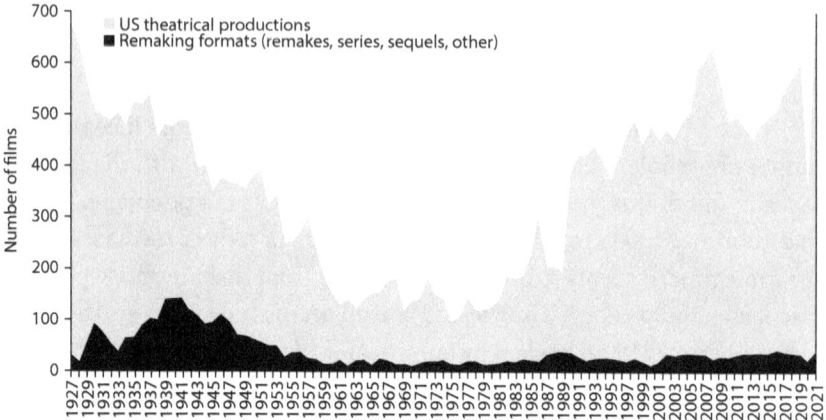

Figure 1. Hollywood Remaking and total US theatrical productions, 1927–2021. *Source*: Hollywood Remaking dataset.

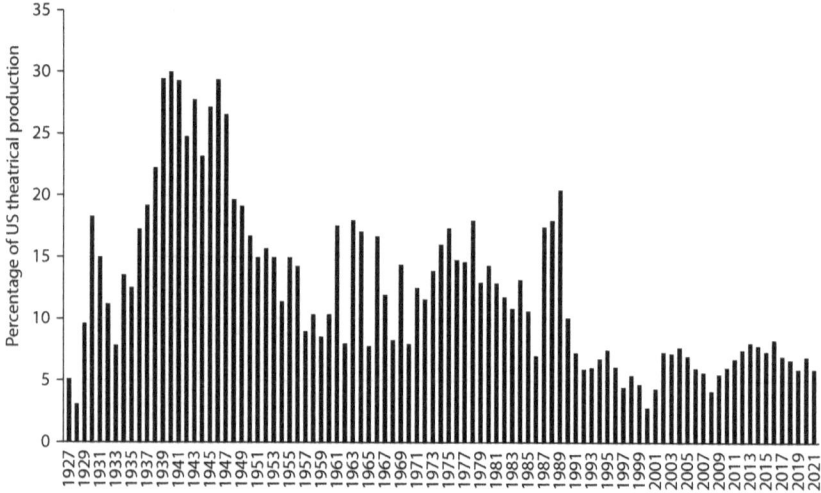

Figure 2. Hollywood Remaking—percentage of total US theatrical productions, 1927–2021. *Source*: Hollywood Remaking dataset.

year 2000 (figure 2). The graph also shows a decrease of remaking formats after the 1940s, a decade when it still averaged 26 percent of total production, to 13 percent on average between 1950 and 1989, and to only 7 percent on average since 1990. Such proportions refute the widely accepted assumption in both academic and journalistic publications that

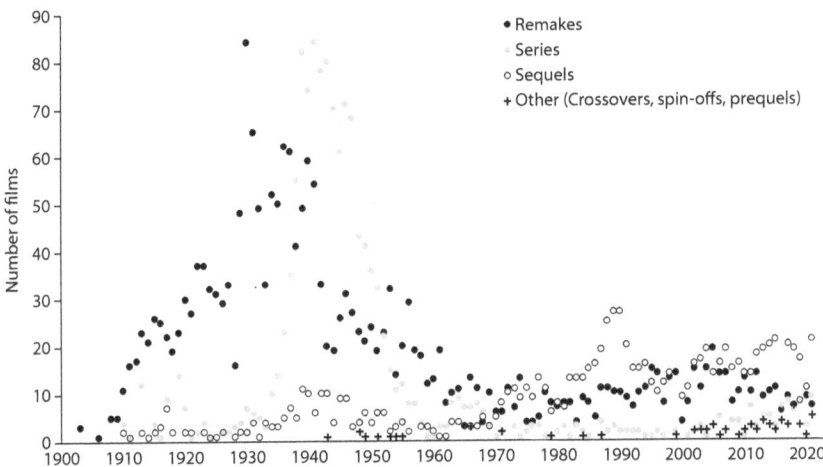

Figure 3. Production of remakes, series, and sequels, and other remaking forms, 1903–2021. *Source*: Hollywood Remaking dataset.

Hollywood remaking is, above all, a contemporary phenomenon. Both the numbers and percentages tell very different stories and firmly locate the heyday of remaking in the past.

The graph can be broken down into film remakes, series, and sequels, in addition to the overall fewer prequels, spin-offs, and crossovers (here subsumed under "other"). This allows us to identify clear peaks and lows that show how industry trends have shifted over more than a century (figure 3). Across the entire time period, the film remake and series constitute the two leading remaking formats, reaching up to eighty-four remakes in the year 1930 and eighty-four series films in 1941. Both formats dominate production in the 1930s and 1940s, before the numbers drop significantly and the sequel rises to prominence in the 1970s. The sequel reaches a first (if much lower) peak at the end of the 1980s, when twenty-seven sequels were released in 1989 and 1990, respectively, and again in the 2010s, when 2016 saw the production of twenty-six sequels. For comparison: only two sequels were released in 1930 and six in 1941, whereas 1990 held only ten remakes and two series films in store; and 2016 has only six remakes and seven series films to show for.

Considering how the distinct remaking formats develop proportionately (figure 4), the film remake stands out as relatively stable over time.

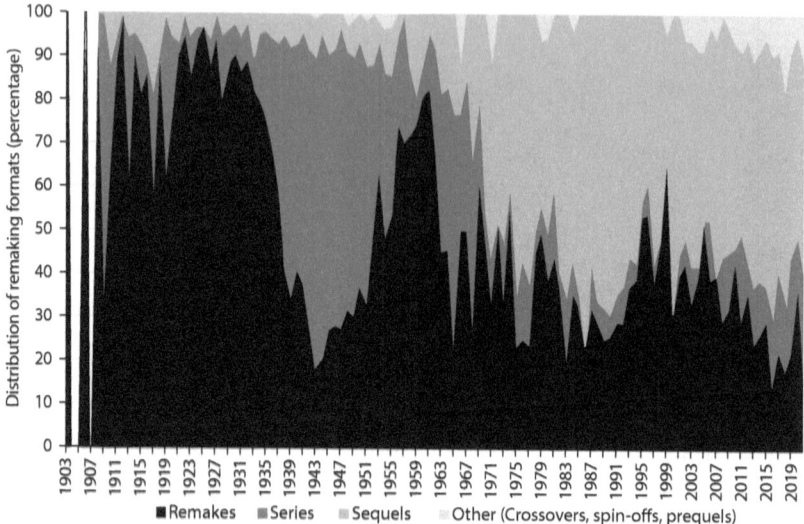

Figure 4. Distribution of remakes, series, sequels, and other remaking forms, 1903–2021. *Source*: Hollywood Remaking dataset.

Despite ups and downs, film remakes never fall below 14 percent (the lowest number in 2016) and make up an average of 50 percent of all remaking formats over the entire period. During the first four decades of the twentieth century, film remakes are clearly the remaking format of choice. Film series, in contrast, dominate production for only two decades (the 1930s and 1940s), when they reach up to 75 percent of all remaking formats in the peak year 1944, and then drop as low as 6 percent in 1959 and 1960. Film series make a short comeback in the 1960s (reaching up to 50 percent of remaking formats in the year 1965), but then decline over the next three decades with zero series films in 1972, 1986, 1998, 2005, and 2007. The numbers also indicate a slow recovery since the 2010s, when series films made up 20 percent, 22 percent, and 21 percent of all remaking formats in 2017, 2019, and 2021, respectively. Sequels played a negligible role until 1970, averaging only 7 percent of all remaking formats, as compared to the 52 percent sequels constitute on average from 1970 onward. Finally, other remaking formats such as crossovers, spin-offs, and prequels are overall less frequent. They become more regular features of Hollywood remaking in the new millennium, averaging 7 percent of all remaking formats since

2000, but they had already peaked in the 1960s and 1970s, making up 12 percent in 1966 and 11 percent in 1971.

What can we make of these numbers? They guide us to production and reception contexts that deserve closer examination. The remake boom in the 1930s, for instance, happened in the wake of a momentous technological innovation: sound cinema. Studios recycled pretested stories from cinema's silent past in order to supply sound-equipped theaters and meet the public demand for talkies. Audiences and critics often welcomed so-called "talker remakes" because they offered an opportunity to revisit favorite stories with the addition of sound and the stars of the day. When television and later playback technologies in the home (VHS, DVDs, and now streaming platforms) began to ensure access to older movies, overall fewer film remakes were produced and attitudes toward them changed. The dataset nonetheless shows that film remakes never disappeared from Hollywood's production slates. They operate differently in a media environment that rewards intertextual proficiency, yet they continue to derive their commercial and cultural value from placing familiar characters and plots in the new technological, cultural, and political contexts of their own time of production.

The film series, meanwhile, is intricately linked to the Hollywood studio system. The series thrived during the 1930s and 1940s in the B-production units of the major studios that delivered product to fill the double bill. The film series rapidly declined in the aftermath of the 1948 Supreme Court decision in the *Paramount* case, which prohibited the studios block-booking practice on which the double bill had relied and effectively dismantled the Hollywood studio system. Hollywood remaking reached a low point during the following two decades (with fewer remakes and series than ever before). The film series never measured up to its previous significance as Hollywood remaking focused on continuity and the kind of serial progression that is typical of the sequel instead of the series' episodic storytelling. When Hollywood remaking makes a comeback in the 1970s, that is, more explicitly serialized sequels enter the limelight. Hollywood experienced a "restabilization . . . after some thirty years of uncertainty and disarray,"[44] and the major studios invested in formulaic, high-profile follow-ups to box-office hits and million-dollar marketing campaigns. Despite Hollywood's conviction that it had found the ultimate success formula, sequels remained highly unpredictable with a fair share of hits and misses and the seemingly unavoidable combination of escalating costs and diminishing returns. Since the late 1990s, however, Hollywood has partly solved these problems by producing sequels that form part of larger transmedia franchises, which are strategically designed to encourage the long-term engagement of audiences with fictional characters and the storyworlds they inhabit and which often include other remaking formats like spin-offs and prequels.

The historical survey provides evidence for what used to be an intuition, namely that remaking has always formed part of Hollywood's movie production, but it also points out common misconceptions about the ubiquity of twice-told tales today and renders industry trends visible. Hollywood remaking has evolved in step with medium-specific technological innovations (in particular the transition to sound), the emergence of new home media (television, VHS, DVD, and streaming platforms), predominant practices of production and distribution (such as the major studios' block booking, for instance), changing marketing strategies, and the general media-ecological conditions of the US film industry at specific times. If overall fewer films that are based on an already familiar story are released today, especially in comparison with the heyday of the film remake and series in the 1930s and 1940s, where does the exasperation with remaking in popular criticism come from, why the fear that it will lead to the death of cinema as an art form? The explanatory power of numbers is limited because they reveal little about the *cultural* visibility of Hollywood remaking and its hold on the imagination. It is therefore necessary to trace competing discursive constructions of Hollywood remaking and to examine the multiple, often contradictory interests of networked stakeholders from production and reception contexts against the backdrop of these industry trends. We also need to analyze how the debates they spark can feed back into the ways in which film remakes, series, and sequels are being made and consumed.

ABOUT THE BOOK

The following chapters propose a theory that is designed to encourage a way of studying (and understanding) Hollywood remaking as an inherently dynamic phenomenon situated between the film industry's economic logic and the cultural imaginary. Remaking is a practice that is firmly rooted in the cinematic past and uses what is already known, familiar, and dear to propel forward the production and reception of new texts into the present and future. On the one hand, this affects how stories are being told, how popular narratives are being managed and creatively developed over long periods of time. On the other hand, such overarching narrative trajectories that are plotted alongside our real-world timeline and refuse to ever really reach full closure intersect with more abstract concepts of time, memory, and identity. By situating the industrial and cultural patterns of Hollywood remaking within their historical contexts, this book sets out to capture the shifting meanings and profound complexities of the practice from the inception of cinema to today's franchise era, while also examining how it becomes productive across multiple sites of production and reception.

Hollywood Remaking follows a three-part structure. The first part (chapters 1 and 2) develops a theory of Hollywood remaking that provides the larger frame of reference for the historical analysis of film remakes in the second part (chapters 3 and 4) and of series, sequels, and franchises in the third part (chapters 5 and 6). Chapter 1 takes Gus Van Sant's 1998 shot-for-shot remake of Alfred Hitchcock's horror classic *Psycho* (1960) as a starting point to engage with remake scholarship and position my own approach within ongoing academic debates. No other remake had previously succeeded in provoking such heated discussion as Van Sant's film. *Psycho* sparked scholarly interest in an industry practice that had long been dismissed as producing purely commercial, derivative, and aesthetically inferior films. I argue that Van Sant's remake confounded and fascinated film scholars because it resisted definitions and categorizations and raised crucial questions about repetition, cinema's temporalities, and how popular media texts stay alive and continue to evolve in the cultural imagination. When academic interest in remaking picked up in the 1980s, following a cycle of Hollywood remakes of French films, scholars imported the vocabulary for their new object of study—the film remake— from the industry and film journalism. The chapter outlines how remake scholarship has moved from attempts to pin down exact definitions, develop theoretical models, and organize remakes in clear-cut taxonomies to more complex considerations of the movies' textual and intertextual status, propositions that challenge the predominant original/remake binary in favor of more dynamic views of how the movies shape each other's meanings, and approaches that factor in extra-textual elements located in the movies' surrounding discourses or in historically specific production and reception practices. Remake scholarship (just like popular film criticism) is frequently still invested in concepts of authorship, authenticity, and originality. However, conceptualizations of the remake that privilege one film (the "original") over the other (the remake) while simultaneously obscuring that both categories in fact constitute each other, have proven as inadequate as considering the remake to be a standalone category in the large-scale system that is Hollywood remaking. In order to carve out a productive theoretical space for coming to terms with the historical evolution and cultural work of the practice, chapter 1 looks beyond the film remake proper and takes into account the growing complexification of remaking that can be directly linked to the rise of television and playback technologies in the home. I argue that these forms of access are responsible for a shift in Hollywood remaking toward more explicitly serialized movies that rely on the viewers' film literacy, memory, and intertextual knowledge.

Insights into how remaking operates as a dynamic practice at the intersection of multiple, often contradictory discourses from production and reception contexts; how it has historically evolved to accommodate the rising level of film-historical knowledge, film literacy, and intertextual proficiency among audiences; and how it has come to rely on the presence of the old in the new raise a number of culturally relevant questions that I address in chapter 2. Constructions of the cinematic past, the historical evolution of meanings, and cultural memory as it relates to the formation of generational and national identities are inevitably ideological in nature because Hollywood remaking always promotes the continuing relevance of certain stories, characters, and cultural values over possible others. At the same time, remaking is a dynamic practice that reactivates movies and meanings and that, at least in theory, comes with an intrinsic capacity to reframe, rewrite, and revise the past so that it can be made compatible with current tastes and attitudes. The chapter uses examples like *Stella Dallas*, *Jumanji*, and all-female reboots to illustrate these theoretical issues.

As I will show, the film remake *Stella* (John Erman, 1990); the belated sequel *Jumanji: Welcome to the Jungle* (Jake Kasdan, 2017); and movies such as *The Invasion* (Oliver Hirschbiegel, 2007), *Ghostbusters: Answer the Call*, *Ocean's Eight* (Gary Ross, 2018), or *The Hustle* (Chris Addison, 2019), which replace white male leads with female actors, all grapple with questions of timeliness and the politics of representation that define their moment—in terms of class (*Stella*), race (*Jumanji: Welcome to the Jungle*), and gender (all movies). Taken together, these individual examples raise broader questions about the serial logic of repetition and variation that drives Hollywood remaking and about its stabilizing function. Is there even room for progressive visions and critical interventions? And what is at stake when movies negotiate cultural, political, and social change? How do conflicting patterns of continuity and change relate to cultural memory, nostalgic longings, and generational identifications? Bringing cultural memory together with generation theory, I also introduce my concept of *movie generations* in this chapter. It assumes that media experiences play a constitutive role for the process of generation building because media representations, repertoires, and technologies together with prevailing media consumption cultures and audience practices hold identificatory potential through which generational belonging can manifest itself. Successive groups of people who grow up sharing not only the same historical, political, and societal experiences but also historically situated media and cultural experiences can share a "we-sense" based on media experiences that are directly related to Hollywood cinema. Using *Ghostbusters* as a case study, chapter 2 theorizes how remaking impacts generational renewal through experiences of "fresh contact"[45] that simultaneously build on, continue, and challenge legacies and established meanings.

Building on the theoretical foundation laid out in the first part, the remaining two parts zero in on specific remaking formats. Historical production trends (based on the Hollywood Remaking dataset) provide the roadmap for these chapters. Chapters 3 and 4 are dedicated to the film remake, looking at the specific moment when the film remake was the leading remaking format during and after the transition to sound (chapter 3), and taking a broader historical view to probe the cultural work of movies that have been remade several times over the course of the twentieth and twenty-first centuries (chapter 4). From the very beginning, repetition shaped the cinematic experience as it facilitated the comprehension of early film, familiarized audiences with the new medium, and established readily recognizable formal, stylistic, and generic conventions. Remakes were instrumental during that early phase and quickly emerged as an effective measure for cinema's progress both as a technological and as a storytelling medium. By reliably (and repeatedly) foregrounding innovation against the backdrop of the already-known, remakes effectively document historical trajectories and accommodate change in an overarching narrative of progress about cinema, culture, and the nation at large. Chapter 3 focuses on Hollywood's transition to sound and talker remakes of former silent hits such as *Anna Christie* (Clarence Brown, 1930) and *Stella Dallas* (King Vidor, 1937), and elaborates how remaking produces temporal markers that help construct a cinematic past—here: the silent era. As I will show, discourses surrounding talker remakes in trade papers and fan magazines were instrumental in making sense of the sound innovation and its impact on filmmaking and film aesthetics. From there, the chapter illustrates how remakes, while invariably the poster child for all that is new, begin to operate as film-historical sites of memory and catalysts for processes of generational identity formations.

While chapter 3 explores the peak period of film remake production during and after the transition to sound, chapter 4 takes a broader historical approach to examine the evolution of remaking over the following decades, when Hollywood begins to release fewer remakes and the time that passes between each iteration increases. My historical statistics show that Hollywood has produced overall fewer film remakes since the 1990s, and that film remakes make up a smaller percentage of total film production amidst a growing trend towards sequelization. Nonetheless, film remakes continue to be a significant economic and cultural force and deserve close attention, especially those movies that have been remade multiple times over the course of many decades. Chapter 4 focuses on three examples that fit this description: *A Star Is Born*, which was made five times over the course of eighty-six years (1932, 1937, 1954, 1976, 2019), *King Kong*, with four iterations within eighty-four years, sequels, crossovers, and spin-offs left aside (1933, 1976, 2005, 2017), and *Invasion of the Body Snatchers*, of which there are four versions within a time span of fifty-one years (1956, 1978, 1993, 2007). I will show how each new version documents cinema's technological advancements, shapes audience perceptions of previous films and film history more generally, and provides a cultural snapshot that highlights the complex balancing between timeless storytelling and the timeliness of visual aesthetics and politics of representation. In all of this, film remakes display a pronounced awareness of their own pre-existence and ultimately come to function as archives—as repositories of memory and knowledge. The many versions of *A Star Is Born*, *King Kong*, and *Invasion of the Body Snatchers*, I argue, fulfill archival functions in that they store, preserve, and classify the cinematic past and make it available to different generations of viewers. They open up a pathway to a collectively shared cinematic past.

Part 3 deepens the discussion of Hollywood remaking by exploring the film series, sequel, and franchise and how they relate to questions of narrative and cultural continuity. The franchise constitutes the starting point for chapters 5 and 6—as a lens through which I first explore the past of Hollywood's more explicitly serialized formats and then turn to their cinematic futures. Chapter 5 examines the trends that mark the history of serials, series, and sequels as they graduated from cheap B-level productions in the Hollywood studio system to high-budgeted A-level productions in the post-studio era. At the center of this historical account is the film series with its formulaic episodes and lack of narrative continuity between one installment and the next. They emerged as the prevalent remaking format in the 1930s and 1940s and are emblematic for Hollywood's highly standardized filmmaking in the studio system. The cinematic seriality of the film series was associated with a cheap, factory-like production mode and the cookie-cutter regularity of the films. The end of the studio system also marked the end of the film series boom and a general slowdown of remaking and the production of serial formats in Hollywood. When cinematic seriality makes a comeback in the post-studio era, it is in the form of big-budget, high-concept blockbusters that are marketed as events. Here, the chapter discusses *James Bond* and *Planet of the Apes* as examples for the reinvention of the series and Hollywood's new focus on sequelization, respectively. The *Bond* and *Ape* movies exist in a transitional space in-between the B-level serial tactics and production patterns of the studio system on the one hand and the A-level seriality of the blockbuster era with high production values and release strategies, a focus on continuity across installments as well as on merchandise, transmedia spin-offs, and adaptations on the other.

Building on the historical evolution of cinematic seriality, chapter 6 traces the rise of the sequel since the mid-1970s and then engages with the industry's ongoing optimization of the sequel and series formats, most recently within the franchise system that has come to dominate Hollywood in the new millennium. If we want to understand how the sequel has once been imagined, *sequelitis* emerges as a key term. The chapter reconstructs the sequelitis discourse surrounding the initially haphazard production of sequels in the 1970s and 1980s, before examining how the term—and ad hoc sequelization—gave way to the idea of franchising and, most recently, to the idea of the forever franchise. With its promise of endlessly renewable stories, the forever franchise has now become the "holy grail" in Hollywood. Exploring Disney's nostalgic reboot of *Star Wars* and the reproduction logics of *Blade Runner 2049* (Denis Villeneuve, 2017), the chapter critically examines the linear, forward-moving temporalities of media texts that might just go on forever. I argue that they are steeped in nostalgia for the (franchise) past and invested in notions of legacy, inheritance, and generational transferal that inadvertently promote conservative and backwards-gazing ideologies.

The book ends with a brief discussion of the concept of the reboot, in which I return once more to the question of how Hollywood's past becomes a usable past through the practice of remaking. I situate the reboot within a recent reorientation of Hollywood remaking in the new millennium that is marked by a general trend away from the film remake and (to a lesser degree) from the sequel. I propose that this development is intricately linked to the conceptual crisis of the film remake after the critical and financial failures of Gus Van Sant's *Psycho* (1998) and Tim Burton's "re-imagining" of *Planet of the Apes* (2001). Both movies foregrounded the difficulties of remaking classic movies that are deeply inscribed in the cultural imagination. In this context, crossovers, spin-offs, and prequels have been gaining momentum as remaking formats that circumvent explicit repetition or linear serial progression. Instead, these movies expand diegetic time and space, provide new perspectives on familiar characters and narrative events, and partake in larger worldbuilding projects. The term *reboot* emerges at the same time, as a "*discursive opportunity* to breathe new life into an established brand identity,"[46] as Joe Tompkins writes. In concluding this book, I want to stress that the "reboot" is not a new remaking category but rather a "remake," "sequel," or "prequel" by another name. Initially, the label emphasized novelty over repetition or continuation, but that has already shifted over the past decade with a number of reboots that are steeped in nostalgia for their franchise pasts. As I will show, we can only fully understand the "reboot" moniker and its dynamic nature, if we consider it within the longer history, industrial logics, and cultural work of Hollywood remaking.

Historically, remaking has been a constant staple of the film industry, but it has also always been in flux, adapting to ever-changing contexts of production and reception. In order to understand this evolution, we therefore need to consider Hollywood remaking as a practice of cultural reproduction that relies on a serial dynamic of repetition and variation *and* pay close attention to the individual remaking formats it generates. *Hollywood Remaking* traces how remaking has evolved as a business practice in the United States, how it has been imagined over time, how it has shaped cinematic aesthetics and cultural debates, and how it has fostered film-historical knowledge and promoted feelings of generational belonging among audience members. To understand how and why remaking seems to dominate the release schedules in our present moment and to grasp why remakes and sequels are so vehemently perceived as posing a cultural threat, it is necessary to go beyond the easy rejections, eloquent dismissals, and endless complaints that inform popular discourses and thwart academic inquiries. Instead, we must give serious consideration to the multifarious meanings of the narrative, economic, and cultural continuities these movies represent.

PART I A Theory of
Hollywood Remaking

1 Making Sense of Repetition

Leo Braudy notes that the term *remake* was "imported to academia from movie journalism and the movie business."[1] Scholars have seized the word and endlessly probed, defined, and redefined the film remake against evolving industrial and critical discourses, thereby contributing to the meaning-making processes that accompany Hollywood's twice-told tales. This means that remake scholarship partakes in the ongoing power struggles over the film remake's aesthetic and cultural legitimacy even though it does not necessarily feed back into its wider production and reception practices. Without overestimating the visibility or impact of academic publications, it seems nonetheless safe to say that scholarly definitions, taxonomies, theoretical models, and cultural studies approaches constitute epistemological forces that help to make sense of the film remake and of Hollywood remaking more generally. They are always concerned with repetition and the specific kind of intertextuality remaking creates, regardless of whether this focus on repetition reinforces or challenges ideas about a movie's status as "original" and the purely commercial (and for some: pointless) existence of its derivatives.

Gus Van Sant's 1998 remake of Alfred Hitchcock's *Psycho* (1960) is emblematic for the ways in which academic knowledge production intersects with industry trends and critical impulses located in film fandom and popular journalism. Van Sant remade *Psycho* almost shot for shot and line by line, closely following Hitchcock's six-week shooting schedule and spending $20 million to make the movie (the 1998 equivalent to Hitchcock's $800,000 budget). At the same time, his version introduces several changes: it is filmed in color and set in the 1990s. Along with new buildings that replace the iconic mansion and motel, the remake presents a new cast of actors (including Vince Vaughn, Anne Heche, Julianne Moore, William Macy, and Viggo Mortensen) who take on the lead roles of Norman Bates (Anthony Perkins), Marion Crane (Janet Leigh), Lila Crane (Vera Miles), Milton Arbogast (Martin Balsam), and Sam Loomis (John Gavin). Furthermore, Van Sant's *Psycho* restores a line of dialogue that had to be removed from Joseph Stefano's original screenplay because, at the time, it violated the Production Code of the Motion Picture Association of America.[2] It also shows more explicit female nudity and sexuality in the case of Marion and Sam's encounter in the opening scene, for example, or when Norman masturbates as he watches Marion undress through a peephole. And it inserts unrelated images—found footage of a naked woman, a cow standing on a road, and clouds in the sky—into the murders of Marion and Arbogast. Thomas Leitch identifies altogether 101 differences between Hitchcock's *Psycho* and Van Sant's, even though the latter is usually considered to be a painstakingly exact remake of the horror classic.[3]

In hindsight, the critical and box-office failure of Van Sant's *Psycho* was not only decisive in ushering in a new era of more complex and more explicitly serialized remaking formats that are gradually replacing the film remake in the new millennium. When Hitchcock fans and popular film critics met the remake with confusion, frustration, and outrage, film scholars, too, engaged in the deconstruction of what one camp considered to be an utterly pointless and pretentious exercise that sullied the legacy of Hitchcock's masterpiece and another camp found to be a misguided experiment that had not dared to go far enough and ultimately failed at duplicating *Psycho*.[4] Van Sant's film "gradually rose to become the (probably) most discussed remake in the history of academic quarterlies,"[5] and it raised pertinent questions about repetition, artistic license, and the figure of the *auteur*, about cinema's "timeless" classics and what it means to remake the past in the present. Amidst the large number of Hollywood remakes, no other film was as successful as *Psycho* in sparking and maintaining scholarly interest in what had been widely dismissed as a purely commercial industry practice that produced derivative and aesthetically inferior films. As "the overwhelming hostility with which Van Sant's *Psycho* was once met upon its release in 1998 is slowly giving way to more moderate analyses and revisionist appreciation of the remake as a unique meta-commentary on American film history, the horror genre, and the practice of remaking,"[6] the film is also becoming a prime example of how the emphasis on repetition foregrounds cinema's complex temporalities and the ways in which popular media texts stay alive and continue to evolve in the cultural imagination.

Frank Kelleter states that "Hitchcock's film led a strange double life in two separate narrative universes . . .: on the one side the realm of film art, where *Psycho* was quickly canonized as a singular work, and on the other side the much less clearly defined domain of popular culture's serial sprawl."[7] Through the perceived redundancy of the shot-for-shot strategy, Van Sant's remake brought these "two separate narrative universes" into view. It challenged cinephile assumptions about the singularity of *auteur* films and instead drew academic attention "to the ways in which *Psycho 60* had *already* been variously 'remade'" in slasher movies like John Carpenter's *Halloween* (1978) and Wes Craven's *Scream* (1996), in Brian De Palma's *Dressed to Kill* (1980), *Blow Out* (1981), and *Body Double* (1984), and in countless other films that reference the famous shower scene.[8] Moreover, the remake highlighted the often-overlooked fact that the Norman Bates story had long been remade and continued in three *Psycho* sequels that were released in the 1980s and also starred Anthony Perkins as Norman Bates.[9] And yet, Van Sant's film never acknowledges the productive afterlife of *Psycho*, as if it pretended to exist in a different reality, where Perkins's Norman Bates had not become a serial character and where the slasher genre that took Hitchcock's *Psycho* as its model had not peaked, declined, and recently been resurrected boasting an additional dose of self-referential humor.[10] With its obsessive repetition— its "re-staging, replaying, re-timing and re-filming" of Hitchcock's horror movie—Van Sant's *Psycho* seems not only oblivious of the cinematic past but also of "the ways in which technical reproducibility has produced particular ideas and forms of repetition."[11] *Psycho*, in short, pushed the limits of the concept of repetition as well as of the film remake and its purpose in the contemporary mediascape.

To be sure, there has never been full agreement in academic circles about what exactly constitutes a film remake. This seems only natural, given that the term originated as an *industrial* and *legal* category and then gained new layers of meaning through its widespread use as a *critical* category in popular film journalism before it finally entered academia. Scholars regard the remake as a *textual, theoretical,* and *cultural* category. Their views mainly differ concerning the remake's boundaries,[12] as they tend to favor either narrow or broad definitions. A remake can consequently be a new version of an already existing movie that announces its remake status through the use of the same (or similar) title and source material, or the term is used to refer to more wide-ranging patterns of repetition and difference in cinema (e.g., the use of allusions and quotations) and other media (e.g., film-to-TV adaptations, videogames based on videogames, fan productions). Despite this variety, the *Psycho* remake nonetheless complicates existing definitions, theoretical models, taxonomies, and cultural studies approaches. Taking *Psycho* as its point of departure, this chapter explores how remake scholars have made sense of repetition and why the usefulness of the film remake as a theoretical category has become increasingly contested in recent years. I will trace a variety of conceptualizations, ranging from complex considerations of the movies' textual properties and intertextual relations, to approaches that factor in extra-textual elements located in the movies' surrounding contexts or in historically specific production and reception practices, and, finally, to propositions that challenge the predominant original/remake binary in favor of a more dynamic understanding of how different versions of the same movie depend on one another and shape each other's meanings. This chapter, in short, provides an overview of the research on film remakes since the 1980s and on its gradual expansion beyond definitions and taxonomies as well as beyond the film remake proper. It then continues to lay the groundwork for a broader understanding of Hollywood remaking and its historical evolution as a serial storytelling practice.

THEORIZING THE FILM REMAKE:
INTERTEXTUAL MODELS AND TAXONOMIES

Since the late 1980s, scholars have made attempts at pinning down definitions of the film remake, initially developing theoretical models and organizing movies in clear-cut taxonomies. For some, "the remake can exist anywhere on an intertextual continuum from allusions in specific lines, individual scenes, and camera style to the explicit patterning of an entire film on a previous exemplar."[13] In general, however, definitions of the remake do not border on a global meaning of intertextuality, as developed by Mikhail Bakhtin, Julia Kristeva, and Roland Barthes, but on the more restricted sense of the term proposed by Gérard Genette, as I will later discuss.[14] There is also a common understanding that, unlike the adaptation, which transfers a work of art from one medium to another by changing its semiotic registers (e.g., from literature to film), the remake always remains within the same medium (film). For Thomas Leitch, "only movies are remade,"[15] but, like all definitions of the film remake and attempts to determine its characteristics and boundaries, this claim, too, has already been challenged. Leitch's position is nonetheless useful if one is interested in examining the historical evolution of the film remake and of Hollywood remaking (understood as a practice that generates Hollywood movies based on Hollywood movies). The medium specificity of the remaking process brings with it an informal (and historically shifting) set of rules that determines what constitutes a remake at a particular point in time and in a given media environment, to what degree it foregrounds repetition, and how it relates to its cinematic predecessor(s).

Maybe not surprisingly, Universal's official *Psycho* website expressed diverging views concerning the rules of remake production in the late 1990s. With the remake, Gus Van Sant "wanted to take on the challenge of truly recreating an incredible, landmark movie, in the same way that different directors repeatedly tackle the material of Shakespeare's *Hamlet* because it is so rich and resonant," the website announced.[16] Van Sant himself confirmed that remaking *Psycho* was, in fact, "like staging a contemporary production of a classic play while remaining true to the original."[17] As James Naremore points out, however, "movies have as much in common with novels as with theater, and Van Sant's *Psycho* is not simply a re-filming of Joseph Stefano's script, but an elaborate quotation of things that were literally printed on another film."[18] If plays like *Hamlet* can be endlessly restaged in the theater and reinterpreted by new performers, this is quite different with a film version of *Hamlet*, which—like the one directed by and starring Laurence Olivier from 1948, for instance—is well-known and has received numerous awards and critical acclaim.[19] The movie's presence lingers on and troubles any attempts to remake it too closely, while readaptations of *Hamlet* that take Shakespeare's play once more as their point of departure must also reckon with it.

When Van Sant explains that "*Psycho* is perfect to refashion as a modern piece," because, "as cinema gets older there is also an audience that is increasingly unpracticed at watching old films, silent films, black and white films,"[20] he is certainly aware of the fact that cinema's technological innovations and changing viewing habits are often the reason behind the production of film remakes. At the same time, however, he ignores "the multiple kinds of repetition made increasingly available through redistribution, re-issue and replaying,"[21] as well as the fact that Hitchcock's *Psycho* is a film "that has haunted American culture's collective consciousness ever since its release."[22] The repetition that Van Sant offers with his version of *Psycho* seems anachronistic because it acknowledges neither the enduring presence and popularity of Hitchcock's movie nor the highly complex intertextual undertaking that remaking has become since the rise of television and playback technologies in the home. Naremore therefore describes Van Sant's *Psycho* as "an intriguing lesson in what not to do with a remake."[23]

As mentioned above, theorizations of the connection between a film remake and one or more previous movies often draw on Gérard Genette's structuralist model of *transtextuality* (a text's relationships with other texts), which he divides into five distinct types: *intertextuality* ("the actual presence of one text within another" in the form of quotation, plagiarism, and allusion), *paratextuality* (which binds a text to its title, preface, notes, illustrations, etc.), *metatextuality* (a "critical relationship par excellence," in which one text comments on another, "without necessarily citing it [without summoning it], in fact sometimes even without naming it"), *architextuality* (a relationship that is "of a purely taxonomic nature," indicated by the title or subtitle of a work), and *hypertextuality* (in which a *hypertext* is derived from an earlier *hypotext*).[24] The last category, *hypertextuality*, has proven particularly fruitful for discussions of the film remake. It posits that the remake is a *hypertext* that is derived from an earlier movie (*hypotext*) through a *transformative process*.

Van Sant's *Psycho* triggered such intense hostility upon its release because fans, critics, and scholars considered the remake's transformations of Hitchcock's movie to be either unnecessary or insufficient. Film critic Roger Ebert found that it was "an invaluable experiment in the theory of cinema, because it demonstrates that a shot-by-shot remake is pointless," and that "genius apparently resides between or beneath the shots, or in chemistry that cannot be timed or counted."²⁵ His colleague Jonathan Rosenbaum was fascinated by the idea but equally underwhelmed by the outcome: "Theoretically, a nearly shot-by-shot, line-by-line remake of any movie could produce something marvelous, fresh, and revelatory, at least if an artist had a viable artistic program to go with it. Practically, I would argue, Gus Van Sant's *Psycho* is a piece of dead meat."²⁶ For film scholar Constantine Santas, the remake came close to "cinematic blasphemy" and its "failure [had to be] attributed primarily to Van Sant himself and to his apparent lack of artistic vision."²⁷

Critical reception of the *Psycho* remake and early scholarly takes are consistent on one point: Van Sant's obsessive repetition drew attention away from the calculated transformations that *Psycho* had actually undergone (color, cast, and 1990s updates) and instead foregrounded how the remake engaged in a "performative resurrection"²⁸ of Hitchcock's film and, indeed, of Hitchcock himself as the *auteur par excellence*. If Leitch describes Hitchcock as "notoriously the first Hollywood auteur ... [and] the last as well, a figure who continues to hover above auteurism's grave,"²⁹ Hitchcock similarly hovers above the remake that so closely resembles his own film and in which the cast "seem[s] haunted, as if repeating the actions of ghosts."³⁰ In 1998, *Psycho* neither met the expectations associated with the film remake nor those of the shot-for-shot, line-by-line remake nor of a Hitchcock remake pure and simple. Instead, it became a unique test case, a hypertext whose troubling familiarity and already circulating "narrative image"³¹ raised questions about how repetition and subtle temporal, spatial, technological, and ideological variations played out between the two *Psychos*.

When Robert Eberwein proposed a preliminary taxonomy of fifteen different kinds of remakes (and further subdivisions), he did not have a category for a shot-for-shot remake like Gus Van Sant's *Psycho* in mind.³² His elaborate taxonomy stands in the tradition of earlier reference works that provide rudimentary definitions and categories for the film remake. Michael B. Druxman, for instance, proposed the distinction between the *disguised*, the *direct*, and the *non*-remake based roughly on the *degree of transformation* and on the extent to which the original is acknowledged in the remake.³³ Building on Druxman, Harvey Roy Greenberg introduced the following three categories: the *acknowledged close remake*, in which "the original film is replicated with little or no change," as in *Ben-Hur* (Sidney Olcott and Frank Oakes Rose, 1907/Fred Niblo, 1925/William Wyler, 1959); the *acknowledged transformed remake*, in which "transformations of character, plot, time, and setting are more substantive than in the acknowledged close remake [and] the original movie is openly, but variably, mentioned as a source," as in *Heaven Can Wait* (Warren Beatty and Buck Henry, 1978), *Always* (Steven Spielberg, 1989), and *Stella* (Jon Erman, 1990); and the *unacknowledged, disguised remake*, in which "major alterations are undertaken in time, setting, gender, or—most particularly—genre [but] the audience is deliberately uninformed about the switches."³⁴ Disguised remakes peaked during the studio system, for example when the plot from *The Mayor of Hell* (Archie Mayo, 1933), about crooked politicians running a reform school that starred James Cagney, was reused in *Crime School* (Lewis Seiler, 1938) with Humphrey Bogart in the lead and in *Hell's Kitchen* (Lewis Seiler, 1939) with Ronald Reagan.³⁵

Unlike Druxman's or Greenberg's attempts to categorize the remake by identifying the *degree of transformation* in comparison to an "original," Eberwein's taxonomy captures the remake's possible *modes of transformation*: technological (silent to sound, color, aspect-ratio; e.g., *Ben-Hur* from 1925 and 1959), geographical (a remake of a foreign film; e.g., *La femme Nikita* [Luc Besson, 1990] and *Point of No Return* [John Badham, 1993]), medial (TV remake, e.g., *Sweet Bird of Youth* [Richard Brooks 1962/Nicolas Roeg, 1989]), as well as changes in gender and race constellations (e.g., *The Front Page* [Lewis Milestone, 1931] and *His Girl Friday* [Howard Hawks, 1940]; *Anna Lucasta* [Irving Rapper, 1949/Arnold Laven, 1958]), temporal and cultural settings (e.g., *A Star Is Born* [William Wellman, 1937/George Cukor, 1954/Frank Pierson, 1976]), and genre (e.g., *Frankenstein* [James Whale, 1931] as a parody in *Young Frankenstein* [Mel Brooks, 1954]).³⁶

Leitch, who approaches remakes from an adaptation studies perspective, is more concerned with the relationship between original movie, remake, and literary source material (or: property) on which both movies are based.[37] The result is a triangular model of intertextuality that lays the groundwork for his taxonomy. Leitch identifies *readaptation*, *update*, *homage*, and *true remake* based on whether the remake "seek[s] to define itself either with primary reference to the film it remakes or to the material on which both films are based," and on whether it "take[s] as its goal fidelity to the conception of the original story or a revisionary attitude toward that story."[38] According to Leitch's taxonomy, then, a remake that evokes the literary source rather than another film version is called readaptation (e.g., Tony Richardson's version of Shakespeare's *Hamlet* [1969]), while a remake that pays tribute to a cinematic referent is an homage (e.g., *Far from Heaven* [Todd Haynes, 2002] as a tribute to *All That Heaven Allows* [Douglas Sirk, 1956]). Both readaptation and homage attempt to be more or less "faithful" to their respective literary and filmic sources. The update and true remake, in contrast, adopt a revisionary stance—toward the literary property in the case of the update (e.g., *William Shakespeare's Romeo + Juliet* [Baz Luhrmann, 1996]) and toward the original movie in the case of the true remake (e.g., *The Postman Always Rings Twice* [Tay Garnett, 1946/Bob Rafelson, 1981]).[39]

Again, Van Sant's *Psycho* resists any easy categorization. It probably comes closest to being an homage, even though Leitch contends that "a faithful homage would be a contradiction in terms (the most faithful homage would be a re-release)."[40] Van Sant, however, "deliberately engages in this 'contradiction in terms,'" Megan Carrigy notes.[41] "Instead of adopting the customary strategies designed to improve its original—readapting, updating, or rethinking the original's source material," Leitch explains in a later piece, "this film was an homage in the specific sense that it did not seriously contest Hitchcock's superiority."[42] But the remake, a near-duplicate of *Psycho*, ultimately reveals the futility of wanting to fit all remakes into fixed universal patterns. As Leitch himself remarks, "All the ingredients of a Hitchcock film would be present except for Hitchcock. But this omission would be the structuring absence of the whole project, the fetish every feature of the new film would systematically evoke or repress by defining itself as the film that uniquely *wasn't* Hitchcock's *Psycho*."[43] In theory, then, *Psycho* is as "faithful," close, or direct a remake as there ever was, conspicuously acknowledging its source and meticulously replicating the "original's" syntactic elements (plot structure, narrative units, character constellation), semantic features (character names, locations, time frame), and style, whereas "free," transformed, or disguised remakes would have made minor or more radical alterations.[44]

Yet, as a remake—made and released in the late 1990s, no less—*Psycho* ultimately defeats its own purpose. Kelleter has even suggested that, despite the manifold (and often fetishistic) ways in which Van Sant's *Psycho* pays tribute to Hitchcock's movie, the remake acts as if it were no remake at all but instead an original creation in "an alternate cinematic universe."[45] As an almost shot-for-shot, line-by-line remake, *Psycho* refuses to play according to the rules that dictate how remakes operate in terms of intertextual referentiality. This is a historically specific concept, currently defined by "the ever-expanding availability of texts and technologies, the tendency of contemporary Hollywood film makers to combine the commercial necessity of generic patterns of repetition with more direct patterns of borrowing (allusion and quotation), and the unprecedented awareness of film history both among film makers and contemporary audiences."[46] The cultural familiarity of movies determines the production and reception of film remakes and how remaking works at specific points in time. As *Psycho* disregards the rules that reign over today's media environment and that demand overall less direct repetition in favor of more complex intertextual structures and the possibility of serial continuation, it also directs attention to the ongoing evolution of Hollywood remaking as well as to the ways in which a film remake is constituted *outside* of the filmic text.

Psycho further hints at the general difficulty of intertextual models and remake taxonomies, namely that "these textual accounts of remaking risk essentialism, in many instances privileging the 'original' over the remake or measuring the success of the remake according to its ability to realise what are taken to be the essential elements of a source text—the property—from which both the original and its remake are derived."[47] Drawing on genre theory, Constantine Verevis argues that "while there is often sufficient semantic and syntactic evidence to suggest that remakes are particular textual structures, film remakes (like genres) 'exist always *in excess* of a corpus of works.'"[48] Remakes come into being as a result of the "broader discursive activity"[49] that surrounds them. They depend on the audiences' "prior knowledge of previous texts and intertextual relationships" as well as their "understanding of broader generic structures and categories," and they are "both enabled and limited by a series of historically specific institutional factors, such as copyright law, canon formation and film reviewing which are essential to the existence and maintenance—to the discursivisation—of the film remake."[50] Daniel Herbert has made a similar argument suggesting that remakes function as a "cultural category"[51] in the same way Jason Mittell has used that term in his work on genre. Mittell writes that "genre is best understood as a process of categorization that is not found within media texts, but operates across the cultural realms of media industries, audiences, policy, critics, and historical context."[52] Remakes, then, cannot simply be located in the filmic text and its intertextual relation to an "original." Instead, they are also always discursively constructed and, as such, sites of contested meaning and cultural power struggles. The movies themselves are active agents in these processes as well, conditioning the discourses surrounding them and shaping culture more broadly. Once purely text-based taxonomies and definitions of the remake give way to historically specific interpretive frames and how they structure intertextual relations, inquiries into film remakes, too, tend to move beyond textual to cultural studies approaches that eventually challenge ideas of an "untouchable original."

THEORIZING THE FILM REMAKE: CULTURAL STUDIES APPROACHES

In their introduction to *Play It Again, Sam: Retakes on Remakes* (1998), Andrew Horton and Stuart McDougal maintain that the film remake is a "special pattern which re-represents and explains at a different time and through varying perceptions, previous narratives and experiences."[53] The film remake invites an engagement with multiple texts as well as with their contexts of production and reception and with their historically specific aesthetics and ideologies. Horton and McDougal's collection marks a shift remake studies has undergone since the late 1990s: from definitions, theoretical models, and taxonomies to analyses that understand film remakes as postmodern and postcolonial forms of engaging with the past and as historical documents in which cultural and social change is negotiated from one film version to the next. In one of the essays, Eberwein criticizes "studies of remakes [that] do not go much beyond a superficial point-by-point, pluses-and-minuses kind of analysis,"[54] and he urges scholars to examine original and remake from a cultural studies perspective instead. Where one approach "treats the original and its meaning for its contemporary audience as a fixity, against which the remake is measured and evaluated," he explains, the other sees the original "as still in process in regard to the impact it had or may have had for its contemporary audience and, even more, that it has for its current audience" and the remake as "a kind of reading or rereading of the original."[55]

Applying the concept of cultural identity that Stuart Hall developed in his essay on Caribbean cinema, Eberwein questions comparative analyses that "posit culturally inflected unity in originals and remakes" because they "assume a fixed timeless cultural identity."[56] According to Hall, any view of cultural identity that emphasizes "the common historical experiences and shared cultural codes which provide us, as 'one people,' with stable, unchanging and continuous frames of reference and meaning, beneath the shifting divisions and vicissitudes of our actual history"[57] needs to be qualified by a second position that takes into account "differences and discontinuities,"[58] the constant transformations of cultural identity, its historical and social contingency. For Eberwein, this means that a comparative approach that wants to comment on the relation between original and remake must do more than identify intertextual references. It has to come to terms with the cultural, political, and social climate that informs the movies' respective historical moments of production and that shapes their forms and meanings at different points in time.

Jennifer Forrest and Leonard R. Koos's collection *Dead Ringers: The Remake in Theory and Practice* (2002) expands this cultural studies perspective. Despite the volume's strong focus on Hollywood remakes of French films, it also contains essays that are exclusively concerned with US cinema and make theoretical, economic, aesthetic, and historical inquiries into Hollywood's remaking practice. Forrest and Koos's introduction provides a brief glimpse at the history of remake production from early film to contemporary cinema, stating that film remakes "reflect the different historical, economic, social, political, and aesthetic conditions that make them possible."[59] Addressing historical and ideological reasons behind the overwhelmingly negative responses to film remakes in the popular press, Forrest and Koos argue that

> while some remakes are demonstrably failures, others are undeniably superb, and almost all interesting for what they reveal, either about different cultures, about different directorial styles and aesthetic orientations, about class or gender perceptions, about different social-historical periods and changing audience expectations, about the dynamics of genre film, or simply about the evolution of economic practices in the industry.[60]

Forrest's essay in this collection examines the beginnings of remake production in the United States;[61] other pieces in *Dead Ringers* and in cultural studies-oriented remake scholarship are generally interested in contemporary film remakes, and particularly in processes of transnational remaking and how they impact representations of culture and gender.

As far as Hollywood remakes of Hollywood movies are concerned, research has mostly focused on horror and science fiction genres (to a lesser degree: westerns, *film noir*, screwball comedies, and melodramas). Certain genres seem to lend themselves to comparative close readings of "originals" and remakes and inquiries into how prevalent meanings, attitudes, and values change over time. This definitely aligns with the common assumption that some Hollywood movies seem to be "especially suited to remaking because they are inherently spectacular and have an elemental, mythopoetic quality," while others supposedly "resist the process, either because they require unique stars (The Marx Brothers, Astaire and Rogers), or because they belong to a particular period of entertainment that is difficult to 'translate' into the present (the Freed-unit musicals at MGM)," or because—like *Citizen Kane* (Orson Welles, 1941) and Alfred Hitchcock's *Psycho*—they "have such artistic prestige and historical significance that remaking them, as opposed to quoting them or borrowing their ideas, seems crass and pointless."[62]

As mentioned above, most critics and scholars ultimately treated Van Sant's remake of *Psycho* as such—a "crass and pointless" endeavor. They constructed an "elegiac discourse" that lamented the remake's "loss of depth" and relentless superficiality.[63] Adrian Martin, for example, found that "the only noteworthy aspect of Van Sant's folly is what its 'experiment' proves: that you can mechanically copy all the surface moves of a screen classic and still drain it of any meaning, tension, artistry, and fun."[64] The remake's "hopelessly wooden and superficial performances,"[65] the treatment of Marion's death in the shower and of Norman's psychosis, and even individual shots and dissolves, these analyses suggest, create a version of *Psycho* that, unlike Hitchcock's movie, is devoid of both: horror *and* meaning.[66] The secrets that structured the plot of *Psycho* in 1960, that indeed served as the source of horror and that Hitchcock famously urged viewers not to reveal once they had watched the movie in the cinema, are no longer secrets in the remake. In fact, the promotional paratexts assumed that audiences were so familiar with the narrative image of *Psycho*, that they would anticipate Marion's death in the shower and know in advance that Norman/Mother is the murderer. The tagline for Van Sant's *Psycho*—"Check in. Relax. Take a shower."—thus triggers audience expectations for the repetition of the shower scene and so does the movie poster that shows a female figure behind a shower curtain (figure 5).

In this context, Leitch remarks that "the most immediately distinctive feature of Hitchcock's film, the shocking unexpectedness of Marion's murder, is exactly what reduces the remake, because it cannot possibly duplicate it, to something like *Psycho* instead of *Psycho* itself, or even *Psycho* updated."[67] As a result, Van Sant's remake is "neither one thing nor another,"[68] namely, neither a Hitchcock movie nor an original horror film. Although "even the small differences have enormous consequences,"[69] Van Sant's *Psycho* seems to offer little for cultural analyses: The strategic updates—costumes, sets, props, and script—remain anachronistic because the narrative itself "seem[s] old-fashioned"[70] in this modernized version. Surely, the very same plot still holds up in Hitchcock's *Psycho*, which critics and scholars consider to have a *timeless* quality and for whom "the perceived banality of *Psycho 98* only served to solidify the place of Hitchcock's *Psycho* in cinema history as a superior and classic masterpiece that stood the test of time."[71] The remake never fully commits to updating *Psycho*, so that "despite the attempt to subtly drag Hitchcock's material into the present day, everything still has a weird early 1960s aura"[72] but neither the depth nor meaning of Hitchcock's movie.

And yet, Van Sant's *Psycho* raises issues that are crucial to our understanding of technological, cultural, and media change as well as the evolution of the horror genre. As with the theoretical reflections on repetition,

Figure 5. The film poster for Van Sant's remake plays on the familiar narrative image of *Psycho* (1960). Cinematic Collection / Alamy Stock Photo.

authorship, and original artistic creations that the remake invites, these issues, too, are raised on a meta-level and encourage an abstract engagement with the shifting temporalities of cinema and spectatorship in the face of technological innovation, changing visual regimes, and technical reproducibility. Carrigy points out that, paradoxically, "Van Sant's *Psycho* reminds us that *the cinema isn't timeless*."[73] The fact that both Hitchcock's movie and the remake circulate in the same marketplace foregrounds that cinema as a medium is always in transition and that the conditions that govern movie production and reception constantly shift and change.[74] Of course, film remakes first and foremost adapt existing material in order to create time*ly* (not time*less*) versions for cinema's contemporary audiences. Along these lines, Naremore himself admits that "for all its continuing interest"—and apparent timelessness—"*Psycho* is no longer a cutting-edge horror film."[75] Rather than exploring what *Psycho* could have looked like had he followed contemporary conventions of the horror film genre, Van Sant relied on repetition with his shot-for-shot strategy and, despite some half-hearted modernizations, ultimately to a horror aesthetics that remains confined to the 1960s.

What Adrian Martin calls the remake's "weird early 1960s aura," then, is not only constituted because *Psycho*'s updates "amount to no more than vague doodling in the margins of the original's image and sound tracks,"[76] but it is additionally underscored by the remake's return to the historical roots of the postmodern horror film. Steve Neale writes that

> the advent of *Psycho* in 1960 is generally regarded as a turning point, as the beginning of something new: as the film which located horror firmly and influentially within the modern psyche, the modern world, modern relationships, and the modern (dysfunctional) family . . . ; as the film which marked a definitive *rapprochement* between the horror film and the psychological thriller and which helped inspire the slasher, stalker and serial killer films of the 1970s, 1980s and 1990s . . . ; and as a film which marked the ending of "classical" Hollywood, and with it the certainty and safety of classical narrative and generic conventions.[77]

Van Sant's *Psycho* is so obsessed with remaking its model as closely as possible that it deliberately refuses to engage with the paradigms Hitchcock's classic set for the transition from classical to postmodern horror. Isabel Pinedo's description of this generic shift corresponds to Andrew Tudor's distinction between pre-sixties "secure" horror (1931–1960) and post-sixties "paranoid" horror (since 1960), and the key characteristics both scholars identify are very similar. Movies following *Psycho*—like *Night of the Living Dead* (George A. Romero, 1968), *The Texas Chainsaw Massacre* (Tobe Hooper, 1974), *Halloween* (John Carpenter, 1978), and *A Nightmare on Elm Street* (Wes Craven, 1984)—"[transgress] the rules of the classically oriented horror film" in such ways that overturning generic conventions becomes itself a recognizable new convention for audiences.[78] These postmodern horror movies locate unremitting violence in everyday life, blur the boundaries "between good and evil, normal and abnormal," question rationality and undermine science and authority, reject narrative closure, and produce a bounded experience of fear in which "body horror" and the "spectacle of the ruined body" speak "to the need to express rage and terror in the midst of postmodern social upheaval."[79]

In the 1990s, the decade when Van Sant's remake of *Psycho* was released, horror movies were also relying on sequelization and "generically self-conscious comedy."[80] As Tudor notes, "The significance of these two features is that they interact to add a further level of reflexivity to the relation between audience and film, inviting the moviegoer to participate in the construction of the horror experience via modes of response which are increasingly self-aware."[81] If sequels had emerged as a distinctive feature of the horror genre in the 1980s, with a string of follow-ups to *Halloween* (1978), *Alien* (Ridley Scott, 1979), *Friday the 13th* (Sean S. Cunningham, 1980), *A Nightmare on Elm Street* (1984), *Child's Play* (Tom Holland, 1988) and many other movies, the trend continued in the 1990s so that "the concept of a 'sequel' . . . has itself become a major convention of the genre, a phenomenon fully understood and, more important, expected and embraced by a generically competent horror audience."[82] Similarly, "the tendency to reflexively generate humour by openly appealing to a knowing audience's familiarity with the genre conventions" has become part and parcel of 1990s horror movies.[83] *Wes Craven's New Nightmare* (1994) and the *Scream* franchise are emblematic of these developments, which invite viewers to make use of their genre literacy in order to derive pleasure from the movies' intertextual playfulness and heightened gaming quality.[84]

Amidst these self-reflexive "neo-stalkers,"[85] Van Sant's *Psycho* seemed already out-of-date when it reached cinemas. As Naremore aptly notes, the remake "resembles nothing so much as a museum installation. Its chief value is on the pedagogical or theoretical level, where it functions, intentionally or not, as a metafilm and reveals a good deal about Hitchcock's specific achievement."[86] In the end, the movie is "academic and not at all scary."[87] Wes Craven's first three *Scream* movies strategically employ their reflexivity and self-consciousness about horror genre and sequel conventions as narrative elements and innovative source of horror.[88] *Wes Craven's New Nightmare* blurs the boundaries between the *Elm Street* movies' reality and dreamworld in new and unexpected ways to achieve a terrifying meta-effect.[89] However, the "meta" quality of Van Sant's *Psycho* differs from these movies. It hinges exclusively on *repetition*, not on a serial logic of one-upmanship that drives sequel production more generally and motivates the movies' self-reflexive maneuvers. Instead of reflecting on the state of contemporary horror cinema or speaking to the viewers' generic competence, the kind of repetition we find in the *Psycho* remake draws attention to questions of timelessness and timeliness, to the long-term evolution of viewing habits, cinematic genres, styles, and technologies, and to the ways in which television and the home video market had already altered the relation between Hollywood movies and their remakes.

While Van Sant's *Psycho* presents a stumbling block for academic inquiries into cinematic reconfigurations of the horror genre, film remakes usually allow to trace generic evolutions within changing contexts of production and reception. Constantine Verevis, for instance, dedicates a chapter of his book *Film Remakes* (2006) to *film noir*, examining the role of two remakes from the 1980s—*The Postman Always Rings Twice* (Bob Rafelson, 1981) and *Body Heat* (Lawrence Kasdan, 1981)—in the development of the neo-*noir*.[90] Focusing on film remakes since the 1970s and a broad concept of remaking that is neither limited to Hollywood movies nor medium-specific, Verevis offers a *contextual model* for studying film remakes and provides a systematic exploration of contemporary film remakes as industrial, textual, and critical categories. He analyzes commercial strategies as well as questions of authorship (*industrial category*), investigates how remakes transform earlier movies and how broader generic structures can also be remade (*textual category*), and shows how audience knowledge, industry discourses, and canon formation contribute to the understanding of film remakes (*critical category*). But while Verevis criticizes that remaking is generally understood as "a one-way process"[91] in which a superior "original" (e.g., Hitchcock's *Psycho*) is reduced to an inferior copy (e.g., Van Sant's *Psycho*), he cannot unfold his theory without relying on the original/remake binary.

Katrin Oltmann, in contrast, challenges the inherently evaluative distinction between original and remake in her book *Remake | Premake: Hollywoods romantische Komödien und ihre Gender-Diskurse, 1930–1960* (2008). To describe her study as an analysis of changing gender discourses in Hollywood's romantic comedies—*The Front Page/His Girl Friday*, *The Awful Truth* (Leo McCarey, 1937)/*Let's Do It Again* (Alexander Hall, 1953), and *Holiday Inn* (Mark Sandrich, 1942)/*White Christmas* (Michael Curtiz, 1954)—does not do justice to the extensive theoretical framework Oltmann establishes before delving into her case studies. She introduces the term *premake* as an alternative to the auratically charged term *original*. According to her, *premake* does not hint at some kind of origin but instead highlights the production process of both movies and simply indicates the temporal positioning of the first film with regard to the remake.[92] At the same time, the remake forms literally part of the term *premake*, symbolizing a circular, rather than linear connection between the films that takes into account how both versions shape each other. Finally, *premake* refers to the idea of the pretext in both its meanings as an earlier text (pre-text) and as a pretext for rereading that earlier text, which enables her to follow Mieke Bal's methodology and perform a "preposterous reading" of different versions. This cultural studies approach "puts what came chronologically first ('pre-') as an aftereffect behind ('post-') its later recycling."[93] Oltmann thus opens up a pathway for dynamic readings of premakes and remakes, their shifting intertextual relations, and the ways in which text and context shape each other in the synchronic and diachronic cultural systems in which they circulate.[94]

Such ideas resonate with recent theoretical approaches that reject essentialist understandings of remaking in favor of broader (and presumably more productive) views. Overall, remake scholarship (like popular film criticism) is frequently invested in concepts of authorship, authenticity, originality, and identity, and places movies in hierarchically organized binary oppositions that pit authenticity against plagiarism, original against copy, art against commerce. These value-laden dichotomies are presented as inherent qualities of movies, naturalizing a rhetoric that privileges one (the "original") over the other (the remake) while simultaneously obscuring that both categories in fact constitute each other.[95] Such deficit-oriented conceptualizations of the remake, based on a linear model that traces the trajectory from a superior "original" to an inferior copy, have proven inadequate when it comes to theorizing the remaking process and the film remakes on their own terms. Alternatively, Oltmann proposes *a circular model* rooted in Sigmund Freud's psychoanalytic concept of *Nachträglichkeit* (afterwardsness), which articulates a temporal loop between past and present that helps to describe how a later event prompts the retroactive attribution of meaning to an earlier event, its belated understanding or even revision.[96] The remake, conceptualized in this manner, is a movie that *creates* an original and enables (as Eberwein has also suggested) the rereading of that original and has the potential to retrospectively transform its meaning in significant ways.[97]

Even though Van Sant's *Psycho* is an unusually close remake of Hitchcock's movie, scholars have argued that its subtle variations highlight the queer subtext of the original, which was all but ignored by critics and audiences when the movie was first released in 1960.[98] By making *Psycho*'s queer sexuality decidedly more explicit, Van Sant's remake engages in a retrospective queering of Hitchcock's film. Such a reading is possible: it places Van Sant's director persona at the center of interpretation and his track record as a filmmaker of the New Queer Cinema with movies like *Mala Noche* (1985), *My Own Private Idaho* (1991), and *Even Cowgirls Get the Blues* (1993), rather than Van Sant's obsession with remaking Hitchcock's *Psycho*. The film remake always disregards narrative closure and, by reactivating a supposedly self-contained, closed work of art (addressing unfinished cultural business and weaving in memories of one or more earlier movies), it self-reflexively engages in a dialectic of past and present, repetition and renewal that shifts attention to the underlying instability of the stories we tell ourselves time and again, and by which we construct identities and communities. As Michael A. Arnzen puts it, "Remakes remind cultures of their own capacity for—and history of—production as they 'remake' the past in order to produce the present."[99] In the process, film remakes undermine textual singularity and swap traditional concepts of authorship, authenticity, originality, and identity for a plurality of meanings.[100]

To distinguish between premake and remake, as Oltmann does, eliminates the haunting presence of the original from theorizations of the remake and replaces its powerful aura with a genuinely intertextual interdependence between different film versions.[101] Oltmann extends this interdependence beyond the filmic texts, evoking "the circulation of social energy" that Stephen Greenblatt describes. What Greenblatt suggests for literary works also applies to Hollywood films: they are "the products of collective negotiation and exchange."[102] More than aesthetic objects, they are *cultural* objects with "compelling force" (or energy), continuously "transformed and refashioned" over time, always in step with the historical contexts and their respective discourses and practices.[103] The focus on the complex cultural and social dimension of the film remake, sets a counterpoint to earlier theoretical models and taxonomies that grappled with definitions and categorizations. It is a decisive step away from narrow textual approaches to what constitutes a film remake toward a conception that not only undermines the idea of the original but ultimately also challenges discussions of the film remake as a site of repetition that is distinct from other remaking formats.

BEYOND REPETITION: COMPLEXIFICATION
AND SERIALIZATION

Existing scholarship, ranging from theoretical models and conceptualizations of the film remake to cultural studies-oriented works, prefers original/remake case studies. Structured around a text-based analysis, such case studies identify patterns of repetition and examine how difference produces meaning. Despite an acute awareness of the movies' intertextual relations, they nonetheless tend to treat both original and remake as individual, self-contained texts and neglect the fact that remaking transforms singularities into multiplicities, into texts *without* "firm limits"[104] or closure that never stop to shape each other's meanings. Leonardo Quaresima observes that "the remake calls into question the very notion of an individual work"[105] but that research has demonstrated a stubborn "backwardness" in addressing this issue. "The critical literature on the remake may seem vast," Quaresima writes, "but it is made up almost entirely of descriptions, or of limited comparative analyses of paired texts, carried out according to the most diverse and unsystematic criteria. Attempts to define the remake are vague and often tautological."[106] To make matters worse, academic analyses of original/remake pairs also overlook that some movies have been remade more than once or otherwise repeated, continued and expanded in sequels, prequels, and spin-offs before they were eventually remade.

The evolution of Hollywood remaking has not yet sufficiently been accounted for in theoretical, textual, and cultural studies approaches that continue to grapple with formulating accurate definitions of the film remake and tend to overlook its historical variability as well as the various intertextual bonds that tie films based on the same material together in a sweeping serial gesture. Frank Kelleter and I have proposed that what counts as a remake changes throughout film history and that "the distinction between a genuine film remake and a sequel, a prequel, or any other type of filmic iteration is more uncertain than these straightforward terms would seem to suggest."[107] Vera Dika speaks of a "crisis around the notion of the 'remake' as a descriptive category"[108] because she detects an intensified "compulsion to repeat already repetitive patterns" in our times. The result is a "potentially dynamic model" in which "the old is not erased but ever present" and serialization emerges as "an overdetermined quality of many contemporary works."[109] These are important observations if one wants to gain a deeper understanding of how the film remake has evolved over time and, more generally, how repetition plays out in the cinematic recycling of familiar material. Historically speaking, what Dika describes is a fairly recent phenomenon, indicating a *complexification* of the remake that results in *more explicitly serialized* movies.

During the inception of cinema, so-called dupes (duplicated positive prints) and early cinematic remakes operated differently. Between 1896 and 1906, before copyright laws for film existed and before moving pictures gained value over the equipment that was necessary to project them, remakes functioned "like new vaudeville acts or fairground attractions, with manufacturers stealing ideas from their rivals and trying to reproduce them."[110] Through copying and outright pirating, multiple, nearly identical versions circulated simultaneously and in direct competition with one another. Remaking played a crucial role in establishing reception practices as well as medium-specific formal, stylistic, and generic conventions.[111] During the classical Hollywood cinema, when studios favored new product and "thought of their films as having strictly current value,"[112] remakes replaced their predecessors with new updated versions that largely recreated familiar material without making any substantial changes. This kind of repetition was designed to meet the demand for new product by bringing popular stories back onto the big screen and to effectively showcase what was new: from cinema's latest technological innovation to fashion, acting styles, film aesthetic, and the stars of the day.

There is a noticeable shift in attitudes toward old movies in the postwar United States, when they become a staple of network television and retrospective movie houses. It is only with the coexistence of different versions and the manifold occasions for repeat viewing in the home, first on television and VHS, later on DVD and online streaming platforms, that film remakes begin to display a self-conscious awareness of their own *preexistence* and of their place in Hollywood's past. Playback technologies in the home, in particular DVDs and what Barbara Klinger calls the DVD's meaning-making "intertextual surround,"[113] have "radically extend[ed] the kind of film literacy—the ability to recognize and cross-reference multiple versions of the same property—that was inaugurated by the age of television."[114] Unlike the earlier practice of remaking that replaced old movies that were no longer in circulation with technologically and aesthetically updated versions, remake production and reception evolved to encourage and reward this kind of knowledge among filmmakers and moviegoers.

Film remakes feature different settings and character constellations, unexpected plot twists and endings as well as intertextual strategies that hold special pleasures for audiences in the know, or the "intertextual viewer," as Quaresima calls the ideal consumer of the remake who takes pleasure in "juxtaposing and comparing."[115] With the simultaneous existence of different versions, in short, remake production and reception begin to accommodate the fact that the past persistently endures into the present and put an emphasis on the movies' serial unfolding rather than their time-bound singularity. While Van Sant's *Psycho* seems to be the odd one out in this scenario, a shot-for-shot experiment that circumvents contemporary expectations about how remakes work and how audience knowledge about Hitchcock's *Psycho*, its three sequels, and the state of the horror genre may affect attitudes toward new renditions, film remakes usually engage in what Frank Kelleter and I have termed *retrospective serialization*.[116] This concept describes the recursive progression that has come to define the production and reception of film remakes. Initially unconnected film versions are retrospectively serialized in Hollywood's remaking process, the singularity of the individual movies is erased, and an *ongoing* narrative emerges instead.

Invasion of the Body Snatchers (Don Siegel, 1956) and its three remakes to date (1978, 1993, and 2007) help to illustrate this point: The plot about an alien invasion during which individual human beings are turned into a collective of emotionless pod people and the story's central themes are not simply repeated but further developed from one version to the next so that the body snatchers story is retrospectively serialized.[117] One tagline for Abel Ferrara's *Body Snatchers* (1993) even announces "The Invasion Continues."

Figure 6. Kevin McCarthy's Miles Bennell in Don Siegel's *Invasion of the Body Snatchers* (left) reappears in Philip Kaufman's 1978 remake—still screaming "They're here! You're next!" (right).

The remakes also feature cameo appearances that imply *continuity* on the level of plot. Kevin McCarthy, who stars as Miles Bennell in the 1956 *Invasion of the Body Snatchers*, reappears in Philip Kaufman's 1978 movie, exactly as viewers remember him: running among cars, warning people, looking for help (figure 6). This scene takes up, and thereby pays tribute to, the intended ending of Siegel's movie, and it suggests "that the action of the remake *follows* that of the original film."[118] This is also implied by the setting of the remake—San Francisco—because it was "one of the major urban destinations of the truckloads of pods on the main highway in the original."[119] Another cameo appearance is that of actress Veronica Cartwright, who plays Nancy Belicec in Kaufman's *Invasion of the Body Snatchers* and Wendy Lenk in Oliver Hirschbiegel's *The Invasion* (2007). As Nancy Belicec, she is the last survivor in Kaufman's movie and thus responsible for a narrative stumbling block. In Hirschbiegel's remake, however, Cartwright's Wendy Lenk is the first person who turns out to be immune against the alien virus, setting the eventually successful search for a vaccine in motion. This innovation adds retrospective causality to what happened in the earlier movie, proposing that Nancy Belicec might have stayed human because she was immune all along. In both cases, then, we seem to learn what happened to the characters after their respective body snatchers stories had already ended, as is typical of the sequel rather than the remake. These intertextual references establish a sense of continuity between one self-contained version and the next, which, in turn, renders the entirety of the body snatchers movies legible as a *serial* narrative that, through the alien invasion trope, has captured the nation's most urgent anxieties over the past fifty years.

Table 1 DVD titles released under the "Double Take: Original & Remake" label

Movie Titles	Original (Director, Year)	Remake (Director, Year)
My Friend Flicka / Flicka	Harold D. Schuster, 1942	Michael Mayer, 2006
Anna and the King of Siam / Anna and the King	John Cromwell, 1946	Andy Tennant, 1999
Cheaper by the Dozen	Walter Lang, 1950	Shawn Levy, 2003
War of the Worlds	George Pal, 1953	Steven Spielberg, 2005
The Fly	Kurt Neumann, 1958	David Cronenberg, 1986
The Magnificent Seven	John Sturges, 1960	Antoine Fuqua, 2016
The Flight of the Phoenix	Robert Aldrich, 1965	John Moore, 2004
Doctor Dolittle	Richard Fleischer, 1967	Betty Thomas, 1998
Planet of the Apes	Franklin J. Schaffner, 1968	Tim Burton, 2001
The Thomas Crown Affair	Norman Jewison, 1968	John McTiernan, 1999
The Crazies	George A. Romero, 1973	Breck Eisner, 2010
Rollerball	Norman Jewison, 1975	John McTiernan, 2002
The Omen	Richard Donner, 1976	John Moore, 2006
Amityville Horror	Stuart Rosenberg, 1979	Andrew Douglas, 2005
Flatliners	Joel Schumacher, 1990	Niels Arden Oplev, 2017

Verevis speaks of a "reciprocity" between successive film versions, which contradicts Leitch's assumption that remakes compete with their predecessors, threaten the old movies' economic viability, and attempt to supersede them.[120] "Contemporary remakes," Verevis states, "*generally* enjoy a (more) symbiotic relationship with their originals."[121] They (re)activate interest in earlier renditions and frequently provide the occasion for rereleasing older movies, for understanding them as originals, and for canonizing them as supposedly timeless classics. This is evident in the ways paratexts and special DVD editions draw attention to earlier movies, so remakes are instantly invested "not only with a narrative image, but with aesthetic (and commercial) value."[122] MGM and 20th Century Fox, for example, have released two-disc DVD sets labeled "Double Take: Original & Remake," which invite viewers to consume two versions of the same movie alongside each other and transform the combination of old "classic" and previously often-maligned remake into a privileged collectible (table 1). These special editions essentially sell an old classic and its remake as a *double feature* within a conceptional framework that fosters intertextual proficiency among audiences and creates knowledge about cinema's overarching aesthetic, technological, and cultural trajectory.

Assembled in the same production package, "Original & Remake" pairs rely on repetition since they actively promote repeat viewing as a practice and encourage audiences to engage in spotting meaningful differences as they relate to the movies' temporal specificities and highlight the artistic autonomy or indebtedness of the remake. What has changed between George Pal's 1953 *War of the Worlds* and Steven Spielberg's 2005 remake? How do the remakes of *Rollerball* and *Flatliners* differ from their respective earlier renditions? Such questions are raised when audiences adopt *a comparative mode of viewing* that directs their attention to the long-term development of cinema's visual aesthetics, CGI and special effects technology, and the role of social critique in sci-fi and horror storytelling. The "Double Take" DVDs might not be among the most elaborate (and expensive) "high-end" editions geared toward film buffs, cinephiles, and academics—the cover design is simple, with little variation between different titles (figure 7), and there are generally very few extras—but they certainly tap into the collector's desire to own a *complete* set. Moreover, it is possible to adapt Klinger's observation about special collector's editions that include rare supplemental features and archival material, because here, too, "the collector has a sense that he or she owns not only the [remake] but also its history."[123] More precisely, the "Double Take" DVD set itself functions as a unique paratext: it derives "extra authority"[124] from the self-contained packaging of "Original & Remake" and tends to transform the remake into an "expandable text,"[125] whose meanings are augmented, reshaped, and, indeed, completed by the film-historical framework the DVD provides.

"Complete Collections," or rather "completist" box sets that contain remakes, sequels, and prequels in one package, operate in a similar manner. Published "after the release of a (presumably) final installment," these DVD sets "retrospectively create and promote . . . almost classical, self-contained structures."[126] The *Planet of the Apes: Evolution Collection* from 2012, for example, includes all seven movies that were released between 1968 and 2011: Franklin J. Schaffner's *Planet of the Apes* (1968) and its

Figure 7. DVD sets assembling film remakes and other remaking forms promote repeat viewing, intertextual proficiency, and film-historical knowledge. Author's collection.

four sequels from the 1970s, Tim Burton's 2001 remake, as well as Rupert Wyatt's prequel *Rise of the Planet of the Apes* (2011). Like many other "complete," "evolution," or "legacy" collections, this DVD set can no longer claim to be comprehensive because Wyatt's reboot of the *Apes* franchise spawned two more sequels (both directed by Matt Reeves): *Dawn of the Planet of the Apes* (2014) and *War of the Planet of the Apes* (2017). Even though the latest movies did not yet exist when the *Evolution Collection* came out, the special edition "still provides a meaningful record of the *Apes* films that bears testimony to how cinematic techniques, sociohistorical concerns, and cultural self-descriptions have indeed 'evolved' over four decades."[127] It serves as a snapshot of a serial narrative, of "a larger, cumulative hypotext"[128] in the making that will continue to produce new installments and resist full closure as long as it remains profitable. Despite its transitory nature, this snapshot speaks to the viewers' desire for closure (at least temporarily, they can own a complete set).

DVD publishing of remakes, sequels, and prequels in the same box set "not only facilitates access to different versions but also enables a mode of reception that foregrounds viewers' second-order engagement with a narrative's media-historical aspects."[129] These collections cultivate a pleasure in repetition and they "are specifically designed for fan cultures obsessed with storing and archiving"[130] because (unlike the "Double Take" DVDs) they are often elaborate, "high-end" affairs with numerous extras designed to produce film-historical knowledge. The seven-disc *The Fly: Ultimate Collector's Edition*—which includes Kurt Neumann's horror classic *The Fly* (1958) and its two sequels, *The Return of the Fly* (Edward Bernds, 1959) and *The Curse of the Fly* (Don Sharp, 1965), as well as David Cronenberg's acclaimed 1986 remake and the sequel, *The Fly II* (Chris Walas, 1989)—comes in an intricate transparent plastic package that has little flies printed all over it. In reference to Cronenberg's movie, the DVDs themselves are stored in a smaller, "telepod"-shaped box that features a lenticular flicker picture of Seth Brundle (Jeff Goldblum) morphing into Brundlefly (figure 7). Just like the TV-on-DVD box sets that Jason Mittell analyzes, this special edition of the *Fly* movies functions as a "collectable media object" that "demands to be displayed, dismantled, used, and discussed" rather than a mere "container for the discs."[131] As a paratext, the box set clearly draws attention to Cronenberg's remake. The 1986 movie is prominently showcased because of the box design and therefore "control[s] and determine[s]"[132] how viewers will approach the *Fly* movies collected in this special edition. Instead of following the chronological order in which the films were released, the DVD box presents the critically most highly acclaimed version as "a point of orientation" from which viewers can explore the variations of the *Fly* narrative by "look[ing] backward and forward."[133] It primes them "that the 1986 film will be 'the best' of the five iterations," while indicating "that the others are necessary viewing if one wants to properly appreciate Cronenberg's masterpiece."[134]

Some box sets seem to deconstruct the notion of an "untouchable original" altogether. The *Jaws Quadrilogy*, including Steven Spielberg's *Jaws* (1975) and the sequels *Jaws 2* (Jeannot Szwarc, 1978), *Jaws 3-D* (Joe Alves, 1983), and *Jaws: The Revenge* (Joseph Sargent, 1987), for example, as well as the *Psycho Collection I–IV* (figure 7), including Alfred Hitchcock's *Psycho* and the sequels *Psycho II* (Richard Franklin, 1983), *Psycho III* (Anthony Perkins, 1986), and *Psycho IV: The Beginning* (Mick Garris, 1990), convert "a once discreet, critically acclaimed, and by now classic film . . . into the first part of a series that is advertised with and by the box set."[135]

Frank Kelleter and I have argued that "rather than canonizing an (already canonical) source text," these DVD collections "highlight its status as an elastic piece of popular storytelling."[136] Again, the box sets themselves lay claim to completeness and closure in order to appeal to viewers—not necessarily with regard to the individual movies (which are mostly self-contained) but concerning their overarching narrative progression. In the case of *Psycho*, Amazon customers, who bought the *Psycho Collection*, have also understood this claim in terms of an expansive storyworld. Indicating, in the review section, that watching either Hitchcock's or Van Sant's *Psycho* had prompted them to seek out the sequels, some of them complained that the 1998 remake or the television show *Bates Motel* (A&E, 2013–2017) were not included.[137] Regardless of whether DVD box sets assemble "Original & Remake" pairs, sequels, prequels, or all of the above, there is certainly a trend toward evoking Hollywood's distant or more immediate past in ways that present audiences with a cumulative hypotext that means more than the sum of its parts. Each new remake, sequel, or prequel is marketed as an "expandable text"[138] that already comes with a past and invites viewers to explore that past, or, to evoke Mittell's notion of the "drillable text," "to dig deeper, probing beneath the surface to understand the complexity of a story and its telling."[139]

Needless to say, the symbiotic relationship between different versions is, above all, driven by economic factors. By the early 1990s, Hollywood studios had already realized that the release of remakes and sequels had great potential for cross-promotion and for monetizing classics and older titles. The theatrical success of remakes such as *Cape Fear* (Martin Scorsese, 1991), *Father of the Bride* (Charles Shyer, 1991), and *Robin Hood: Prince of Thieves* (Kevin Reynolds, 1991) stirred videocassette sales and rentals of the movies' predecessors: *Cape Fear* (J. Lee Thompson, 1962), *Father of the Bride* (Vincente Minnelli, 1950), and *The Adventures of Robin Hood* (Michael Curtiz and William Keighley, 1938).[140] In light of these developments, studios worked on more sophisticated piggybacking strategies, and repackaging older titles to coincide with the release of the next remake or sequel was promising and profitable.[141] If audiences were familiar with *Chinatown* (Roman Polanski, 1974), *48 Hrs.* (Walter Hill, 1982), and *Gremlins* (Joe Dante, 1984) from watching the movies on television or videocassette, the corporate reasoning went, they would also flock to the cinemas to see the belated sequels, *The Two Jakes* (Jack Nicholson, 1990), *Another 48 Hrs.* (Walter Hill, 1990), and *Gremlins 2: The New Batch* (Joe Dante, 1990). Videocassettes in particular were thought to function as "a trailer for the sequel" and important advertising tool.[142]

This remains true for the ancillary markets of DVDs, Blu-Rays, and streaming platforms. Yet, rather than operating as a memory aid that ensures brand-name recognition, the coexistence of old and new now asks viewers to engage with a movie's and Hollywood's past, to accumulate knowledge about material from the popular storytelling repertoire, and to reflect on how it has evolved over time, in terms of the cinematic past and with regard to the viewers' personal life trajectories. The presence of the old in the new, I argue, has left its mark on how repetition operates in Hollywood today and on how stories are being told. Under the impact of television and home media technologies, the film remake is becoming less of a *self-contained* text and more explicitly *serialized*, with allusions, intertextual references, and an increasing postmodern self-awareness that take audiences back and forth between multiple versions, ultimately hinting at some sort of continuity across distinct media-historical, cultural, and autobiographical moments. References to earlier movies firmly ground each new remake in the present while also establishing a baseline for audiences against which technical achievements can be appreciated (e.g., special-effects technology in the *King Kong*, *The Fly*, or *Ghostbusters* remakes), cultural change is rendered legible (e.g., the allegorical treatment of contemporary anxieties in the different versions of *Invasion of the Body Snatchers* or *Planet of the Apes*), and recontextualizations turn into meaningful historical or theoretical comments (e.g., in the remakes of *A Star Is Born*, *You've Got Mail* [Nora Ephron, 1998], and Gus Van Sant's *Psycho*). Where heterogeneous audiences with varying degrees of familiarity, knowledge, and expectation used to be the norm, paratextual framing, industrial and critical discourses, and the movies themselves seem to dictate that remake literacy and intertextual proficiency are becoming less of an option and more of a requirement.

If we acknowledge the more overtly serialized nature of the film remake, it is indeed possible to speak about a "crisis around the notion of the 'remake' as a descriptive category."[143] What is more: definitions that do not consider the historically dynamic discourses and operating principles of the film remake will also fail to realize that the already fluid boundaries between the film remake and other remaking formats continue to dissolve in contemporary Hollywood cinema. There is a long list of movies that elude clear-cut categorizations, including the *Invasion of the Body Snatchers* remakes, which contain elements of the sequel, or movies such as *The Godfather Part II* (Francis Ford Coppola, 1974) and *Psycho IV: The Beginning*, which qualify as sequel and as prequel. Both movies alternate between two parallel plotlines: one is set in the present and continues the story from the earlier movie(s) and the other is set in the past, focusing on events that have occurred before the diegetic time of other movie(s). *The Godfather Part II* juxtaposes the rise of young Vito Corleone (Robert De Niro), who immigrates to America and establishes the family business in New York, with the fall of his son Michael Corleone (Al Pacino), who destroys the mafia family after his father's death. In *Psycho IV*, fifty-eight-year-old Norman Bates (Anthony Perkins) has been released from the mental institution, and lives in a beautiful house with his loving wife. Upon learning of his wife's pregnancy, he plans to murder her in order "to protect the world from this aging bad seed known as Norman Bates." Desperate, he calls into a radio talk show to share his troubled past, leading to a series of flashbacks that present Norman's childhood with his schizophrenic mother and the origins of his split personality. The film thus contrasts the construction of his deterministic cage and his struggle to break free from it.

Ongoing narrative continuity and seriality have been gaining importance over the past decades, so it seems logical to adopt the broader concept of *Hollywood remaking*, which, while limited to texts that belong to the same medium, reaches beyond the film remake proper and its unique reliance on repetition to include series, sequels, prequels, spin-offs, and so on. The longevity of many long-running film franchises clearly hinges on their capacity for *multiplication* and *serialization* in a constantly changing mediascape, which is why they often embrace different forms of cinematic iteration. As mentioned above, nine *Planet of the Apes* movies have been released over the past fifty years, among them four sequels, a film remake, and a prequel trilogy that has recently rebooted the franchise. *Star Wars* is another example where this kind of flexible storytelling—moving forwards, backwards, and sideways in a persistent fictional world—has become a defining element of the franchise's enduring existence and profitability. This may seem confusing, yet studios, filmmakers, audiences, and critics share a common understanding that *the film remake* repeats and updates an already familiar story; *the sequel* continues the story of one or more characters; *the prequel* inverts the temporal relationship of the sequel by presenting what happens *before*, not *after*, the events of a previous movie; *the spin-off* redistributes the focus of an earlier work; *a crossover* places characters or other defining elements from unrelated works into the context of a new story; and *a franchise* may include all of the above and more.

These categories themselves are not set in stone and have recently seen a number of additions that film critics and scholars consider more adequate for describing how repetition with a difference plays out on screen in the franchise era. *Reboot* is a relatively new term for movies that relaunch an expensive, creatively depleted, or dormant film franchise by breaking with the continuity of a narrative in order to start over with radically redesigned characters and storylines as well as the inherent promise of textual, aesthetic, and technological novelty. *Batman Begins* (Christopher Nolan, 2005) and *Casino Royale* (Martin Campbell, 2006) have been trailblazers for this Hollywood trend because of how they reinvented their heroes and succeeded in reviving the *Batman* and *James Bond* franchises. A decade later, *Star Wars: The Force Awakens* (J. J. Abrams, 2015), *Terminator: Genisys* (Alan Taylor, 2015), and *Creed* (Ryan Coogler, 2015) also rebooted their franchises in the sense that they generated new, long-term revenue and interest. However, they did not break with the franchise past but instead embraced it, relying on the return of beloved characters (and actors) as well as recognizable narrative and aesthetic codes that served both to foreground their investment in the past and to bind audiences to overarching, decades-spanning narratives. These movies remake *and* continue familiar stories, combine old and new characters, and evoke the enduring cultural and historical significance of the franchise. They display a pronounced nostalgia for the franchise past that does not match earlier definitions of the reboot, so that neologisms such as *requel* (a portmanteau combining reboot and sequel) and *legacyquel* (blending legacy and sequel) have popped up in popular film criticism and academic journals to differentiate what "reboot" actually means.

Labels that originate in the movie industry as well as in popular film criticism—from film remake to legacyquel—fulfill important communicative functions and activate expectations associated with a particular kind of Hollywood movie. They also enter academic debates about repetition, intertextuality, originality, and—more recently—seriality. As scholars, however, we must be wary of taking these labels at face value. They facilitate the communication about industry trends and reception practices, but instead of relying on them as descriptive or critical categories, we should rather treat them as another object of study and sharpen our analytical tools in order to understand how they shape the movie industry and culture more broadly. Any investigation of remaking as a historically evolving practice that produces a variety of formats through repetition and variation, "while not being required to participate in typological controversies, needs to study them as part of the research field itself. If that is done, scholastic distinctions and debates become visible as lively forces within a larger network of actors that sustains this particular storytelling culture."[144] Examining Hollywood remaking from a historical and cultural studies perspective, in other words, cannot exclusively rely on the analysis of production trends and imaginative frameworks but also needs to consider academic definitions and approaches. These have rapidly evolved since the 1980s and provide an epistemological basis for understanding the power struggles around the aesthetic and cultural legitimacy of Hollywood remaking. If remaking is further considered to be a serial storytelling practice, as I propose here, it is possible to examine the long-term unfolding of popular narratives across the cinematic past as well as changing cultural, social, and political points in time, and to ask how film remakes as well as sequels, prequels, spin-offs and reboots intersect with cultural memory, lived experiences, and processes of individual and collective identity formation.

2   Hollywood's Usable Past

In the comedy *Neighbors* (Nicholas Stoller, 2014), there is a scene in which thirtysomething Mac Radner (Seth Rogen) talks about superheroes with his younger neighbor Teddy Sanders (Zac Efron). Mac clings on to the last vestiges of his youth, as he and his wife, Kelly (Rose Byrne), raise their newborn daughter in a suburban family home; Teddy just moved in next door with his Delta Psi Beta fraternity. Joining one of the loud, drug-and-alcohol-filled frat parties at Teddy's house, Mac strikes up a conversation about Batman (figure 8):

> MAC: Hey, who's Batman to you? Like, when you think of Batman, who's Batman?
> TEDDY: Are you kidding me?
> MAC: Christian Bale?
> TEDDY: Christian Bale.
> MAC: Michael Keaton is Batman to me.

They go on to quote lines from *Batman* (Tim Burton, 1989) and *The Dark Knight* (Christopher Nolan, 2008), imitating the recognizable "bat-voices" of the two actors: Michael Keaton's low, guttural "I'm Batman" and

Figure 8. "Who's Batman to you?"—Mac's (Seth Rogen) superhero talk with Teddy (Zac Efron) is not only about taste but also about time-bound media experiences and generational belonging.

Christian Bale's throaty growl of "Where is she?" during the interrogation scene with the Joker (Heath Ledger). Mac and Teddy's respective preferences for these cinematic iterations of Batman, made almost twenty years apart, encapsulate the insurmountable distance between the new dad and the college student. It stands in for their different outlooks on life that fuel the conflict between them and drive the plot of *Neighbors*. And yet: even though they do not identify with the exact same Batman character from the exact same movie, Mac and Teddy still have a pop-cultural reference point in common. Hollywood remaking—including reboots and the repeated reinvention of superheroes like Batman—creates *a continuum of shared memories and experiences* (based on the mythical stability of Batman and his fictional world), while also *anchoring individual memories and experiences in time and space* (namely when Michael Keaton's earlier portrayal of Batman is more appealing to a viewer than Christian Bale's).

The short dialogue from *Neighbors* and its central question, "Who's Batman to you?" draws attention to the cultural functions of Hollywood remaking. In the movie, remaking is a topic of casual conversation, but precisely as such it signals how the practice is deeply enmeshed in everyday life, where it organizes the passage of time along viewers' lived experiences, different life stages, and overall aging process. The short conversation therefore gives an impression of how remakes, sequels, and reboots help audiences navigate the vast realm of popular culture and shape the ways in which viewers imagine themselves as mnemonic communities. Mac and Teddy each remember Batman movies from their respective childhoods and identify more closely with one specific version (or what ultimately amounts to their favorite and, therefore, the "best" iteration) of the Caped Crusader. The preference for either Michael Keaton's charismatic onscreen presence or Christian Bale's somber portrayal of Batman, I argue, is not merely a question of taste but instead determined by time-bound media and cultural experiences that partake in defining and shaping generational identities.

The central aim of this chapter is to explore how Hollywood remaking establishes connections between *time*, *memory*, and *identity* and to probe the nostalgic element inherent in this complex constellation. Contemporary Hollywood cinema relies on each of these three axioms to sell new products that are based on the already-known. They determine industrial and critical discourses surrounding remaking today; make up the imaginative framework in which producers and creative talent, critics, and audiences come to understand remakes, sequels, and franchises; and, through long-term meaning-making processes, affect how people remember themselves in a rapidly changing world. Remaking transforms the cinematic past into a *usable past*. The term was originally coined by cultural critic Van Wyck Brooks in his influential essay "On Creating a Usable Past" (1918), which is concerned with the literary history of the United States. Brooks writes: "The present is a void, and the American writer floats in that void because the past that survives in the common mind of the present is a past without living value. But is this the only possible past? If we need another past so badly, is it inconceivable that we might discover one, that we might even invent one?"[1] In the tradition of pragmatic progressivism, a usable past is indeed "an invention or at least a retrospective reconstruction *to serve the needs of the present.*"[2] The term leads a productive afterlife in historiography and memory studies, gravitating around questions like "what *we* do *with* the past" (an instrumentalist view that stresses the politics and power dynamics involved in maintaining or debunking particular versions of the past) and "what that *past* does for *us*" (a functionalist understanding that foregrounds individual and collective identity constructions in relation to the past).[3] Both takes are relevant when it comes to Hollywood remaking, where serial patterns of repetition and variation construct, preserve, and challenge the cinematic past, while also providing recurring reference points that compel audiences to position themselves within a complicated matrix of personal experiences, cultural memory, and national history.

To be sure, what constitutes a usable cinematic past—that is, a cinematic past with "living value"—varies considerably for different cultural agents. For the movie industry, for instance, it takes on a literal meaning considering that Hollywood exploits its studio vaults and archives in order to recycle old material and renew its economic and cultural value in the present. On the level of production, remaking enables filmmakers and producers to situate themselves and their work within film history by paying homage to, or by updating, improving, and critically revising earlier versions of a movie. In more abstract terms, the popular storytelling material that remaking reactivates in the present also plays into Hollywood's self-descriptions, when movies provide historical markers that make it possible to track and measure cinema's technological, aesthetic, and cultural developments in comparison to older versions. On the level of reception, remaking structures time for viewers because it brings back points of identification at different life stages. Here, the "living value" of the cinematic past means that the recurring presence of certain characters, plots, and storyworlds over many years and decades helps viewers to orient themselves in the world and, as I will show, to construct a coherent sense of self. More broadly speaking, Hollywood's usable past also leaves its mark on the nation's cultural imagination because remakes, sequels, and long-running franchises emerge as sites where conservative and progressive ideologies are negotiated again and again.

Focusing on *Stella Dallas*, *Footloose*, *Jumanji*, and the recent Hollywood trend to produce all-female reboots, the first part of this chapter explores how remaking deals with shifting meanings, cultural values, and attitudes and examines the critical potential of cultural reproduction. The discussion centers on remaking's long-term engagement with ideas of continuity and change as well as on a set of questions about timeliness and the politics of representation that Hollywood raises with each new remake, sequel, and reboot: Does the story hold up? Are the plot and characters still relatable? How does the movie respond to and shape its specific cultural and historical moment? How does it relate to contemporary "structures of feeling," to "meanings and values as they are lived and felt"?[4] What kind of cultural work does it perform for the present? With the complex negotiations that transform Hollywood's past into a usable past in mind, the second part of the chapter zeroes in on how remakes and sequels organize the passage of time both on the collective level and for individual viewers and analyzes the identificatory potential that popular culture holds and sustains over the course of our lives. I argue that through the repetition and serial unfolding of narratives over extended periods of time, Hollywood remaking encourages the prolonged reception of and engagement with fictional characters and their storyworlds and thus offers structures and meanings for the self. Remaking draws on the cinematic past to build a repertoire of shared media texts that partakes in the shaping of selfhood and in the construction and maintenance of communal coherence. Taking the cue from memory studies' work on the relationship between memory and media as well as generation theory's interest in formative media experiences, I suggest that Hollywood remaking constructs a "we-sense" through shared experiences, memories, and attachments. Remakes, sequels, and reboots can prompt the formation of what I call *movie generations*. Within this conceptual framework, I will study the backlash against Hollywood's recent remaking cycle, which brought back generation-defining movies and television shows from the 1980s, and against the female-led *Ghostbusters: Answer the Call* (Paul Feig, 2016). My focus is on the "ruined childhood" trope that dominated film reviews and fannish discourses and on how remaking these formative media texts mobilized deep-seated feelings of (white) nostalgia. Moving to the latest *Ghostbusters* movie, *Ghostbusters: Afterlife* (Jason Reitman, 2021), the chapter contends that time, memory, and identity have become such important parameters in Hollywood that they have effectively altered the nature of remaking in the new millennium and paved the way for the *nostalgia franchise*.

MANAGING CONTINUITY AND CHANGE: REMAKING, TIMELINESS, AND THE POLITICS OF REPRESENTATION

Hollywood remaking produces continuity. Film remakes and sequels always come to form part of *ongoing* narratives—irrespective of their own claims to novelty, originality, and status as standalone works of art. The three *Body Snatchers* remakes to date, for instance, repeat the story of the first movie, while also continuing and gradually expanding it in each new rendition; the *Jaws* sequels turn the fish-eats-man formula into a family saga around the Brody family's recurring encounters with great white sharks; and even Christopher Nolan's dark and gritty reboot of Batman can never entirely divest itself of earlier renditions of the fictional world of Gotham City and the villains against which Batman fights. Remaking puts trust in the viewers' intertextual proficiency, their ability to connect multiple versions and derive pleasure from recognizing similarities and differences. It does not matter whether the movies are explicitly serialized on the level of plot, however, because processing familiar material in new historical contexts renders the entirety of movies based on that material legible as *serial texts* that evolve over time. What is being continued here, in other words, does not automatically have to involve the movies' sustained storyworlds and the narratives that unfold on-screen. Rather, the process of recontextualization goes hand in hand with a serial progression that manifests itself at one remove from the diegetic level. By inscribing movies into the overarching narrative that is Hollywood's—and, in extension, the nation's—history, remaking creates *cultural continuity*. The term *second-order seriality*[5] captures how remakes, sequels, and reboots self-reflexively document cinema's development and how these movies produce a sense of coherence as they foreground continuity and a theme of inevitable progress that also defines the historical master narrative of the United States.

According to Frank Kelleter, serial storytelling "supports a practical *regime of continuation*."[6] Serial narratives that endlessly generate follow-up possibilities by translating repetition into difference, he writes, "play an important part in creating systemic trust in the improbable reality of their own—and hence their own culture's—persistence."[7] This means the continuation of stories we already know contains a promise of "infinite futurity" that extends to the culture at large and to its capitalist system of cultural production.[8] Hollywood remaking, too, "has a stabilizing function, as each new variation reinforces the entire system of cultural self-generation and furthers the culture's belief in its own existence and continuity."[9] Remaking builds trust that the constantly changing world in which we live will nevertheless remain the world we know.

What distinguishes the serial narratives that remaking produces from those in other serial media with regular daily or weekly rhythms (newspapers, radio, and television) is their extended duration and their stance toward the past. Hollywood remaking stresses continuity by weaving a historical thread around and through the cinematic past that reaches out into the present and future. And in doing so, remaking calls attention to the passage of time in a manner that foregrounds *change*. Remakes, sequels, and reboots thus serve as a mode of timekeeping: each new version of an already familiar story stands in for a specific moment in terms of its cultural, social, and political dynamics, as well as its position in film history, which is defined by industry trends, technologies (e.g. sound, color, widescreen, 3-D, CGI, motion capture), performers, narrative structures, and visual aesthetics, politics of representation, and, more generally, the medium's affordances and constraints at the time.

To negotiate continuity and change, and to promote the enduring relevance of certain characters and storyworlds as well as the cultural sensibilities they represent over possible others is an inherently ideological and political act. The capacity of Hollywood remaking to reactivate old movies and meanings invariably comes with *a critical potential* to reframe, rewrite, and revise the past so that familiar material is in keeping with the zeitgeist. New versions process cultural change as they adapt familiar stories to current tastes and attitudes and negotiate norms and values that are embedded in historically changing cultural, social, and political contexts. However, this critical potential tends to be counterbalanced by the specter of continuity. Because remaking always combines the reassuringly familiar and the new, it can never veer off too far from the established narrative. In the end, the critical potential nonetheless distinguishes film remakes and sequels from old movies with a "classic" label that, as Barbara Klinger puts it, "serves strategically to defend the status of the old product in the contemporary world of media consumption" and deflects any criticism regarding outdated representations of gender roles and racial stereotypes.[10] To be sure, "immortal films" like *Citizen Kane* (Orson Wells, 1941), *Casablanca* (Michael Curtiz, 1942), or *It's a Wonderful Life* (Frank Capra, 1946) have certainly undergone material and semantic transformations each time they have been rereleased, restored, or adapted to new media formats throughout their long existence, as Klinger also reminds us.[11] Yet, in comparison to movies that are remade, continued, expanded, or revised at different points in time, these films ultimately remain the same self-contained, "timeless" classics with relatively stable meanings. Hollywood remaking produces serially evolving narratives with *new texts* in *new contexts* that can accommodate change (and usually do so, albeit to varying degrees). Remaking, in other words, introduces a "timeliness" factor that can be measured and evaluated along the conservative and progressive tendencies of the movies' representational politics.

Take *Stella* (John Erman, 1990), the third version of *Stella Dallas* after Henry King's 1925 silent movie starring Belle Bennett and King Vidor's 1937 sound film remake with Barbara Stanwyck in the leading role, which was nominated for two Academy Awards. Made more than half a century after the first remake, *Stella* stars Bette Midler in the heartrending melodrama about a loving, working-class mother who has a daughter by upper-class Stephen Dallas and eventually gives her up to him and his new partner with the intention that the girl can climb up the social ladder. Producer Samuel Goldwyn Jr. and screenwriter Robert Getchell were eager to modernize the story so that "audiences accept it on today's terms."[12] Stella and Stephen have an affair but never marry, and she raises their daughter on her own as a single working mother who earns her livelihood as a barmaid. According to director John Erman, this remake is less "about social classes ... [and] more about breaking away from an economic prison."[13] A *New York Times* report from the film set similarly confirmed the presumably progressive stance of the movie: "When [Stella] decides to banish her teen-age daughter to Dr. Dallas's yuppicdom, it's not for class as such. It's to let [her] ... escape the poverty cycle, drugs and a hoodlum boyfriend."[14] Upon its release, *Stella* received overall mixed reviews, but critics, who disliked it, did not see how the story could speak to modern audiences and found it a "hopelessly dated and ill-advised remake."[15]

To be sure, *New York Times* critic Frank S. Nugent had already made a similar complaint when the Barbara Stanwyck remake had opened at Radio City Music Hall in the summer of 1937. Nugent thought that the 1923 novel that inspired the movie had aged badly: "It seems unlikely that historians of the future will find Olive Higgins Prouty's *Stella Dallas* among the imperishables of literature. It is too dated a piece for that. Too apt to grow sere and withered by time."[16] And yet, Nugent found a timeless quality to the story, simply because "mother love and sacrifice, which are at the heart of the Prouty work, are durable dramatic commodities, as irresistible and compelling today as they were in 1923, when the novel first appeared, or as they were in 1925, when a still-voiceless screen brought the book to some semblance of dramatic life."[17] Reviews were more critical of the 1990 remake, however, questioning both the timelessness and timeliness of the melodrama: "Fifty-three years later, the world has changed so drastically that the bare bones of *Stella Dallas* don't even begin to support this story," Janet Maslin noted in the *New York Times*.[18] "Single mothers are not unusual; class barriers are not unbridgeable; little birds routinely fall farther from the nest."[19] *The Village Voice*'s Georgia Brown criticized the movie's anti-feminist premise and conservative backwardness in her review, pointing out that because Stella, once she finds out that she is pregnant, refuses to either marry Stephen, have an abortion, or receive his child support, essentially acts like "[a] real guy's gal! This is what feminists mean about melodrama serving patriarchal structures."[20] Writing for *New York* magazine, film critic David Denby tied his verdict that "contemporary" *Stella* "doesn't add up anymore"[21] to larger concerns about Hollywood's usable past: "There's a clear danger in the constant retooling of creaky old movie plots—the likelihood that the social conventions that existed when the material was first generated, and that gave the story some connection with a contemporary audience, will have evaporated by the time of the second or third remake, leaving the story hanging in the air."[22] On both the production and reception sides *Stella* elicited contradictory views about the progressive promise of Hollywood remaking, about how repetition, variation, and the serial evolution of familiar stories over long periods of time can actually manage continual readjustments to ever-changing cultural, political, and social contexts and their highly unstable meanings.

Craig Brewer's 2011 remake of *Footloose* (Herbert Ross, 1984) turned out to be very similar in this regard. While Brewer's movie is strikingly faithful to the 1980s musical drama about teenager Ren McCormack (Kevin Bacon) who moves from the big city to a small town and fights to overturn the town's ban on music and dancing—so much so, in fact, that Roger Ebert admitted, "I was wickedly tempted to reprint my 1984 review, word for word"[23]—the remake is much less critical of religious zeal than its earlier counterpart. This is why, in their *Los Angeles Times* review, Steven Zeitchik and Amy Kaufman wondered whether "*Footloose* [has] been given a conservative makeover."[24] They wrote: "It's probably a stretch to say the new *Footloose* . . . panders to the religious right. But the movie fits a heck of a lot more comfortably in Rick Perry's America."[25] In an interview, Brewer told them, "I didn't really feel like this was the time to demonize faith in terms of the narrative . . . like it was important that this be about teenagers against God, because I don't know if that is relevant today."[26] According to Zeitchik and Kaufman, the remake raised a lot of questions among film critics and commentators when it was first announced, most importantly, "How do you remake a movie that was at times hostile to religion for today's mainstream American audience? Now we have our answer: You don't."[27]

Despite disagreement about how repetition and variation play out in terms of progressive or conservative ideologies, *Stella* and *Footloose* seem straightforward examples of how Hollywood puts the cinematic past (that is, already existing material that ideally continues to be "irresistible and compelling" to contemporary audiences) to use in shifting cultural and media landscapes. Other remakes and some long-running film franchises are certainly more committed to addressing societal change than these two cases. This is evident in their efforts to update gender and racial representations, revise problematic legacies, and trade outdated stereotypes for a more inclusive, diverse, and empowering array of heroes and heroines in more accepting fictional worlds. Movies like *The Invasion* (Oliver Hirschbiegel, 2007), *Ghostbusters: Answer the Call*, *Ocean's Eight* (Gary Ross, 2018), or *The Hustle* (Chris Addison, 2019), for instance, have replaced white male leads from past renditions with female actors. Disney's new *Star Wars* movies feature multiracial, multiethnic, and multinational casts. *Jumanji: Welcome to the Jungle* (Jake Kasdan, 2017), which continues the story of *Jumanji* (Joe Johnston, 1995) after twenty-two years, functions as a belated sequel that is likewise "hyper-aware of the future it has stepped into."[28]

The story of a magical (and deadly) game that traps its players until they finish it, is retold not as a story of grief, loss, and fear but as a comic action-adventure in which a mismatched group of teenagers embarks on a journey of self-discovery. In the first *Jumanji*, Judy (Kirsten Dunst) and

Figure 9. Judy, Peter, Alan, and Karen form an unlikely, all-white family in *Jumanji* (1995). The characters in *Jumanji: Welcome to the Jungle* (2017) are more diverse and appeal to younger, global audiences.

Peter's (Bradley Pierce) parents have recently died in a car accident, and, when Alan (Robin Williams) returns to the real world after having been stuck in the Jumanji jungle all by himself for twenty-six years, his family is gone as well. While Judy, Peter, Alan, and his childhood friend Sarah (Bonnie Hunt), whom the three track down to finish playing the game, form an unlikely, all-white family until their world eventually turns back to normal, *Jumanji: Welcome to the Jungle* has a much more diverse cast and set of characters that appeals to younger, global audiences and speaks to the newly discovered bankability of inclusivity in Hollywood (see figure 9). Four teenagers—fearful nerd Spencer (Alex Wolff), the high school's football star Fridge (Ser'Darius Blain), bookish introvert Martha (Morgan Turner), and the popular girl and Instagram addict Bethany (Madison Iseman)—find themselves in a *Breakfast Club*-style detention scenario. They are cleaning out the school's basement, when they come across an old video game console and cartridge (Jumanji has mysteriously transformed from a board game into a video game in this sequel). Once each of them has selected an avatar, they are sucked into the game and into the bodies of their new digital selves: Spencer turns into the muscular and charismatic archeologist Dr. Xander "Smolder" Bravestone (Dwayne Johnson), Fridge transforms into the short, whiny zoologist Franklin "Moose" Finbar (Kevin Hart), Martha finds herself in the body of Lara Croft-inspired martial arts expert Ruby Roundhouse (Karen Gillan), and, Bethany becomes overweight, middle-aged Professor Sheldon "Shelly" Oberon (Jack Black).

The teenagers' plunge into the cursed jungle and the body-swap situation invert the premise of 1995's *Jumanji*, tone down the danger of playing the game in the real world (where wild animals wreaked havoc on a small town, and Judy, Peter, Alan, and Sarah had only their one life to lose), and put a funny twist on the familiar story. The sequel's creative play with repetition and variation, in particular its "delightfully clichéd . . . racial inclusion" and reliance "on tropes to poke fun at millennials, feminists, and the body issues that come with the Instagram-curated world that we live in,"[29] serves to brand *Jumanji: Welcome to the Jungle* as ideologically progressive. Since the digital avatars are cast against the teenagers' real-world selves, involving bodily changes, gender bending, and the reversal of defining character traits, the movie humorously exposes and disrupts social expectations about conformity and heteronormativity. At the same time, however, and despite the movie's apparent "hyper-awareness" about representations of gender, race, and sexuality, its punchlines still depend on binary gender identities that pit supposedly natural masculine and feminine qualities against each other, on Blackness as a source of humor, and on women as objects of the male gaze.

It is framed as hilarious, for instance, that Dwayne Johnson's imposing physical stature, bravery, and strength do not add up with Spencer's geekiness and insecurity, or that Bethany's being trapped in Jack Black's body creates a camp, girly gay man. The comic effect is achieved because these characters do not live up to toxic ideals of "real men," which also means that "binary gender roles are still so embedded in the fabric of society that questioning them and playing with them is a guaranteed route to a cheap laugh."[30] When Fridge's alter ego in the video game, Franklin "Moose" Finbar, succumbs to his major weakness and eats pound cake at a bazaar, he expects an allergic reaction and screams in panic, "Am I still Black?!," before he explodes and loses one of his three lives. While the movie embraces racial diversity, it also resorts to Black stereotypes to elicit laughs. And when Martha notices her avatar's sexy outfit, she exclaims: "Why am I wearing half a shirt and short shorts in the jungle?!" Meant as a tongue-in-cheek comment on the ridiculously revealing and impractical costumes of action heroines in video games and Hollywood movies, this joke about female sexualization and objectification also articulates what feminist media scholar Rosalind Gill has described as a "postfeminist sensibility" that pervades contemporary media culture. Martha's transformation into Ruby Roundhouse follows a makeover paradigm that is presented as self-improvement and as an empowering experience "in which the objectifying male gaze is internalised."[31] Her ironic remark is certainly critical of sexualized costume designs, yet her avatar keeps wearing the skimpy outfit throughout the jungle adventure. This is not surprising, though, because "in postfeminist media culture irony has become a way of 'having it both ways'"[32]—feminist values are explicitly embraced yet voiced in a contradictory manner.

Both the body swap premise and digital world of the video game in *Jumanji: Welcome to the Jungle* serve as distancing devices that make it indeed possible to have it both ways, to combine the movie's progressive politics with contradictory representations of race, gender, and sexuality. The sequel's knowing play with clichés is a nod to the 1990s (when the first *Jumanji* movie was released), to video game culture, and to the conventions of Hollywood's action-adventure movies. It also generates comic situations through the preposterous disconnect between such outdated stereotypes and contemporary sensibilities. Gender flips, racial inclusion, and a growing awareness that representation matters are progressive moves in an industry, where "some of the biggest, most prominent, most popular media franchises are [still] overwhelmingly white centered and male driven."[33] With repetition and variation as its main operating principle, Hollywood remaking can foreground representational shortcomings and accommodate broader social, political, and cultural changes that occur within a generation's time, while holding on to what has proven economically successful and grown near and dear to audiences in the past. As a derivative practice that thrives on repetition, remaking preserves old (and sometimes old-fashioned) stories; as an innovative and creative undertaking, remaking updates familiar material and can partake in fashioning more diverse and inclusive narratives and fictional worlds.

Daniel Herbert observes that "the drive to represent a variety of different kinds of people can lead to new and potentially empowering forms of creativity within a franchise,"[34] and there is no doubt that the progressive impulse behind the female-led *The Invasion*, *Ghostbusters: Answer the Call*, *Ocean's Eight*, and *The Hustle* as well as the diverse cast of *Star Wars: The Force Awakens* (J. J. Abrams, 2015) and *Jumanji: Welcome to the Jungle* have an impact on Hollywood's representational practices. These movies resonate with current cultural concerns while also capitalizing on the progressive visibility of women, people of color, and non-heteronormative sexualities. They are specifically designed to engage historically marginalized groups eager to see themselves represented on the big screen and to reach large domestic and global audiences. And yet, while the growing visibility of Hollywood heroes who are not white men is changing contemporary cinema's storytelling practices and visual aesthetics, discursive constructions that frame this visibility as progressive, political, and empowering deserve special scrutiny. Visibility has long been associated with the struggle of marginalized groups for recognition, for political and cultural change, and for social justice. "To demand visibility," feminist media studies scholar Sarah Banet-Weiser writes, "is to demand to be seen, to matter, to recognize oneself in dominant culture."[35] As with other media (old and new), however, progressive representations of race, gender, and sexuality in Hollywood movies paradoxically threaten to turn the larger political project of visibility on its head. These movies offer points of identification and promote empathy, but the visibility of women, people of color, and non-heteronormative sexualities also "fundamentally shift[s] politics of visibility so that visibility becomes *the end* rather than a means to an end."[36]

Jumanji: Welcome to the Jungle, for instance, supports feminist values, celebrates racial diversity, promotes body positivity, and is accepting of nonbinary gender identities. But the sequel's video game world and digital avatars also assert Hollywood's ideology of "colorblindness" and the belief that race no longer matters in a "post-racial" America.[37] The fact that a white, lanky teenage boy (Alex Wolff's Spencer) transforms into an imposing Black man (Dwayne Johnson's Dr. Bravestone) goes entirely uncommented on in the movie, making both roles racially neutral. Colorblind racism frames race and racial difference as belonging to the past. "As an ideology," Ashley ("Woody") Doane writes, "colorblindness 'feels good' because it describes the United States as a society that has successfully transcended its racist history; it also absolves Americans, particularly white Americans, of any responsibility for social change to address racial inequality."[38] Furthermore, the movie's main storyline effectively works against its progressive agenda. By temporarily switching their bodies with the digital avatars during the Jumanji video game, the teenagers ultimately work on becoming their best selves in the real world, a transformation that is itself structured around the themes of confidence and empowerment. Presented as individual choice (you can become whoever you want to be), this transformation follows a neoliberal logic of self-optimization that absorbs ideas about diversity and inclusivity, and thereby effectively weakens the political edge of the movie's representational scheme.[39]

The Invasion, to turn to one of the examples in which a woman plays the leading role occupied by men in earlier renditions, puts the focus on divorced single mother and psychiatrist Dr. Carol Bennell (Nicole Kidman). This fourth, gender-swapped version of the body snatcher story articulates a critique of patriarchy and of "aggressive masculinity as the root of human conflict and misery."[40] Balancing career and motherhood, Carol describes herself as a "postmodern feminist" in a key scene of the movie, but her self-understanding and "having it all" attitude are threatened during the alien invasion that spreads like a virus and turns humans into emotionless pod people. Carol tries to avoid infection and protects herself and her son Oliver (Jackson Bond) from her changed ex-husband, Tucker (Jeremy Northam), who wants to persuade Carol to join the growing mass of pod people by making her feel guilty about her professional ambitions. He presents her career as the reason for their failed marriage and broken family: "I was third on your list. That can't happen in our world." Carol's struggle to remain human thus also "becomes a struggle to be vigilant in resisting patriarchal pressures to be dutiful wife first."[41] *The Invasion*'s progressive gender theme means that with Carol "the female lead character in the body snatcher movies develops from a romantic interest that will eventually betray the male protagonist into a strong heroine who succeeds in saving herself, her child, and the entire world."[42] At the same time, the remake engages in a postfeminist discourse that takes feminism "into account,"[43] positing that gender equality has *already* been achieved and only comes under attack when extraterrestrials want to conquer Earth. While neutralizing "the masculine propensity for violence"[44] that fuels global conflicts, the alien invasion also brings back (repressed) patriarchal ideals as the basis of harmonious (family) life. Unlike the three earlier versions, this body snatcher movie has an upbeat ending (a vaccine against the alien virus is developed from Oliver's blood) that restores the world—and postfeminism—as we know it.

Released in 2007, *The Invasion* wears progressive politics on its sleeve and constructs a postfeminist plot around the gender swap that is the

Figure 10. Erin (Kristen Wiig) visits Abby (Melissa McCarthy) and Holtzmann (Kate McKinnon) in the Paranormal Studies Lab and reads an online comment. With the joke, *Ghostbusters: Answer the Call* (2016) also calls out the hostile fan reactions surrounding the production of the movie.

remake's most radical innovation. In comparison, *Ghostbusters: Answer the Call*, *Ocean's Eight*, and *The Hustle*, which arrived in cinemas a decade later, come across as ostensibly nonchalant about switching to all-female casts. Of course, these movies coincide with a resurgence of interest in feminism—a *popular* feminism that is intricately entwined with postfeminist ideas and whose new visibility coincides with an intensification of misogyny in recent years.[45] True to postfeminist ideology, they take it for granted that women should star in the same roles previously occupied by (mostly) white men and pretend that gender does not matter when it comes to remaking familiar stories from the past. There are only occasional, if half-hearted, reminders that gender inequality still exists and structures our cultural, political, and economic lives. *Ghostbusters: Answer the Call* mentions the gender bias in academia, for instance, by referring to the double standard surrounding women on the tenure track and engages with the social and political implications of the gender switch, by critically commenting on the sexism and racial politics of the first movie as well as on social media as a site where misogyny has come to thrive (figure 10). *Ocean's Eight* engages in a peculiar kind of feminist trailblazing, when mastermind Debbie Ocean (Sandra Bullock) motivates her female partners in crime right before a jewel heist at the Met Gala: "Somewhere out there, there's an 8-year-old girl lying in bed, dreaming of being a criminal. Let's do this for her." And the *Hustle* remake—a female-led version of the comedies *Bedtime Story* (Ralph Levy, 1964) and *Dirty Rotten Scoundrels* (Frank Oz, 1988) in which Anne Hathaway and Rebel Wilson take on the roles of sophisticated con artist and less refined, amateur rival once played by David Niven/Michael Caine and Marlon Brando/Steve Martin—operates on the sexist premise that "no man will ever believe that a woman is smarter than him."

Still, these movies have trouble playing up their new gender dynamics in meaningful ways. Despite their progressively feminist posture, they tend to put an emphasis on "female empowerment and sisterhood . . . as individual, economic imperatives and personal acts of revenge"[46] and depend on male approval. All living cast members of *Ghostbusters* (Ivan Reitman, 1984) make guest appearances in the 2016 remake. In *Ocean's Eight*, Debbie awkwardly hovers around the grave of her dead brother Danny Ocean (George Clooney), who recruited a group of criminals for spectacular heists in Steven Soderbergh's *Ocean's Eleven* (2001) and the two sequels *Ocean's Twelve* (2004) and *Ocean's Thirteen* (2007). Danny haunts this all-female heist movie: Debbie repeatedly visits his tomb, "half-expecting him to crawl out," and audiences, too, "spend the film anticipating his appearance."[47] These remakes, sequels, and spin-offs prominently put women in leading roles, but they are not *about* women. Rather, they "require women to relive men's stories instead of fashioning their own," remarks Amanda Hess in the *New York Times*.[48] "And they're subtly expected to fix these old films, to neutralize their sexism and infuse them with feminism, to rebuild them into good movies with good politics, too. They have to do everything the men did, except backwards and with ideals."[49]

Remaking is a method to review and revise the white male viewpoint that continues to dominate Hollywood productions: female-focused new versions of familiar stories as well as more diverse and inclusive casts offer a progressive vision (and a promise) for the future while also operating as a corrective to the cinematic past. Because of its serial dynamic, remaking is able to negotiate change with recourse to already familiar material, to well-known characters, plots, and fictional worlds. But the logic of repetition and variation at the heart of remaking comes with its own constraints. In order to meet the audiences' demand for movies that are both fresh and comfortingly familiar, Hollywood seldom diverges from what has proven successful in the past. As a result, updated representations of gender, race, and sexuality in contemporary remakes, sequels, and spin-offs come across as both powerful critical interventions *and* as contradictory and, in the end, meaningless projects that only tinker on the surface of progressive politics.

Regardless of whether the new visibility of female leads and characters of color is in and of itself empowering for individual viewers or productive of broader social, cultural, and political change, it is surely not popular with all audience members as misogynistic and racially motivated backlashes against *Ghostbusters: Answer the Call* and Disney's *Star Wars* movies have shown. Despite angry voices that claim otherwise, however, remaking never erases the past but always evokes it, throwing into sharp relief how things once *used to be*. Therefore, it can trigger a nostalgic desire for a time and space that no longer exists and presumably never existed in the first place (at least not as it is being remembered in the present). Hostile fan reactions are a reminder of what is at stake when Hollywood movies refuse complete closure and continue to unfold as serial texts that can constantly readjust their narrative options in accordance with the current political climate, the latest societal developments, and contemporary cultural discourses. Such reactions also redirect our attention away from the politics of representation and visibility to the ways in which individual and collective identities are constructed in relation to the cinematic past, and, more importantly, to the question of how remaking affects cultural memory, nostalgic longings, and a sense of (self-)continuity that help sustain these identities in the present and into the future.

MOVIE GENERATIONS: MEMORY, NOSTALGIA, AND GENERATIONAL IDENTITIES

Hollywood remaking constructs a cinematic past in which serially evolving narratives become sites of ongoing cultural work, expressing and shaping how a culture thinks about itself and how individuals position themselves within that culture. Remaking produces historicizing accounts that stress continuities between the past and the present, while it also handles historically shifting meanings, attitudes, values, and ideologies in each new film version. By recycling material from cinema's popular storytelling repertoire, remaking thus performs a stabilizing function, reassuring viewers that what they remember from the past, what they know and care about, continues to be meaningful in the present and future. But by providing contemporary variations on already familiar themes, remaking simultaneously advances a narrative of unstoppable progress—in the ways the latest remake or sequel enacts social, cultural, and political change or responds to technological innovations—that is likely to challenge the idea of stable memories and meanings. Even though Hollywood produces *shareable* media texts as it renews movies from the past for younger generations of viewers, remaking nevertheless tends to stir nostalgia for "untouchable originals," for movies to *remain* a product of their time (just like their audiences want to see and understand themselves as a product of that time). I argue that this is where remaking enters the interconnected realms of memory, time, and identity, and where Hollywood movies emerge as tightly bound up with ideas about cultural transmission and generational belonging.[50]

According to Marita Sturken, "memory establishes life's continuity; it gives meaning to the present, as each moment is constituted by the past. As the means by which we remember who we are, memory provides the very core of identity."[51] But memory is never only a matter of personal recollection; it is always socially produced and shaped by collective contexts. The concept of *cultural memory* describes how the individual and the collective interact to construct versions of a shared imagined past that can be transmitted from one generation to the next through objects, images, monuments, commemorative traditions, and institutions.[52] It defines the discursive frames for individual as well as collective identity formations. A wide array of media—including Hollywood movies—actively generate memories that link individuals to a collectively shared past. Cultural memory studies has examined the complex relationship between memory and media, showing how movies, television shows, photographs, and digital images operate as "technologies of memory" (Marita Sturken) that constantly produce and reproduce memories. Media objects, in short, affect how we remember the past and understand our own life story within the larger historical structures of a culture.

For Susannah Radstone and Katharine Hodgkin, media objects serve as "memory props" that help sustain the self. They stress that beyond the representational value alone, it is the affective qualities of the media objects that aid in recognizing past experiences and in "propping the subject."[53] This is closely linked to what José van Dijck calls "mediated memories," namely *"the activities and objects we produce and appropriate by means of media technologies, for creating and re-creating a sense of past, present and future of ourselves in relation to others."*[54] From mediated memories it is easy to arrive at "the production and dissemination of memories that have no direct connection to a person's lived past and yet are essential to the production and articulation of subjectivity."[55] Alison Landsberg introduces the term *prosthetic memories* for such recollections: they are "produced by an *experience* of mass-mediated representations" and can be worn "like an artificial limb."[56] Landsberg explains that the bodily, sensuous, and affective nature of prosthetic memories enables an engagement with the past that reaches beyond individual subjectivity and "becomes the basis for mediated collective identification."[57] Cultural memory studies is mainly interested in mediated memories of historical events, especially media representations of violent and traumatic experiences (World War I, the Holocaust, 9/11), and examines how media sustains firsthand memories of such traumas but also *makes* memories that can be collectively shared and transmitted along generational lines.[58]

Building on the concept of cultural memory and theoretical approaches to memory and media, I propose that media objects that are not concerned with histories of violence and trauma or momentous events from the nation's past can also fuel processes of individual and collective identity formation. Popular culture brims with stories that have been retold so many times that their fictional characters and storyworlds form stable elements of a culture and of everyday life. Hollywood remaking produces media objects that are unique vessels of memories and meanings. Remakes, sequels, and long-running franchises function as "sites of memory" (*lieux de mémoire*), to use Pierre Nora's suggestive term. Again, I am neither referring to Hollywood's treatment of a historically remembered past here, the "memory-making fictions" (Astrid Erll) of period dramas, historical films, or retro movies, nor to movies that have memory as their subject matter or instances of genre memory. Instead, I am concerned with the distinctive temporal relationship that remaking establishes between movies and viewers. Through its combination of repetition and innovation, remaking always conjures up the past, mediating memories on the diegetic level (*intertextual memory*) but also in a more abstract sense, where they invoke the real world and lived experiences outside the movies (*extratextual memory*).

Intertextual memory means that movies remember earlier versions of themselves and lay out their own past for audiences to explore: film remakes contain traces of the past that refer viewers back to one or more previous renditions, and sequels rely on the viewers' serial memory in order to continue a story. Intertextual memory involves a variety of memory prompts, ranging from the repetition of entire plots or plot elements to the restaging of iconic scenes to the return of familiar actors in familiar roles to flashbacks, cameo appearances, and self-referential comments. In addition, such connections between movies are often foregrounded in the movies' paratexts (promotional material including posters, trailers, interviews, advertisements, etc.), popular film criticism, and academic publications. If remaking thrives on intertextual memory that points viewers to the cinematic past, it simultaneously triggers extratextual memory—memories that are not contained within the movies themselves but that viewers come to associate with them, with the era in which the movies were first released, and with their own personal lives at the time.

By and large, remaking thus creates little time machines that take viewers on a journey into the past. The engine of these time machines is the persistent return of *King Kong*, *Invasion of the Body Snatchers*, *Planet of the Apes*, *Ghostbusters*, and *Star Wars* to cinemas over the course of many years and decades. Each new movie version provides viewers with an entry point to the cinematic—and, in extension, to their own personal as well as the cultural and national—history. Remaking invites viewers to travel back in time, to remember specific iterations in their historic moment, and to realize that they are not alone with their memories but belong to a group of people that has also lived and aged alongside popular media texts that remain relevant in the present and will likely continue to exist in the future. I call such groups of people *movie generations*: *mnemonic communities that share a "we-sense" based not only on the same historical, political, and societal experiences but also on historically situated media and cultural experiences.* They grow up watching the same Hollywood movies in cinemas and at home, are familiar with the same actors and stars, and use the same media technologies. Remaking enables the formation of movie generations because by recycling material from the cinematic past it not only extends the identificatory potential of characters, plots, and themes beyond their immediate historical contexts but also imbues movies with a wide-reaching "recruiting power."[59] Through remaking, in other words, movies emerge as catalysts of generational identities.

Movie generations theorizes the concept of generation neither as a marketing category nor in terms of biological reproduction. Leaving kinship relations as well as the steadily growing list of popular generational labels like "boomers," "Gen Xers," and "millennials" aside, the idea behind movie generations takes German sociologist Karl Mannheim's *The Problem of Generations* (1928) as its point of departure.[60] In his essay, Mannheim develops a theory of generational identities that stresses the importance of collectively shared memories. For Mannheim, generation-defining intellectual, social, and political events that are experienced during one's formative years shape how members of roughly the same age group construct who they are and how they locate themselves historically. They share a common *Zeitheimat* (W. G. Sebald): a nostalgically imagined "home in time" that fosters a sense of belonging, and that one can always travel back to by taking a trip down memory lane. Despite his insistence that only memories based on firsthand experiences (e.g., the bodily experience of World War I) can produce generational units (e.g., the war generation as a "lost" generation), Mannheim acknowledges that works of art (and their mediated memories) can become "vehicles of formative tendencies"[61] and shape generational identities (e.g., Erich Maria Remarque's *All Quiet on the Western Front* as a generation-defining text that rhetorically produces the war generation as a "lost generation").[62]

The concept of movie generations combines these ideas with recent findings, which suggest that media experiences play a constitutive role for the process of generation-building because media representations, repertoires, and technologies together with prevailing media consumption cultures and audience practices hold identificatory potential through which generational belonging can manifest itself.[63] I propose that Hollywood movies—specifically those that have repeatedly been remade, continued, expanded, and revised—have "group-forming potency"[64] and provide insights into the mechanisms of generation building, in particular the double logic of generationality and genealogy. Sigrid Weigel makes such a distinction, maintaining that generation is never only about contemporaries who share the same experiences (*generationality*). Beyond this horizontal (or synchronic) understanding, the cultural concept of generation also has a vertical (or diachronic) dimension that involves ideas about inheritance and heritage, cultural reproduction and transmission, and, eventually, the continuity of culture (*genealogy*). According to Astrid Erll, "generationality and the rhetoric of genealogy appear as flipsides of social identification. . . . no generationality without its genealogical other" (e.g., the "lost generation" as unthinkable without "the old men," that is "the older generation of parents, teachers, and politicians" against which the young men who fought in World War I define themselves as a group).[65] The formation of movie generations similarly depends on both "contemporaneity and transmission."[66] Remaking enables movie generations to recognize themselves as such in the ways their movie version differs from previous or later installments (as in "Who's Batman to you?"). But remaking also keeps pop-cultural texts alive and in circulation over long periods of time and provides successive groups of viewers with points of access to a shared storytelling history and common repertoire (to which ultimately all iterations of Batman belong).

Central to my thinking through popular culture and Hollywood remaking in terms of memory and generation is Mannheim's notion of *fresh contact*. He explains that, given the "continuous emergence of new participants in the cultural process," generational experience is constituted in the formative moment when individuals "come into contact anew with the accumulated heritage."[67] Remaking thoroughly complicates the idea of fresh contact because it is a practice that does not simply preserve supposedly timeless classics and offers them up as a treasure trove of cultural heritage that can be handed down from one generation to the next. Rather, remaking is all about timeliness and serially evolving narratives that introduce novelty and additional layers of meaning as they repeat the already-known. Of course, fresh contact necessarily implies that there are different vantage points in the process of generational renewal because fresh contact "always means a changed relationship of distance from the object and a novel approach in assimilating, using, and developing the proffered material."[68] With remaking, to be clear, fictional characters, storyworlds, and themes both maintain and renew their identificatory power across generations, yet the movies that new age groups encounter during their formative years never remain the same. Each movie generation has its own (usually: favorite) movie version that creates a we-sense among group members. Remaking revives the memory of these formative media objects from the past each time Hollywood releases a new movie that is the version of fresh contact for the next generation of viewers. As a result, remakes, sequels, and reboots connect past and present as they simultaneously build on, bolster, and challenge the lasting legacy of material that audiences—then and now—can relate to. Bringing back *Stella Dallas*, *Invasion of the Body Snatchers*, *Footloose*, *Jumanji*, *Ghostbusters*, and *Star Wars* at distinct historical moments effectively foregrounds how the years pass and the times change. Each new iteration of these Hollywood movies shapes a movie generation and helps viewers to sustain a sense of self across different life stages (childhood, youth, adulthood, and late life).

Given that remaking balances continuity and change in order to attract and satisfy as large an audience as possible, it seems almost paradoxical that remakes, sequels, and reboots are now so often met with alarm and perceived as an outright threat. Of course, Thomas Leitch's argument that film remakes in particular "are parasitic on their original films" and "typically threaten the economic viability of their originals"[69] no longer holds in today's media landscape. In our current moment, Hollywood counts on the "symbiotic relationship"[70] between different film versions to increase the economic, aesthetic, and cultural value of both the remakes and the movies they remake rather than pose an existential threat to older renditions. Yet this does not cancel out the fact that fans, tastemakers, and cultural gatekeepers regularly perceive remakes as well as sequels and reboots as genuinely disruptive forces. These authorities engage in a discourse of threat that is unrelated to economic concerns about the movies' performance in a shared marketplace and focuses on their impact on cultural memory and generational identity instead. Popular film criticism has been especially vocal in formulating fears that remakes, sequels, and reboots will supersede their predecessors, interfere with their cultural legacies, and transform their meanings. Some critics vent their general dislike of remaking by calling out Hollywood's obsession with the "destructive regurgitation" of "untouchable originals,"[71] others think of remaking as an attack on their childhood memories: they experience the practice as an intrusion into the subtle ways in which favorite movies can shape and confirm one's worldview and self-concept throughout life.

When a number of feature films and television series of the 1980s made their comeback on the big screen in the new millennium—including movies such as *Miami Vice* (Michael Mann, 2006), *Friday the 13th* (Marcus Nispel, 2009), *The Karate Kid* (Harald Zwart, 2010), *The A-Team* (Joe Carnahan, 2010), *Footloose* (Craig Brewer, 2011), *21 Jump Street* (Phil Lord and Chris Miller, 2012), and *RoboCop* (José Padilha, 2014)—this return to the 1980s elicited overwhelmingly negative responses from the Anglo-American film critic community.[72] In the *Independent*, Guy Adams lamented that watching the new versions "gave rise to that all-too-familiar feeling that accompanies the desecration of a childhood memory: anger, resentment, and a deep, almost primeval sense of sorrow."[73] To watch *The A-Team*, he wrote, "is to have a sledgehammer taken to rose-tinted memories," and the remake of *The Karate Kid*, "which my generation watched over and over on the family Betamax, has fallen victim to a grimly predictable makeover."[74] The discourse surrounding Hollywood's 1980s remaking cycle oozed nostalgia for movies and television shows that film critics now remembered as generation-defining cultural touchstones and, of course, for a simpler (childhood) past. Whereas the old movies triggered memories that could take viewers back in time to an idealized, collectively shared pop-cultural past that was, in effect, responsible for who they had become and how they understood themselves in the present, the new Hollywood movies looked like "an effort to trammel the memories of an entire generation."[75]

Memories shape identities and a sense of self during the course of our lives, and, over time, popular culture—the movies and television shows we watch, the novels and comic books we read, the music we listen to, and the video games we play—becomes thoroughly entangled with these memories. The reactions to Hollywood's recent remaking trend indicate that we are likely to form sentimental attachments to media objects that belong to (and eventually come to represent) a formative period in our lives—in the case of film critic Guy Adams: *The A-Team* and *The Karate Kid* as childhood favorites. Yet, more often than not, it is the release of a remake or belated sequel that reminds viewers of those childhood movies in the first place. Remaking calls up an array of memories and, in doing so, evokes nostalgia for specific pop-cultural products (movies and television shows from the immediate past), their moment in time (as part of 1980s popular culture and specifically *not* as timeless classics), their historically located media technologies (as in repeatedly viewing *The Karate Kid* "on the family Betamax"), and ultimately for that younger, carefree version of the self (the child). Therefore, the choice of movies that are being remade matters—and not only for studio executives with an eye on the bottom line or in terms of the timeliness of the material and the movies' politics of representation. Remaking supports the formation of *generational canons* that, in turn, serve viewers to recognize themselves *as generational communities*. The *A-Team* movie, the *Karate Kid* remake, *Footloose, 21 Jump Street, RoboCop*, and the rest of the 1980s remaking cycle, in other words, produce collective identification and reinforce feelings of generational belonging. This holds true for the older viewership that knows these movies from the 1980s as well as for younger audiences. For the older generation, the new versions repackage childhood memories along with the beloved movies of that time and simultaneously renew the movies' personal and cultural significance. Members of the next movie generation, who situate themselves at the opposite end of the decades-spanning temporal spectrum that remaking creates, add their own memories and meanings as they link the latest versions to their own lived experiences in the present.

The "ruined childhood" trope that Guy Adams employs when he writes about *The A-Team* and *The Karate Kid* deserves closer examination if we want to understand the recursive relationship between memory, nostalgia, and identity in the overall context of Hollywood remaking. The trope was certainly not new at the time Adams's critique of the 1980s remaking cycle was published. It first emerged in angry fan responses to the *Star Wars* prequel trilogy (1999–2005)[76] and has since gained momentum in online fandoms, mainstream media outlets, and increasingly in the alt-right's "metapolitics,"[77] kindling heated discussions whenever Hollywood announces that it has another reboot or remake in the works. In the context of the misogynist and white supremacist ideologies of men's rights activists and the alt-right, such "narratives of loss and cultural 'ruin'"[78] claim that popular feminism and diversity pose a threat to the legacies of franchises that have upheld hegemonic masculinity, whiteness, and heteronormativity in the past. Encapsulating fears that "woke" Hollywood is sacrificing the opportunity "to retransmit preferred masculine identities and privileges, making the[m] inheritable down the cultural line"[79] in favor of representing cultural change, the "ruined childhood" trope has thus become a symbol of white male and even white nationalist identity formations.

The reactions surrounding the 2016 *Ghostbusters* movie are a case in point: mostly white, male-identifying fans of the franchise so vehemently rejected the new version that think pieces and academic articles began to dissect the irritating behavior born from a sense of fan entitlement and kicked off debates about nostalgia and toxic fan practices. Self-proclaimed fans of the two 1980s movies, *Ghostbusters* and the sequel *Ghostbusters II* (Ivan Reitman, 1989), orchestrated an online campaign to make the trailer for *Ghostbusters: Answer the Call* "the most 'disliked' movie trailer in YouTube history."[80] After the release of the movie, Black cast member Leslie Jones became the target of abuse on Twitter, where online trolls inundated her account with sexist and racist hate speech, pornography, and memes.[81] In response to the harassment on the platform, Twitter permanently suspended the account of Milo Yiannopoulos, technology editor for the right-wing news website *Breitbart* and notorious alt-right internet troll.[82] He had published a scathing review of *Ghostbusters: Answer the Call* on *Breitbart* that singled out Jones (and her character Patty) and then led the barrage of prolonged online abuse toward Jones on Twitter. And, not unlike Yiannopoulos in his review, many *Ghostbusters* fans repeatedly claimed that the gender-swapping reboot destroyed cherished memories of one of their favorite childhood movies.[83] They were widely viewed as aggressive, misogynistic, and racist fanboys who "oppose[d] progressive change"[84] and weaponized their childhood to protect a beloved fan object. Media scholar Derek Johnson uses the term *fantagonism* to describe "the antagonistic ways fans relate to one another, producers, and the text."[85] In its most extreme form, the kind of "fantagonism" provoked by *Answer the Call* resonates with the "Great Replacement" theory of white nationalism,[86] yet even less extreme attacks on the film were often rooted in a desire to preserve an endangered white masculinity.

Writing from a fan studies perspective, William Proctor argues that fans' claims of "childhood ruination" should be taken seriously. *Answer the Call* he contends can indeed overwrite the 1980s movie and with it "a deified (and reified) icon of childhood, a nostalgic conduit with which to view the formation of social identity, formative memory and personal history."[87] This implies that the all-female *Ghostbusters* destabilizes a sense of ontological security white, male fans had previously attained by repeatedly engaging with the 1980s movies. And, borrowing sociologist Anthony Giddens's phenomenological concept for how people cope with modernity's risk culture, Matt Hills explains how fandom supports "basic trust in self-continuity and environmental continuity."[88] That trust can be disrupted if fans feel that their fan object is coming under attack. When a subsection of outraged fans alleged that *Answer the Call* ruined their childhood, "such intensity seems, on the face of it, nonsensical and melodramatically overblown," writes Hills, "yet it is also of a piece with 'excess-as-authenticity' or 'feels culture,' where intense emotionality is, discursively and culturally, valued as possessing at least a claim to (fannish) authority."[89] In the case of *Ghostbusters*, the 1980s movies form part of the lives of longtime fans and determine their generational (and gendered) identification. Their fan culture, including fan practices and the performance of fannish authority, relies on the unconditional stability of *Ghostbusters* as an almost sacred, unalterable fan object. In this scenario, remaking undoes stability even though it brings back familiar material as a persistent point of reference. Remaking always explores possibilities of variation and continuation, introducing change that is never limited to the new version at hand but retrospectively affects the meanings and memories of previous movies as well. That is why a radically different take on *Ghostbusters* is perceived as threatening both the beloved fan object and the fans' self-narrative that is so deeply enmeshed with it.[90]

If routines establish the framework of ontological security and help sustain continuity and a coherent narrative between past and present selves, change can cause an existential crisis with regard to the temporal unfolding of self-identity.[91] Hollywood remaking apparently constitutes such a moment of crisis for fans and popular film critics—from the all-female *Ghostbusters* to the 1980s remaking cycle to the *Star Wars* prequels. *Ghostbusters* fans clearly lashed out against *change*, and they did so in a particularly antagonistic manner, hurling hatred and vitriol at the movie itself, at director Paul Feig, and at the female cast starring in the reboot. Their misogynistic and racist comments are shocking but somehow hardly surprising in a deeply divided cultural and media landscape, where the empowerment of women and people of color is promoted and widely embraced on one side and simultaneously dismantled and delegitimized on the other.[92] Hollywood, it seems, is acutely aware of the complex and contradictory contemporary panorama and increasingly strategic about how remaking must balance continuity and change for movies to appeal to large audiences and become domestic and global box-office hits without alienating older generations of viewers. This is no longer only about the symbiotic relationship remakes and sequels establish with their respective predecessors because marketing and reviews draw attention to earlier versions, communicate the narrative image of the new movie, and invest it with aesthetic and commercial value.

In the case of *Ghostbusters: Answer the Call*, the industry implemented conflicting strategies to handle and incorporate the hostile activism of the white, male fan faction. As Derek Johnson shows, they pushed back against "fantagonism" by reasserting the professional authority of the creative talent but simultaneously contradicted this disciplinary measure by speaking to the fans' nostalgia and centering the promotional campaign around "endorsements and cameos from the surviving cast members and producers of the original 1984 film."[93] Even so, *Ghostbusters* has shown that marketing and intertextual tidbits (like the involvement of actors Bill Murray, Dan Aykroyd, and Ernie Hudson and their public approval of the movie) barely suffice to lend legitimacy to progressive updates of familiar material and appease audience members with a tendency toward cultural conservatism (brought to the fore by a fannish sense of loss). Under such circumstances, Hollywood appears to have doubled down on the cinematic past and reconfigured the role time, memory, and identity play in today's media environment. The aim is to carefully negotiate progressive and conservative ideologies and to produce more explicitly serialized movies that incorporate nostalgic longings for the past but can still be shared across movie generations, that update movies in accordance with the social norms and cultural sensibilities without threatening to erase childhood memories or rendering favorite movies from that time in one's life obsolete.

Ghostbusters: Afterlife (Jason Reitman, 2021), the movie that followed *Answer the Call*, is a good example of how serialization can be tactically used as course correction that helps to carry on the franchise. This

Ghostbusters installment completely ignores the 2016 reboot and serves as a direct sequel to the first two movies from the 1980s. The trailer (which *Ghostbusters* fans praised on social media) reveals that *Afterlife* puts the emphasis on legacy, takes inspiration from the Netflix series *Stranger Things* (2016–), and (like that hit show) is steeped in nostalgia for the 1980s. *Afterlife* is written and directed by Jason Reitman, son of the director of *Ghostbusters* and *Ghostbusters II*, Ivan Reitman. In interviews, Jason Reitman established his position of authorial power by presenting *Afterlife* as a father-son affair and by foregrounding his own nostalgic memories of and fannish devotion to the *Ghostbusters* franchise as necessary credentials to direct the sequel: "I've always thought of myself as the first *Ghostbusters* fan, when I was a 6-year-old visiting the set," he told *Entertainment Weekly*.[94] "I remember being on set and seeing them try out the card catalog gag for the first time when the library ghost makes them come flying out. I remember the day they killed Stay Puft and I brought home a hardened piece of foam that just sat on a shelf for years. I was scared there was a terror dog underneath my bed before people knew what a terror dog was."[95] These childhood memories shaped him, Reitman insisted, and they also made him wonder about someday making his own *Ghostbusters* movie.[96] He promised, "We are in every way trying to go back to original technique and hand the movie back to the fans"—a statement that sparked outrage on social media and forced Reitman to explain himself because the expression "hand the movie back to the fans" was understood as another dig at the 2016 reboot and endorsement of the toxic *Ghostbusters* fanbase and their misogynistic and racist behavior.[97]

Meanwhile, Ivan Reitman, who is a producer of *Afterlife*, was touched that his son wanted to join the family business and spoke of "a passing of the torch both inside and out."[98] The notion of legacy is not limited to director duo that treats the franchise like a family heirloom, but also central to the plot of the latest *Ghostbusters* movie: a single mother (Carrie Coon) and her two kids, Trevor (Finn Wolfhard) and Phoebe (Mckenna Grace), move to their late grandfather's old farm house in Summerville, Oklahoma. The trailer suggests that Trevor and Phoebe are the grandchildren of Egon Spengler, once the Ghostbusters' most brilliant scientist (played by Harold Ramis, who died in 2014). When the kids discover the iconic ECTO-1 vehicle, ghost traps, jump suits, and other strange equipment, they find out who their grandfather really was (a Ghostbuster!) and eventually follow in his footsteps hunting ghosts and saving the rural small town that has become their new home. The trailer contains numerous Easter Eggs and subtle call-backs to the past but does not feature any of the original cast members who have committed to reprise their roles in the movie.[99] Instead it focuses on Trevor, Phoebe, and their new friends, who represent the next generation of Ghostbusters.

Kids fighting supernatural evil in an American small town is, of course, also *Stranger Things*'s storytelling recipe and the connection to Netflix's original series (2016-) is further reinforced by the tone, visual style, and retro aesthetic of *Afterlife*, as well as the fact that actor Finn Wolfhard is known for his breakout role as Mike Wheeler on the show. In addition, *Afterlife* and *Stranger Things* share a nostalgia for the 1980s. *Stranger Things* is set in the 1980s, or rather, what amounts to an idea of the decade cobbled together from bits and pieces of popular culture. In the second season, Mike, Dustin (Gaten Matarazzo), Will (Noah Schnapp), and Lucas (Caleb McLaughlin) even dress up in *Ghostbusters* costumes for Halloween. The show does not reconstruct a historical past, however, but a glossy "pastness,"[100] a mediated—anachronistic—1980s-ness for the present. The show, Cherise Huntingford writes, "encourages us to remember—*or at least think we remember*—its hair-scrunchies-and-synth-pop mise-en-scène, asphyxiating its [Stephen] King-esque plot in the distilled neon goo of Eighties pop culture—a falsified nostalgia for a time that only ever existed on screen."[101] Made in the new millennium, *Stranger Things* brings millennial sensibilities to the 1980s it nostalgically recreates on screen, so that the decade is "completely alien to Ronald Reagan's era" and allows for "a fresh, multicultural point of view that emphasizes diversity and ways of being *not* normal."[102] Stripped of what would make a return to the actual 1980s unappealing for a large part of today's viewership, the show's nostalgia is literally "memory without pain," in Paul Monaco's words, "recollection sweetened, mystified, or mythified."[103] It creates an alternate, revisionist, and improved sense of the historical past in which sexism, racism, and other forms of oppression and exclusion have no place. In *Stranger Things*, the 1980s become an almost progressive decade structured along mediated representations of iconic images and music from the pop-cultural past. This certainly speaks to the "waning of historicity" that Fredric Jameson describes,[104] in which "nostalgia substitutes a memory of history with a memory of the *idea* of history."[105] But it also highlights the politics of the nostalgia mode, specifically in the ways that erasures in the present can draw attention to the social injustices of the past.

Judging from the trailer, *Afterlife* is holding Netflix's narrative blueprint upside down, bringing the 1980s (and 1980s content) back into the new millennium (not vice versa) and infusing the franchise's 1980s past with an almost mythical quality. Here, nostalgia has everything to do with picking up the legacy of the "original" Ghostbusters in the present, with mobilizing, mediating, and modifying memories. The sequel's sentimental attitude toward the 1980s is more than a narrative device, though; it is profoundly evocative, tapping into the emotional connections that viewers build with their childhood media and making these connections available for new movie generations. The seriousness and pathos the trailer conveys are unexpected given the tone set by the first *Ghostbusters* movie. As one critic put it, "The trailer endeavors to create reverence for a very irreverent film, in which Dan Aykroyd gets his dick sucked by a ghost, among countless other indelible gags."[106] The growing popularity (and: profitability) of *ongoing narratives* makes such radical, retrospective transformations possible (and, perhaps, necessary in order to continue the story in a way that balances nostalgia with present-day sensibilities). Like *Stranger Things*, *Afterlife* summons nostalgia for something that never was, or at least not quite like what viewers remember. Having kids follow in the footsteps of the 1980s Ghostbusters creates a powerful narrative premise that appeals to younger and older movie generations alike: whereas younger viewers can discover the Ghostbusters story along with Trevor and Phoebe, the setup also encourages older viewers to remember their childhood and to relive their own first encounter with the team of paranormal exterminators. The new characters are therefore an invitation to approach the franchise with genuine curiosity and to see the fictional world of *Ghostbusters* with wondrous eyes.

With its emphasis on both continuity and generational renewal, *Afterlife* effectively operates as a "legacyquel," but the movie also qualifies as a "requel" (or, what is sometimes called a "soft reboot"). It deliberately neglects elements of the first two movies that are likely considered problematic today and disregards the 2016 movie altogether in order to revitalize the franchise and its memory, meanings, and identificatory power in the present. However, as film critic Jeremy Gordon has remarked, erasing parts of the cinematic past is not an easy undertaking. "The new *Ghostbusters* can't pay homage to the original in a vacuum," he writes. "Thanks to the blowback against the 2016 reboot, all its creative choices seem like explicit political decisions. Sick of lady Ghostbusters? Well, here's two white guys in lead roles. Sick of new stuff? Well, here's a bunch of the old."[107] In contrast to *Stranger Things*, *Afterlife*'s nostalgia centers on a sense of loss and becomes politically charged as a manifestation of *white* nostalgia. On the level of plot, the Ghostbusters of the past have to be brought back to life in the present. The movie explicitly mourns the loss of Egon Spengler (Harold Ramis), Peter Venkman (Bill Murray), Ray Stantz (Dan Aykroyd), and Winston Zeddemore (Ernie Hudson) by dwelling on Egon's haunting presence in the farmhouse, for example, and the museum-style exhibition of the iconic ghostbusting equipment in the shed. In connection with the backlash against the all-female *Answer the Call*, however, this nostalgic stance toward the past also risks promoting the rhetoric of restoring white, male cultural and political dominance that pervades white nationalist discourse and also constitutes the main message of Donald Trump's populist campaign slogan "Make America Great Again." White nostalgia encapsulates the belief that for white, heterosexual men the past was better than the present because "the changes molding modern America have marginalized them economically, demographically, and culturally."[108] Political correctness, popular feminism, immigration, and growing diversity are perceived as threats to white male identity and to the nation. *Afterlife*'s focus on "restoring" the *Ghostbusters* franchise plays into such white nostalgia discourses.

With its highly conservative and politically controversial course correction following the toxic fan reactions and disappointing box-office performance of *Answer the Call*, *Afterlife* deliberately reboots the *Ghostbusters* franchise as a "nostalgia franchise."[109] Like *The Force Awakens*, *Terminator: Genisys* (Alan Taylor, 2015), *Creed* (Ryan Coogler, 2015), and *Jurassic World* (Colin Trevorrow, 2015), which had already done so in 2015, *Afterlife* recalls and exploits the past, blending old and new to reach multiple generations of viewers. The movie's nostalgic appeal is not only derived from reconnecting with familiar characters and their storyworld but also from a pervasive cultural fascination with the 1980s and its generation-defining popular culture. Unlike *Answer the Call*, which took a fresh, tongue-in-cheek approach to the franchise with its in-jokes and cameos, its gender swap and fanboy villain (whom the women defeat by shooting a giant, evil version of the iconic ghostbusters logo in the crotch), *Afterlife* relies on nostalgia to maintain long-term continuity and as a method of renewal. As it summons up the past, the movie also responds to "an affective yearning for a community with a collective memory, a longing for continuity in a fragmented world."[110] The longing for continuity goes hand in hand with a growing need for stable memories and meanings. This may not necessarily be the case with superheroes like Batman or any other serial figure that "needs no explanation, no introduction, and no elaborate framing"[111] because it is *already* familiar and because it never really changes. In Hollywood it is common practice that actors who play iconic serial figures like Batman, James Bond, Sherlock Holmes, and Tarzan are more or less replaceable so that a question like "Who's Batman to you?" inevitably calls up memories of a specific performer, movie, and moment in time. Nostalgia franchises, however, blur such clear temporal demarcations when they bring the stories, characters, and actors from the past into the present.

Hollywood's marked preference for serialization in recent years also means that nostalgia franchises preserve that more abstract sense of continuity, which extends beyond the fictional world on screen and is entangled with the viewers' subjective experiences and memories. By committing to the franchise past rather than renouncing it, by telling ongoing stories that look back at a nostalgia-tinged franchise past and account for the years that have passed in real life, movies like *The Force Awakens*, *Terminator: Genisys*, *Creed*, *Jurassic World*, and now *Ghostbusters: Afterlife* can function "as a soothing remedy for viewers' increasingly fragmented and disorienting experience of contemporary life."[112] At the same time, however, the movies' backward-gazing temporality raises questions about the politics of the nostalgia franchise. Even though they generally make a point of reimagining the white and male-led *Jurassic*, *Star Wars*, *Terminator*, *Rocky*, and *Ghostbusters* franchises as ostensibly more diverse and inclusive, their narrative continuity over many decades and into the future can often only be maintained through the repetition and generational renewal of white characters, plots, and themes. This renewal is informed by ideas of legacy and inheritance, passing-of-the-torch rituals, and a pervasive sense of nostalgia that invariably normalize conservative politics alongside progressive updates and revisions. Hollywood remaking has always been concerned with constructing a usable cinematic past, with inventing "classics," "untouchable originals," and legacies that "serve the needs of the present."[113] Yet the ways in which movies become entangled with our memories and sense of self is constantly changing—just like the practice itself is constantly adapting to the current moment. If we want to fully understand how we arrived at today's nostalgia franchise, we need to take a closer look at the evolution of Hollywood remaking over the past century, at historical trends, and at distinct remaking formats.

PART II Film Remakes

3 Cinematic Pasts and Presents

In the history of Hollywood cinema, most film remakes were produced during and following the transition to sound (1927–1931), when old silent hits had their comebacks as talkies. Even back then, however, film remakes were no novelty—remaking had been a well-established industry practice long before Hollywood converted to sound. In fact, film remakes had already figured prominently in early cinema, when "the practitioners of the new medium imitated each other in their quest for subjects that would show off their marvelous machines."[1] Thus, Biograph's *Empire State Express* (1896) and Edison's *The Black Diamond Express* (1896) remade the Lumière brothers' short film *Arrivée d'un train* (1895) to promote the companies' film technologies: the Biograph and the Vitascope. Like Edison's *Clark's Thread Mill* (1896) and Biograph's *The Sausage Machine* (1897), which were respective remakes of the Lumière brothers' *La sortie des usines* (1895) and *Charcuterie mécanique* (1895), these early one-shot films continued a nineteenth-century tradition that displayed technological inventions as public entertainment.[2] They presented film projection as spectacle, demonstrating what the new machines could do, rather than serving as a storytelling medium. It is in this sense that Tom Gunning has described early cinema from 1895 to 1906 as a "cinema of attractions."[3]

These first short films repeated lifelike motion, magic tricks, and acts from other forms of popular mass entertainment—vaudeville, in particular, where film exhibition was one among the many numbers on the program. Filmmakers imitated, copied, and remade the products of rival film companies in order to meet the public demand for moving pictures and as a business strategy that undercut their competitors. As a result, *repetition* shaped the cinematic experience and ensured that audiences knew what to expect when they went to see the moving pictures. Early cinema's presentational approach assumed that audiences had prior knowledge of the film's subject or simple narrative, often relying on cultural intertexts from traditional fairground and vaudeville entertainment. Live narration, music, sound effects, spoken dialogue from behind the screen, or intertitles were intended to clarify plots based on the logical progression of events, whereas certain genres (like the trick or chase film) were self-explanatory.[4] In any case, remaking facilitated audience comprehension of early cinema, which, as Charles Musser writes, "could not present a complex, unfamiliar narrative capable of being readily understood irrespective of exhibition circumstances or the spectators' specific cultural knowledge."[5] From the outset, remaking thus "worked to create a tradition in which audiences were educated, and upon which filmmakers could expand."[6] Within the first years of film exhibition and consumption, the quick succession of nearly identical remakes familiarized audiences with the new medium and film-viewing practices, "produc[ing] the recognition necessary for the creation of a cinematic language."[7]

Remaking informed early film reception—"the 'proper' relations among viewer, projector, and screen, the peculiar dimension of cinematic space," which, according to Miriam Hansen, "were part of a cultural practice that had to be learned."[8] But it also played a crucial role in establishing medium-specific formal, stylistic, and generic conventions.[9] Edwin S. Porter's one-shot film *Uncle Josh at the Moving Picture Show* (1902), a remake of Robert W. Paul's British film *The Countryman's First Sight of the Animated Pictures* (1901), illustrates both functions. The film that Porter made for Edison is one of three "Uncle Josh" films that belong to the genre of the country rube, "a stock character in vaudeville, comic strips, and other popular media."[10] Hansen writes that "early cinema seized upon the encounter of supposedly unsophisticated minds with city life, modern technology, and commercial entertainment as a comic theme and as a way of flaunting the marvels of that new urban world."[11] Seated in a box at a vaudeville theater, Uncle Josh watches three films in a moving picture show. These shorts are existing Edison productions that represent popular early genres: *Parisian Dancers*, *The Black Diamond Express*, and *The Country Couple*. But Uncle Josh does not remain in his seat for long once the projection starts: he leaves his box as soon as a dancer appears on screen, jumps back in for cover when a train suddenly approaches, and eventually takes down the screen in a fit of anger during the country couple's lovemaking scene, thereby revealing the kinetoscope operator. The humor derives from Uncle Josh's inappropriate response to the moving pictures he mistakes for reality, which is framed as a mode of reception that is no longer acceptable. The short thus chronicles the audience's learning process by contrasting it with the country rube's "deviant and excessive behavior"[12] upon encountering film for the first time. Simultaneously, the combination of various genres and styles in the films-within-the-film attests to the existence of readily recognizable cinematic conventions. In addition, Hansen detects an "underlying assertion of 'progress'" here that extends to the three shorts themselves, since they appear primitive in comparison to the more evolved representational techniques used in *Uncle Josh*. Hence, she suggests that "even at this early stage the cinema's sense of its own, albeit brief, history is inscribed" in its films.[13]

This chapter takes up and expands Hansen's idea, arguing that such instances of *self-historicization* become a defining feature of Hollywood cinema and, more specifically, of Hollywood remaking. If "cinema writes its own history with remakes, sequels, or prequels—and . . . does so within the evolving network of expectations, recognitions, allusions, variations, and reinterpretations that makes these iterations possible and keeps them in circulation," as Frank Kelleter and I have suggested,[14] film remakes play a leading role in this kind of cinematic self-historicizing. They constitute a particularly effective means of mapping cinema's progress since they reliably foreground what is new against the backdrop of the already-familiar. Focusing on Hollywood's film remake production during and after the transition to sound, this chapter examines how so-called *talker remakes* operate as film-historical markers and generational reference points as they draw the line between—and, indeed, help invent—the silent and sound era. Talker remakes, I argue, actively constructed and preserved an ephemeral cinematic past. The first part of the chapter is concerned with the coverage of Hollywood's talker remakes in trade papers like *Motion Picture News, Film Daily*, and *Variety* and fan magazines such as *Photoplay, Screenland*, and *Modern Screen*. These paratexts provided interpretive frameworks for making sense of the transition to sound and its impact on Hollywood cinema, both on the level of individual films and stars and within a larger film-historical context. Based on industry news items, film reviews, contests, and fan letters that were printed in these publications, I reconstruct the commercial, cultural, and critical attitudes that accompanied the unprecedented surge of film remakes that followed on the heels of the sound innovation. The chapter then goes on to explore how film remakes emerge as agents of memory and modernization. Toward the end of the 1930s, fan magazines framed talker remakes not only as movies that ensured the permanence of popular stories but simultaneously creating a generation-defining narrative of technological progress around them that distanced the silent past from the sound film present. Photo spreads and quizzes encouraged direct comparisons between silent movies and their sound film remakes, as they tested, refreshed, or imparted knowledge about film history and the effects of the sound innovation.

THE REMAKE BOOM DURING THE TRANSITION TO SOUND

Uncle Josh at the Moving Picture Show was soon followed by longer and more complex multiple-shot films that had become the norm after the rise of narrative film around 1902. Remaking continued to be a staple of the rapidly growing film industry. In fact, remaking played a significant role in the legal and cultural legitimization of film in the United States because a series of copyright infringement cases in the first two decades of the twentieth century contributed to its recognition as new medium, commodity, and art form.[15] As the films themselves became more profitable than the equipment with which they were made and projected, the repetition of content needed to be regulated. Copyright law put an end to piracy practices and unauthorized copying, and, with a growing number of literary and stage adaptations, remake rights became linked to a written source (not another film version). Still, repetition remained a mainstay of cinema: film cycles and early genre films reused existing material, and film serials relied on repetition-based formulas to lure audiences into the movie theaters for each week's new episode. It was only during Hollywood's transition to sound that the film remake gained prominence over these other popular forms of repetition.

In the 1928 October issue of the fan magazine *Screenland*, Martin Martin wrote that "Hollywood has gone Talking Picture crazy"[16] and predicted a boom in film remake production. Martin, who wrote a column that regularly supplied readers with the latest gossip from the movie sets, shared rumors about the construction of new sound-proof stages, actors' voice tests, and Warner Brothers' growing value in the stock market. With a look at Hollywood's production slate, Martin commented: "It is becoming fashionable to remake the stories that were successes."[17] Martin was right about the coming wave of talker remakes. A year later, the industry publication *Motion Picture News* reported that "a minimum of 70 Remakes" was scheduled for the 1929–1930 season and projected a lineup of more than 125 remakes for the following season.[18] From today's perspective such numbers seem outrageous (for comparison: the average number of film remakes released in the 2010s was 10 per year). But there were plenty of reasons that justified the unprecedented production of film remakes during the transition to sound. Recycling old stories that had already registered as successes with audiences meant that the major studios could control the risk of financial or aesthetic failure that came with the introduction of the new sound technology. Since the coming of sound posed formidable economic and technological challenges for the film industry and radically changed the cinemagoing experience, playing it safe with tried and proven material from the recent cinematic past was widely considered to be the best approach. The majors could turn to their film libraries and use the motion picture rights to novels, plays, and literary works they had previously acquired in order to showcase the sound innovation against the backdrop of well-known stories. Producing talker remakes often involved renegotiating dialogue rights, so that a studio's decision to remake a silent movie from its library did not necessarily mean cutting costs but rather managing risks in times of uncertainty.[19]

In 1930, Philip Scheuer of the *Los Angeles Times* explained the current remake boom with "the new adaptability of old tales to the sound medium."[20] He also pointed out that three years into the sound era, "there is no organized procedure to remakes. Sometimes, in the 'reshooting' of a semiclassic like *Anna Christie*, both the title and text are scrupulously retained; at other times, only the title or only the text. More usually, both are changed."[21] Especially in the period between 1928 and 1931 when sound was gradually introduced, "films [were] more like tests than texts,"[22] film historian Donald Crafton reminds us. Studios were eager to engage "with active but unpredictable consumers"[23] and wanted to learn about their tastes and moviegoing habits. Talking trailers, for example, addressed cinemagoers directly and asked them to share their preferences with the theater manager who would then pass them on to the studios.[24] Adding sound to silent hits made remaking an attractive, low-risk strategy for studios, and they often built elaborate marketing campaigns around the talking debut of their stars.

GARBO TALKS, NOVARRO SINGS:
STARS, FANS, AND TALKER REMAKES

This was the case for MGM's biggest draw, Swedish actress Greta Garbo. Crafton writes that "Garbo feared that her Swedish accent might impair her work in sound and wanted to delay as long as possible."[25] She made her long-awaited talking debut in the above-mentioned *Anna Christie* (Clarence Brown, 1930), a pre-Code drama about a young Swedish American woman and former prostitute, who reunites with her estranged sea captain father and falls in love with a young sailor. When she reveals her past, both men abandon her, but they eventually return and forgive her. Based on the play of the same name by Eugene O'Neill, *Anna Christie* had already been adapted to the silent screen in 1923. That movie, produced by Thomas H. Ince and directed by John Griffith Wray, starred Blanche Sweet as the heroine and George F. Marion as her father—a role he had also played in the first Broadway production of *Anna Christie* and now reprised in the 1930 remake. The remake was produced in English, German, and, additionally, as a silent version (all starring Garbo), which was common in 1930, because many movie theaters still had to be wired for sound. MGM constructed a large-scale promotional campaign around the slogan "Garbo Talks!" The two words were printed in newspaper and magazine ads, displayed on theater marquees, billboards, and cars. In July 1930, *Motion Picture News* reprinted a cartoon from the *Illinois Siren* (a college humor magazine, written, edited, and published monthly by students at the University of Illinois) that commented on MGM's campaign (figure 11). It shows a couple standing outside a movie theater decorated with large banners that have the slogans "GRETA TALKS" and "GARBO TALKS" printed on them. One of them remarks, "I was afraid of that," thereby ridiculing the simplicity of the message and the excitement MGM wanted to create around Garbo's first talking picture using only these two words. The cartoon also exposes many moviegoers' unfounded skepticism about her speaking voice and foreign accent.

Anna Christie turned out to be a critical and box-office success for MGM, earning rave reviews and three Academy Award nominations. *Variety* called it "great artistically and tremendous commercially. In all departments a wow picture"[26] and referred its readers back to the silent movie to point out the technological and artistic accomplishments of the talker remake. "Comparison is inevitably suggested with the silent version made by Thomas Ince eight years ago with Blanche Sweet and William Russell," the review read.[27] "If in its day Ince's inaudible version was an artistic milestone, the same story, plus dialog and Clarence Brown's superfine direction, is *another marker along the path of cinematic progress.*"[28] Like most trade publications, *Variety* too, dedicated a substantial part of the review to commenting on Greta Garbo's voice. After all, "'Garbo Talks' is, beyond quarrel, an event of major box office significance."[29] Or, as Peter Vischer put it in the *Exhibitors Herald-World*: "When Greta Garbo speaks, it becomes a matter of importance in the motion picture world."[30]

Apart from the trade papers, fan magazines had also anticipated this moment. *Talking Screen*'s short review of the *Anna Christie* remake began with the observation that "every single human being who admires Greta Garbo has been waiting with baited [sic] breath for the sound of her voice on the talking screen."[31] The movie heightened the suspense by making audiences wait just a little longer before they finally heard Garbo speak for the first time. "She does not appear in the first reel of *Anna Christie*,"

Figure 11. MGM's promotional campaign for the talker remake of *Anna Christie* centered on the simple slogan "Garbo Talks!" Cartoon from the college magazine *Illinois Siren* reprinted in *Motion Picture News*, July 19, 1930: 41. Image courtesy of the Media History Digital Library, http://mediahist.org.

Talking Screen disclosed. "It is not until the scene has shifted to the back room of the saloon that the door opens and Greta stands there. Then—you wait for her first words! And they come—deep, resonant, splendidly befitting this woman of exotic mystery and depth."[32] The fan magazine had previously covered Garbo's talking debut and engaged its readers with articles about female actors' vocal talents and the question "Who's the Best Talkie Bet?" The film industry on the whole "was making itself heard loudly, if not well," *Talking Screen* reported.[33] "Angel voices thundered when they should have trod delicately on the public tympana. Tiny feminine stars squeaked in moments of overwhelming pictorial tenderness."[34] MGM, the most conservative studio during the transition to sound, wanted to avoid such technical problems that had led the moviegoing public to "[stuff] fingers in its ears and [wish] dismally that the squawkies would strain their vocal organs beyond repair," and experimented "to eliminate the hissing and booming" before fully committing to the sound film business.[35] The studio's hesitance paid off. *Talking Screen* included MGM's biggest star Greta Garbo as one of the "Best Talkie Bets" a couple of months before the premiere of *Anna Christie*: "We hear that Greta's voice is deep, resonant, unforgettably expressive—the most wonderful voice in Hollywood."[36] But in the end, the fan magazine let the readers decide whether Garbo or other silent film stars like Norma Shearer, Mary Pickford, Lois Moran, Dolores Costello, Myrna Loy, Janet Gaynor, Clara Bow, Anita Page, and Lupe Velez earned "the widely contested title of Best Talkie Voice."[37]

The late 1920s had seen a proliferation of fan magazines that catered to what Crafton has called "Americans' movie craziness."[38] *Talking Screen*, *Photoplay*, or *Screenland* offered fan-oriented coverage about what was happening in Hollywood, on set and behind-the-scenes, but they also suggested that fans might have some degree of control over the direction in which the film business would develop. They claimed to speak for their audience (who were mostly female readers under twenty-five) and started to cultivate fan response.[39] Crafton describes fan magazines "as mediators of a complex web of exchange between the industry, the commercial world, and the consumer . . . [and] as filters through which ideas about the movies emerged."[40] By weaving elaborate narratives around the question of whether or not a star would be able to master the microphone, fan magazines encouraged readers to express their opinions and take part in their favorite Hollywood star's triumphs or hardships during the conversion to sound.[41] Greta Garbo's talking pictures kept moviegoers speculating about the future of her career as a movie star—and so did Mexican American actor Ramon Novarro's. Interestingly, both Garbo's and Novarro's sound film debuts were linked to talker remakes—and both were

Figure 12. This contest in the fan magazine *Screenland*, emphasized Ramon Novarro's voice and musical talent. It asked readers to pick a movie Novarro should remake as a sound film. "A Gift from Ramon Novarro," *Screenland* (September 1930): 61. Image courtesy of the Media History Digital Library, http://mediahist.org.

framed in terms that matched the novelty of sound with the novelty of hearing the popular actors' accented voices for the first time, thus constructing their exotic otherness around the technological innovation.

In 1930, *Screenland* held a contest that presented sound film remakes of Novarro's "silent screen successes" as ideal vehicles to boost his talkie career.[42] The contest filled a double-page spread and invited readers to choose whether they wanted to see Novarro return in a remake of *The Prisoner of Zenda* (Rex Ingram, 1922), *Scaramouche* (Rex Ingram, 1924), *Ben-Hur* (Fred Niblo, 1925), or *The Student Prince* (Ernst Lubitsch, 1928). By picking the right movie, the contest suggested, fans might have an impact on the actor's career. The prize for the best letter was an autographed guitar that was also featured on the pages. Three photos showed Novarro, in traditional Mexican attire, holding and strumming a Dobro amplifying gift guitar, the model that he himself owned and played (figure 12). The text underlined Novarro's musical talent, explaining that "the versatile and musical Ramon Novarro offers a gift in keeping with his personality—a musical instrument. We all know that Novarro studied voice culture before the movies learned to talk, and that he plays several instruments."[43] Everything about the contest—the prize question, the gift guitar, the photos, and the short accompanying texts—advertised the actor's fine singing and speaking voice and creating a narrative around the star-persona in which his outstanding vocal qualities would enable Novarro to continue making a smooth transition into the sound film era.

The Novarro contest illustrates how *Screenland* engaged its readers, signaling that fans could actively participate in Hollywood's transition to sound and have a say in the studios' decisions concerning which movies to remake as talkies. Fan magazines also printed letters that contained specific suggestions for movies that readers wanted to see remade and for which they would buy a ticket. Such published letters were often awarded small prizes, which means that we cannot be sure about their authenticity: they might have been written by staff members or freelance authors with an eye on the prize.[44] Leading fan magazines like *Photoplay* paid up to ten dollars in prize money each month for the best letter published in full. At *Modern Screen*, the editor invited readers to send letters with their suggestions:

> Dear Friends: Right now Hollywood is making more effort to win your approval than ever before. . . . Perhaps you have hit on the type of picture which would be a tremendous success and which you would like above all others. It may be a new type of story. *Or a new treatment of an old type of story*. Whatever it is, I'd be glad to have your ideas. Come on, now, drop me a line and pour out your ideas.[45]

When readers proposed titles for talker remakes, they tended to promote a good story that would benefit from a talkie treatment rather than a vehicle for a particular Hollywood star. In the July 1933 issue of the *New Movie Magazine*, Jack Kleinman from Chicago was convinced that "a lot of fans will flock to the box office to see . . . new pictures made from the best pictures before the talkies."[46] Talker remakes of *The Lost World* (Harry O. Hoyt, 1925) and *The Volga Boatman* (Cecil B. De Mille, 1926), Kleinman wrote, "would be a great help to the box-office in these days of depression."[47] In the January 1934 issue, Mrs. Effie Myers from Williamsport, Indiana, wrote that she hoped to see a sound version of *Ben-Hur*. "I hardly think it needs to be remade (in my opinion the acting and filming couldn't be improved upon)," she conceded in her letter to the *New Movie Magazine*, "but with the addition of sound it would be superb—what a thrill seeing [this picture] again would bring!"[48] Film critics, too, compiled lists of movies that Hollywood should consider remaking as talkies. Chester B. Bahn, film critic of the *Syracuse Herald*, suggested in July 1934 that the following titles be "remade with present-day stars in the cast and the added advantages of modern technical developments": *Birth of a Nation, Hunchback of Notre Dame, Covered Wagon, Ben-Hur, Variety, Sea Hawk, Quo Vadis, If I Were King, Robin Hood, Little Old New York, If Winter Comes, Dorothy Vernon of Haddon Hall, Scaramouche,* and *Peter Pan*.[49] Overall, there seemed to be a consensus among those who suggested film titles that sound would be an improvement and make the film remakes worthwhile.

RECYCLING STRATEGIES TO FEED THE MAW OF EXHIBITION

It was expensive to wire the movie theaters for sound and, for the technology to work effectively, they needed to be equipped with air-conditioning. "The coming of sound necessitated acoustic control inside the theater, leading to the end of open doors and noisy ventilation fans," Donald Crafton explains.[50] "Quiet air conditioning not only improved the noise level but enabled theaters to remain open year-round. This increased the demand for movies, led to the cancellation of the traditional winter recess in Hollywood, and opened the door for more independent product."[51] During the 1930s, when the "Big Five" major studios (MGM, Paramount, RKO, Warner Bros., and 20th Century Fox) controlled the production, distribution, and exhibition of movies in a vertically integrated film industry, Hollywood made between four hundred and five hundred movies per year for eighty to ninety million Americans who went to see double features at least once a week.[52] Each movie ran through the major studio's run-zone-clearance system that divided the movie theaters into first-run, second-run, and later-run houses. According to Vinzenz Hediger, "an average film took two years to descend the ladder of the distribution system, from urban first run in prestigious palaces to lower-run and rural theaters. After their two-year distribution period most films were withdrawn and disappeared into the vaults of the studio."[53] Because the system "favored rapid turnovers" and was "almost fully geared to novelty,"[54] the majors always needed new content and put much time and effort into story acquisition and development. Despite the fact that MGM, Paramount, RKO, Warner Bros., and 20th Century Fox "had story departments in New York, Hollywood, and Europe that systematically searched the literary marketplace for suitable novels, plays, short stories, and original ideas,"[55] however, there was a perceived story shortage and recycling old properties became a standard operation when it was difficult to find fresh material for the talkies. As Eric Hoyt points out, "the demand for tested story material created a lively market for the buying and selling of remake rights."[56] In contrast to today, where Hollywood studios hold on to their properties, "the industry's commonsense belief was that trading story rights among studios was both necessary and advisable: necessary because of the shortage in suitable screen stories; advisable because the remake of another producer's film would likely reach a slightly different, and hopefully bigger, audience."[57]

The industry's trade publications followed the perceived shortage of suitable talkie material closely and printed news items about the studios' search for remakable properties in their vaults. These publications were crucial agents in analyzing and making sense of the remake boom that was set in motion by the sound innovation, constituting a framework that actively negotiated the meanings and implications of the talkie for the US film business. By 1930, trade papers provided long lists of the remakes that studios had scheduled on their annual production slates, published production news about individual remakes that were being filmed as well as rumors about future projects, and printed statements from leading industry figures. Universal boss Carl Laemmle Jr., for example, told *Motion Picture News* in January of 1930 that "silent successes of other years, remade with sound and dialogue, are registering heavily at the box-office," adding that "shortage of talker story material, which producers are reported as viewing with concern, can be and is being overcome, to a large extent, by the remaking of pictures upon which the public has put its stamp of emphatic approval in other years."[58]

In October of 1930, the leading industry publication *Film Daily* published a Bell Syndicate opinion piece written by playwright and screenwriter Robert E. Sherwood, who was "surprised that there have not been more [remakes of old silent pictures in talking form]."[59] He argued that "in view of the widely advertised shortage of stories in Hollywood . . . it would seem to be logical to go through the files and resurrect all the acknowledged triumphs of earlier days."[60] Many articles expressed such views in which the film remake emerged as the perfect remedy for Hollywood's insatiable hunger for fresh talkie material. The message was often cast in a language that evokes vivid images of zombie-like resurrections from the dead and of tomb raiding and adventurous treasure hunts in the studios' archival vaults. In February of 1929, *Motion Picture News* reported that many past successes were currently being "exhumed" by the studios.[61] Other news items spoke of "box office successes of former days [that] are to be reborn"[62] and of producers who were "digging deep"[63] — either to find a lost gem in "the veritable Treasure Chest"[64] the studio had accumulated in the past two decades, or to "Rattl[e] the Skeleton" and "unearth old material for talkers."[65] The choice of words speaks volumes about how Hollywood understood its own history at the time and it shows that the transition to sound transformed the value of the studios' silent film libraries "from collections of properties that could be profitably recirculated as copies to collections of properties that could be used for the production of derivatives"[66] — especially remakes.

Yet, even if the production of talker remakes seemed logical (given the shortage of story material and the public demand for talkies), it was obvious that the film industry had difficulties fathoming in which direction it was heading. The projection from the beginning of 1930 that more than 125 remakes would hit theaters in the 1930–1931 season had to be revised toward the end of the year. The *Film Daily* noted "a general trend away from remaking,"[67] with ultimately only fifty-three remakes in the 1930–1931 season and another drop to seventeen and then nine remakes scheduled for the following two seasons.[68] My Hollywood Remaking dataset reveals that the final numbers were not as low as the *Film Daily* predicted (figure 13). The year 1930 clearly stands out as a monumental year for film

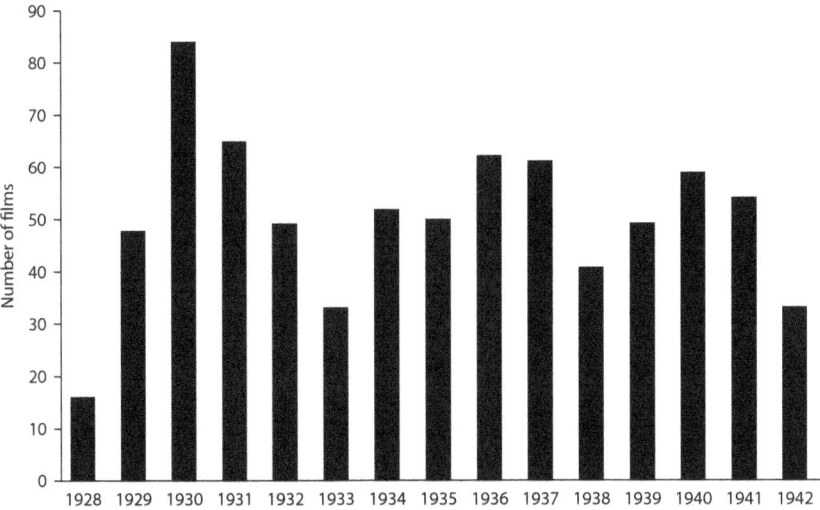

Figure 13. Production of film remakes, 1928–1942. *Source*: Hollywood Remaking dataset.

remakes with a total of eighty-four releases. In the following three years the numbers decrease (1931: sixty-five remakes, 1932: forty-nine remakes) until they reach the lowest number of the decade in 1933 (thirty-three remakes). But remakes remained at an overall very high level, making up 17 percent of total film production in the United States in 1930, 13 percent in 1931, 10 percent in 1932 and still 7 percent in 1933. They reach another peak in 1936 (sixty-two remakes) and 1937 (sixty-one remakes), when the sound film celebrated its tenth anniversary—the occasion for another cycle of talker remakes.

These ups and downs on the production slate indicate that audience reaction was unpredictable and that talker remakes quickly turned out to be anything but a safe bet, even if the original silent film had been a hit. In the article "Remake Question Still Puzzling Studio Chiefs" from November 1930, *Motion Picture News* stated that some remakes "have made money at the box office," some "have not grossed any great amount, but are out of the red," and "others have not measured up to the standards of good pictures and have suffered accordingly."[69] These different outcomes confused studio heads. While they were nonetheless convinced that "any good picture will register at the box-office regardless of whether or not it has been made previously,"[70] distributors were not so sure about the talker remakes' moneymaking potential. *Variety* reported that "distributors are trying to reach a conclusion whether it is worth while making remakes in dialog."[71] During the third year of talkers, Hollywood continued to rely heavily on remakes because of the lack of new material, but the film industry also recognized that titles, audience memory, and timing were important factors to consider when studios aimed for a box-office smash.

THE REMAKE QUESTION: TITLES, AUDIENCE MEMORY, AND TIMING

In 1930, Hollywood producers and exhibitors disagreed about releasing talker remakes of silent movies under new titles (*disguised remakes*). Producers feared that there might be too many talker remakes on the marquees and began "digging up new story names and eliminating all mention in advertising, etc., of what the remakes are based on," whereas exhibitors protested that this practice meant "[throwing] away the most valuable part of the property."[72] Unlike the producers, they were convinced that old titles "would mean something at the box office"[73] and threatened to play the new movies under their old silent titles anyway. Trade papers, too, were opposed to changing old titles and warned that retitling silent hits was a practice audiences would not accept: "To remake in dialog, as it is claimed some producers think of doing, the former silent under a different title, as a decoy, may be dangerous. That might seriously imperil the good will of any theatre playing the deceptive talker. That it is a remake can not be hidden. Though the local critics failed to mention it, the public will recognize and talk."[74] By the mid-1930s, the question of whether or not to release new movies under the same old title was as urgent as ever. In 1935, the *Film Daily*'s eponymous trade columnist "Phil M. Daly" wrote, "You'd be surprised to learn how many pix are disguised under another name,"[75] and a year later, critic Don Carle Gillette outright condemned retitling and warned that changing a title would do more harm to the business than keeping it: "The bad will created in apparently trying to fool the public by offering an old story in disguise is likely to be more costly to theaters than any possible loss of patronage due to fans recognizing the story if it is announced under its original title."[76] Instead, Gillette's reasoning went, studios would do well if they capitalized on the familiarity of the title. "A big hit of the past, remade and presented under its original title with popular stars of today, has the double box office value of a story reputation and current marquee names."[77]

Retitling persisted in Hollywood as a common practice, though, and was met with growing criticism by fans and critics toward the end of the decade. In the *Film Daily*, Chester B. Bahn stated that "as a matter of business, it's okay to take up a successful picture of yesterday and remake it."[78] But he also stressed that "remakes should be presented honestly."[79] Meanwhile, movie fans charged the industry with "false advertising and unethical tactics," as Harold Heffernan reported in the *Baltimore Sun* in July 1939.[80] A woman from Shreveport, Louisiana, planned to campaign for a state law that would make it an offense to "exhibit . . . any film play that has been previously exhibited under a different title, unless such exhibition is plainly advertised as a remade version."[81] The woman declared that, during the past several months, she had come across "at least fifteen motion pictures which she saw anywhere from ten to two years ago, and which she was led to believe were new stories when she paid her money at the box office."[82] Like other moviegoers, she felt cheated and was angry that she had been lured into the theater under a false pretense and ended up paying good money for a movie she already knew. "To my way of thinking, this is dishonesty," the woman complained.[83]

> Certainly it is false advertising and shows a complete lack of ethics and fair play with the people who make the motion picture industry's existence possible. While I do not object to the showing of remade pictures when they are plainly advertised as such—*Beau Geste* and *The Hunchback of Notre Dame* are examples—I do believe the motion picture industry would profit immensely along artistic and financial paths if producers would clean their shelves of old story properties and concentrate on new subjects instead of those that are definitely antiques.[84]

Commentators found that the Shreveport woman's campaign was likely to register as yet another threat to the film industry, which was already grappling with shrinking movie audiences at the time. Apparently, regular patrons stayed away from theaters "because producers have stubbornly persisted in making gangster pictures . . . , because of the many remade stories parading under different titles . . . and because of poor stories or double bills."[85] Business insiders thought that disguised remakes were responsible for an audience loss of at least 10 percent. And yet, the studios continued their production, announcing plans to release three times more remakes in comparison to previous seasons.[86]

"Hollywood always seems to resort to the remake in a tight spot," Heffernan mused and explained that "there are scores of works on the shelves of each studio that are considered 'standard' for periodical revisions."[87] As a rule, titles of famous plays and literary classics were never altered, but some producers evidently held the belief "that title changing is essential when reusing any screen material."[88] In October 1935, *Variety* analyzed why remakes fared poorly at the box-office and found that one reason was because the moviegoing public "has a great memory for titles."[89] *Variety* explained, "It's [the] old story that [the] public wants something new, and now with pictures being sound it's more so than ever. . . . Even if they did not see a pic in silent days, or even if it were made in early days of sound, they sort of shy away saying 'we want nothing shopworn.'"[90] When the title promised something new, however, many remakes became "memory tests"[91] before the audiences' eyes. In his review of the Philo Vance detective movie *Night of Mystery* (E. A. Dupont, 1937), a remake of the early sound film *The Greene Murder Case* (S. S. Van Dine, 1929), the *Motion Picture Daily*'s Red Kann therefore questioned "the general effectiveness of remakes of well known mystery tales disguised as new stories by a new title."[92] He himself guessed the murderer early on and predicted, "It will not take long for those who saw the original . . . to realize this is the same broth warmed over, but with a different cast. The flavoring is identical in a dish differently presented that easily may not be so good."[93]

Movie fans, too, complained about remakes of movies they still remembered. Mrs. Frank Kurlick from East Hartford, Connecticut, for instance, aired her discontent in *Photoplay*'s letter column. "Something must be done about the new evil perpetrated by the movie moguls—remakes of pictures that movie-goers have not yet forgotten," Kurlick wrote in the 1941 May issue of the fan magazine.[94] She was irritated that Hollywood had remade the romantic drama *One Way Passage* (Tay Garnett, 1932) under the new title *'Til We Meet Again* (Edmund Goulding, 1940) and wondered: "Why should I pay to see a story, however beautiful, that I know beforehand?"[95] Some months later, in the December issue, Sue Anna from Lexington, Kentucky, asked this set of questions in a letter that won *Photoplay*'s ten-dollar prize: "Why all the remakes of pictures still easily remembered by most movie-goers? . . . Doesn't Hollywood have any original stories left? Hasn't the public indicated that the story is the important thing—regardless of stars—and that no matter how good a story is, it gets stale with too much retelling?"[96] Nevertheless, Sue Anna did not condemn Hollywood's remaking practice altogether. Instead, she proposed that studios "go a little further into the years," in order to find "something worth reviving" that "has been forgotten by all but a few and would be something new to the present generation."[97]

Even though Hollywood cinema had only a brief past (and an even briefer sound film past), memory had already become a tricky thing that affected how audiences responded to remakes. Without the novelty of sound, critics found "remakes of films that have been great successes cannot avoid the handicap of comparison."[98] In *Hollywood*'s review column, for example, Llewellyn Miller argued that the 1940 remake of *A Bill of Divorcement* (George Cukor, 1932) suffered in comparison "because there is a haunting memory of other faces and voices."[99] A review of *Beau Geste* (William A. Wellman, 1939), the talker remake of the 1926 movie about three brothers who join the French Foreign Legion, admittedly praised the new version as "a spectacular and engrossing action film . . . which keeps impressionable audiences on the edge of their seats."[100] Yet it also pointed out shortcomings that had nothing to do with the movie itself. The remake failed because it could not reproduce the affective quality that the review attributed to the 1926 *Beau Geste*: "Memory is apt to linger more fondly on the fine features and many a movie-goer who remembers that first version will probably insist that this 1939 remake does not quite recapture the striding vigor and terrible suspense of its predecessor."[101]

Another review of *Beau Geste* made a similar argument: "*Beau Geste* will be a moneymaker. There is such an inherent vitality in this Percival Wren story that, given anything in the way of expensive production, it seems impossible to imagine how it could fail. But *Beau Geste* will be a disappointment to exhibitors who remember the silent version, and to many patrons whose memory is also long."[102] While both reviews recognized the timeless appeal of the movie's theme and the great box-office potential of the talkie, memories of the silent film version interfered with any wholehearted approval of the new *Beau Geste*. In this case, the addition of sound comes nowhere near to compensating for what seems to get lost in the remake. To be sure, already in 1930, *Los Angeles Times* film critic Philip K. Scheuer wrote that "those of us on the outside who really treasure the memory of certain silent masterpieces of the past are sometimes taken aback by the blitheness with which talkie men announce a 'new version' of an old classic."[103]

With remakes abounding in the early sound years and throughout the 1930s—"no company has been immune to the remake virus," the *Motion Picture Herald* noted in April 1937—both movie fans and critics often found fault with Hollywood's reliance on old properties.[104] "Those having the longest or most retentive memories are most wrought up," the trade paper observed. Yet it also chided, "All seem to forget that times change and so do people and stories."[105] This view was also common among fans, who welcomed remakes of their favorite movies. The debate in *Photoplay*'s letter column, where readers like Mrs. Kurlick and Sue Anna had complained about Hollywood's penchant for remakes, took a different turn, when Clarence Thornbey from Nebraska defended the practice in 1942's May issue and directly addressed the criticism of his fellow fans: "In 'Speak for Yourself' and other various columns I have read articles that start out 'Why all the remakes of old pictures? Aren't there any new stories in Hollywood?' etc. Don't those people that write that stuff ever realize that the younger generation likes to go to shows too? They like to see famous stories on the screen no matter how old they are, just so they're entertaining."[106] Following this train of thought, remaking was no dishonest moneymaking scheme but a legitimate filmmaking practice that helped construct a cinematic past and archive for future generations.

At a time, when movies were a strictly ephemeral experience, "a time-specific and place-bound encounter, subject to contingencies of programming and local performance,"[107] remakes preserved good stories and kept them in circulation. Audiences could watch a movie while it played in a theater near them, but once it was taken from the bill, it would most likely never return. During the silent era, it had been common that major productions like Cecil B. DeMille's *The Ten Commandments* (1923) would run for up to sixty-two weeks, but such opportunities for repeat viewing dwindled when the US film industry converted to sound and first-run engagements were reduced to only a few weeks or days.[108] Vinzenz Hediger writes that "old films held little value" in the Hollywood studio system and that rereleases or reissues "were usually limited to a few major films, particularly to those that had been box-office successes during their original release."[109] Popular silent films like *The Birth of a Nation* (D. W. Griffith, 1915), *The Phantom of the Opera* (Rupert Julian, 1925), *Ben-Hur*, and *The Big Parade* (King Vidor, 1925), for instance, were rereleased with new synchronized music scores and added dialogue sequences in the early sound years, but the exhibition of silent films decreased throughout the 1930s and was extremely rare by the end of the decade.[110] Remakes offered the chance to (re-)watch popular stories from Hollywood's recent past as modern sound films and with the stars of the day. And yet, for many fans and critics remakes and memory seemed to collide. Was a successful remake a matter of timing? And if so, how much time had to pass between one version and the next?

Pondering why remakes flopped at the box-office, *Variety* speculated in September 1930, "It may be that a sufficiently long period has not elapsed between those silents chosen for the remakes, and the remade talkers."[111] If moviegoers had seen a popular silent movie not too long ago, a talker remake would most likely fail to replicate or even surpass that experience. "Evidently the impression with them is that the addition of sound and dialog do not make it worth while to sit through the picture a second time," *Variety* explained.[112] "It's like a forgotten play or song."[113] In January 1931, the trade paper counted a total of 134 remakes that had been released since 1928 and compiled a list with the studios, titles, and years that had passed between a silent production and its sound film remake. Based on this data, *Variety* recommended an interval of at least seven years between two movies: "Under four years is almost suicidal for remakes, certainly without drastic changes in story and a camouflage title."[114] The best timing remained a burning question throughout the 1930s, motivating industry insiders and critics to join in the discussion. In the *Film Daily* column "Along the Rialto," "Phil M. Daly" argued in November 1935 that a ten-year interval would be best given that "every ten years a new audience is presented for films."[115] And with an eye on the release of *Raffles* in 1939—the fourth version after 1917, 1925 and 1930—director Sam Wood likewise suggested that "every really great story should be remade as a picture every 10 years."[116] Chester B. Bahn reviewed and qualified Wood's statement in the *Film Daily*, adding "for safety's sake": "It all depends who remakes it."[117] In general, however, Bahn found the ten-year interval between remakes that Wood proposed "a reasonable interlude" and went on to explain the math: "There's a sizeable turnover in the film audience in a decade, considering that the film audience, broadly speaking, has a 10 to 60 age limit. If that holds true, remakes after 10 years actually are 'originals' to some 20 per cent of the film audience."[118]

The timing and frequency of remakes in Hollywood eventually raised questions about movie generations, about the timeliness and timelessness of popular stories, and, most importantly, about whether film was an art form (on a par with literature and theater) or a mere commodity. Those who championed original ideas and were critical of Hollywood's reliance on remakes drew comparisons between the film and the automobile industry, pointing out that the car manufacturers' commercial success depended on the continued production of new and improved models. *Variety*, for instance, proposed the following cure for "headaches and nights of worry" caused by the unpredictability of remakes:

> Picture producers could best pattern production ideas after automobile people who have their engineers working on new ideas and never try a remake because it was good the year before. They come through with something new and attractive each year in improving their output. Picture people have creative brains at their disposal to do likewise for them in story material, or have it available on the world literary market, so should make use of these advantages in discreet fashion.[119]

Others supported remakes as a good business practice *and* because of their artistic value. In many ways, this reasoning went, remakes resembled the kind of repetition audiences were already familiar with from theater productions and the literary marketplace.

In *Film Daily*, Don Carle Gillette argued in June 1936 that "the remaking of a hit story of ten, fifteen or even twenty years ago, provided the subject still has interest for present-day moviegoers, is just as good business as the legitimate stage practice of reviving certain plays decade after decade or the publishing of new editions of classic literary works."[120] Two years earlier, in 1934, Gillette had made the case for "a permanent repertory of screen classics."[121] "Although the motion picture is still pretty much of an infant alongside the various arts," he explained, "its amazing precocity has fructuated into so much that is of lasting artistic merit, aside from entertainment value, that the time has come to give a thought to a permanent repertory of screen classics."[122] Despite its short history in comparison to the stage, literature, and other arts, "the screen has the resources to match any of them."[123] Gillette's notion of "screen classics" contradicts today's understanding of the "classic" label and such a movie's relatively stable identity as a historical—yet timeless—cultural object.

> The idea is not to re-release these outstanding pictures periodically, but to remake them every five or ten years with casts composed of the reigning favorites of the day and with the added advantages of whatever new improvements in technique may be developed in the interim. Out of some 10,000 features produced in the last 17 years, at least 1,000 had story value of a more or less perennial nature. If remade only once every ten years, it would still provide 100 practically sure-fire stories each season—and they could be made at a considerable saving in cost.[124]

The "screen classics" Gillette imagines are not about remembering, repeating, and revitalizing individual, self-contained texts that can lay claim to being considered aesthetically, historically, or culturally significant. Instead they involve the regular *renewal* of "outstanding pictures" based on their "story value." The singular, timeless quality of a good story is to be preserved in and through its multiple versions, each of which creates new economic, aesthetic, and cultural value as it modernizes and modifies *not the story* but *its rendition* in terms of cinema's technological affordances and by starring popular actors "with current marquee value."[125] Gillette was convinced that such screen classics would "draw the fans, both new and old" and bring producers "as near as [they] can ever hope to get in making pictures with pre-assured profit."[126]

Commercial imperatives, popular entertainment, and art come together in this vision, where great stories were to be remade every five or ten years so that each movie generation would have its own up-to-date version. As Gillette explains: "Among today's generation of movie-goers are many who never saw *Prisoner of Zenda, Tol'able David, Thief of Bagdad, When Knighthood Was in Flower, La Boheme, Seventh Heaven, Madame X, Beau Brummel, Monsieur Beaucaire, The Big Parade, Beau Geste, Green Goddess, In Old Arizona, Showboat* and other similar caliber hits that are as good stories in one generation as in another."[127] Gillette's idea of "screen classics," in short, does not promote stable texts and meanings in the form of a singular, original object but multiplicities that ultimately construct a different kind of stability—*and continuity*—over time. The repertoire of movies to be remade again and again ties the question of timing ("At what intervals should these movies be remade?") to concepts of generation, memory, and the emergence of film as cultural heritage. Despite the many and often contradictory discourses in the 1930s about what Hollywood's practice of recycling existing material meant for cinemagoers, the movie business, the concept of originality, and the evolution of film as an art form, it became clear that remakes did not merely connect the cinematic past and present—they partook in *creating* a cinematic past and present and made cinema's progress tangible.

FROM SILENT PAST TO SOUND FILM PRESENT

By the time the film industry began to commemorate the transition to sound as a milestone of cinema's progress, talker remakes had become intricately linked to the construction of silent cinema as a bygone era. Talker remakes represented the modern sound age, while their precursors belonged to another time, the silent era. The labels had caught on quickly and the movies associated with them eventually functioned as structuring devices, marking different stages in a constantly progressing film history that thrived on technological innovation. Talkies were considered to embody cinema's evolution toward a mature art, and they fit right into the discourses of scientific progress that were prevalent in the late 1920s and 1930s. As Donald Crafton notes, "Talkies were readily plugged into [the] popularly constructed circuit that connected new developments in transportation (electric trains and elevators), communication (telephone and radio), and labor-saving and leisure-time appliances (the phonograph).

Like other electrical technologies, sound film was on the cusp of modernity."[128] If talkies had "an aura of modernity and inevitability,"[129] talker remakes of old silent hits put cinema's progress on display for the world to see. These movies invited direct comparisons between the silent past and the sound film present. Through repetition, talker remakes recalled the past, but their central technological innovation—sound—along with the stars and fashion of the day, current acting styles and film aesthetic, firmly located them in the present. Talkies were modern and talker remakes even more so *because they reminded audiences that they were modern.*

Fan magazines like *Modern Screen*, *Photoplay*, and *Screenland*, which "'fanned' consumers' desires to learn more about movies and to become 'fanatic' about their screen favorites,"[130] encouraged the juxtaposition between the silent past and sound film present by framing cinema's conversion to sound as a generation-defining event. The 1936 February issue of *Modern Screen*, for instance, set stills from silent movies side by side with stills from their respective talker remakes (figure 14). The heading "Yesterday—Today" spread out over the double page, with "Yesterday" printed on the top of the left page and "Today" on the right, the spatial distance of the two words conveying the temporal distance between past ("Yesterday") and present ("Today"). This was further reinforced by the text and illustrations arranged to the left and right of the photos. "Yesterday" is printed in a serif typeface that creates a vintage look and stresses the word's semiotic relationship to a time that has already passed. This retro effect is also used for the text printed in the lower left corner: "Remember these great scenes in silent films?"[131] The question establishes a connection between "Yesterday" on the one hand and the silent era on the other, and, directly addressing *Modern Screen*'s readership, provides the context in which the photos on the double page should be read: Silent films belong to the past, to memory. The illustration on the left emphasized this idea as it shows a drawing of a female figure wearing a long, heavily draped, corseted outfit of the late Victorian era, finished with a broad feathered hat and an umbrella. On the right page, the word "Today" is printed in an elegant Art Deco typeface with stylized, geometric shapes that stand in sharp contrast to the vintage font on the left. The modern, sans-serif lettering is picked up in the lower right corner, where the text—referring back to the question on the left—reads: "And now each finds voice in a modern version."[132] The text and font on the

Figure 14. For fan magazines, the release of talker remakes presented an opportunity to revisit the cinematic past. "Yesterday—Today," *Modern Screen* (February 1936): 44–45. Image courtesy of the Margaret Herrick Library.

right represent the modern age of the talkies. The illustration of another female figure shows a woman with a streamlined silhouette, who wears a fashionable 1930s clutch coat with wide shoulders and a narrow waist. The coat reaches below the knee and is trimmed with a stylish fur collar and cuffs. Her look is complete with a small hat, gloves, and a dog on a leash.

Twelve movie stills were juxtaposed at the center of the double page—with scenes from the silent movies always placed on the left and the same scenes from the talker remakes on the right. Short captions provided information about the titles and stars as well as the years of the silent movies. For instance: "In 1917, William Farnum and Jewel Carmen did *A Tale of Two Cities.*—Today [1935], Elizabeth Allen and Donald Woods play the same epic lovers."[133] Greta Garbo reprised her role as Anna Karenina in the talker remake *Anna Karenina* (Clarence Brown, 1935), which she had also played in the silent movie *Love* (Edmund Goulding, 1927). J. Warren

Kerrigan, who starred in *Captain Blood* (David Smith, 1924), was replaced by Errol Flynn in the sound film version (Michael Curtiz, 1935). The roles Douglas Fairbanks and Mary McLaren played in *The Three Musketeers* (Fred Niblo, 1921) were revived by Walter Abel and Margot Grahame in the talkie (Rowland V. Lee, 1935). Joan Crawford and House Peters' *Rose-Marie* (Lucien Hubbard, 1928) was remade with Jeannette MacDonald and Nelson Eddy (W. S. Van Dyke, 1936), Wilma Banky and Ronald Colman's *The Dark Angel* (George Fitzmaurice, 1925) with Merle Oberon and Fredric March (Sidney Franklin, 1935).

Modern Screen prominently placed the two oldest silent movies—*A Tale of Two Cities* (1917) and *The Three Musketeers* (1921)—at the top, since the stills set side by side with the talker remakes from 1935 best captured the distance between the movies in terms of fashion, acting style, and film aesthetic. The other examples cannot be categorized as easily: The stills are very similar even if they feature different actors (except for Greta Garbo) and the time that has passed between one version and the next is merely eight years in two cases (*Rose-Marie* and *Anna Karenina*) instead of eighteen (*A Tale of Two Cities*) and fourteen (*The Three Musketeers*). Yet, it is clear that the fan magazine wanted to present the sound innovation as a catalyst for change and talker remakes as agents of modernization. In order to do so, *Modern Screen* resorted to the suggestive layout, fonts, and illustrations described here, prompting its readers to recognize themselves as belonging to a movie generation that exists in a modern sound age clearly distinct from the old-fashioned silent era.

If talker remakes marked the difference between past and present, they also established a connection between the two. The generational identification with the new movies and the sound film era, that *Modern Screen*'s double page endorsed, required film-historical knowledge about silent pictures that were no longer accessible to most contemporary moviegoers. By the mid-1930s, only a few silents still circulated in the free market; some were forever lost to nitrate fires, others were intentionally destroyed by the studios to free up storage space for new material and to reduce the risk of fires.[134] *Modern Screen*'s "Yesterday—Today" framed silent hits as outdated, yet, in order to fully appreciate the modern sound film versions, readers were encouraged to take a comparative stance and revisit (or learn about) the cinematic past.

Remembering the silent era *through* film remakes became a regular feature of fan magazines so that paratexts surrounding Hollywood's talker remakes ultimately bestowed permanence on ephemeral silent pictures, fostered proficiency in film history, and engaged in remembrance work. *Photoplay*, for example, published the movie quiz "Match Them If You Can" in the 1938 November issue to test how well its readers knew the cinematic past. The objective was to match film stills from twenty silent pictures of the late 1910s and early 1920s with scenes from their contemporary remakes and fill in details about both movies. The pairings, randomly arranged on a double page around a short text with instructions for taking the quiz, included *Stella Dallas* (Henry King, 1925/King Vidor, 1937), *Maytime* (Louis Gasnier, 1923/Robert Z. Leonard, 1937), *If I Were King* (J. Gordon Edwards, 1920/Frank Lloyd, 1938), *Sally, Irene and Mary* (Edmund Goulding, 1925/William A. Seiter, 1938), *Robin Hood* (Allan Dwan, 1923/Michael Curtiz, 1938), *Prisoner of Zenda* (Rex Ingram, 1922/John Cromwell, 1937), *Tom Sawyer* (William D. Taylor, 1917/Norman Taurog, 1938), *Holiday* (Edward H. Griffith, 1930/George Cukor, 1938), and *Camille* (Ray C. Smallwood, 1921/George Cukor, 1937).

In the accompanying text, *Photoplay* distinguished between a "'flash in the pan' film, which is seen by many audiences and then consigned to oblivion" and "those perennial classics that live forever in the form of 'remakes'—new versions of old films that are often remade two or three times."[135] The fan magazine thus introduced and defined—in one short sentence—the term *remake* and explained how such movies preserved "perennial classics" for future generations of viewers. Considering that one needed to know at least 75 percent of the answers to pass the test, *Photoplay* expected its readers to be familiar with Hollywood's practice of remaking former box-office hits. Everyone who knew 85 percent of the answers, one could read in the instructions, was on a par with the magazine's movie experts. *Photoplay* also rewarded in-depth knowledge of the silent films: one could win a total of ten points for each question—five points for the film title, three points for the names of the actors in the old film, and two points for the names of the actors in the new version.

Like *Modern Screen*'s "Yesterday—Today," "Match Them If You Can" presented the release of talker remakes as an occasion to remember Hollywood's silent films. Once more, the transition to sound was framed as a momentous innovation with a lasting impact on filmmaking and film aesthetics. Both in the layout of the double page and in the answers section, the remakes figured more prominently than their distant originals and (like *Modern Screen*) *Photoplay* privileged identification with the contemporary sound film versions. At the same time, the fan magazine was also invested in film-historical knowledge production that established silent films as the baseline against which readers could measure Hollywood's progress. The quiz showcased talker remakes as a gateway to the cinematic past—a reason to recall the stars and stories of a bygone era in the present moment and a timely reminder of the strides film had made as an art form. In this sense, fan magazines like *Modern Screen* and *Photoplay* created an interpretative framework for understanding the transition to sound that both accommodated and reinforced the ways in which Hollywood imagined itself and its historical trajectory, especially approaching the tenth anniversary of sound on screen.

In the 1930s, photo spreads for specific talker remakes also contained prompts to remember the silent movies on which the remakes were based. In its 1937 August issue, for instance, *Screenland* published "Return of *Stella Dallas*" to direct attention to the release of the sound film starring Barbara Stanwyck in the title role (figure 15). The word *return* in the heading, stills from the 1925 version, and the explanatory captions on the page conjured memories of the silent hit. "That girl's here again—Stella herself, famous screen heroine of twelve years ago, revived by Barbara Stanwyck," the text announced, and the captions informed readers about the who is who "in the first version" and "in the modern edition."[136] "Remember that silent screenplay of *Stella Dallas*, produced by Sam Goldwyn over a decade ago, with Ronald Colman and Belle Bennett . . . in leading rôles?" *Screenland* asked.[137] "Now Goldwyn brings it all back to us, with Stanwyck as the colorful *Stella*, Anne Shirley as her daughter, *Laurel*, John Boles as *Stephen*."[138] The fan magazine promoted the remake as a modern take on the melodrama, encouraging readers to reflect on the differences between both movies. "What change hath time and talkies wrought!" *Screenland* marveled, with the archaic "hath" in the exclamation encapsulating the temporal and technological distance that separated the silent and sound film versions of *Stella Dallas*.[139]

In fact, the talker remake itself operates (albeit much more subtly) as an agent of memory and modernization. Early in the 1937 version, when

Figure 15. Fan magazines advertised both the timelessness of a story and the timeliness of the talker remake. "Return of Stella Dallas," *Screenland* (August 1937). Image courtesy of the Media History Digital Library, http://mediahist.org.

working-class Stella and upper-class Stephen first meet and fall in love in the small factory town of Millhampton, Massachusetts, in 1919, the couple goes to the movies. There is no equivalent for this scene in the 1925 version, which means that their "date" can also be read as a self-reflexive comment that the remake makes about its own origins in silent cinema and, more generally, about the cinematic past. On the walk home, Stella tells Stephen that she wants to be "like the people in the movie, all well-bred and refined." She will, of course, utterly fail at adapting to upper-class ways of life. This key scene therefore sets up the conflict, which eventually leads to Stephen's separation from Stella and her motherly sacrifice: She gives up her daughter Laurel to Stephen and his new wife Helen so as to enable the girl's entrance into high society. Jennifer Parchesky notes that "Stella becomes an object lesson in how *not* to look and behave even as the elegant styles of Laurel and Helen—and off-screen representations of Stanwyck herself as working girl risen to glamorous star—suggest alternative models."[140] Contemporary reviewers remarked that the anachronism of Stella's garish outfits and vulgar behavior is implausible "in an era when magazines, radios, newspapers and motion pictures dole out fashion hints by the bushel."[141] Stella's excess seems preposterous, but it serves to tell a story in which her working-class background threatens the upward social mobility of her child. According to Parchesky, "For Stella's sacrifice to have any value, the audience must accept the premise that she cannot possibly assimilate to her daughter's world."[142]

Stella's attempts to fit in ultimately amount to nothing more than a "layering of incongruous styles [that] makes her violation of taste readily apparent to all classes."[143] On the way home from the movie theater, Stephen tells Stella that she does not have to change for him because he likes her just the way she is and that "it isn't really well-bred to act the way you aren't." Stella is presented as "most attractive and sympathetic when at her most natural," in this remake, "specifically in moments of maternal suffering like the train scene and the final street scene, where soft focus and subtle toplighting make her apparently make-up-free face radiant and light up her frizzy hair like a halo."[144] One could also argue that this is when Stella behaves and looks like a woman and mother with whom contemporary audiences are supposed to identify, whereas the person she pretends to be—based on idealized notions of the glamorous upper-class life she has internalized from Hollywood movies of the silent era—is embarrassing and alienating. Stella and high society are portrayed as a bad match, but she does not fit into the modern present of the sound film remake either, a time marked by "the triumph of consumer culture's displacement of genteel notions of taste with external standards of fashion."[145] By including the scene at the movies and her admiration for the refined characters on the silent screen, the remake presents Stella as a woman, who—once her youth and beauty start to fade—becomes not only lost in her fantasies about upper-class distinction and the lure of unattainable elegance and taste. She is also stuck *in time* and will never be able to adapt to the modern age that her daughter Laurel, Helen, and Stephen navigate so effortlessly.

The remake's reference to silent cinema can be understood as a nod to the first *Stella Dallas* movie, which the 1937 sound version both recalls and replaces. To a certain extent, it anticipates the self-conscious awareness of their own preexistence that film remakes begin to display once different versions circulate simultaneously in the same cultural system because of television and home video technologies, as I discuss in chapter 1. At the time, however, such meta-commentaries that connect the cinematic past and present are more commonly located in paratexts and surrounding discourses rather than in the movies themselves. Remakes, in other words, strongly focused on repetition as a device that foregrounded what was new, whereas the idea of progress that technological innovations inscribed into the movies was communicated in paratexts that explicitly invoked the cinematic past. This means that talker remakes (including *Stella Dallas*) closely remade their silent predecessors (keeping plot structures, narrative units, character constellations), which in turn showcased the movies' addition of sound and dialogue as groundbreaking novelty. As remakes, these talkies therefore operated in a predominantly *additive* manner (it is *Stella Dallas* plus sound) instead of taking a *transformative* stance (it is *Stella Dallas* but set in 1990, as is later the case in the Bette Midler vehicle *Stella*) or a *revisionist* approach (possibly: *Stella Dallas* as a feminist reimagining of the maternal melodrama). In 1937, paratexts like *Screenland*'s "Return of *Stella Dallas*" were invested in advertising both the timelessness of the story and the timeliness of the remake. "Return" points out the compelling nature of the heartrending tale about motherly love and sacrifice, based on Olive Higgins Prouty's novel *Stella Dallas* that was first serialized in the *American Magazine* (1922) and subsequently published in book form (1923), while also highlighting the remake's modern aspects, in particular the sound innovation and the new actors taking on the familiar roles. This takes place against the backdrop of the silent film version so that the comparison directs the readers' attention to the cinematic past and serves to situate the talker remake within the sound film present (and the readers right along with it). The information that Samuel Goldwyn returns as the producer of *Stella Dallas* meanwhile establishes a continuity between past and present and comes with the promise that the updated sound film version starring Barbara Stanwyck also has the fabled "Goldwyn touch."

Following the heyday of the film remake with talkie versions of old silent hits in the 1930s, Hollywood cinema continues to chart its own evolution as a technological medium and as a cultural force through film remakes. Whereas *Uncle Josh at the Moving Picture Show* evoked cinema's brief history in one single short (regarding reception practices as well as the new medium's artistic potential and affordances), feature films and their remakes begin to present longer historical trajectories and take active part in a kind of cinematic self-historicization that centers on ideas of ongoing modernization and unstoppable technological and cultural progress. To tell these more abstract stories (at one remove from what is happening on screen), film remakes establish connections between cinematic pasts and presents. Each new rendition of familiar material works toward remembering, storing, and archiving what has come before, toward producing memories and meanings, and toward constructing and communicating the cinematic past. Of all the different forms of cultural reproduction that come out of Hollywood, film remakes thus stand out as the most uniquely suited for documenting *change* over time. This is not surprising, since "technological innovations ... such as sound, color film, special effects ... and computer digitalization, are often the reason behind testing new (and often expensive) ground with pretested stories,"[146] and the film remakes' serial strategy of repetition and variation lends itself to tweaks and updates that incorporate shifting norms and values of a culture. If Hollywood keeps remaking the same movies, repeating and replaying popular stories over the course of fifty, sixty, eighty years and more, film remakes end up structuring the time by which we live, marking film-historical, cultural, and generational sequences.[147] Every single film remake is a product of its time and immediately recognizable as such; yet, it also always contains *traces* of the past and mobilizes memories that refer viewers back to earlier versions, to the moment in time these earlier versions represent, and to the cultural, political, and biographical contexts in which they belong.

4   The Remake as Archive

Film remakes invite a comparative mode of viewing that prompts audiences to engage with the cinematic, cultural, and national past and to position themselves within that past based on the popular culture they consume. As I discussed in the previous chapter, the three short films that are shown in Edwin S. Porter's self-referential *Uncle Josh at the Moving Picture Show* (1902)—*Parisian Dancers*, *The Black Diamond Express*, and *The Country Couple*—constitute an early example of a movie that contains literal traces of the past. In general, however, film remakes tend to function in more subtle ways. During Hollywood's Golden Age, the close repetition of narrative and filmic elements was key to winning over audiences with a new version of a popular story, while also showcasing cinema's latest innovations. At the time, explicit references to the past were often located outside the movies, in the paratexts and discourses that surrounded them. Today, this is still the case—from promotional material to press coverage and critical reviews to the bonus features, making-of documentaries, and audio commentaries on DVDs and Blu-rays that serve as "entryway paratexts,"[1] instructing viewers not only how to understand the remake at hand but also how to understand its *history*. What has changed since the rise of television and home video technologies is that film remakes are produced with intertextually proficient viewers in mind: the movies themselves frequently manifest a marked self-awareness and comprise instances in which they remember their own past and suggest viewers do the same. Such fundamental shifts in how film remakes work and produce meaning (including about themselves and their place in film history) necessarily imply that, if we want to understand film remakes, we have to think of Hollywood remaking as a dynamic practice that evolves in tandem with industry trends, technological innovations, stardom, visual regimes, and the medium's affordances and constraints, as well as broader cultural, social, and political developments. Film remakes are inextricably bound up in questions of temporality, of memory, knowledge production, and the ways in which notions of the past and present are called up in each new rendition of the same old story.

Thus, every version of *Stella Dallas* (1925, 1937, 1990), *A Star Is Born* (1932, 1937, 1954, 1976, 2018), *King Kong* (1933, 1976, 2005, 2017), and *Invasion of the Body Snatchers* (1956, 1978, 1993, 2007) stands in for a specific period in film history defined by cinema's state-of-the-art technology, visual aesthetics and narrative style, popular stars, and politics of representation. At the same time, each rendition resonates with the historically specific sensibilities, preoccupations, and cultural anxieties that shape its respective context of production, and it encourages viewers to recognize themselves as members of a movie generation. The first version of *Stella Dallas* (Henry King, 1925), for example, is a product of the silent era that has come into being and is remembered as such *because* of the sound film remake from 1937.[2] The *King Kong* movies act as markers for cinema's evolving visual effects: from stop-motion animation and rear projection (in the 1933 movie) to large-scale animatronics (in the 1976 version) to motion capture, digital imaging, and keyframe animation (in the last two iterations from 2005 and 2017). *A Star Is Born* offers recurrent variations on the myth of the American star-making machine, prominently featuring popular female actors and singers in the role of the rising star—Constance Bennett as Mary Evans (1932), Janet Gaynor (1937) and Judy Garland (1954) as Esther Blodgett, Barbra Streisand as Esther Hoffman (1976), and, in the most recent remake, Lady Gaga as Ally (2018). And *Invasion of the Body Snatchers*' allegorical story about an alien invasion that threatens to turn humans into a collective of emotionless pod people has lent itself to re-imaginings like few others. The movies address the threat of communism in the Cold War era, McCarthyism, the alienating effects of capitalism, conformism, postwar radiation anxiety, the return of "brainwashed" soldiers from the Korean War, and masculine fears of "the potential social, political, and personal disenfranchisement of postwar America's hegemonic white patriarchy"[3] (in the 1956 version); they deal with anxieties caused by changing personal relationships and a lack of faith in government authorities after the Vietnam War and the Pentagon Papers, the Watergate scandal, and President Richard Nixon's fall (in the 1978 remake); they process worries about the consequences of bio-chemical warfare and the exposure of American soldiers to toxic chemicals during Operation Desert Storm (which caused the Gulf War syndrome), environmental concerns and preoccupations with toxic waste (in the 1993 remake); and they take up the threat of bioterrorism in a post–9/11 and post-SARS context (in the 2007 remake). Each version shifts with the zeitgeist and replaces former cultural anxieties with more contemporary and urgent ones, always inviting multiple readings.

If chapter 3 engaged with the heyday of film remake production during and after the transition to sound, this chapter takes a larger historical perspective in order to trace how remaking evolves over the next decades, when Hollywood begins to release fewer remakes and generally more time passes between each iteration. Film remake production comprises fourteen remakes on average per year between 1940 and 2021, with as many as fifty-nine remakes in 1940, and as few as three remakes in 1965 and four in the year 2000 (figure 16). Since the overall production numbers vary significantly during this time period, it is important to consider film remakes in relation to Hollywood's total movie output. Film remake production constitutes up to 15 percent of US film production in 1961 (12% in 1940 as well as 11% in 1941 and 1956 are other peaks) and falls as low as 1 percent in the new millennium (in the years 2000, 2008, 2016, 2018, 2019, and 2021). The Hollywood remaking dataset indicates a trend away from the production of film remakes since 1990, when remakes only make up 2 percent of the total film production on average per year. These findings align with what we already know about the stronger focus on serialization and Hollywood's preference for sequels and franchises in the new millennium. Nonetheless, film remakes remain an important economic and cultural

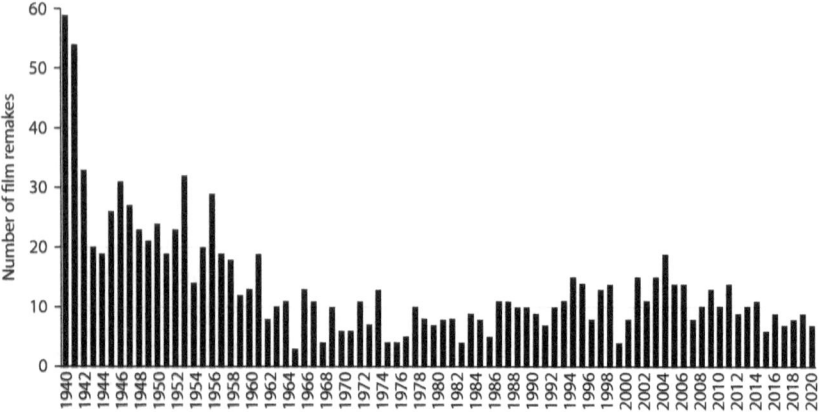

Figure 16. Production of film remakes, 1940–2021. *Source*: Hollywood Remaking dataset.

force and deserve our close attention, especially those movies that have been remade multiple times over the twentieth and twenty-first centuries. Focusing on *A Star Is Born*, *King Kong*, and *Invasion of the Body Snatchers*, this chapter shows how every new version continues to chronicle the history of cinema's technological evolution, to shape audience memory of and knowledge about film and film history, and to operate as cultural snapshots oscillating between the timelessness of a good story and the timeliness of visual aesthetics and politics of representation. It is in this sense, I argue, that the film remake can ultimately be imagined as archive.

There is a common understanding of the term *archive* that most scholars, librarians, and archivists share, namely that the archive is a physical place where documents and artifacts are kept.[4] As a repository of knowledge, the archive traditionally fulfills four basic functions: "storage, preservation, classification, and access."[5] This means the archive is an institutional space that collects and stores selected objects that it wants to keep for future reference. It also protects these objects from damages that occur as the result of use and aging and restores the wear and tear wrought by time. The archive further records objects, and describes, indexes, and classifies them according to established systems of knowledge organization. Finally, it makes these objects accessible for future generations who can search the archive, find information, and thus make connections between the past and present. Historically, the archive can be understood as "a key institutional 'site' of memory with an intertwined history with modernity and the birth of the state apparatus," as Jussi Parikka notes.[6] With regard to the rapidly changing media environments in the age of digitization, however, the meaning of the concept has started to shift. The archive, Parikka suggests, "is now increasingly being re-articulated less as a *place* of history, memory, and power, and more as a dynamic and temporal network, a software environment, and a social platform for memory—but also for remixing."[7]

From a theoretical perspective, archival discourse has been influenced by the works of Michel Foucault and Jacques Derrida, who were the first to almost completely detach the archive from the concrete physical space and its conventional definition. Foucault sees it as a "system of discursivity";[8] Derrida claims that "the archive . . . is not only the place for stocking and for conserving an archivable content *of the past*" but that "the technical structure of the *archiving* archive also determines the structure of the *archivable* content even in its very coming into existence and in its relationship to the future. The archivization," Derrida writes, "produces as much as it records events."[9] Both Foucault and Derrida have drawn attention to the constructedness of the archive and expanded the concept, thereby providing new ways of thinking about history and memory. Across the disciplines, the concept of the archive has become a central concern in the past decades, leading simultaneously to the conflation and inflation of the term.[10] In any case, the concept of the archive promises to be particularly fruitful in the field of cultural memory studies from which I want to draw for my analysis of the remake as archive. The overall growth of scholarly interest in the concept of the archive, for example, can be linked to what Pierre Nora has identified as the archival impulse of our times—the desire to collect and preserve everything.[11] According to Nora, "modern memory is, above all, archival. It relies entirely on the materiality of the trace, the immediacy of the recording, the visibility of the image."[12] Nora speaks of *lieux de mémoire* or sites of memory in this context[13]—a concept that Etienne François and Hagen Schulze have taken up and specified to mean "long-standing, trans-generational focal points of collective memory and identity."[14]

I suggest that these ideas of the archive can open up new perspectives for our understanding of Hollywood cinema and its ongoing interest in self-historicization, and in particular how this manifests in film remakes. This chapter, then, explores how exactly the remake functions as archive and film-historical site of memory, addresses issues like remembering, forgetting, and canonization that are crucial to cultural memory studies, and examines how the remake becomes productive in processes of movie-generational identity formations. I argue that the remake is a repository of knowledge about Hollywood history that opens up a pathway to a collectively shared cinematic past. To be sure, I am not interested in the creation of actual film archives and *cinemathèques* here. Rather, I use the term *archive* in a metaphorical sense, suggesting that the remake itself stores, preserves, and classifies the cinematic past, making it accessible to different generations of viewers. In doing so, the remake fulfills important cultural functions that still need to be fully explored and simultaneously problematizes the ways in which Hollywood privileges certain narratives through repetition and thus legitimizes existing power structures and dominant ideologies.

HOLLYWOOD TAKES "JUST ONE MORE LOOK"

In the latest version of *A Star Is Born* (Bradley Cooper, 2018), troubled country rock singer Jackson Maine (Bradley Cooper) falls in love with Ally (Lady Gaga), who works as a waitress, sings in a drag bar, and has almost given up her dream of pursuing a professional music career. After the night they first meet—spent in bars, talking, and singing—Jackson's limousine drops Ally off at her house. As she walks away from the car, Jackson lowers his window and calls out to her.

JACKSON: Hey!
   ALLY: What?
JACKSON: I just wanted to take another look at you.

The scene quickly became an internet meme, but, more importantly, some variation of it can be found in every version of the ill-fated love story that

A Star Is Born tells. The earliest movie, *What Price Hollywood?* (George Cukor, 1932), based on a magazine story written by Adela Rogers St. Johns, provided the inspiration for the first *A Star Is Born* (William A. Wellman, 1937) that was made less than five years later. In *What Price Hollywood?*, waitress Mary Evans (Constance Bennett) is discovered by alcoholic Hollywood director Max Carey (Lowell Sherman). She becomes a star and marries playboy Lonnie Borden (Neil Hamilton). Yet as Mary's dreams come true, her marriage threatens to fall apart, and Max's life and career are on a downward spiral. Before he commits suicide in Mary's house, Max tells her: "Mary, I just wanted to hear you speak again, that's all." This is fitting, considering that Mary has had her breakthrough on Hollywood's sound stage. The subsequent retellings of the story as *A Star Is Born* center on a fading male (movie or music) star who propels an unknown female artist to stardom, and "I just wanted to hear you speak again" becomes the "just one more look" line.

In the 1937 version, actor Norman Maine (Fredric March) says it to Esther Blodgett (Janet Gaynor), a farm girl from North Dakota who wants to become a movie star. They meet at a cocktail party where she works as a waitress and, when he brings her home, Norman asks her: "Do you mind if I take just one more look?" In the 1954 musical version (again directed by George Cukor), a drunk Norman Maine (James Mason) lurches onstage while Esther Blodgett (Judy Garland) is performing a song and dance act. She incorporates him into her routine thus preventing him from embarrassing himself and disrupting her show. Sobered up, he tracks her down at an after-hours musicians' hangout on Sunset Boulevard later that night and eventually drives her home. Before he leaves, Norman says, "Hey, I just want to take another look at you." And in the 1976 version, which moves the story from its original film industry setting to the music business, John Norman Howard (Kris Kristofferson) goes to a small bar after his concert is over. Here, Esther Hoffman (Barbra Streisand) performs as lead singer of the Oreos. John is drunk and argues with a waitress, ruining Esther's act. When a bar fight breaks out, Esther sneaks John out through the back door and he insists on driving her home in his limousine. The famous line comes much later in this movie, when the two meet again at a radio station and he calls out to her: "Hey Esther . . . I was just taking another look." In each iteration of *A Star Is Born*, the male lead thus

Figure 17. "One more look" is a recurring line in the multiple versions of *A Star Is Born*.

utters a version of "just one more look" as a peculiar farewell that simultaneously marks the beginning of a romance *and* foreshadows its tragic end. The men repeat the line again before they kill themselves (just as in *What Price Hollywood?*). The 1976 version is the only exception in this regard, but the idea is still echoed in the song "With One More Look at You" that Esther sings at the end of the movie as a tribute to her dead husband (figure 17).

"Just one more look" is a curious phrase that brims with meaning beyond *A Star Is Born*'s often-recycled storyline. In the movie, it serves to take stock of the love affair—at its budding beginning and what it promises to be and again at its doomed end, when "just one more look" turns into a tender assessment of what that love has been. There is more to this, however, because with each new version of the *A Star Is Born* formula Hollywood also takes another good look at itself. In the *Atlantic*, Todd S. Purdum writes: "For more than 80 years, right up to this month's premiere of Bradley Cooper and Lady Gaga's latest remake, *A Star Is Born* has been the urtext, the *film à clef* in which Hollywood has sought to explain (and, by extension, to justify) itself—to itself, and to the world."[15] *A Star Is Born* certainly has moments in which Hollywood critically assesses itself, but, at the same time, it also always recreates and sustains a powerful myth of fame and stardom. This is the very reason why it is so intriguing to take "just one more look," to produce and watch yet another remake of *A Star Is Born*. In the 2018 movie, Bobby (Sam Elliott) tells Ally how his late brother Jackson used to say that music is essentially twelve notes between the octave and then the octave repeats: "It's the same story, told over and over. Forever." Because it is a remake in which Bobby repeats Jackson's words—adding that "all any artist can offer the world is how they see those twelve notes"—they are as much about music as they are about Hollywood and about stories like *A Star Is Born*. As remakes, these movies enable us not only to observe the mythmaking at work but also Hollywood's self-historicization in and through the movies it repeats time and again. These remakes invite us to examine the enduring appeal of the same old story and to interrogate why and how repetition and variation matter when that story is told over and over in ever-changing industrial and cultural contexts.

In *A Star Is Born*, "just one more look" is at once a line that is full of *expectations* (when the couple falls in love) and one of *knowledge and memory* (approaching the suicide of the male star at the end). I want to suggest that, at a more abstract level, film remakes can be envisioned in a similar way. This is not to say that remakes should be read as Hollywood's tragic romance with its own past (even though some critics would probably subscribe to this idea). Instead, remakes are cultural products that draw their inspiration and own cultural value from taking another look at the past, from a promise of timelessness and timeliness that raises expectations on the one hand (that stories still resonate with contemporary audiences, that themes still matter, that technological, narrative, visual, and representational updates are in keeping with the zeitgeist) and that create repositories of knowledge and memory (about Hollywood, film history, a collectively shared cinematic past, about cultural and political contexts, about generational sequences, and about the self and its place in all of this) on the other. If we accept the idea that remakes operate as repositories of knowledge and memory, it is only a small leap to think of them as archives and imagine how *they store, preserve, classify, and provide access to the cinematic past.*

ARCHIVAL FUNCTIONS OF THE REMAKE: STORAGE AND PRESERVATION

Storage and preservation are two archival functions that are already evident in the talker remakes I examined in chapter 3. Think of the subtle manner in which movies like *Stella Dallas* call up memories of earlier versions and of the silent era, for example. Talker remakes offered a remedy against cinema's ephemerality: as studio libraries—the actual physical spaces, where film reels were kept—became "engines for the production of derivatives,"[16] new talkie versions of old silent hits *stored* and *preserved* cinema's popular stories by bringing *Stella Dallas* and other audience favorites back onto the big screen for the world to see. In this way, talker remakes worked to build and preserve a cinematic past and storytelling repertoire while also shaping the ways in which Hollywood imagined its own history (namely as a narrative of technological progress). Storage and preservation continue to be two key cultural functions of film remakes because they always contain some earlier version(s) as they repeat, update, and revise the already-seen. With the advent of television and playback technologies in the home and the copresence of the old and the new, the repetition of familiar titles, plots, and themes as well as iconic scenes and signature lines relies on and maintains instantly recognizable textual relations, which, in turn, speaks to the ways in which film remakes have come to mobilize expectations, knowledge, and memory.

A Star Is Born's "just one more look" is a concrete example of how remakes establish connections to their predecessors. The line activates the story's cinematic past. It constitutes a moment in which the remake communicates that it knows about other versions of *A Star Is Born*, that it remembers its own history. The same is true for *King Kong* when Peter Jackson's 2005 remake of the movie about a giant ape that is captured and brought to New York to be exhibited as the "Eighth Wonder of the World," restages one of the most memorable scenes in film history: Kong on top of the Empire State Building. Kong is attacked by airplanes and, mortally wounded from their gunfire, eventually falls off the skyscraper. While there are other iconic moments from the 1933 *King Kong* that the remake replays, it is this scene that encapsulates how Jackson's movie pays tribute to the first film by closely replicating shots, dialogues, and the creature's sounds and movements. It renders these elements legible as points of reference that connect past and present, showcase the new as pathway to the old, and effectively transform the remake into an archive of the cinematic past.

When the same stories are retold time and again over the course of many decades—like *Stella Dallas* (three times in the last sixty-five years), *A Star Is Born* (five times in eighty-six years), *Invasion of the Body Snatchers* (four times in fifty-one years), and *King Kong* (four times in eighty-four years, sequels, crossovers, and spin-offs left aside)—the remakes' archival functions are newly emphasized with every novel rendition. Each time a movie is remade, the archive grows and the connections run deeper, inviting intertextually proficient viewers to find and follow traces of the past, to probe the story's unfolding up until the latest iteration. My claim that remakes *store* and *preserve* the cinematic past is easily compatible with the idea that remakes produce cumulative hypotexts,[17] in which multiple versions and layers of meaning add up to serially evolving narratives that never reach full closure. To think of remakes as archives further opens up a historical perspective beyond the fictional worlds at hand and provides a glimpse at the cultural work remakes perform. This also means to acknowledge that remakes are involved in *processes of classification*: they (1) develop increasingly complex systems of intertextual references, (2) prompt canon formation, and (3) structure time as they mark film-historical, cultural, and generational sequences.

ARCHIVAL FUNCTIONS OF THE REMAKE: CLASSIFICATION

First, remakes mediate memories on the diegetic level through *intertextual references* to earlier versions: As mentioned above, *King Kong* movies recall and repeat elements of past renditions, when they tell their own version of the underlying "Beauty and the Beast" formula and thus encourage the viewers' systematic engagement with *difference*. Remakes conjure up their own past in this manner and want viewers to discover that past as well. But they also carve out and nurture broader intertextual relations from one version to the next. For instance, Joseph Conrad's 1899 novella *Heart of Darkness* about Englishman Marlow's journey up the Congo river, into the heart of Africa, and his encounter with colonial agent Kurtz provides the subtext for the first *King Kong* movie from 1933. This subtext is then made more explicit in the 2005 remake and especially in the latest retelling from 2017, *Kong: Skull Island* (Jordan Vogt-Roberts, 2017). In Peter Jackson's *King Kong*, two characters discuss the book onboard the *Venture*, as the ship makes its way from Manhattan to Skull Island. The young deck hand and notorious thief Jimmy (Jamie Bell), who has "borrowed" a copy of Conrad's *Heart of Darkness* from the New York Public Library, asks the Black first mate Ben Hayes (Evan Parke): "Why does Marlow keep going up the river? Why doesn't he turn back?" Hayes's response includes a lengthy quote from the book that serves to frame their own expedition as a quest for knowledge and—mobilizing postcolonial analyses of Conrad's work—tries to curb the racial undertones of *King Kong* and its metaphorical representation of Black masculinity as monstrous and obsessed with whiteness, especially with white women. In the 2005 remake, Naomi Watts plays that white woman, but her Ann Darrow has more agency than the female characters in earlier renditions and forms an emotional bond with Kong—an idea that the 1976 remake already explores but that this version renders much more convincingly (also because of Andy Serkis's motion-capture performance of the giant ape).

Twelve years later, *Kong: Skull Island* eventually turns the subtext into text when it models the familiar story after Francis Ford Coppola's *Apocalypse Now* (1979), the famous film adaptation of Conrad's novella that transposes *Heart of Darkness* onto the Vietnam War. *Kong: Skull Island* was released as the second movie of Legendary Pictures' recently created *MonsterVerse*, a shared cinematic universe that comprises a series of monster movies about Kong and Godzilla. As such, *Kong: Skull Island* is probably appropriately different from other *King Kongs*, yet it can never fully escape the "anxiety of influence" (to borrow Harold Bloom's felicitous term) the earlier versions generate. Film remakes do not operate as self-contained texts, even though—like *Kong: Skull Island*—they are usually conceived and produced as such. Instead, they are forever tethered to the past and bound up in retrospective meaning-making processes that are fueled by the serial dynamic of repetition and variation. Today more than ever, film remakes build on knowledge and memory to position themselves within expanding systems of intertextual references and within a cinematic past that they simultaneously help define.

Second, remakes partake in *the construction and maintenance of film canons*: they create "classics," inscribe movies into film history, and keep their memory alive. Peter Jackson's *King Kong* is a good example of a remake that is invested in highlighting the achievements and continued relevance of its predecessor, in shaping the memory and afterlife of the 1933 version, that is, while deliberately omitting another (the 1976) remake from the celebratory account it puts forward in the movie itself (which stays very close to the 1933 *King Kong*) and in the surrounding paratexts and promotional material (in particular the special features dedicated to exploring the groundbreaking visual effects of the first movie). Similarly, *Invasion of the Body Snatchers* (Don Siegel, 1956) is a movie whose enduring presence in the popular imagination can be attributed as much to its "combination of a central metaphor for the monstrous that, like the vampire or zombie, is sufficiently flexible to accommodate multiple interpretations with a style and structure that is admirably economical even as it is highly expressive"[18] as to its remakes. The B-movie garnered little critical attention upon its release in 1956 but saw a steady increase in popularity and cultural importance over the following decades that eventually culminated in its inclusion in the National Film Registry at the Library of Congress.[19] At the time, *Invasion of the Body Snatchers* had already been remade twice: by Philip Kaufman in 1978 and Abel Ferrara in 1993. Another version, Oliver Hirschbiegel's *The Invasion*, followed in 2007. While the role television reruns have played in making Siegel's *Invasion of the Body Snatchers* a "classic" should not be underestimated, the remakes have certainly done their part as well. At different points in time, they have revived interest in the movie by pointing out its timelessness against the timeliness of their own interpretation of the body snatcher material and inspired new critical discussions, academic investigations, and rereadings of the 1956 movie.

Third, remakes inevitably draw attention to *the passage of time (structuring film-historical, cultural, and generational sequences)*, when they return older movies to the limelight, putting them into canons and (back) on the map of film history. We can see this happening on a smaller scale with the talker remakes and the ways in which they reinforce the distinction between the silent past and the sound film present. Again, the remakes' unique cultural functions of providing temporal structures and chronicling change are much more pronounced, however, when movies are remade more than once over long periods of time. They become orienting beacons, simultaneously operating as stable points of reference that bring back familiar stories such as *A Star Is Born*, *King Kong*, and *Invasion of the Body Snatchers* in different film-historical, cultural, and biographical contexts, and as timekeeping mechanisms, since each new iteration demarcates the moment in which it was first produced and released. Of course, remakes themselves deal very differently with the passage of time between one version and the next. *A Star Is Born*, for instance, makes little effort to update or revise its tragic love story, even though each movie is set in the present of its own time of production. This strategy serves to emphasize the timeless quality of *A Star Is Born*. Yet the most recent remake—while generally adored as a successful retelling by film critics who praise Lady Gaga's and Bradley Cooper's performances as well as the cinematography and soundtrack—has also provoked criticism. As Aja Romano writes in her review for *Vox*, "superb filmmaking and a regressive, even harmful narrative can co-exist in the same work."[20] Romano finds it "deeply frustrating" that a story which has always really been about the man (not the woman's rise to stardom) and a "relationship built on a huge power imbalance and lack of female agency . . . has reappeared, with all its problems, at a moment when we're taking a hard look at the very kinds of power imbalances and consent issues within the industry that this film reifies, and even romanticizes."[21] Despite its claim to timelessness, *A Star Is Born* hence raises questions about the timeliness of the remake in 2018 amidst the #MeToo and #Time's Up movements and invites not only comparisons with earlier renditions of the same story but also reflections on the persistent appeal of the (pernicious) myths about Hollywood, stardom, and female success that are at the heart of the movie.

The *King Kong* films, too, rely on the timeless allure of the story about the giant gorilla, yet the remakes approach the passage of time in their own way. Except for the 1976 movie, which has a contemporary setting, the remakes take place in the past: Peter Jackson's 2005 version is set during the Depression (just like the 1933 *King Kong*) and the 2017 rendition maps the story onto the time of the Vietnam War. Kong himself is a powerful, "primitive" figure of the past that is confronted with modernity: modern civilization, modern urbanity, modern entertainment, modern warfare. This modernity—deeply embedded in colonialism, racial oppression, and capitalism—threatens and ultimately kills Kong.[22] According to David Crow, "Kong's cinematic language is written in a vocabulary of the past. The better film versions are always looking back at times gone by. . . . By gazing backward, only then does Kong's reign resonate in the here and now."[23] Not everyone agrees with Crow's view, however. After the release of the 2005 remake, some critics and scholars have pointed out that Peter Jackson's decision to keep the Depression-era setting of the first movie instead of bringing the story into the twenty-first century would diminish *King Kong*'s cultural impact. Yet, the remake certainly comments on its own cultural moment in how it deals with the past and negotiates the tension between timelessness and timeliness that poses a genuine challenge for all remakes.

Jackson's *King Kong* does not reconstruct the 1930s as a historical past but constructs a glossy 1930s "pastness" for the present.[24] The Depression becomes a site of nostalgia, the past a (retro) style. Michael Millner notes that "whereas the original version uses the Depression as a scene and situation to escape," Jackson's opening montage conjures images of Depression-era New York in which "the city is bright, rich, opulent; economic suffering is pushed aside."[25] This is a past designed for contemporary audiences. "One should not be dispirited by this representation of economic depression but rather encouraged to nostalgically revel in the period reconstructions: the elaborate 1930s costumes, the antique cars, and the bright lights of a long-gone Broadway. The moment is more Jazz Age than Depression Era. Or perhaps the moment is more our own, dressed up in inter-War costume."[26] Indeed, *King Kong* produces an idea of the 1930s that seems to exist "beyond real historical time."[27] This is the "nostalgia mode" that Fredric Jameson describes as a symptom of the postmodern "waning of historicity."[28] In the nostalgia mode, he writes, history becomes "a vast collection of images";[29] it is replaced by simulation and pastiche, reduced to stereotypes that lack depth and political meaning but that render the past consumable in a present in which it is often difficult to hold on to a sense of (temporal) continuity. We live in "a postmodern state of information flow, media imagery, flexible accumulation, market volatility, global production, and accelerated consumption, in a postmodern culture of surface, simulation, fragmentation, and instantaneity"[30] that affects how we organize time and memory and how we experience the world in which we live.

For Valerie Frazier, *King Kong*'s focus on the Depression prevents the remake from offering meaningful cultural and political commentary of the current moment: "In his single-minded efforts to render a new historical re-reading of the 1930s, Jackson divests Kong of any currency in the twenty-first century."[31] According to Frazier, this failure to address the present is further emphasized because "many of the racist subtexts of the original have been eradicated, sanitized, or made politically correct."[32] Jackson "works to diffuse or downplay racist readings of *King Kong*, readings that stereotype or exoticize the black other"[33] by replacing the dark-skinned natives of Skull Island with a more diverse, racially indeterminate group of red-eyed zombies and by adding the Black shipmate, Ben Hayes, as an authoritative and paternal figure. Hayes's character serves to "erase postcolonial undertones of third-world exploitation, perpetuating the myth that capturing Kong is an enterprise in which men of any color have an equal chance of gain and profit."[34] Tellingly, Hayes is one of the first crew members to be killed by Kong, thus undermining the remake's own elaborately introduced post-racial message.

In many ways, both Millner and Frazier's readings of Jackson's *King Kong* echo Jameson's ideas about the "crisis in historicity" that marks our postmodern lives. But Frazier's criticism seems paradoxical, when she argues that the movie cannot engage in current debates because it is set in the past, and that it is not political enough because of its investment in contemporary notions of political correctness. It is precisely the contradictions and the entanglement of progressive and conservative ideas (about race, gender, colonialism, and capitalism in the age of globalization) that constitute the movie's meaningful comment on both the past *and* the present. Jackson's movie—just like any other film remake—is always also an eloquent document of its time. It revisits "unfinished business" of the past in ways that inevitably resonate with and shape contemporary concerns and therefore deserves our critical attention. *King Kong* or the latest *A Star Is Born* may need some unpacking for a thorough understanding of how remakes engage with and structure the passage of time in terms of cinema's technological evolution, ongoing cultural change, and the constant formation of new movie generations (because one is set in the past and the other changes so little with regard to its predecessors). But there are also films like *Invasion of the Body Snatchers* that wear their commitment to providing a timely interpretation of a seemingly timeless story on their sleeve.

Each *Body Snatchers* remake contains one key scene, early in the movie, in which a character diagnoses contemporary cultural anxieties and concerns to help explain people's seemingly paranoid delusions that their relatives are not their relatives, and another one, later in the movie, in which a spokesperson of the pod people presents the pod-state as a utopian (or: dystopian—depending on one's vantage point) alternative to the status quo.[35]

When Miles Bennell (Kevin McCarthy), the protagonist of Don Siegel's *Invasion of the Body Snatchers* from 1956, asks psychiatrist Danny Kaufman (Larry Gates) about what is happening in the small town of Santa Mira, he suggests that people are suffering from "an epidemic mass hysteria" caused by "worry about what's going on in the world." This deliberately vague first assessment thus captures many political and social preoccupations of the 1950s, from "the 'Red Menace,' which crystallized around the activities of Senator Joseph McCarthy; . . . learning to cope with the consequences of a modern, urban, technologically bureaucratized society; and the pervasive fear of atomic annihilation"[36] to concerns about social conformity and the crumbling of white patriarchy in postwar America. Once he has become an emotionless pod, Danny Kaufman paints the alien takeover as a painless rebirth "into an untroubled world," in which everyone is the same, and where love, desire, ambition, and faith do not exist.

In the 1978 remake, psychiatrist David Kibner (Leonard Nimoy) offers an updated explanation for the rising number of people who claim that their partners are not their partners. Speaking of "some kind of hallucinatory flu that is going around," he sees a trend of "unstable relationships" at the heart of the problem and tells Elizabeth Driscoll (Brooke Adams), who is concerned about her boyfriend's suddenly distant behavior:

KIBNER: People are stepping in and out of relationships too fast because they don't want the responsibility. That's why marriages go to hell, the whole family unit is shot to hell. . . . You're jumping to a very bizarre conclusion. That this man you live with has been replaced by somebody else. Isn't it more likely that you want to believe he's changed because you're really looking for an excuse to get out?

In a later scene, Kibner—now a spokesperson of the pod people—promises Elizabeth and Matthew Bennell (Kiefer Sutherland): "You will be born again into an untroubled world. Free of anxiety, fear, hate." The remake comments on the erosion of the social fabric and a lack of faith in government authorities that characterize the 1970s in the wake of the Vietnam

War and the Watergate scandal. "The CIA? The FBI? They're all pods already," Jack Belicec (Jeff Goldblum) exclaims before he turns into a pod himself. It is also telling that the San Francisco Public Health Department, where Matthew and Elizabeth work, never comes to the rescue and that Matthew's "heroic impulse" to fight the pod people all by himself is ultimately insufficient.[37]

Abel Ferrara's 1993 remake projects the familiar *Body Snatchers* story onto an army base, where the head of the medical corps, Major Collins (Forest Whitaker), worries about "people at the infirmary, who are exhibiting extreme delusional fixations. People afraid to sleep. People afraid to deal with family members. Afraid of them. Exhibiting paranoia about others, about other people's identities. People afraid of themselves." He suspects that the symptoms are caused by exposure to toxic chemicals on the military base and wonders: "Can they affect brain patterns? Can they interfere with chemo-neurological processes? Can they foster psychoses, paranoias, narcophobias? . . . Can they alter one's view of reality?" The remake thus addresses environmental concerns and preoccupations about toxic waste, but it also processes the unexplained chronic illness associated with veterans, who were exposed to toxic chemicals during the Gulf War (1990–1991), known as the Gulf War syndrome. In the other key scene, in which the alien invaders present their vision of the world, General Platt (R. Lee Ermey), who has already turned into a pod, says: "When all things are conformed, there will be no more disputes. No conflicts. No more problems. . . . It's the race that's important, not the individual." As Barry Keith Grant points out, "The main horror strategy of the film is that the military mentality, emphasising collective action and unthinking obedience to orders, makes it impossible to distinguish professional soldiers from those who are pods."[38] *Body Snatchers* suggests that the pods' fascist ideology is compatible with the military. No one knows when General Platt became a pod person because his behavior never really changes. Neither does the soldiers' automatic, emotionless "Yes, sir" provide a clue as to whether they are pods or humans.

The latest remake to date, Oliver Hirschbiegel's *The Invasion*, offers yet another take on these two scenes. When Wendy Lenk (Veronica Cartwright, who also played Nancy Belicec in the 1978 version) tells her psychiatrist Carol Bennell (Nicole Kidman) that she thinks her husband is not her husband, she treats her regular patient as in any other session, telling her that "nothing you say in this office is stupid or crazy" and prescribing her an anti-psychotic. Wendy's problem seems to be "normal" for our times and apparently Carol's profession requires her to be rational, cold, and emotionless (as if she were a pod already). It is only when she worries about her son Oliver (Jackson Bond) that her maternal instincts kick in, she steps out of her professional role, googles the phrases "my husband is not my husband" and "my son is not my son," and starts to panic.

The diagnostic of the situation, which tends to offer insights into the historically specific cultural anxieties and preoccupations of the movie's time of production, does not come from a doctor in *The Invasion*, but from Russian ambassador Yorish Kaganovich (Roger Rees), which makes this remake more explicitly political and highlights the movie's global premise. At a dinner party, he asks Carol: "Can you give me a pill? To make me see the world the way you Americans see the world? Can a pill help me understand Iraq or Darfur, or even New Orleans?" Yorish's criticism of US foreign and domestic politics—of the "preemptive" US-led invasion of Iraq as part of the War on Terror that was launched by the US government in response to the 9/11 attacks, of the US government's position in the ongoing Darfur conflict, and of the response to Hurricane Katrina and the flooding of New Orleans in 2005—is muffled when he gives his provocative questions a philosophical twist. Yorish observes that civilization in general is "an illusion, a game of pretend" to "hide our true self-interest," and that a world without violence and atrocities would not be human. His words both anticipate the global peace treaties signed under the temporary alien rule and justify Carol's violent killing and injuring of pod people in order to save her son as a quintessentially "human" response. Yorish's generalization is not only highly problematical in how it reframes what it means to be human, it also distracts from his earlier critique of government action. The theme is nonetheless central to *The Invasion*, where the authorities are not merely out of reach, as in the other versions of the story, but are active agents in the alien takeover while pretending to protect public health and safety.

Carol's ex-husband Tucker Kaufman (Jeremy Northam) is the director of the Centers for Disease Control and Prevention (CDC) and one of the first people infected by the alien life form, which enters the blood stream like an intelligent virus and turns humans into pod people once they enter the REM phase in their sleep. Tucker exploits his position and the CDC structures to spread the virus under the guise of flu inoculations. Instead of preventing an epidemic, he causes it, preparing for the global takeover of the aliens. But when he wants to convince Carol and their son Oliver to join the pod people, his arguments are not delivered calmly, nor are they about making the world a better place. As a pod, he has a patriarchal, antifeminist, and surprisingly personal agenda, claiming that Carol's careerism is responsible for their failed marriage—something that apparently cannot happen in a society of pod people. This is a meaningful departure from the established narrative patterns, just like the possibility of reversing the transformation with the help of a vaccine (developed by an international team of scientists that works secretly underground) and the ambiguous restoration of the status quo at the end of *The Invasion*. The remake firmly situates itself within a post–9/11 and post-SARS context, allegorically addressing the threat of bioterrorism and a deep-seated skepticism about the government's ability to deal with such potential crises.

Taken together, each film version projects the anxieties and urgent cultural, social, and political themes of its own time of production onto the *Body Snatchers* story. In this way, they do not only process continuity and change but also become temporal markers and reference points for different generations of viewers. The movies emerge as unique pop-cultural products in which personal experiences, cultural memory, and national history converge to be revisited time and again, to be brought back for close inspection, updates, and revisions. These aspects are connected to yet another archival function that remakes perform: *making the cinematic past accessible.*

ARCHIVAL FUNCTIONS OF THE REMAKE: ACCESS

Access is an archival function of the film remake that is not only linked to the rise of what Barbara Klinger calls "home film cultures."[39] Playback technologies have certainly made the cinematic past more easily accessible and enabled viewers to become film collectors and cultural archaeologists. If chances to rewatch a favorite film once depended entirely on prolonged first-runs, reissues, and remakes, or, later, on inflexible television program schedules, VHS, DVD, and online streaming platforms have seemingly lifted all external constraints and created individualized possibilities for film consumption, repeat viewing, and explorations of the cinematic past. In terms of memory and knowledge production, however, it is important to look at how paratexts provide access to the cinematic past. Paratexts establish a remake's connection to earlier renditions. They are never just about the remake at hand but always also about its history. Paratexts, I suggest, *activate* the remake's archival function by encouraging viewers to remember or discover earlier versions and by inviting them to reflect on the development of cinema as a medium. This is not only true for the photo spreads, contests, quizzes, and reviews that I analyzed in chapter 3. These paratexts accompanied the release of talker remakes in Hollywood's Golden Age and provided an interpretative framework for understanding the transition to sound and what it meant in terms of cinema's technological progress. Today, paratexts still function in a similar manner.

Take Frederick James Smith's review of Cecil B. DeMille's talker remake *The Squaw Man* (1931) in the *New Movie Magazine*, for instance. It says very little about the actual movie but presents facts about two earlier renditions: "This is Mr. De Mille's third production of *The Squaw Man*. It was the first film he ever made, back in 1912. Dustin Farnum played the title role then. In 1919 he made it again, with Elliott Dexter as the Englishman who married an Indian girl. Both these versions of the old Edwin Milton Royle melodrama were silent films, of course. Now, in 1931, comes *The Squaw Man* as a talkie."[40] Smith provides information that DeMille had already directed the same movie twice, who starred in these earlier renditions, and on whose play all three versions were based. In doing so, he displays his knowledge about the cinematic past (distinguishing himself as an expert) and imparts this knowledge to the readers, thus engaging in film-historical knowledge production and remembrance work. Today's reviews of *A Star Is Born* are not very different in that regard. It is almost impossible to find one that does not mention that the 2018 movie is "a remake of a remake of a remake,"[41] or that presents it alternately as "the latest version of [an] old Hollywood chestnut"[42] and as "a millennial take on [a] Hollywood warhorse."[43] These reviews always frame Bradley Cooper's *A Star Is Born* in reference to the cinematic past, adverting audiences to the fact that this story has already been told in 1937, 1954, and 1978, featuring Janet Gaynor, Judy Garland, and Barbra Streisand as the rising stars, and explaining that "each generation has its own version of . . . [the] timeless tale."[44] Most reviewers also mention *What Price Hollywood?* as a precursor to the tragic love story, thereby displaying their in-depth knowledge of Hollywood's recycling mechanisms and reaffirming their authority as film critics. The information they provide about the movie's past can shape and enrich the viewing experience, as it creates extra layers of meaning and adds intertextual pleasures to the filmic text, but, most importantly, it draws connections to Hollywood's past and helps to keep it alive in the present.

Reviews of remakes have always offered a pathway to the cinematic past, making times gone by accessible for different generations of viewers by recalling the various iterations of one and the same story. As television and home media technologies have enabled the copresence of old and new film versions and fostered remake literacy and intertextual proficiency, this kind of knowledge production and remembrance work has also become part and parcel of DVD paratexts such as making-of documentaries, commentary tracks, and bonus features. These supplementary materials explicitly invite the viewers' active engagement with a remake's and, by extension, Hollywood's past within the film-historical framework that the DVD provides. On the *Invasion* DVD, for instance, the short documentary "We've Been Snatched Before" and the making-of featurette "*The Invasion*: A New Story" emphasize that the 2007 movie is a modern retelling of familiar material and simultaneously justify the existence of the remake by pointing to the timeless appeal of the premise and apparent "need" for regular updates. "This is one of those stories that gets retold every 15, 20 years for a reason," screenwriter David Kajganich explains, and Mike Davis (author of *The Monster at Our Door: The Global Threat of Avian Flu* and one expert among many, who were interviewed for the documentary) states that "*Invasion of the Body Snatchers* is a wonderful tale that has almost Shakespearean mobility from one period to the next. You can constantly revisit it because the kind of core obsession about infection remains the same."

The special features included in the Deluxe Extended DVD Edition of Peter Jackson's *King Kong* operate in much the same way. It pays tribute to the 1933 version (most explicitly in the "King Kong Homage" featurette but also in making-of material that directs the viewers' attention to the first *King Kong*) and offers an object lesson in the historical evolution of visual effects technology. In the making-of, which takes audiences behind the scenes and informs them about the production process (especially the use of digital filmmaking tools and the technique of motion-capture), Jackson foregrounds the groundbreaking special effects of the first *King Kong* and explains how they influenced his decision to become a filmmaker and led him to work on a remake—first as a kid, constructing miniature models of Kong and the Empire State building for his own stop-motion animation, and then as director of *Lord of the Rings* fame, using the latest visual effects technologies. "What *King Kong* does," Jackson says in the making-of, "is it totally inspires you to think about the trickery of films. You know, it's the wonderful escapist use of special effects." What the abundant bonus material on the *King Kong* DVDs does is it invites audiences to think of the movie *as a remake*. *King Kong* is a movie with a past, these paratexts announce. Engaging with that past, "drilling down"[45] into the text to understand how *King Kong* has evolved over time and how the remake positions itself within film history and with regard to the other *King Kong* movies, activates the older renditions in the present and creates additional intertextual pleasures for audiences. It is probably telling that the bonus material on the Deluxe Extended DVD Edition belongs to what Jackson calls the "*King Kong* Archives." The designation is programmatic in that it establishes a repository of behind-the-scenes material that documents the production process of the 2005 movie. Yet, considering the numerous references to earlier versions of *King Kong* that make up the interviews and images of the bonus features collected here, the remake itself becomes the archive that provides access to the cinematic past.

This chapter has analyzed the cultural work of movies that have been remade time and again in the twentieth and twenty-first centuries. Through repetition and innovation, these versions of one and the same story are able to foreground change and hence document the long-term evolution of film history, culture, and the nation at large. But understanding the film remake as archive also means to ask which stories are being archived through the practice of Hollywood remaking. What kind of knowledge, ideologies, and myths are being preserved in the popular storytelling repertoire that film remakes help to construct and sustain over time? Such questions also concern series, sequels, and long-running franchises that are more overtly interested in establishing continuity. In a study of Hollywood remaking that considers the film remake as merely one of many formats that emerge from an industrial process of recycling already-familiar material, exploring the film remake and its historical evolution from early cinema to the digital era in its own right yields important insights. It helps us grasp how the film remake's distinct serial dynamic of repetition and variation unfolds in popular culture and how it ultimately serves cultural and mnemonic functions by structuring historical, social, technological, biographical, and generational time. However, focusing exclusively on the film remake does not provide a complete picture of Hollywood remaking. In order to fully understand the process of innovative reproduction that has structured Hollywood cinema from the very beginning, we also need to look at more explicitly serialized remaking formats such as the series, sequel, and franchise.

PART III Series, Sequels, and Franchises

5 Cinematic Seriality from "B" to "A"

In April 2002, *Newsweek* published "Franchi$e Fever!," an article in which movie expert John Horn identified a sea change in how the film industry worked: Whereas moviemaking used to be "a gambler's profession, where million-dollar wagers are laid down, and often lost, with lightning speed," studios had become more risk-averse, and were "trying to make the movie business as predictable and profitable as serving up Mocha Frappuccinos."[1] For Horn, "the studios [were] behaving more like Starbucks than Caesars Palace,"[2] as they built on pre-awareness and churned out high-concept movies that audiences would easily recognize as belonging to a brand. "They're called franchise films," Horn wrote, "and they are revolutionizing the way Hollywood does business."[3] The fundamental critique of the piece is clear (and familiar): instead of developing creative, risky, and challenging projects from scratch, Hollywood relied on tried-and-true material, on remaking enduring, presold properties. With reference to the coffeehouse chain Starbucks, Horn framed this approach in terms of franchised business operations that are located outside the culture industry.

Media scholar Derek Johnson has shown how the idea of franchising, which was perfected across retail and service industries in the postwar United States (think: fast food, laundromats, car washes, hotels, and accounting services), was borrowed and adapted to shape, manage, and imagine "the multiplied replication of culture from intellectual property resources."[4] As a corporate strategy in retail businesses, franchising is based on an "agreement between stakeholders—a franchisor who develops the system and a franchisee who invests independently in that system."[5] If someone wanted to become a franchisee and open a McDonald's restaurant, for instance, they had to pay a license fee for the right to operate the business under a shared, corporate trademark and agree to follow the rules of the larger corporation (from preparing a hamburger or a milkshake to arranging the chairs and tables in one's own establishment). Both parties benefitted from the system, as Johnson points out: "franchisors could develop new products and markets with little capital risk and without the administrative headaches of managing so many outlets; independent franchisees gained national identities and proven merchandising programs."[6] During the franchise boom of the 1950s and 1960s, the business model was quickly institutionalized in the United States, and franchising became part of the cultural imaginary.

After a wave of mergers and acquisitions that began in the 1960s and culminated in the 1990s, Hollywood has been dominated by media conglomerates which own the major studios as just one of their many business branches. This development brought tectonic shifts in structure and economics as Hollywood embraced industry logics that are now largely framed in terms of franchising. To be sure, retail franchising and media franchising are not the same. Whereas retail franchising is about "vertical integration across production, distribution, and sales," about creating new outlets where uniform products can be sold to local consumers, media franchising is concerned with "horizontally multiplied production of media related through some shared, familiar content."[7] Profitability, in other words, does not depend on the distribution of the exact same product but on *content differentiation*, ideally across a variety of media platforms. "The point of [media] franchising is to connect intellectual property resources with producers who can generate new kinds of products," Johnson explains.[8] This also means that "while franchise products like Coca-Cola and McDonald's hamburgers are mass produced—each item coming off the assembly line should be identical to the next—it would be more accurate to consider franchised media content as *serially* produced."[9] Yet, it is precisely the idea of serialization that conjures up images of Fordism, of filmmaking as an assembly-line production that follows standardized, rigid structures and proven formulas to endlessly produce and reproduce popular commodities.

If John Horn thought the studios were behaving like Starbucks serving fancy coffee drinks that are made following specific recipes that consumers know and love, his comment refers to both the industry's desire to produce sure-fire hits and to audience taste. Those who enjoy their Mocha Frappuccino fared badly in this comparison, since Horn aimed to expose Hollywood's reliance on money-making hit film formulas as incompatible with ideals of creativity and originality. This was, in fact, how many critics made sense of franchising around the turn of the millennium. They imagined franchising as a relatively new phenomenon that "revolutionized" the film industry (as Horn puts it here) and radically changed the ways in which movies were being made and consumed. For Horn, the film industry had succumbed to franchise fever, but for *Variety*'s Peter Bart, for instance, *franchise* was nothing more than "a convenient buzzword."[10] Instead of a radical shift in the movie business, he saw "a confusion in semantics": "Because of the franchise mania, it's become downright gauche to acquire a plain old property anymore—it always has to be a series of properties."[11] The term *franchise* had turned into a statement of intentions and a promise of profits. But the underlying goal to develop persistent brands, to exploit properties in the cinema and across the various business branches of the large media conglomerates that owned the studios, was not always easy to achieve, and so "all sorts of wannabe franchises have been quickly banished from memory."[12] According to Bart, "*Godzilla* was going to be reborn as a franchise until people saw the [1998] movie. The surprise hit *Speed* was slated to become a series of *Speeds*—until audiences had a look at *Speed 2*."[13]

The point is that "franchising" had entered industrial and popular discourse in the 1990s and quickly taken hold of the imagination. By the early 2000s, *franchise* had become a ubiquitous term in Hollywood and shorthand for a successful business model in a notoriously high-risk business. The concept behind franchising, however, was not new at the time. "From the late 1970s onwards, studios began pursuing this strategy with greater dedication than they had in the past," Stuart Henderson reminds us, adding that "the studios' ambitions for franchise construction, and their understanding of how this might be achieved, preceded the arrival of the new format by many years."[14] The case for a more far-reaching historical continuity could be made, in which the high-concept and big-budget approach to the sequel that Hollywood adopted in the 1970s as well as the production of film series in the 1930s and 1940s, with recurring characters that audiences knew from serialized comic strips, radio plays, or dime novels, present precursors of today's franchises. Such accounts foreground cinema's serial heritage and hint at an ongoing perfection of the industrialized film production process, but, even so, it is important to acknowledge that there is no straightforward progression from film series to sequel to franchise. The sequel never replaced the series entirely and, of course, both the series and the sequel continue to exist in the franchise era. Instead of definite genealogies, the history of the film series, sequel, and franchise exhibits a persistent entanglement of the novel and the familiar as it adapts to shifting industry patterns and reception practices. The through-line here is Hollywood's reliance on seriality—on repetition, variation, and continuation in the form of recurring characters, ongoing stories, and consistent fictional worlds.

Approaching the film series and sequel as distinct (yet closely connected) variations of Hollywood remaking and as crucial building blocks for the film franchise allows us to ask questions about the complex meanings and cultural work of *continuity*: How is it that sequels and series have become synonymous with the promise of endless reproducibility? What role does long-term continuity play regarding commercial viability but also for the management of serially evolving narratives with transgenerational appeal? How can decades-spanning serial texts such as *Star Wars*, *Rocky*, and *Blade Runner* maintain narrative continuity and stick to consistent characters and fictional worlds in the face of cultural change and social justice debates? How does Hollywood's preference for ongoing narratives impact constructions of time, memory, and generational belonging? Through the lens of Hollywood remaking, it becomes possible to critically examine Hollywood's investment in sustaining industrial, narrative, and cultural continuity over long periods of time, to offer nuanced, historical accounts of the film series, sequel, and franchise, and to address the second-order seriality that comes into being when long-running franchises work at one remove from the diegetic level, where they establish meaningful industrial, aesthetic, cultural, and political continuity. This chapter traces the history of cinematic seriality in Hollywood from cheaply produced film serials and series (B-level productions) in the studio era to high-budgeted film series and sequels (A-movies) in the post-studio-era and thus lays the groundwork for an exploration of the subsequent rise of the sequel and the film franchise in the next chapter.

FACTORY FARE: THE FILM SERIES IN THE STUDIO ERA

If film remakes schooled early cinema audiences in the consumption of the new medium film and worked to create a cinematic language through formal, stylistic, and generic conventions,[15] it was the film serial that brought episodic structures, continuing storylines, and long-form narratives to the movie theaters. From the 1910s to the television boom in the 1950s and 1960s, serials supplied viewers with short, weekly installments over two to four months that showed the thrilling adventures of serial queens, detectives, policemen, and superheroes. In the silent era, film serials such as *What Happened to Mary* (Edison, 1912), *The Adventures of Kathlyn* (Selig, 1913), and *The Exploits of Elaine* (Pathé, 1915) consisted of twenty highly formulaic "chapters"; sound film serials like *Dick Tracy* (Republic, 1937), *Batman* (Columbia, 1943), and *Superman* (Columbia, 1948), which were geared at juvenile audiences, had twelve to fifteen chapters.[16] According to Ilka Brasch, film serials were "the result of highly economized, compartmentalized, and efficient production processes that perfected Hollywood's appropriation of a Fordist division of labor."[17] The dialectic of repetition and variation that is the driving force behind popular culture's serial narratives, found expression in the film serial's rigid narrative formulas and the rearrangement of familiar elements. Convoluted, meandering plots stubbornly resisted closure by introducing outrageous twists and cliffhanger endings. Brasch speaks of the film serial's "anecdotal storytelling": "Each serial picks a range of anecdotes, and each episode arranges them differently within its formula . . . . serial queens, large inheritances, mystic objects, jungle adventures, wild animals, dangerous vehicles, noted detectives, daring children, complex machines, and menacing contraptions populate the screens in ever-new combinations."[18]

This narrative sampling and recycling, in which film serials engaged, offered a glimpse at the experience of modernity,[19] but, as the conventions of classical Hollywood cinema began to be codified, it stood in contrast to classical narrative logic and style. Jared Gardner writes that "Filmmakers came to privilege causal relations over framed experiments in startling effects, as narrative episodes were deliberately transformed from charged fragments into agents in the interlocking chain of classical narrative. The industry trained audiences to privilege continuity, resolution, and closure—and to reject as 'bad film' the fragments, the gaps, the illogical connections of early film."[20] Whereas the film serials were increasingly excluded from lavish movie palaces during the silent era, disappeared from the trade papers after the conversion to sound, and were eventually dismissed as children's fare,[21] the film series with their self-contained episodic structures occupied a different position in the film industry and the popular imagination. There were early examples like Biograph's *Jones* series, which included eleven films directed by D.W. Griffith that were released in 1908 and 1909, or Kalem's *Girl Spy* series, which ran for two years from 1909 to 1911 and contained at least six films directed by Sidney Olcott. These series already featured "recurring, consistent characters in unconnected stories."[22] While serials and sequels also revisit characters from earlier installments, the *lack of narrative continuity* between one film and the next distinguishes the film series from these two other forms.

Gene Gauntier, who was both the writer and heroine of the *Girl Spy* series about a Confederate girl who cross-dresses as a soldier to spy on the North, later recalled in the *Women's Home Companion* that the first film

> made a tremendous hit and exhibitors wrote in for more. Thus began the first series made in films and I kept them up for two years until, tired of sprains and bruises and with brains sucked dry of any more adventures for the intrepid woman, I married her off and ended the war. And I thought this would be the finish. Not so! The demand for them still came in and I was compelled to come back with one called *A Hitherto Unrelated Incident of the Girl Spy*. There is always a way, in pictures.[23]

From early on, series narratives thus came with the built-in option for continuation even if final closure seemed to have been achieved, for adding new adventures and bringing back well-known characters to meet the popular demand for more. The success of the *Girl Spy* series inspired Kalem to develop its formula for film serials centering on courageous young female protagonists, which provided weekly thrills from the mid-1910s onward.[24]

Each standalone film of the *Jones* series revolves around Mr. and Mrs. Jones (always played by the unbilled John R. Cumpson and Florence Lawrence) and their domestic life as a middle-class couple. Mr. Jones regularly propels himself into humorous situations that threaten to upset his marriage, but by the end of every film, the conflict is resolved and the family harmony restored. This series is all about narrative containment, and there is no explicit narrative continuation from one installment to the next. Henderson points out that this was "possibly the first film series to revisit characters over a series of episodes without recourse to preexisting source material," and that later entries in the *Jones* series assumed that regular viewers had retained information about the characters across multiple films and that the resulting familiarity with the Joneses would have enhanced their enjoyment of the latest film.[25] "By striking this balance, in which characters do not develop but nonetheless become known quantities with associated traits, Griffith's films are absolutely typical of the series format which was quickly becoming a staple of film production in North America."[26]

It was not until the 1930s, however, that studios fully committed to the series production model. In response to the financial pressures of the Great Depression and the increasing demand for movies, Hollywood institutionalized double-bill programming and highly rationalized B-film production, thus creating the conditions under which the film series would flourish. The film series became the predominant remaking format in Hollywood between 1938 and 1951 (figure 18). That is, during those years, the studios produced more series films than film remakes, on average sixty-three per year, with numbers as high as eighty-two series films in 1939, eighty-four in 1941, and eighty in 1943, and as low as thirty-two in 1951—the last year in which the production of series films superseded the production of film remakes, marking the end of the series' reign in the cinema. In the period between 1938 and 1951, series films alone constituted up to 20 percent of the total film production in the United States (in 1943) and maintained a consistently high percentage on the release schedule

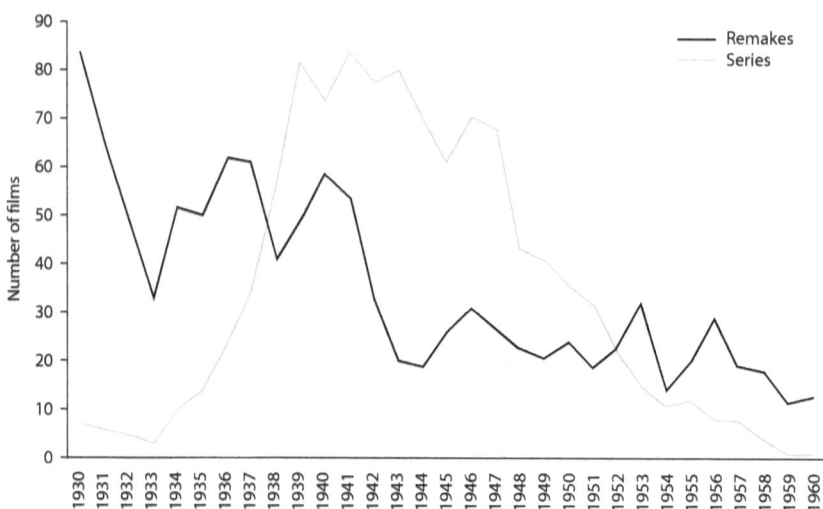

Figure 18. Production of film remakes and series, 1930–1960. *Source*: Hollywood Remaking dataset.

over several years (17% in 1939, 1941, 1944, and 1945; 19% in 1946; and 18% in 1947), before the numbers began to decrease in 1948.

This was the studio era, in which the five majors ("Big Five")—MGM, Paramount, RKO, 20th Century Fox, Warner—and the three minors ("Little Three")—Columbia, Universal, and United Artists—dominated the American film industry. The Big Five were fully vertically integrated, controlling the production, distribution, and exhibition of their films, whereas the Little Three focused on production and distribution without owning large theater chains like the majors. It was the time of contract players, block-booking, blind-bidding, and the run-zone-clearance system—all of which guaranteed not only the production but also a market for low-budget fare like the film series. Studios employed actors under exclusive long-term contracts. In turn, they decided in which movies they would appear and defined their careers and star images. Studios sold their films to exhibitors in large packages (or blocks) of thirty or more, which meant that if exhibitors wanted to show the studios' desirable A-movies, they had to accept the lesser movies of the package, too, with no option to pick and choose titles. Exhibitors were also forced to book films sight-unseen if production had not yet begun and often knew little more about the movies they were scheduling for the coming season than the title, cast, and a short description. The run-zone-clearance system ensured that studio-owned theater chains were the first to show the studios' new movies at the highest ticket price. When a period of time had passed after the first run at a lucrative downtown picture palace (clearance), the movies moved on to gradually smaller and less profitable second-, third-, and, eventually, final-run theaters (with a clearance between each run). Ticket prices dropped as the movies passed from one venue to the next and through the corresponding zones, which divided the market into geographical areas ranging from urban centers to small towns to rural communities.

The film series emerged as a popular and predictable product in the studio era because it could minimize costs and risks for the studios and build a devoted audience that was likely to return for future installments. "Once successfully launched, the series creates loyal and eager fans who form a core audience. By keeping production costs in line with this ready-made demand, series pictures are almost guaranteed a profit," writes Tino Balio.[27] And while Henderson detects some resemblances between "the manner in which studios in the 1930s set about establishing series from the first film onwards" and "the more contemporary practice of franchise building from the 1990s onwards," he emphasizes that "the speed and relatively low budgets with which these films were produced set them clearly apart from what came later."[28] During the peak in film series production, films belonging to a series were released twice a year on average, and series often sustained themselves over more than a decade. However, the production rate could vary considerably, depending on the studio. For instance, the most prolific film series—*Hop-Along Cassidy* (1935–1948, Paramount/United Artists), *The Durango Kid* (1940–1952, Columbia), and *The Three Mesquiteers* (1936–1942, Republic)—released up to ten westerns per year and a total of sixty-six, sixty-five, and fifty-one entries over the course of their respective thirteen-, twelve-, and six year-runs. The installments that studios seemed to be cranking out with cookie-cutter regularity were meant to fill out the double bill that offered cinemagoers two movies for the price of one: a cheaply produced B-movie (rented at a flat fee) and a high-budgeted A-movie as the main feature (rented at percentage deals).

Not all B-movies were film series, of course, but considering the financial and temporal constraints under which B-movies were being made, "with diminished budgets, shooting schedules and production values, and with miniscule promotional muscle," film series "possessed certain advantages over other B-product," as Frank Krutnik remarks.[29] Many film series were based on "original properties [that] already enjoyed a thriving serial existence before they reached cinema," so that films featuring familiar serial characters from other media like Blondie, Sherlock Holmes, or Charlie Chan could build on audience pre-awareness.[30] Krutnik also notes that "where non-series B-films had to stand on their own, ostensive seriality provided an insurance policy that could cover any liabilities in the individual film."[31] In more practical terms, seriality also enabled studios to further heighten the speed and lower the cost of film production, because they could reuse what was already there. "Not only the casting but the sets, props, music, even the story formula itself could be standardized, rendering what was already a low-budget enterprise that much more efficient and economical."[32]

Not all B-movies were film series, and not all film series were B-movies. MGM produced and exhibited its *Thin Man* series (1934–1947), including six films with William Powell and Myrna Loy as married detective duo Nick and Nora Charles, and a *Tarzan* series with six films (1932–1942), based on Edgar Rice Burroughs's stories and featuring Johnny Weissmuller as jungle hero Tarzan together with Maureen O'Sullivan in the role of Jane, as A-grade series. Because the *Thin Man* and *Tarzan* films only came out every two or three years and had high production values, Henderson suggests that they have "more in common with today's franchises than most of [their] contemporaries."[33] Unlike the majority of the series installments that bolstered the bottom half of the double bill, the *Thin Man* and *Tarzan* films also "exhibit an intention to maintain narrative continuity and develop their characters across the series," which moves them closer to the sequel than the series format.[34] However, such distinctions remain fuzzy and these films would generally be referred to as series rather than sequels.

Based on the level of narrative cohesion and continuity between individual installments, Henderson distinguishes between three types of series: *conceptual series* such as Warner's *Gold Diggers* (1933–1938) and MGM's *Broadway Melody* (1935–1940) that "repeat basic narrative situations and reassemble certain key talent . . . but never carry over characters or continue narrative strands from previous films"; the *series film proper*, as the most common type, focusing on detectives (such as Charlie Chan, Sherlock Holmes, Mr. Moto, Boston Blackie, and the Falcon), adventurers (such as Cisco Kid and Red Ryder), or comic characters (such as Torchy Blane and "Mexican Spitfire" Carmelita Fuentes) "which are carried over, often into similar, repetitive situations, but within discrete narrative units"; and *series with continuity* like MGM's long-running *Hardy* family series (1937-1958) and *Dr. Kildare* (1938-1941), as well as the higher-budgeted *Thin Man* and *Tarzan* series mentioned above, that acknowledge chronology in some way or other, either through intertextual memory of events, relationships, or characters from earlier installments, or because the characters develop over time "through education, marriage, parenthood or the ageing process."[35]

The distinction between *film series proper* and *series with continuity* is thus largely tied to the genre, to the types of characters, and to the longevity of the respective film series. Detective films, westerns, and adventure and horror series often featured what Shane Denson and Ruth Mayer call a *serial figure*: an iconic, flat, recurring character that is *"familiar*, even if one has never dealt explicitly with the figure before."[36] In the film series proper, serial figures "arrive on screen fully developed and remain largely unchanged from one film to the next," so that the main appeal of the series does not lie in observing characters grow over time.[37] Limited to "serial iteration, recurrence, and looping," they instead generate novelty and excitement "through a new case or adventure which introduces some combination of new supporting characters, new locations and a new narrative enigma, all of which are specific to that film and do not recur in future episodes."[38] Family series, in contrast, are interested in how characters behave in their domestic settings and in how they change as they approach different life stages. Even when the characters lead extraordinary lives, "narrative development and life development go hand in hand" in the family-centered series and foreground a sense of continuity and growth that is rooted in time going by. Thus, film series that are mainly committed to self-contained, episodic structures without ongoing storylines can usually not escape the kind of continuity that the passage of time brings with it. Columbia's *Blondie* series (1938-1949), for instance, sees the birth of Blondie's (Penny Singleton) daughter Cookie (Marjorie Ann Mutchie) and witnesses as Blondie's older son grows from three-year old "Baby Dumpling" into a teenager, who is eventually called by his real name, Alexander (Larry Simm).

The Andy Hardy films, *Dr. Kildare*, the *Thin Man* series, *Tarzan*, and *Blondie* along with Paramount's *Henry Aldrich* series (1939–1944), MGM's *Maisie* (1939–1947), and a number of popular B-series produced overarching storylines through the chronologies of family life and the theme of biological reproduction. To be sure, Hollywood sequels, though less numerous than film series at the time, were already well-versed in establishing narrative continuity through kinship and life-cycle relations, as brides, wives, sons, and daughters took over the big screen. From early examples of the silent era such as *The Squaw Man's Son* (E. J. Le Saint, 1917), following Cecil B. DeMille's 1914 version of *The Squaw Man*, or the lavishly produced sequels *Don Q, Son of Zorro* (Donald Crisp, 1925) and *The Son of the Sheik* (George Fitzmaurice, 1926), in which Douglas Fairbanks and Rudolph Valentino returned after their respective box-office hits *The Mark of Zorro* (Fred Niblo, 1920) and *The Sheik* (George Melford, 1921) to play dual roles of father *and* son, to studio-era B-movies such as Universal's horror sequels *Bride of Frankenstein* (James Whale, 1935) and *Son of Frankenstein* (Rowland V. Lee, 1939), *Dracula's Daughter* (Lambert Hillyer, 1936) and *Son of Dracula* (Robert Siodmak, 1943) to the *Four Daughters* (Michael Curtiz, 1938), who became *Four Wives* (Michael Curtiz, 1939), and then *Four Mothers* (William Keighley, 1941), sequels used to be family affairs. From the 1970s onward, by the way, such titling practices and serialization strategies came to be replaced by the sequel's love for numbers and a stronger focus on delivering more of the same. Yet, as we will see in chapter 6, the long-term sequel production that has emerged from this industry trend and that sustains narrative continuity by following characters and unfolding their stories over many decades, often resorts to the kind of kinship relations we already find in earlier sequels and studio-era series. They become storytelling engines for contemporary franchises and inadvertently transform them into family-centered undertakings, even if the more mundane implications and heteronormative values associated with such kinship relations contradict what the genre, theme, plot, and characters might once have stood for.

CINEMA VS. TELEVISION: HOLLYWOOD'S "BIG PICTURE" APPROACH IN THE POST-STUDIO ERA

The family series was among the last to disappear from the cinemas when the studios abandoned the production model in the 1950s. Universal still released ten *Ma and Pa Kettle* films (about a rural couple with fifteen children that wins a brand-new model home in a radio jingle contest) from 1947 to 1957, but already at a lower frequency of only one film per year instead of two or three. The end of the series boom in cinemas was ushered in by the Supreme Court decision in the *Paramount* case in 1948 and the rise of television in the postwar United States. The *Paramount Decree* was the outcome of a landmark antitrust case that challenged the major and minor studios' control of the American film industry and their monopolistic practices. A series of consent decrees had already limited block-booking and prohibited blind-bidding before the 1948 decision forced the major studios to divest themselves of their theater chains and thus effectively ended the vertical integration of production, distribution, and exhibition on which the studio system was built. Having lost their ready-made markets and the guaranteed revenue streams from the studio-owned movie theaters, the Big Five moved away from the factory-style mass production of movies, long-term contracts, and the producer-unit system toward what Janet Staiger has called the "package-unit system," with short-term, "film-by-film financing and planning" that relied on the "industry-wide pooling of labor and materials" and "intensified the need to differentiate the product on the basis of its innovations, its story, its stars, and its director."[39] Major studios cut back on production and released overall fewer movies and proportionately fewer film series, serials, and sequels, which dropped to an all-time low in the 1950s and 1960s.[40]

Amidst the seismic shifts in the film industry brought on by the forced divestiture of theater chains, serials and film series moved from the big to the small screen, where seriality became the central structuring principle.[41] In the postwar United States, more and more families were buying television sets and came to prefer the economic advantages, selection of programs, and comfort of stay-at-home entertainment. They watched television instead of going to the cinema on a regular basis. The baby boom and white migration away from the cities with their large downtown picture palaces to the mushrooming suburbs "contributed to the erosion of the nation's moviegoing habit on which both the studios and theatres had previously been able to rely."[42] Average weekly cinema attendance plummeted from eighty-two million in 1946 to forty-two million in 1952 to twenty million in 1966, where it remained for the next decades at less than a quarter of the soaring numbers from 1946.[43] The shrinking audiences had much to do with the postwar cultural ideal of the middle-class, suburban, nuclear family and a new importance of the home. With reference to a key term from Cold War foreign policy, Elaine Tyler May speaks of "domestic containment" to describe "the way in which public policy, personal behavior, and even political values were focused on the home."[44] The rise of television formed part of this cultural change, and television programs, too, actively promoted the turn to domesticity and the private, to heteronormativity and traditional gender roles.

The major studios moved into television production to secure an alternative source of revenue and by the mid-1950s, they had come to put "pre-existing materials [and] many of the organizational methods of the old studio system . . . to new uses," producing B-film genres like western and detective series for the small screen and adapting film series such as *The Thin Man* (MGM/NBC, 1957–1959) and *Dr. Kildare* (MGM/NBC, 1961–1966) to the new medium.[45] Henderson explains that "series such as the Hardy family and Ma and Pa Kettle were obvious prototypes" for the television soap operas and sitcoms that "were quickly colonised by the new, domestically situated technology."[46] He further suggests that the virtual abandonment of long-running family series that focused on everyday situations and often followed characters through different life stages "has something to do with the industry's waning interest in the adult female moviegoers who were central to its success in the 1930s and 40s, and its subsequent preference for courting the attention of teenage boys."[47]

Within this new industrial context, the cinematic seriality of the studio era, when the "dream factory" produced serials and film series at low budgets and high production rates, became a thing of the past. While majors continued to produce episodic content in their newly established television divisions, the film industry also pursued strategies to differentiate its product from black-and-white television by focusing on the release of fewer, lavishly produced feature films for the big screen that were intended to lure audiences away from their television sets at home and back into the movie theaters. Since the early 1950s, such large-scale productions have been referred to as "blockbusters," even though the term is now "most readily associated with the dominant commercial forms of modern, mainstream, 'postclassical' or 'post-studio' Hollywood."[48] Following the slogan, "Make Them Big; Show Them Big; Sell Them Big,"[49] biblical and historical epics like *The Ten Commandments* (Cecil B. DeMille, 1956) and *Ben-Hur* (William Wyler, 1959), war films like *The Bridge on the River Kwai* (David Lean, 1957), or musicals like *The Sound of Music* (Robert Wise, 1965) cost at least three times as much and were considerably longer than the average Hollywood movie made at the time. They used cinema's latest technology in color, widescreen, stereophonic sound, and 3-D, which they showcased through special distribution and exhibition practices—especially the roadshow that limited the movie's first release to a select few theaters with higher ticket prices before its general release.[50]

There are several reasons why these older blockbusters neither spawned sequels nor continued as film series. First, the preferred "big picture" genres—biblical or historical epics, and adaptation of Broadway musicals—"were not easy targets for sequelisation, for both formal and logistical reasons."[51] It was always easier and less costly, for instance, to adapt another, already existing Rodgers and Hammerstein musical than to develop a sequel to *Oklahoma!* (Fred Zinneman, 1955) or *South Pacific* (Joshua Logan, 1958) from scratch (which would not only have required a new story and screenplay but also original musical numbers).[52] Moreover, audience familiarity with biblical stories and exceptional historical events, the tragic endings of movies like *West Side Story* (Robert Wise/Jerome Robbins, 1961) and *Dr. Zhivago* (David Lean, 1965), and the unlikelihood of being able to reassemble the large, all-star casts of movies like *Around the World in 80 Days* (Michael Anderson, 1956) and *It's a Mad, Mad, Mad, Mad World* (Stanley Kramer, 1963) for a follow-up each posed their own difficulties for future continuations.[53] Second, the "big pictures" had to remain "exceptions to the norms of production and release"[54] for the roadshow's prestige mode of exhibition and inflated ticket prices to be justified. Any kind of serialization would have distracted from the movies' special status as a spectacular blockbuster. "It is contemporary Hollywood (dating from the mid-1970s) which has become dependent on the regular production of blockbusters as its principal mode of operation," Sheldon Hall contends.[55] As we will see, this shift also includes the regular production of blockbuster sequels. Finally, the high-budget musicals and epics of the 1950s and 1960s remained standalone movies *because* seriality became intricately linked to the new medium television.[56] If Hollywood wanted to differentiate its product from television's stay-at-home entertainment and sell its large-scale productions as unique events, seriality and any of its cookie-cutter connotations (mass-produced, standardized, inexpensive, and all the same) were not an option.

Hollywood's "big picture" approach was extremely risky, and while some productions, like *The Sound of Music*, turned out to be spectacular box-office hits, there were also spectacular failures such as *Cleopatra* (Joseph L. Mankiewicz, 1963), *Dr. Dolittle* (Richard Fleischer, 1967), or *Star!* (Robert Wise, 1968). By the end of the 1960s, it had become clear that a business model that was based on the revenue from a few successful "big pictures" was unsustainable in the long run. All major studios plunged into the red during this decade and became candidates for conglomerate takeovers or diversified to become conglomerates themselves. Hall writes that "as a result of their losses, several of the studios changed corporate ownership or executive management; a number temporarily stopped production; most 'rationalised' their corporate structure, assets and operations; and almost all announced radical new economies and revised production policies."[57] In this industrial context and after a "brief period of thrift in the early 1970s, the studios once again became committed to blockbuster-oriented production policies."[58] This development also brought cinematic seriality back into the limelight as a means to minimize corporate risk. The result was an uptick in sequel production and, ultimately, the dawn of the franchise era.

SERIAL PURSUITS: SERIES AND SEQUELS
IN THE POST-STUDIO ERA

Stuart Henderson writes that, from the perspective of today's franchise era, "in which many of the highest-budget, highest-earning films are either sequels or attempts to initiate a multi-film series, it is hard to conceive of the extent to which the equivalent releases from the early 1950s through to the late 1960s were, with a handful of noteworthy exceptions, stand-alone events."[59] To be sure, the studios' focus on producing self-contained "big pictures" on the one hand and adapting cinema's successful serial formulas for television on the other did not mean that seriality had completely disappeared from the movie theaters. Instead, it became a staple of cheaply, mostly independently produced "exploitation" films that provided product for a large number of cinemas "whose demand for features was no longer met by the major studios and their low-volume, high-budget mindset."[60] The teen movie cycle of the late 1950s and early 1960s as well as the Black action films (pejoratively known as "Blaxploitation"), violent vigilante movies, and pornographic films (or: "Sexploitation") from the early 1970s catered to specific segments of the moviegoing audience.

Gidget (Paul Wendkos, 1959), a comedy about a teenage girl who gets to know California's surf culture during her summer vacation, not only spawned two sequels, *Gidget Goes Hawaiian* (Paul Wendkos, 1961) and *Gidget Goes to Rome* (Paul Wendkos, 1963), but also inaugurated a cycle of beach party movies, including *Beach Party* (William Asher, 1963), which developed into a popular conceptual film series. Independent producer American International Pictures (AIP) made these movies for teen audiences and the growing sector of drive-in movie exhibition.[61] Low-budget "Blaxploitation" films such as *Cotton Comes to Harlem* (Ossie Davis, 1970), *Shaft* (Gordon Parks, 1971), and *Super Fly* (Gordon Parks, 1972) were initially aimed at Black urban moviegoers but became crossover box-office hits, reaching a mainstream audience. They each inspired several sequels and a sequel-heavy action movie cycle featuring Black detectives, prostitutes, gangsters, and bounty hunters dealing with crime, drugs, and violence in the inner city. Brutal vigilante revenge movies were also big at the box office in the early 1970s, when "the Nixon administration (self-destructively, it turned out) urged Americans to 'get tough on crime.'"[62] These movies, focusing on "populist heroes [who] took the law into their own hands to fight against crime, corruption, and authoritarian bureaucracy,"[63] included *Billy Jack* (Tom Laughlin, 1971) and *Walking Tall* (Phil Karlson, 1973) with their respective sequels. Feature-length porno films also became a popular genre after the new rating system of the Motion Picture Association (MPA) had replaced the Hays Code in October 1968. X-rated movies like *Deep Throat* (Gerard Damiano, 1972) and French import *Emmanuelle* (Just Jaeckin, 1974) launched the "porno chic" trend for mainstream audiences and generated "Sexploitation" sequels and imitations.

David A. Cook observes that in the early 1970s, "once-marginal exploitation genres . . . became important factors in the American film market; but by the decade's end, most exploitation product had migrated to home video."[64] Hollywood's major studios would adopt innovative production and release tactics of low-budget exploitation cinema, especially *saturation booking* (the mass release of movies on the same day), *four-walling* (distributors rent entire movie theaters for a flat fee and do not share the revenue with exhibitors), and *massive television advertising* (when most studios still spent their money on print media). These tactics played a decisive role in creating the modern Hollywood blockbuster, but they also informed the evolution of the sequel. However, the studio system's factory-like production mode and preexisting approaches to cinematic seriality remained influential in the post-studio era as well.[65]

The launch of the *James Bond* series in 1963 and the four sequels following on the heels of the box-office success of *Planet of the Apes* (Franklin J. Schaffner, 1968) are rare examples of the major studios' serial endeavors at the time—before they turned to the high-concept, high-budget, and sequel-oriented production mode that has come to characterize the blockbuster era from the mid-1970s onward. Through the lens of Hollywood remaking, the *Bond* and *Ape* movies occupy a transitional space because they rely on serial strategies and production patterns of the studio system while also indicating a "B" to "A" trajectory of cinema's serial formats in terms of production value and release strategies, a growing interest in creating and maintaining continuity across installments, and the importance of merchandise and transmedia spin-offs and adaptations. These characteristics, to be clear, have become standard in Hollywood's franchise era, but they were far from conventional in the 1960s and 1970s.

The *Bond* series, of course, was not really invested in narrative continuity until the *Casino Royale* (Martin Campbell, 2006) reboot and the subsequent movies starring Daniel Craig as secret agent 007—*Quantum of Solace* (Mark Foster, 2008), *Skyfall* (Sam Mendes, 2012), *Spectre* (Sam Mendes, 2015), and *No Time to Die* (Cary Joji Fukunaga, 2021)—introduced ongoing storylines and serial memory to the traditionally episodic structure of the film series and, for the first time, created a complete story arc for Craig's James Bond. When United Artists released *Dr. No* (Terence Young, 1963) as the first movie based on author Ian Fleming's series of spy novels, it set the pattern for a consistent *James Bond* formula, in which 007 arrives on screen as an already fully formed character—a serial figure that returns film after film without ever changing, always ready to accomplish the next mission and to fight against villains in the name of her majesty the queen.

According to Jennifer Forrest, film series like *James Bond* are not only open-ended (without any real beginnings nor ends) but also suspended in time.[66] What she describes as the "absence of true diegetic chronology" allows viewers to consume individual movies in any order.[67] But it also means that, within their fictional worlds, characters like James Bond are not affected by the passage of time, by the process of aging, or, in Umberto Eco's words, "by the law that leads from life to death through time."[68] The removal of such temporal constraints on the diegetic level creates an "eternal present"[69] for the *Bond* series and ensures its—potentially endless— existence through the generative principle of repetition and variation. Over the course of six decades, 007 has appeared twenty-seven times on the big screen and was portrayed by seven different actors (Sean Connery, David Niven, George Lazenby, Roger Moore, Timothy Dalton, Pierce Brosnan, and Daniel Craig) in order to maintain the static attributes and perpetual youth (or: immortality) of the unchanging series character. Even when Daniel Craig's James Bond does, in fact, die in *No Time to Die*, his death does not end the series. On the contrary, it ensures its survival. The movie itself announces that "James Bond will return" in the series' signature title card that regularly follows after the movie's end credits (figure 19). This is a promise that sets up the future of the Bond series, without Daniel Craig but very likely featuring a once more reinvented (if still recognizable) secret agent.

Even though James Bond generally operates as a fixed serial figure, the Daniel Craig movies (especially *No Time to Die*) have tried to update the character and bring him into the current moment. The world around James Bond has so radically changed that his misogyny and sexist treatment of women are no longer acceptable today. As a reminder: in *Goldfinger* (Guy Hamilton, 1964), Sean Connery's Bond forces himself on the character Pussy Galore (Honor Blackman), despite clear verbal and visual

Figure 19. The series' signature title card promises that James Bond will have a future.

cues of the woman's lack of consent. In *Thunderball* (Terence Young, 1965) Connery's character uses physical force to coerce nurse Patricia Fearing (Molly Peters) into kissing him, suggesting that if she sleeps with him, he will refrain from sharing information that could get her fired. In *Diamonds Are Forever* (Guy Hamilton, 1971), Connery's Bond aggressively removes a woman's bikini top and strangles her with it. And the list could go on. In *GoldenEye* (Martin Campbell, 1995), which features Pierce Brosnan in the role of Bond and the first female M (Judy Dench) as chief of the Secret Intelligence Service, she describes Bond as "a sexist, misogynist dinosaur, a relic of the Cold War, whose boorish charm [is] wasted on me." Yet, the film still treats women as Bond Girls, as sex objects and trophies that Bond needs to dominate and possess.

When Daniel Craig's new James Bond movie was announced, in short, critics found 007 "too toxic for the #MeToo era" and suggested that "Time's up for ... this most enduring of characters"[70]—referencing two social justice movements fighting sexual harassment and sexualized violence that gained global prominence following the sexual-abuse allegations against Hollywood producer Harvey Weinstein in October 2017. But in the end, Craig's Bond in *No Time to Die* convinced many that this thoroughly conservative "exemplar of bygone gender norms and ... tuxedo aficionado in a casual age" might indeed have a hidden "radical streak" that resonates with contemporary concerns: "A sense of self-hatred and doubt about his mission is precisely what gave his turn in the iconic role its edge, and what made this era's version of a very old franchise feel, at times, genuinely challenging," writes Alyssa Rosenberg in the *Washington Post*.[71]

In many ways, the long-running *James Bond* series shows the mechanism of repetition and renewal at work and draws attention to its embeddedness in social, cultural, and political contexts. As social norms and political attitudes change over time, the persistence of a serial figure like James Bond depends on the successful negotiation between past and present and, ultimately, on some sense of serial evolution, continuity, and character growth that seems at odds with Bond's iconic familiarity and the series' formal preference for "serial iteration, recurrence, and looping."[72] The James Bond movies of the 1960s were released at regular intervals, with pauses that were long enough to allow each movie to be marketed as an event. According to Henderson, this strategy would "become the template for the production and distribution practices which would later govern Hollywood's approach to blockbuster-scale seriality in the coming decades."[73] He further observes that the movies' "eschewal of narrative continuity between instalments" is a debt to the studio-era film series but, already at the time, this choice "would increasingly seem, if not outmoded, then certainly no longer the norm."[74]

Planet of the Apes opted for a different approach in the early 1970s, when it tried to establish continuity between the four sequels *Beneath the Planet of the Apes* (Ted Post, 1970), *Escape from the Planet of the Apes* (Don Taylor, 1971), *Conquest of the Planet of the Apes* (J. Lee Thompson, 1972), and *Battle for the Planet of the Apes* (J. Lee Thompson, 1973). Once the first movie, based on the novel *La planète des singe* (1963) by French author Pierre Boulle, had found a studio (20th Century Fox) willing to take the risk of financing a science-fiction spectacle with talking apes and was eventually released in 1968, it became an extraordinary commercial and critical success. The final scene in which Charlton Heston's character—astronaut George Taylor—comes across a half-buried Statue of Liberty on the beach of the "Forbidden Zone" and realizes that he has not landed on an alien "Planet of the Apes" after all but on a future Earth, is considered "one of the most effectively shocking in the history of cinema."[75] It has entered the cultural imaginary as a shorthand for the threat of a nuclear apocalypse in its immediate Cold War context, and has, since the 1980s, also been invoked by Greenpeace to protest nuclear testing as well as by other groups "to describe and debate issues ranging from urban decay to the Bosnian Civil War to international trade to gun control."[76] Retrospectively, the famous ending also renders *Planet of the Apes* legible as an early example of climate change fiction (or cli-fi), if considered with our growing preoccupation with the climate crisis in mind. The dramatic ending, in short, left room for interpretation—and for a number of sequels.

After the success of the first film, writes Eric Greene, 20th Century Fox "requested a sequel. And another. And another. And another. And another."[77] Still, producing these *Apes* movies and creating continuity between them was not as straightforward as Greene's comment suggests. The first sequel, *Beneath the Planet of the Apes*, ends with the final destruction of the world and everyone living in it because Fox initially did not plan on investing in another follow-up. When this movie proved to be another hit, Fox changed course and sent a telegram to screenwriter Paul Dehn, saying "Apes exist. Sequel required."[78] But how could he continue the story if the world and characters people already knew no longer existed? *Planet of the Apes* exemplifies the conundrum of time-space continuity that comes with sequelization, especially if the sequel is merely an afterthought, conceived after the success of an earlier movie and, more often than not, in spite of that movie's narrative closure. Dehn found a creative solution for *Escape from the Planet of the Apes* by having three of the intelligent Chimpanzee characters escape and travel back in time with Taylor's abandoned spaceship. Dr. Cornelius (Roddy McDowall), Dr. Zira (Kim Hunter), and Dr. Milo (Sal Mineo) land in the United States, in the year 1973, where the rest of the movie is set. The time travel into the viewers' present bestows new urgency on the themes of racial conflict, nuclear destruction, animal rights, and ecological devastation. Since Fox was now convinced that there was a continuing market for the *Apes* films, *Escape* had an open ending to facilitate maintaining continuity in a follow-up. The next sequel, *Conquest of the Planet of the Apes*, unfolds almost twenty years later, in 1991, with Cornelius and Zira's grown son Caesar at the center of the plot. Whereas *Conquest* ends with Caesar proclaiming the birth of the "Planet of the Apes," the final installment, *Battle for the Planet of the Apes*, brings the story full circle with its return to the dystopian future and radioactive ruins of the "Forbidden Zone" that viewers encountered in the first movie.

The complex chronology that Dehn developed for the *Apes* movies in order to create continuity between the installments has remained largely untouched by a short-lived live-action television series (CBS, 1974) and an animated television series (NBC, 1975–1976) that followed on the heels of the last *Apes* movie; by Tim Burton's reimagining of *Planet of the Apes* (2001), which failed to resonate with contemporary anxieties and could not relaunch the *Apes* franchise in the new millennium; or by the prequel *Rise of the Planet of the Apes* (Rupert Wyatt, 2011), which, dramatizing timely fears of genetic engineering and the possibility of a viral pandemic, eventually succeeded in reigniting interest in the *Apes* material and spawned two more sequels, *Dawn of the Planet of the Apes* (Matt Reeves, 2014) and *War for the Planet of the Apes* (Matt Reeves, 2017).[79] Burton's movie loosely remakes the first film, with a confusing (and much criticized) open ending. The movie concludes with astronaut Leo Davidson (Mark Wahlberg) leaving the distant Ape planet through an electromagnetic storm that brings him back to Earth. But as he crash-lands on the steps of the Lincoln Memorial in Washington, D.C., he finds the features of Abraham Lincoln replaced with those of General Thade (Tim Roth)—the brutal chimpanzee military commander Leo had fought on the Planet of the Apes. In his analysis of the Burton remake, Constantine Verevis contends that "the remake of *Planet of the Apes* has a twist ending *because* the original does."[80] Even if the ending "might make little narrative sense, . . . it makes perfect remake sense," because it "underlines the cultural memory of the original ending and emphatically secures the authority and influence of the cult original."[81] In contrast, the prequel movies are not interested in "reimagining" or transforming the first *Planet of the Apes* movie. Set before the narrative events of that film, they repeat the premises from *Conquest of the Planet of the Apes* (in *Rise*) and *Battle of the Planet of the Apes* (in *Dawn* and *War*) and jointly tell the story of how Earth became the Planet of the Apes.

However, made more than three and even four decades apart, none of these later films is invested in creating narrative continuity with the first *Apes* movies, even though they certainly produce seriality effects that manifest themselves at one remove from the main plot and fictional world of the *Apes* franchise. In their entirety, the *Apes* films tell *an ongoing story of cinema's technological and aesthetic evolution that encourages viewers "to identify, however nostalgically, with a specific standard of commodity production that has come to define their age group's experience of popular culture."*[82] From John Chambers's groundbreaking prosthetic makeup in 1968 and Rick Baker's new design in the Tim Burton remake to the combination of motion capture and digital animation in the latest movies—the advances in technology and visual effects invariably construct a story of progress that almost naturally extends to the cultural and political concerns that inform every single *Apes* movie. Possibilities for revisiting the older films, spotting intertextual connections, and drawing comparisons to the latest versions render this progress visible and invite viewers to position themselves along its straightforward course—with regard to the specific technological, aesthetic, cultural, and political moment that these movies stand in for.[83]

Beyond such overarching narratives of change and movie-generational belonging, the first *Planet of the Apes* and its four sequels—along with the early *James Bond* and sequel-heavy exploitation films—complicate notions of the sequel's linear trajectory from "B" to "A" in the post-studio era.[84] In fact, none of the examples discussed here is radically different from earlier serial endeavors. Instead they combine old and new, mixing strategies of the studio era's producer-unit system with contemporary commercial and aesthetic practices. Taken together, they are evidence of how the film series and sequel diversify along with the film industry following the *Paramount Decree* and the rise of television as popular stay-at-home entertainment. While the independently produced exploitation films were low-budget, high-volume affairs (reminiscent of B-movie production), the Bond and *Apes* films had overall higher budgets and were marketed as events (like the studio-era A-movies and early blockbusters). Furthermore, they anticipate a generic shift, with studios spending big money on action-adventure, science fiction, fantasy, and horror stories (that would have been B-level products in the studio era), instead of making prestige historical epics, musicals, war films, or westerns.[85] And yet, *Beneath the Planet of the Apes*, for instance, had a smaller budget than *Planet of the Apes* since it relied on recycling strategies (for sets, costumes, and ape masks) that were typical of the film series production in the studio era.[86] Henderson also writes that "the efficient regularity with which the subsequent three films . . . were produced by a team of regular collaborators ([producer Arthur P.] Jacobs, [screenwriter Paul] Dehn, actors Roddy McDowall and Kim Hunter, make-up designer John Chambers and art director William Creber among others), financially supported by a single studio, recalls the factory-like approach of the Seitz Unit at MGM."[87]

These echoes of the studio system were countered by an overall higher production value, the *Apes*' focus on establishing continuity between the films, and a new interest in merchandising. Even though George Lucas and *Star Wars* are often credited with starting the film merchandising boom, the sale of film-related products already played an important role for both Bond and *Apes*.[88] Scott Higgins writes that models of 007's Aston Martin and various toys and gadgets (such as the James Bond Action Pen, for example), "promised to bridge the gaps between the individual films" and supported "long-term serial engagement with an inhabitable fantasy."[89] *Apes* merchandise, ranging from trading cards and action figures to model kits, soaps, records, and books, reached their peak in 1974, when the television series was released, and fulfilled similar functions. Overall, then, *James Bond* and *Planet of the Apes* hint at the direction in which the sequel would continue to evolve, laying out production, release, and marketing strategies as well as aesthetic and narrative trends that become much more pronounced in the following decades. As the major studios became part of horizontally integrated media conglomerates, the sequel, too, embarked on "a haphazard progression towards the franchise-oriented landscape"[90] that we know today. As we will see in the next chapter, *sequelitis* and *forever franchise* emerge as important key terms if we want to fully understand what happens next. Focusing on Hollywood's investment in sustaining industrial, narrative, and cultural continuity through sequels and film franchises, we can further investigate the impact of ongoing narratives on constructions of time, memory, and generation as well as the persistence and malleability of dominant ideologies in popular culture.

6 From Sequelitis to the Forever Franchise

According to the *Guardian*'s film critic Ben Child, "a third *Blade Runner* movie is as inevitable as the robot revolution."[1] With *Blade Runner 2049* (2017), Denis Villeneuve had delivered a long-awaited sequel to Ridley Scott's science fiction classic from 1982, but even though the movie turned out to be a critical success, another follow-up seemed unlikely because of its disappointing box-office take. To be sure, there are several unresolved narrative strands in *Blade Runner 2049*, which indicate that the movie had been made with plans for further installments in mind. Convinced of *Blade Runner*'s brand value and the unbroken appeal of the dystopian future in which both movies take place, Child contends: "If Ridley Scott's film can get a triumphant sequel after more than three decades, a box-office fizzle won't stop the series."[2] Both Scott and Villeneuve have stated that they are interested in telling more *Blade Runner* stories. "I've got another one ready to evolve and be developed," Scott said in 2018;[3] and Villeneuve stated in 2020 that he found the *Blade Runner* world "such an inspiring place" that he would be ready to make another—standalone—movie.[4] "The problem I have is the word 'sequel,'" the director said in an interview: "I think cinema needs original stories. But if you ask me if I'd like to revisit this universe in a different way, I can say yes. It would need to be a project on its own. Something disconnected from both other movies. A detective noir set in the future. . . . I wake up sometimes in the night dreaming about it."[5]

Villeneuve's aversion to the word *sequel* calls up familiar discourses that privilege "original stories" over any form of Hollywood remaking (here: the sequel) and emphasizes the creativity and artistic integrity of the filmmaker. Yet Villeneuve's take on the original/remaking binary seems not as clear-cut as Steven Spielberg's, for example, who had called sequels "cheap carnival tricks"[6] in 1975 and refused to make another *Jaws* movie at the time. And while he eventually directed one *Jurassic Park* and two *Indiana Jones* sequels later in his career, Spielberg now finds that they are not as good as his "originals" and remains adamant that he would never direct a remake of *Jaws* or any other of his movies.[7] Villeneuve, in contrast, wants to make another *Blade Runner* movie after having already directed one sequel. It might seem paradoxical that he develops his idea of "original stories" within the confines of already-existing material and fictional storyworlds. Yet, judging from his statement (and his 2021 remake of *Dune*), the director is obviously not opposed to practices of remaking per se. Unlike Spielberg, who was convinced that sequels "reduced moviemaking as an art to just a science,"[8] Villeneuve seems bothered by the *narrative continuity* that the sequel mandates and the resulting creative constraints, rather than by an overarching business model that prioritizes repetition and serialization.

Two points can be made about this observation: First, directors' attitudes toward remaking have changed from reluctance or outright rejection to produce follow-ups in the 1970s and 1980s, when sequelitis was an omnipresent buzzword, to the whole-hearted embrace of film franchises and the imperative of continuation, expansion, and serial renewal that reigns supreme in contemporary Hollywood cinema. The 2017 release of the *Blade Runner* sequel, thirty-five years after the first movie premiered in theaters, and both Denis Villeneuve's and Ridley Scott's desire to revisit this fictional world follow in the footsteps of this development, which has also ushered in the rise of the franchise auteur. By the early 2000s, studios increasingly trusted "directors whose commercial track records were as yet unproven, but who had established something resembling 'auteur' credentials," with their biggest releases and presold properties.[9] Peter

Jackson's *The Lord of the Rings* trilogy, Sam Raimi's *Spider-Man* films, Bryan Singer's *X-Men* movies, or Christopher Nolan's reboot of *Batman* were all framed as the (indie) filmmakers' vision and personal interpretation of familiar source material. Toward the end of the decade, the promise of creative freedom and authorial control along with the studios' increased investments in restarting and reviving dormant franchises, began luring established directors, like Ridley Scott, to revisit their own movies. *Prometheus* (2012) and *Alien: Covenant* (2017) mark Scott's return to the franchise that began with his film *Alien* in 1979 and was initially followed by three sequels that were each directed by a different filmmaker: *Aliens* (James Cameron, 1986), *Alien³* (David Fincher, 1992), and *Alien Resurrection* (Jean-Pierre Jeunet, 1997). For *Blade Runner 2049*, Scott ultimately served as an executive producer and helped develop the story, but he let Denis Villeneuve direct the sequel because he was still working on *Alien: Covenant* at the time. Scott explains that he had never wanted to make follow-ups to any of his films but that his opinion had changed over time: "We try not to repeat ourselves . . . that's why I never did a sequel to *Alien* for another 20 years, and then I thought 'Do you know what, I'd better go back to this.'"[10] *Blade Runner*, too, offered enough material to tell another story, and Villeneuve, as the new director, seized the opportunity to inhabit the world that Scott had created and make it his own.

The second point is that Villeneuve's criticism of the sequel is unmistakably embedded in the franchise logic that informs today's film industry. While sequels have paved the way for Hollywood's franchise boom, they can now be both a revitalizing element *and* a stumbling block for long-running film franchises. I have stated elsewhere that *the sequel is a repetition-based continuation or extension of a closed (or partly closed) narrative that relies on recurring characters and is defined by the chronological relationship to its predecessor as well as a high degree of narrative continuity: events in the sequel occur after events in the earlier film and what happened in the earlier film continues to be meaningful in the sequel.*[11] As we will see, film franchises, which thrive on audience preawareness and the seemingly infinite possibilities of serial spread and sprawl across time and different media platforms, still depend on the long-term binding function of sequels with their familiar characters and sequentially progressing story arcs. However, there is a tendency to move away from the rigidity of narrative continuity to a more flexible, modular mode of storytelling that focuses on shared fictional worlds (or: cinematic universes). Superhero movies set in the *Marvel Cinematic Universe* (MCU), Disney's *Star Wars* spin-offs, or the King Kong and Godzilla movies of the *MonsterVerse* follow this modular logic that has become key to securing the franchises' enduring existence and profitability. In a return to a more conventional film series setup typical of classical Hollywood cinema, these movies trade sequelization for more explicitly self-contained, episodic structures. This is precisely what Villeneuve envisions with a possible detective *noir* that does not possess direct narrative links to the previous *Blade Runner* movies but takes place in the same, carefully designed dystopian future audiences already know.

The discussions about the potential futures of *Blade Runner* draw attention to the ongoing evolution of the sequel and series formats, most recently within the franchise system that has come to dominate Hollywood over the course of the last two decades. To understand franchising and its emphasis on audience familiarity with characters and storyworlds, it is necessary to go back in time and trace its emergence, along with the complex evolution of the film industry and intertextual relations as well as the expansive and inclusive dynamics that feed into processes of cultural reproduction. In chapter 5 I showed that, by the early 2000s, *franchise* had become a convenient buzzword to make sense of Hollywood remaking, and franchising was widely imagined as the expansion and multiplication of cultural production across different media over time. This chapter argues that franchising entails a rethinking and optimization of sequelization as a more predictable and therefore (ideally) more profitable industry practice, arguably as a more legitimate model of cultural reproduction, and as an elaborately designed intertextual experience in which each individual product deepens and enriches a shared storyworld. But in order to get there, we first have to consider the rise of the sequel in the 1970s and 1980s and the sequelitis discourse, which frames follow-ups as shallow, standardized entertainment that lacks any artistic value or critical potential. The focus is on how producers, audiences, and film critics made sense of the production trend and the sequel form, and how the emerging discourses and cultural practices played into the movies' serialization strategies and increasingly self-referential maneuvers.[12] From there, the chapter moves on to explore the idea of the forever franchise and examines how it is structured around the concept of the shared universe, time, and nostalgia. Further engaging with these ideas, I will finally return to *Blade Runner 2049* and probe the politics behind its narrative continuity and a reproduction logic that follows linear time and introduces a generational element to push the story forward.

POTENTIAL HIT FILM FORMULA:
SEQUEL PRODUCTION IN THE 1970S AND 1980S

The rise of the sequel in the 1970s and 1980s takes place in the industrial context of conglomerization. At the time, steadily rising production and marketing costs for high-profile blockbusters turned filmmaking into an increasingly risky proposition. Following the industry logics of conglomerate Hollywood, studio heads with bottom-line prudence considered sequels to popular movies relatively safe investments in a notoriously unpredictable business. Producing a follow-up reduced the amount of time and money that went into the development of a movie and the repetition of a successful formula guaranteed that even if the sequel did not prove to be another hit, it would at least not tank at the box office. Conglomerization went hand in hand with horizontal integration, which meant that the parent companies to which the film studios now belonged "provided not only a safety net for large investments—losses in theatrical film divisions could be offset by the profitability in other areas—but an incentive as well: the popular success of a blockbuster can be 'spun off' into the various ancillary markets in which the studios also have interest."[13] The driving force behind this development was the corporate belief in *synergy*, which held that if the same content is produced across divisions in different media and for different markets, the products (movies, novels, comics, music, toys) would promote each other and generate overall more income. Within this scheme, sequels could renew interest and build long-term audience loyalty, and thus worked toward establishing a "brand" and then sustaining it over time. Sequels seemed to be the closest thing to a sure-fire moneymaking formula that Hollywood had to offer, and studio heads and producers certainly agreed that the industry math demanded follow-ups,[14] even if the story did not.

Conglomerization also favored wide-release strategies (or: saturation booking) that required a much larger number of prints and massive publicity campaigns with print and television advertising. As we have seen in chapter 5, simultaneous openings at different cinemas had already been a staple of exploitation cinema, "where it was used to generate quick profits before negative word of mouth could set in."[15] But the strategy was now adopted to screen blockbusters at hundreds of cinemas across the country at the same time and to turn these movies into highly anticipated events no one wanted to miss. Spielberg's *Jaws* is often credited with successfully establishing the model, in which a movie's opening weekend performance determines its box-office success. Again, sequels (including several follow-ups to *Jaws*) promised to function exceptionally well under these changed exhibition and marketing conditions. Instant name recognition and audience pre-awareness leveled the financial risk at the heart of Hollywood's expensive hit-or-miss investments. Sequels were presold properties that came with built-in audiences: from the start, moviegoers knew what these movies were about; sequels simply needed to remind them of what they had already watched and liked before, playing on their familiarity with the stories, characters, performers, and themes. Sequels, in other words, could appeal to audiences by evoking memories of a previous film, kindle a longing for more of the same, and simultaneously manage expectations. They epitomized the financial advantages of product familiarity, also and especially considering the power and reach of Hollywood's marketing machine. Or, as Universal Pictures president Frank Price put it: "We spend millions of dollars to make something unknown into something that is known. A non-sequel starts from zero. A sequel is a guaranteed reward."[16]

In theory, sequels seemed to make the studios' financial risk more calculable. In practice, however, they were a black box. Even though studios invested in high-profile follow-ups to spectacular box-office hits and marketed them with multimillion-dollar ad campaigns, sequels were an *afterthought* in the 1970s and 1980s, conceived, created, and released after a self-contained movie, which usually delivered narrative closure without built-in sequel options, had proven popular with audiences. Such ad hoc sequel production was informed by hunches, gut feelings, and rules of thumb based on experiences the film industry was making at the very same time that the sequel trend was taking hold. By the early 1990s, studio executives expected sequels to earn up to 60 percent of the profits accrued by the prior movie.[17] But such guesstimations had regularly failed to anticipate the diminishing returns that inevitably greeted sequels number three, four, or five, and they were equally inept at predicting when sequels would outperform their predecessors at the box office. In Hollywood, "nobody knows anything," as Oscar-winning screenwriter William Goldman famously put it.[18] Not surprisingly, it was a small sensation when economist Thorsten Hennig-Thurau and his team proposed actual mathematical formulas to calculate the monetary value of sequels in relation to non-sequels in 2009.[19] They proved that sequels generated higher average box-office revenues and involved overall less financial risk for studios than a similar movie in the same genre if the sequels adhered to the continued participation of stars and filmmakers, similar budgets, release dates, and distribution intensity.[20] Even so, the "nobody-knows" mantra still persists today, as Hennig-Thurau and Mark B. Houston note in a more recent publication that calls out the industry's reluctance to embrace theory and data analytics to determine economic success.[21]

In the 1980s, movies such as *Rocky III* (Sylvester Stallone, 1982), *The Karate Kid Part II* (John Avildsen, 1986), and *Lethal Weapon 2* (Richard Donner, 1989) outperformed their predecessors and foregrounded the sequel's moneymaking potential, and hit film sequels also boosted the fortunes of independent production companies, helping them to flourish among the major studios. This was the case with Carolco Pictures and the *Rambo* action movies about Vietnam veteran John Rambo, which studio president Peter Hoffman described as "the most important sequel series not owned by a major studio," explaining that it enabled the company to invest in other projects.[22] The *Nightmare on Elm Street* sequels likewise provided New Line Cinema with "stability and cash flow,"[23] earning it the moniker "The House that Freddy Built"—with reference to Freddy Krueger, the *Elm Street* serial killer (played by Robert Englund). In Hollywood's new conglomerate order, ancillary markets like television and home video also became important sources of revenue for blockbusters with soaring production and marketing costs. Sheldon Hall describes them as "a new set of 'runs' [that] has taken the place of the one maintained under the vertically integrated studio system, with the theatrical market *in toto* now effectively occupying the place of first run and the various ancillaries functioning as subsequent runs."[24]

Sequels promised handsome profits in ancillary markets, especially home video and pay-cable—"the principal growth areas throughout the 1980s."[25] The presale of television and home video rights based on the sequels' recognizable titles, allowed companies to line up revenues in advance. Once the low-budget sports drama *Rocky* (John Avildsen, 1976), starring then unknown Sylvester Stallone as boxer Rocky Balboa, proved to be a box-office sensation and triple Academy Award winner, television rights for *Rocky II* (Sylvester Stallone, 1979) and *Rocky III* sold for $21 million and $28 million, respectively, before the movies were even released in theaters.[26] The growing home video market similarly relied on recognizable titles, but its relationship with the sequel was more explicitly symbiotic. Sequels often enlivened VHS sales of their predecessors, while those same videocassettes also promoted the next installment and built audience anticipation for the sequel.[27] Rob Friedman, marketing chief at Warner Bros., explained that the company relied on VHS to bridge the time gap between *Gremlins* (Joe Dante, 1984) and *Gremlins 2: The New Batch* (Joe Dante, 1990) and to attract a transgenerational audience: "A lot of kids have seen the first one on video; many kids at the young end of the first movie are within our target for the second; and a lot of parents at the top end of the spectrum will bring their kids to see this one."[28]

It is easy, then, to see why the film industry fell in love with sequels: as a readily recognizable property capable of accumulating immense profits in movie theaters and ancillary markets, sequels demonstrated—again, at least in theory—that repetition plus variation equaled hit film formula. Sequels were an investment in the future of an intellectual property that built on that property's successful past to create and then maintain audience loyalty over time. Like film serials and series, sequels that continued familiar stories with familiar characters (and actors) in familiar settings or situations, capitalized on what Roger Hagedorn has described as the binding function of serial narratives.[29] Unlike film serials and series, however, sequels tended to combine cinematic seriality with high-concept, big-budget event movies to attract and engage mass audiences over the course of many years.

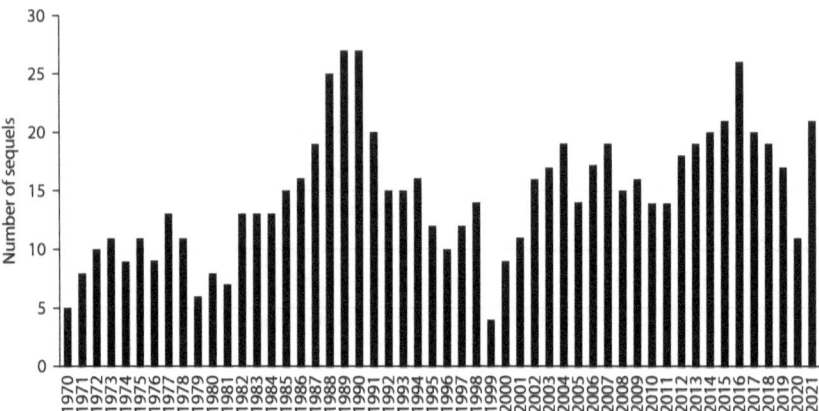

Figure 20. Production of sequels, 1970–2021. *Source: Hollywood Remaking* dataset.

Sequels leaped to the top of the production slate during the 1970s and 1980s. Averaging 52 percent of all remaking formats per year between 1970 and 2021, it is clearly the preferred remaking format in contemporary Hollywood cinema. During that period, fifteen sequels were released on average each year. Though the numbers vary, with peaks of twenty-seven sequels in 1988 and 1989 and twenty-six in 2016 as well as a low of only four sequels in 1999 (figure 20), they fluctuate considerably less than those of the film remakes and series. On average, sequels make up 5 percent of total film production in the United States each year, reaching as high as 11 percent in 1975, 12 percent in 1988, and 14 percent in 1989, and falling as low as 1 percent in 1999.

Through large-scale advertising campaigns, merchandising, and theatrical, home video, and TV releases, sequels became highly visible cultural products that provided pop-cultural reference points for audiences. From an industry point of view, the mode of serial storytelling associated with the sequel was probably as close as Hollywood would ever get to a self-preserving hit film formula. Paradoxically, though, if a sequel lived up to its box-office potential, the next installment had to deal with escalating costs, which then typically led to diminishing returns and, eventually, to the end of sequel production. This is so because sequels are always driven by *a serial logic of one-upmanship*: they follow an intensification-oriented principle of repetition and innovation in order to retell a familiar story in an enhanced and therefore potentially new way.[30] Precisely because the sequel actively recalls and imitates its predecessor but cannot repeat the pleasure of the first viewing experience, it tries to compensate by "amplify[ing] certain recurring elements, delivering more of the same with an emphasis on 'more.'"[31] This was common practice in the film business: "When you do a sequel, it has to be better than the first," 20th Century Fox president Sherry Lansing noted.[32] Consequently, the repetition and intensification of successfully established elements of distinction dramatically increased the budget from one movie to the next.

Even before Hennig-Thurau and his team came up with mathematical formulas, industry wisdom held that the secret to sequel success was "when all the cast members return, the director is retained and the script doesn't wander too much from the original premise."[33] However, this kind of repetition also inflated above-the-line costs, as actors, directors, and creative talent demanded higher salaries for their involvement in follow-ups. Intensification strategies geared toward innovation—more stars, more stunts, more explosions—further added to the overall production costs of the movies. Thus, even sequels that outperformed their predecessors sometimes turned out to be less profitable because they cost so much to make and market. When sequels failed at the box office, they could even prove a liability for studios instead of functioning as a cushion against risk. Throughout the 1970s and 1980s, declining cost-profit ratios and outright failures like *The Exorcist II: The Heretic* (John Boorman, 1977), *More American Graffiti* (Bill L. Norton, 1979), or *Grease 2* (Patricia Birch, 1982) thus challenged the idea that sequels were sure-fire hits.

THE UNCANNY SUCCESS OF FORMULAIC FARE:
SEQUEL RECEPTION

As trade papers closely monitored the sequel trend in the 1970s and 1980s—printing figures and graphs, as well as interviews with studio heads, marketing executives, and Hollywood insiders—film critics devoted much time and energy to theorizing sequel reception. Dave Kehr remarked in 1983 that it had been "a summer of Sunday newspaper think pieces on sequels," and that "most of the critics who have written on the sequel phenomenon have come to the same conclusion: that the proliferation of Roman numerals means that Hollywood is in a deep crisis of creativity—that no one in Hollywood seems capable of an original thought."[34] Kehr echoes the sequelitis criticism of the time. Yet he felt that audiences, too, held their share of the blame. "In spite of its shuddering lack of originality, the summer of 1983 will set a new record for box-office receipts. Clearly, somebody out there likes sequels—they aren't being shoved down unwilling throats. Audiences now seem to be buying movies much the way they buy toothpaste: on the basis of a familiar brand name."[35] The effect instant name recognition apparently had on audiences—so cherished by the industry—annoyed and puzzled Kehr. In what is highly reminiscent of the Frankfurt School's critique of the culture industry,[36] he reproached moviegoers for displaying the same consumer attitude toward cultural products they would typically exhibit towards mass-produced everyday commodities. At the same time, however, he also saw the need to understand sequels and their appeal: "Sequels, clearly, are here to stay for the foreseeable future, which means it's probably time to stop deploring them and find out what they really are."[37]

Why, then, did moviegoers flock to the theaters to watch the latest sequel? How come they were so eager to revisit familiar characters and storyworlds? Ticket sales suggested that audiences welcomed "the reassurance of the familiar."[38] Besides offering a form of risk management to the studios, sequels seemed to fulfill a similar function for audiences. As Caryn James explained in the *New York Times*, moviegoers "who enjoy *Ghostbusters* or *Lethal Weapon* minimize the risk of boredom, of wasting their own time and money, by heading for the sequel."[39] The sequel cultivates specific expectations that circle around the audiences' familiarity with a movie's premise, characters, and storyworld and the promise to combine the repetition—and possibly intensification—of signature elements with the thrill of a new adventure. Such expectations build audience loyalty in ways that film critics associate not so much with cinema as with another medium: television. According to this reasoning, sequels appealed to moviegoers who were conditioned by the comforting rhythm of television series, to which they "tune[d] in week after week to see the same characters do the same type of thing."[40] James spoke of "an affection for the familiar bred largely these days by television,"[41] and in the *Los Angeles Herald-Examiner*, Gregg Kilday pointed out that moviegoers were "eagerly lining up to see movies that repeat movies they have already seen" because they had been "weaned on episodic television."[42]

Film critics interpreted the sequel trend in terms of a growing convergence between cinema and television, foregrounding episodicity and repetitiveness as the common traits Hollywood sequels shared with television series, regardless of their medium-specific temporalities and patterns of production and reception. Audiences could set aside specific times and days each week to follow their favorite TV shows, but there was no direct equivalent of appointment television in the movie theater. Since the sequel used to be an afterthought, moviegoers had no way of knowing whether, when, and how specific characters would return to the big screen. At the same time, the rise of the sequel in the 1970s and 1980s clearly indicated that if audiences grew attached to a character, they were likely to display the same loyalty to Hollywood sequels featuring that character as they would toward the next episode of a popular television show. Apparently, it did not matter that films were released several years apart rather than in a weekly rhythm. References to television's episodicity and repetitiveness may have aimed to unravel the mystery of the sequel's success with audiences, but they were nonetheless steeped in value judgments. Tying cinematic seriality, in particular the sequel's combination of a self-contained episodic structure with continuing narrative strands, to television's serial modes set Hollywood's sequel-oriented cinema on a par with a mass medium that was considered to have a much lower cultural status. Such comparisons, in other words, were also rhetorical maneuvers aimed at denigrating both Hollywood's aesthetic credibility and the tastes of the moviegoing public. Above all, film critics identified the sequel trend as threatening the production of creative and original screen stories: "With seven film sequels now on screen and *A Nightmare on Elm Street 5: The Dream Child* opening next week, this season has set the record for unoriginal material," Caryn James complained in 1989, the year she described as "the hysterical culmination of a decade that has included the *Star Wars* trilogy, three Rambos, four Rockys, four Supermans, two Beverly Hills cops."[43]

Although film critics portrayed them as part of the sequelitis problem, sequel audiences were not easy to please. Their long-term loyalty typically centered on enduring characters of the action-adventure genre that were associated with specific (male) stars, but moviegoers were frequently perceived to "carry on a love-hate relationship" with those characters.[44] According to *Die Hard* screenwriter Steven E. de Souza, "They adore these characters and don't want them to change at all.... But then they're disappointed and resentful if the sequel is a knockoff of the original."[45] Despite the irresistible pull of the sequel, this kind of disappointment seemed to be writ large over every follow-up coming out of Hollywood. The sequel supposedly lured its audiences with the promise of repetition and innovation but could not satisfy their expectations. Scholarship on literary sequels ascribes the drawing power of sequelization to "a deep unconscious nostalgia for a past reading pleasure."[46] Terry Castle, for example, points to the contradictory impulse that drives readers' desire for a sequel that is exactly the same, yet different: "Their secret mad hope is to find in the sequel a paradoxical kind of textual doubling—a repetition that does not look like one, the old story in a new and unexpected guise."[47] Applying these ideas to the film sequel, Todd Berliner has proposed that "the almost inescapable failure of sequels results from the fact that, at the same time a sequel calls to mind the charismatic original, it also recalls its absence, fostering a futile, nostalgic desire to reexperience the original aesthetic moment as though it had never happened."[48] The sequel thus cannot "*restore*" its predecessor but "only *remind* us of the original film and continually and conspicuously fail to reinvoke that initial pleasure."[49]

This reading is particularly convincing in the case of *The Godfather Part II* (Francis Ford Coppola, 1974), the one prominent exception among sequels because it is generally considered superior to Francis Ford Coppola's first mafia film and ranked as one of the best movies of the decade. Berliner attributes the sequel's (albeit not immediate) critical success to "an inventive approach to sequelization," explaining that "the film incorporates into its plot the very nostalgia, dissatisfaction, and sense of loss that sequels traditionally generate in their viewers, thereby giving thematic resonance to audiences' inevitable disappointment with movie sequels."[50] *The Godfather Part II* self-reflexively links its own sequel status to the loss of the godfather and the subsequent decline of the Corleone family dramatized through the plot. Looking beyond the *Godfather* example, however, disappointment seems to be the default response of film critics (and scholars) rather than the moviegoing public. To limit sequel reception to a general sense of disappointment (on the part of the critics and scholars) or a feeling of reassurance (on the part of the moviegoing public), however, is to ignore the pleasures of cinematic seriality. Besides enjoying the comfort of the familiar, sequel audiences find satisfaction in the predictability of formulas involving recognizable characters, plots, and themes, and derive pleasure from the ways in which patterns of repetition trigger memories and reward intertextual knowledge.[51] Long-term serial involvement also brings satisfaction as each new installment enriches characters and deepens their narrative worlds over time, providing Rocky Balboa, *Alien*'s Ellen Ripley (Sigourney Weaver), or *Die Hard*'s John McClane (Bruce Willis) with a consistent and consistently elaborated past, present, and future in their respective fictional environments. This is not about the *loss* of an "original," then, but about the *serial pleasures* inherent in the possibilities of repetition, variation, and continuation.

If film critics in the 1970s and 1980s were eager to explore the rise of the sequel and understand its uncanny success with audiences, their think pieces remained within a framework of cultural criticism that shaped the discursive construction of textual hierarchies between a supposedly "original" work of art and the sequel as a derivative, unabashedly commercial, and therefore artistically invariably inferior product. Their overwhelming dismissal of the sequel on aesthetic grounds and on account of its barely disguised commercial imperatives was "strongly invested in the idea of the feature film as a self-contained work of art that has transcended its commodity status."[52] Following this logic, the *work-bound aesthetic* they associated with the self-contained "original" was entirely different from the *serial aesthetic* of the sequel. The traditional three-act structure of movies (beginning, middle, and end) that provided "the pleasure of a well-rounded, gratifyingly concluded plot"[53] was allegedly fast disappearing as Hollywood came to prefer "movies that already have one foot in the sequel."[54] Open-endedness replaced narrative closure as plot threads were left dangling to be picked up in the next installment, and explicit serialization strategies (flashbacks, the repetition of signature lines, recurrent situations, etc.) established an intertextual dependence on one or more earlier films. Movie titles featuring Roman or Arabic numerals were emblematic of this serial aesthetic, demonstrating beyond doubt that the sequel ran counter to the critics' ideal of a standalone "original." While film critics thus condemned the industry's penchant for endlessly repeating a winning formula rather than creating supposedly original works of art, sequels grappled with the creative challenges of perpetual renewal that were usually overlooked in sequelitis criticism.

"IT'S OKAY, I'VE DONE THIS BEFORE":
SELF-REFLEXIVE SEQUELS

Hollywood sequelization during the 1970s and 1980s was unlike the preplanned sequel production that picked up steam in the 1990s. By the turn of the millennium, sequels made up multipart literary adaptations as in the case of the *Lord of the Rings* and *Harry Potter* movies, or they had come to form part of large transmedia franchises revolving around well-known serial characters, in particular comic superheroes (as in the *X-Men* and *Spider-Man* films). From the outset, these franchise movies were designed as a limited long-term investment, with multiple-picture contracts that secured the continued involvement of creative talent in a string of sequels as a means of preventing rising costs (which had so often meant the end of sequel production in the past). Conceptualized as serial installments that eventually added up to a self-contained whole, these movies were hence fundamentally different from the earlier unplanned sequels that followed on the heels of a box-office hit. And they did not yet aim for the carefully orchestrated transgenerational extension that is at the heart of the forever franchise some twenty years later, building on decades-spanning attachments to characters and storyworlds, on notions of legacy and inheritance, and on generational transferal to secure the existence of a long-running franchise into the future.

In the 1970s and 1980s, the sequelization of a standalone movie without built-in sequel options often had a paradoxical effect: if the success of a movie could be traced back to certain elements that distinguished it from other movies within the same genre, these elements were likely to be repeated in the sequel(s) and therefore gradually lost the novelty that had made the first movie a hit.[55] Sequelization required "what was previously novel to become formulaic, for variation to become repetition,"[56] and this imposed powerful limitations on the follow-up. After directing three *Karate Kid* movies in the 1980s, for example, John Avildsen was convinced that film critics had it all wrong when they dismissed sequels as lackluster carbon copies: "It takes extraordinary creativity to make a sequel," he stressed. "It's a real challenge to come up with stories and situations that will hold an audience's attention and be true to the film's original. They are harder to make because you don't have that element of surprise, that element of freshness of an original."[57] The narrative possibilities of the sequel were shaped and restricted by what Hollywood thought audiences expected to see. This usually meant keeping the sequel within the parameters of the first movie in terms of genre and style, as well as continuing a narrative strand from that movie and combining it with a new line of action that put a familiar character in a familiar situation—thus intensifying the repetition according to a serial logic of one-upmanship.

The Karate Kid Part II, for instance, repeats and expands the underdog story of Daniel LaRusso (Ralph Macchio) and his trainer Mr. Miyagi (Pat Morita) from the 1984 surprise hit *The Karate Kid*. Daniel is again threatened by a bully, trains hard following Mr. Miyagi's nontraditional methods, and eventually emerges as the unlikely winner of the climactic fight against his enemy in the final act. This time, however, the movie is set in Okinawa (instead of California), and Daniel has a new love interest. He practices different karate moves (the drum technique replacing the signature crane kick of the first movie), and a higher-stakes fight eclipses the tournament in *The Karate Kid* (it is a life-or-death situation rather than a mere competition). The sequel further expands the underdog formula by revealing details about Mr. Miyagi's mysterious past—a plotline that provides a narrative link between both films while simultaneously developing Daniel's and Mr. Miyagi's respective characters and their mutual friendship. The next sequel, *The Karate Kid Part III* (John Avildsen, 1989), presents yet another take on the formula with a revenge plot motivated by Daniel's winning the tournament in the first movie (which is therefore both pre-text and pretext for this installment), and it tests the friendship between Daniel and Mr. Miyagi. Like its predecessor, this sequel has a self-contained, episodic structure that provides closure, and, at the same time, it constructs and maintains—through recurring characters, situations, and themes as well as ongoing (or reactivated) plotlines—a larger, long-term serial arc (or what Henderson calls "macro-fabula")[58] that provides continuity and justifies the existence of the sequel(s).

The buddy cop movie *Lethal Weapon* (Richard Donner, 1987), to give another example, was followed by three sequels—*Lethal Weapon 2, 3,* and *4* (Richard Donner, 1989, 1992, 1998)—that all revolve around the narratively closed but increasingly spectacular adventures of mismatched LAPD detectives Martin Riggs (Mel Gibson) and Roger Murtaugh (Danny Glover), featuring progressively more explosions, action scenes, and stars in supporting roles. The relationship between Riggs and Murtaugh and their individual situations evolve over the course of the films as the two become buddies, with Murtaugh giving up the idea of retiring from the police force, and Riggs, haunted by his wife's death that made him unpredictable and suicidal, eventually starting a new family. This is "storytelling on the go"[59] in the sense that relatively minor plotlines of a self-contained movie are picked up and continued in order to construct ad hoc a serially progressing narrative framework in which the sequel's new episodic adventure takes place. Over time, the *Lethal Weapon* movies thus build "a cumulative narrative of integration and normalisation."[60]

Some sequels struggled to combine the serial and the episodic to create meaningful narrative continuity. Even though Hollywood made a rough distinction between sequelizable (usually character-driven) and sequel-proof (usually theme-driven) movies,[61] the industry math would still demand follow-ups of the latter kind. After Steven Spielberg's *Jaws* became an instant box-office sensation in 1975, producers Richard D. Zanuck and David Brown quickly realized that the movie called for an "obligatory sequel"[62] and started work on the first of altogether three follow-ups. Yet, by focusing repeatedly on the Brody family and their various encounters with ever bigger and more spectacularly dangerous sharks, the overarching narrative connecting *Jaws* and its three sequels ultimately transforms the successful fish-eats-man formula into a family saga. By the fourth installment, *Jaws: The Revenge* (Joseph Sargent, 1987), which deals with Ellen Brody's (Lorraine Gary) personal vendetta against yet another great white, the course that the fish-eats-man formula had taken was the object of much ridicule. "Why hasn't this family moved to Nebraska?" Caryn James wondered in her review. Two years later, another sequel—*Back to the Future Part II* (Robert Zemeckis, 1989)—mocked *Jaws'* seemingly

Figure 21. Back to the Future Part II (1989) mocks Hollywood's seemingly unlimited potential for self-renewal.

unlimited potential for self-renewal when time-traveling Marty McFly (Michael J. Fox) arrives in the year 2015 to see a movie marquee advertising *Jaws 19* (figure 21). To be sure, *Back to the Future* tried to avoid the sequel label by describing itself as a trilogy instead—a self-contained story in three parts, with a work-bound aesthetic that distinguished its installments from the endlessly generated sequels film critics had come to associate with Hollywood's unstoppable recycling mania. *Back to the Future* thus playfully evokes sequelitis criticism and simultaneously eludes it.

Managing audience expectations for familiarity and renewal as well as competing demands for continuity and closure, and for characters that evolve but never change, the sequel begins to show a high degree of self-awareness in the 1980s, often commenting on its own status as sequel. Lianne McLarty has argued that "this self-consciousness is . . . to be expected from a phenomenon that depends on the existence of a previous text (or texts) for its motivation."[63] Yet the Terminator's "I'll be back," John McClane's amazement at how "the same shit [can] happen to the same guy twice" in *Die Hard 2* (Harlin, 1990), or Martin Riggs's exclamation "We're back, we're bad, you're black, I'm mad" in *Lethal Weapon 2* are more than postmodern gimmicks. As McLarty suggests, they certainly constitute "a playful exchange between producers and consumers in which both sides not only know the rules, but know the other knows they know."⁶⁴ These self-referential cinematic moments, in other words, reward audience memory and intertextual knowledge. At the same time, I argue, they explicitly foreground the process of sequelization on a meta-level, where they generate and reinforce ideas about sequel conventions and the role repetition and variation play in these movies.

This kind of postmodern self-awareness temporarily breaks the narrative flow to take audiences back and forth between individual installments and to refer them both inside and outside the fictional worlds the characters inhabit. Such comments always make sense within the movie (the Terminator does return, McClane has found himself in a similar situation before, and the unstable Riggs and his Black partner Murtaugh take on a new case), but they also serve to establish narrative continuity between movies and to augment our sense of the Terminator, McClane, or Riggs as consistent characters with personal histories.⁶⁵ Broadly speaking, then, these comments signal to audiences that sequels know about their pasts and (potential) futures, and that they will extend existing narratives accordingly. The sequels' self-awareness comes as no surprise. As Frank Kelleter has pointed out, all serial narratives display "an intense tendency toward *self-observation*."⁶⁶ Sequels, too, pay permanent attention to their narrative possibilities of repetition and innovation. During the 1970s and 1980s, they did so largely in step with, and in response to, industrial and popular discourses that either championed the sequel as the ultimate hit film formula or lambasted the trend as evidence of Hollywood's money-grubbing impulses and creative exhaustion. Sequels eventually became products of their own reception, embodying the paradoxical discursive constructions I have outlined.

In the larger scheme of things, the 1970s and 1980s provide a snapshot of the ongoing evolution of the sequel as a specific instance of Hollywood remaking that structures cultural reproduction around repetition, variation, and—most importantly—continuation. Initially, the film industry struggled with the unpredictability of the assumed hit film formula, but by the 1990s, sequelization had become a strategy to expand and multiply popular properties across media and time that largely took place within the optimized framework of the franchise. The industry, in other words, began to imagine preplanned sequels in terms of franchising, and popular film criticism followed suit, gradually abandoning the sequelitis discourse. In 2004, *Variety*'s Todd McCarthy observed: "A funny thing has happened in the movie business: Sequelitis is no longer a disease."[67] *Lord of the Rings*, *Harry Potter*, and *Spider-Man* had served "satisfying seconds" that delivered "the right mix of the fresh and the familiar."[68] In his 2002 *Newsweek* piece "Franchi$e Fever!," John Horn was more critical of the commercial impulse behind the studios' risk-averse strategy of "churning out stories that are so easily identifiable that they can be completely understood by their titles alone . . . rather than focusing on challenging dramas or dark comedies."[69] Even though Horn framed his dislike in familiar terms—lack of creativity, sequels as undisguised commodities, uninspired entertainment that is neither "thrilling" nor "satisfying"—he still conceded that audiences can derive pleasure from follow-ups and pointed out the potential of long-term serialization—in case audiences loved what they saw and actually wanted more. After all, "franchises should be the greatest, most enchanting thing that ever happened to audiences. What could be better than a movie that never ends?"[70]

ENTER THE FOREVER FRANCHISE: SHARED UNIVERSES, TIME, AND NOSTALGIA

Attempts to sustain franchises not only over a limited period of time, but to renew them and extend their life span over many decades and potentially further into the future have created a scenario in which stories might indeed go on forever. One observer saw the 2008 release of *Iron Man* (Jon Favreaux, 2008) as a key moment in terms of where Hollywood was heading. In the movie's post-credits scene, Tony Stark (Robert Downey Jr.) meets Nick Fury (Samuel L. Jackson), who tells him, "Mr. Stark, you've become part of a bigger universe. You just don't know it yet."[71] These words anticipate the expansive serialization strategies that the *Marvel Cinematic Universe* (MCU) has pursued over the past decade, beginning with *Iron Man* and *The Incredible Hulk* (Louis Leterrier) in 2008, and—after Disney bought Marvel Entertainment in 2009—continuing with almost thirty superhero blockbusters, twenty television shows (on ABC, Hulu, Netflix, and Disney+), short films, comic books, and web-series to date.

As Felix Brinker has shown, the MCU relies on a "multi-linear model of serialization," in which "the adventures of superheroes such as Iron Man or Captain America [unfold] across nominally separate film series—but, at the same time, all films ... [are] set within a shared storyworld that allow[s] their plots to overlap and intersect."[72] MCU's narratively interconnected series of superhero movies quickly became a model for other studios in search of endless story possibilities. Disney itself perfected the shared universe approach after it acquired Lucasfilm and the rights to the *Star Wars* franchise for $4 billion in 2012.

George Lucas's prequel trilogy (1999–2005) begins some thirty years before the events of the first film—retrospectively retitled *Star Wars: Episode IV—A New Hope* (George Lucas, 1977)—and focuses on the Jedi training of Anakin Skywalker (Hayden Christensen) and his subsequent fall to the dark side. Given that the prequels were financially successful but generally unloved as follow-ups to the original trilogy, Disney aimed at strategically designing future installments that would "[reinstill] widespread popular excitement for the very idea of *Star Wars*"[73] and bind different generations of viewers to the multipart story and various modular extensions it planned to tell. The intertextuality that links Disney's *Star Wars: Episode VII—The Force Awakens* (J. J. Abrams, 2015) to the *Star Wars* franchise distances it from the prequels and moves it back into the direction of the original trilogy, picking up the story about thirty years after the destruction of the second Death Star by the rebel alliance in *Star Wars: Episode VI—Return of the Jedi* (Richard Marquand, 1983).

If Marvel's shared superhero universe depends on a rapidly expanding and increasingly complex intertextual network, in which every new installment and transmedial iteration is becoming "required viewing" for audiences, Disney opted for a more streamlined serial logic when it brought *Star Wars* back in 2015. The release schedule included the new trilogy as well as spin-offs and standalone movies that are not directly connected to the other movies or earlier releases, but exist in the same fictional world and take place on the same timeline. For *Star Wars*, the shared universe approach means "an arguably infinite well of adaptable stories."[74] In a *Wired* piece, Adam Rogers predicted that "you won't live to see the final *Star Wars* movie," if Disney were to successfully exploit the idea and produce an "infinite series," with "a new *Star Wars* movie every year for as long as people will buy tickets."⁷⁵ The concept of the shared universe is still new to Hollywood, as Rogers points out: "Marvel prototyped the process; Lucasfilm is trying to industrialize it."⁷⁶ It has caught on and obviously also clicked with directors Ridley Scott and Denis Villeneuve, who, as mentioned, have both expressed interest in making another *Blade Runner* movie that does not directly continue Rick Deckard's story but is set in the same universe of *Blade Runner* and *Blade Runner 2049*.

In contrast to the MCU, where the interconnectivity between movies featuring individual superheroes, crossover movies (in which they team up), television shows, and comics, demands a high degree of audience engagement and has become almost impenetrable for casual viewers or outsiders, *Star Wars* follows a more inclusive storytelling approach with its shared universe. Central to the *Star Wars* model are a sense of narrative continuity across individual installments, the assurance of a persistent storyworld, and linear seriality that arranges events along a consistent, progressing diegetic timeline, which distinguish it from MCU's serial spread and sprawl with parallel universes and alternate timelines. The emotional investment in familiar *Star Wars* characters and the fictional world they inhabit can thus be transferred over time, from one generation of viewers to the next. This is how sentimental attachments and nostalgic longing become the fuel of the forever franchise, propelling it ahead into the future. The passage of time and a nostalgic gaze at the past are consequently at the center of *Star Wars*' efforts to become a forever franchise.

In the MCU (and the comic books it is based on), time is effectively suspended because the superhero's defeat of the latest threat always restores the status quo. "Comics universes," Rogers notes, "really only expand along the y- or z-axes . . .—more characters or more locales. Robert Downey Jr. can play Iron Man for only so long. If you want to keep making Marvel movies, you're going to need a new Iron Man or a new universe."⁷⁷ Visual effects, in particular postproduction techniques of digital de-aging, have solved some narrative problems by erasing time from the faces of actors whose characters travel in time or are shown in flashbacks.⁷⁸ But they all remain essentially unchanging serial figures, who proliferate across different media and whose "flatness and iconicity" go hand in hand with "recognizable images, . . . plots, phrases, and accessories that, once established, can be rearranged, reinterpreted, recombined, and invested with new significance."[79] Even if the MCU has a complex diegetic chronology, with time travel and some characters who do actually age (Peter Parker/Spider-Man graduates from high school and college, for example), timelines are neither consistent nor linear. They slide as needed to regularly update the eternal present of the superheroes and let them stay forever young. The passage of time, in other words, does not really matter.

The serial unfolding of *Star Wars* over many decades is different in this regard. Time passes in these movies and that has consequences: "Han Solo, Princess Leia, Luke Skywalker, and the legacy actors playing them can grow from callow youth to wise old age and then pass the torch.... The universe can extend for 10,000 years forward and back from the moment Luke blows up the first Death Star."[80] Because actors Harrison Ford, Carrie Fisher (who passed in 2016), and Mark Hamill reprised their roles and returned as visibly aged (yet still recognizable and comfortably familiar) characters in *The Force Awakens*, they bridged the long gap between the original *Star Wars* trilogy (1977–1983) and Disney's sequel trilogy (2015–2019), and ultimately merged diegetic and extra-diegetic time,[81] bringing the fictional characters, actors, and audiences into one and the same temporal space. The passage of time in these sequels not only anchors all *Star Wars* movies in the fictional time and space of the galaxy far, far away, it also serves to "synchronise the amount of time which has passed in our own lives with that of the characters"[82]—and actors.

Long-running franchises that acknowledge the passage of time through the return of aged characters and actors—among them *The Force Awakens*, *Terminator: Genisys* (Alan Taylor, 2015), *Creed* (Ryan Coogler, 2015), *Jurassic World* (Colin Trevorrow, 2015), *Blade Runner 2049* and *Ghostbusters: Afterlife* (Jason Reitman, 2021), to name just a few—historicize the trajectory from *then* to *now*. They foreground technological, political, and cultural continuity and change, operate as catalysts for individual and collective memories as they link audiences to a shared mediated past, and encourage generational identification with popular media texts. In these cases, nostalgia tends to be strategically inscribed into the franchises as a transgenerational selling point, so *the forever franchise is also always a nostalgia franchise*.[83] For the film industry, nostalgia ensures the long-term profitability of *Star Wars* and other decades-spanning franchises by constantly renewing the economic and cultural value of past products as they simultaneously drive future productions. Hollywood exploits its past and promotes it as culturally relevant and shareable across generations. For audiences, the particular appeal of nostalgia might not necessarily lie in the yearning for an idealized past and the reactionary tendencies and escapism that are commonly associated with it.[84] Research suggests that nostalgia can help construct and maintain a coherent, consistent sense of identity in times of technological, social, and political change and function as a slowing mechanism that affects how we experience time.[85]

If this is so, nostalgia franchises seem to have a stabilizing function for a broad spectrum of the audience. Nostalgia is not only targeted at older viewers who have aged along with the franchise. It may also be evoked by association, that is, regardless of whether or not audiences have actually experienced the past that is referred to. Sentimental attachments to specific media texts, characters, and fictional worlds can be transmitted across generations through "nostalgia-by-proxy."[86] This is central to the nostalgic return of *Star Wars*. On the level of narrative, *The Force Awakens* heavily relies "on *A New Hope* for its structure, themes, and even set pieces,"[87] while the sequel form provides the chance to bring back beloved characters (and actors) from the first movies that were absent in the prequels. *The Force Awakens* further shows allegiance to the franchise beginnings through a nostalgic visual style and a conspicuous retro-sensibility. These narrative and aesthetic maneuvers mobilize particular *Star Wars* codes and generate a "constant thrill of recognition"[88] that ultimately operates as a catalyst for memories and sentimental identification with the franchise and its past. *The Force Awakens* is deeply invested in creating this kind of nostalgia as an inclusive experience that appeals to audiences across generations by evoking the enduring relevance of *Star Wars* as a pop-cultural phenomenon and simultaneously reinforcing this status for the sake of future installments.

It is important to note that the involvement of original cast members after such a long time directly impacts the reproduction logics of sequels that make up forever franchises. On the one hand, the time gap between the films cannot simply be ignored, but must be accounted for in the plot in order to answer to the sequel's imperative of narrative continuity. This means that until the digital de-aging of actors in post-production becomes standard in Hollywood and urgent moral and philosophical questions

Figure 22. Star Wars: The Force Awakens (2015) is nostalgic about the franchise past.

surrounding the digital resurrection of deceased actors are eventually resolved,[89] the actual, biological aging of an actor like Harrison Ford also dictates corresponding continuities for his iconic roles in the *Star Wars, Blade Runner,* and *Indiana Jones* movies. On the other hand, the passage of time requires intertextual memory prompts: the past must be recalled in the present. Even sequels that are released in relatively quick succession tend to refer back to preceding movies, for example, in the form of flashbacks or through the repetition of plot and aesthetic elements that serve as orientational beacons and convey the impression of a linear temporal progression between one movie and the next. With longer gaps between installments, however, such connections are intensified and nostalgically charged.

By bundling moments of narrative and aesthetic recognition, *The Force Awakens* specifically evokes intertextual and extratextual memories of the franchise past and stresses how it intersects with the audiences' lived experiences. When Han Solo and Chewbacca (Peter Mayhew) finally find their long-lost spaceship in *The Force Awakens*, they board the *Millennium Falcon*, and, after taking a sentimental look around, Han Solo says, "Chewie . . . we're home" (figure 22). The sentence marks the characters' first on-screen appearance in the movie and evokes a nostalgic sense of homecoming that extends beyond the scene to include audiences. Han Solo and Chewbacca then bump into Rey (Daisy Ridley) and Finn (John Boyega), who had stolen the spaceship on a junkyard to escape from the planet Jakku. Rey recognizes Han Solo and shouts in amazement: "This is the Millennium Falcon? You're Han Solo?!" Her exclamation establishes both the spaceship and Solo as the stuff of legends, as famous in the *Star Wars* universe as they are in the real world. In this way, Rey stands in for *Star Wars* fans, who finally get to see their childhood heroes (again), as well as for a younger generation of fans, who can now, at long last, partake in a new chapter of the ongoing Skywalker Saga. *The Force Awakens* thus inscribes *Star Wars* reception and fandom into the narrative continuity, thereby foregrounding the cultural legacy of the franchise through a new generational voice that connects past and present.

Because persistent storytelling means to acknowledge the passage of diegetic and extra-diegetic time (including the aging of popular characters and actors), the ongoing cultural reproduction that forever franchises strive for through future-oriented narrative continuity tends to be embedded in plots of generational succession that are structured around nostalgic returns and the passing of the torch from withering heroes to their younger successors. Consequently, I argue, generational renewal becomes the storytelling engine of the forever franchise, often aligning cultural reproduction with biological reproduction and the heteronormative ideology of *reproductive futurism* (to borrow queer theorist Lee Edelman's term).[90] The linear, forward-moving temporalities of the forever franchise hence are often steeped in nostalgia for the past *and* seem to prescribe an investment in an idea of legacy that deserves critical attention.

REPRODUCTION LOGICS, LINEAR TIME, AND ENDLESSLY REPETITIVE FUTURES

Blade Runner 2049 is a belated sequel that depends on the interworking of repetition and continuation, on cultural familiarity, and a nostalgic longing for the past. As mentioned earlier, it is one among recent sequels that rely on the return of well-known characters (and actors) as well as on the repetition of narrative and aesthetic codes that foreground the movie's past and bind audiences to overarching, ongoing stories. Film critic Matt Singer has proposed the term *legacyquel* to describe such movies.[91] The notion of legacy contains the promise of endlessly renewable franchises (or: forever franchises), but it also accommodates the passage of time between one film and the next through the theme of generational succession. This theme, I argue, is intricately linked to the sequel form and its linear understanding of time. In the case of *Blade Runner 2049*, the sequel's formal characteristic of linear time (or: "straight time")[92] paves the way for the unfolding of the story across generations. The ideology of straight time scripts heteronormative timelines and produces what Elizabeth Freeman has called "chrononormativity"[93]—a normativity that is defined by a reproductive, generational, and unerringly future-oriented relation to time. However, as we will see, the kinship relation between familiar and new characters that the sequel suggests overrides key assumptions of the first *Blade Runner* movie. To be sure, reproduction is a central concept in both movies. Yet, whereas *Blade Runner* is concerned with the artificial production and reproduction of humans and memories and the question of what ultimately distinguishes man from machine, *Blade Runner 2049* complicates the understanding of reproduction both through the sequel form *and* the theme of biological reproduction. As a result, I argue, the movie ultimately subscribes to a politics of reproductive futurism.[94]

The first *Blade Runner* is set in rainy Los Angeles in 2019, where police officer Rick Deckard (Harrison Ford) is tasked with tracking down and eliminating four replicants. These Nexus-6 models have come to Earth from the off-world colonies to force their "creator" and CEO of the Tyrell Corporation, Eldon Tyrell (Joe Turkel), to extend their preprogrammed lifespan of four years. Deckard's investigation leads him to Rachael (Sean Young), a new prototype with implanted memories. Rachael thinks she is human and only becomes aware of her own status as a replicant in the course of the movie. As Deckard kills the renegade replicants one by one, but ultimately escapes with Rachael, the movie raises ethical questions about memory, identity, and what it means to be human. In the sequel, set in the year 2049, LAPD police officer K (Ryan Gosling) tracks down and kills Nexus-8 replicants. He himself is a model of the newer, more obedient Nexus-9 series, which now live together with humans on Earth, but are not recognized as equals. When K comes across a box of mortal remains, a serial number engraved on the bones reveals that they are Rachael's and that she died during childbirth. Thus begins the search for the unlikely replicant offspring. K's mission is to kill it in order to prevent a replicant uprising and possible war. CEO Niander Wallace (Jared Leto), who took over the production of replicants after the bankruptcy of the Tyrell Corporation, senses the economic potential of such a child and sends his assistant Luv (Sylvia Hoeks) to find it. As K follows the leads that eventually bring him face to face with Deckard (Harrison Ford), the child's father, he begins to question his own (implanted) childhood memories and identity. However, as it turns out, he is not Rachael and Deckard's child, but the memory engineer Dr. Ana Stelline (Carla Juri). The film ends with the family reunion of father and daughter.

The long gap of thirty-five years between the two movies and the fact that *Blade Runner 2049* was conceived as a sequel (not a remake) are significant because they determine the repetition-based continuation of the story—with recurring characters, a fixed chronological relationship to the previous film, and narrative continuity. As a sequel, *Blade Runner 2049* continues the story of *Blade Runner* but at the same time reproduces and intensifies what has already happened and what audiences have already seen: the unmistakable cityscape of the future, science fiction technology from flying cars to K's holographic companion Joi (Ana de Armas), the film noir-style detective story, suspenseful chases and action scenes. To a certain extent, this is inscribed in the DNA of the sequel form, which, despite the development of plotlines, is primarily concerned with the repetition and amplification of familiar elements. The passage of time between one film and the next—again on both the diegetic and extra-diegetic level to accommodate the return of actor Harrison Ford as a visibly aged and disheveled Rick Deckard—pave the way for the story to unfold across generational lines and establish the sequel's temporal logic in terms of a reproductive futurism.

Coined by queer theorist Lee Edelman, reproductive futurism describes how the institutions of family, heterosexuality, and biological reproduction create heteronormative temporalities that affirm the existing social order and preserve it for the future.[95] In this context, any form of queerness is perceived as a threat to the status quo, as incompatible with the general consensus. Reproductive futurism is central to political discourses and informs narrative traditions that are "committed to development and unfolding, to the logics of evolution and descent, of emergence, of reproduction, of hereditary transmission, of generation and tradition, of improvement and multiplication, of (life's) purpose, of living on or surviving,"[96] and generally foreground the figure of the child. Accordingly, the child itself embodies a logic of repetition that fixes social order and identities for the future. Following Rebekah Sheldon, "The figure of the child stands in for a futurity that strips the future of everything but repetition and yet insists that repetition is progress."[97] The sequel's formal characteristic of linear temporal progression introduces a possible future into the *Blade Runner* story, which presents a radical departure from the dark and gloomy fictional world of the first film that so clearly had *no future*. Against all climate calamities and bleak end-time scenarios, *Blade Runner 2049* is committed to the future through the central role of Rachael and Deckard's child—a future that propagates heteronormative ideas of family and procreation.

This has implications for the development of the themes from the first movie and retrospectively offers new, innocuous readings of what once happened in *Blade Runner*. At a time when a man who publicly boasted about sexually harassing women was elected to the White House and the abuse scandal around film producer Harvey Weinstein sparked the #MeToo movement, *Blade Runner 2049* reinterprets an uncomfortable *Blade Runner* scene with Rachael and Deckard—a rape scene rather than a love scene. They are both at Deckard's place. He tries to kiss her, but she recoils and tries to flee from the apartment. Deckard follows Rachael and angrily slams the apartment door with his fist, grabs her and pushes her against a window. He then urges her to say "Kiss me" until Rachael finally complies and, as the scene fades to black, transforms from cool *femme fatale* into Deckard's lover. In view of their child, Deckard's physical violence is rendered inconsequential, the past is reframed, and the scene is turned into a romantic encounter. At some point in the sequel, Deckard is even told that Rachael was specifically designed so that he would fall in love with her and conceive a child. In *Blade Runner 2049*, the miracle child thus dispels any doubts about Rachael's consent and retroactively negates her agency.

Replicants had nothing to do with processes of biological reproduction in the first *Blade Runner* movie and were concerned solely with their own survival beyond the programmed expiration date. In the sequel, Rachael has become a mythical symbol through the birth of her baby. When she first appears in the movie, Rachael is frozen in time: unaged since the first movie, she stands opposite Deckard, thereby foregrounding how old *he* has become (figure 23). Young and old are juxtaposed, highlighting the trajectory from then to now on the level of plot. While Harrison Ford reprises his role as Deckard, Sean Young does not star in the sequel. What

Figure 23. Blade Runner 2049 (2017) juxtaposes old and young, original and copy.

we see is a fully digitally made unaged version of herself. The British visual effects studio Moving Picture Company (MPC) scanned the form of the actor's skull to make a digital model of Rachael's head, which was then combined with footage and images of Young from the 1980s. The digital head was later grafted onto stand-in actor Loren Peta and another actor was hired to re-create Young's voice.[98] In *Blade Runner 2049*, Rachael's resurrection is short-lived, however. Wallace confronts the captured Deckard with this clone of Rachael to get information about the whereabouts of the replicant child. But Deckard is confused and seems to realize that resurrecting the past in the present is impossible. "Her eyes were green," he tells Wallace, imposing a death sentence on Rachael (Luv immediately executes her). Rachael is already dead at the beginning of *Blade Runner 2049*, yet she must die again. She is simultaneously decoupled from the story and absolutely necessary for its development. For a film that apparently does not want to be considered a copy of its original, although it is deeply indebted to it, the treatment of the artificial woman and mother Rachael raises complex questions regarding the reproduction logic of *Blade Runner 2049*, not least because of the figure of the child that is so central to it.

Rachael's child is the first of a new species of artificial humans, a miracle of posthuman evolution, on which a group of replicant activists living underground in the bleak world of *Blade Runner 2049* project their hopes for a better future, and that gives rise to the possibility of a revolution (a subplot that is not further pursued). For, according to this logic, it is no longer only memories and emotions that make replicants human. Rather, it is their ability to reproduce biologically. K's romantic relationship with the holographic Joi, who, far removed from any reality in this fictional world, enacts the illusion of a heterosexual partnership with archaic gender roles for him (appearing as submissive 1950s-style housewife, who serves K dinner to the sounds of Frank Sinatra, and as erotic playmate) remains not sex- but childless. Yet even for K, it is natural birth that constitutes the existence of a soul and therefore signals that replicants could be equal to humans. Wallace, meanwhile, hoping for good business from biological reproduction, fetishizes the female womb of his creations. There is a scene in which he takes one look at the naked body of a newly fabricated female replicant and then stabs her in the abdomen with a knife because she is infertile and he, as god-like maker, has not yet achieved his goal with her. As Shama Rangwala aptly notes, this scene emphasizes "the desired (and, frankly, transphobic) future based on reproduction in the womb"[99] to which *Blade Runner 2049* is committed. In the desolate *Blade Runner* world, which already seemed doomed in the first movie and in which, three decades later, neither plants nor animals thrive, children are suddenly omnipresent through the theme of reproduction—and with them the promise of a future in which the present constantly reproduces itself. Protein farms breed maggots as the basis for the food supply on Earth, while the dream of a better existence in the off-world colonies seems to be over in the sequel. In this context, the figure of the child represents continuity through generationality and is typical for the shift in focus that Sheldon has identified in narratives of the Anthropocene: "from the child in need of salvation to the child who saves."[100]

K's search for clues unearths various memory objects that are directly linked to the mysterious replicant child: a baby sock, a photograph of a woman holding a newborn, and a wooden toy with a birth date engraved on it. These objects trigger K's own childhood memories and, believing himself to be Rachael and Deckard's son, lead him to an orphanage located in the middle of an endless garbage dump, where a few hundred shaven-headed, neglected children sort scrap metal. As it later turns out, however, K did not experience the childhood he recalls. They are memory implants based on the experiences of Dr. Ana Stelline, who was hidden in the orphanage as a child and grew up there undetected and unaware of her real identity. Isolated from the outside world, Ana now designs memories as a memory maker for Wallace's industrially produced replicants. When K visits her during his investigation, Ana is working on a memory of a birthday party, depicting in great detail children crowding expectantly around a table, watching as the birthday girl blows out the candles on the cake. "If you have authentic memories, you have real human responses," she tells K about the process, which is primarily used to manage the replicants and bring a stable product on the market. And yet the memories Ana creates have nothing to do with the world of *Blade Runner 2049*. Like Rachael and Joi, Ana ultimately serves to provide anachronistic notions of social coexistence that revolve around family, heterosexuality, and reproduction for the future. Taken together, the retroactive reinterpretation of the past (in the case of Rachael), the digital simulation of a heteronormative relationship (Joi), and prosthetic memories that once again focus on the figure of the child (Ana) serve to normalize and at the same time underscore the sequel's nostalgic positioning with respect to *Blade Runner* and to familiar gender scripts.

What *Blade Runner 2049* does, in the end, is present us with an endlessly repetitive future. We see it in the ways the sequel foregrounds the theme of reproductive futurism; and we see it when the sequel integrates anachronistic images of a mythic past. The birthday party, complete with cake and candles, is just one example. Ana also designs memories of a forest, and the contrast between the lush green of her trees and the only other tree in the movie—a propped-up dead tree in a devastated landscape under which K finds the box with Rachael's bones—could not be more striking. In other scenes, set in the radioactive ruins of an abandoned, orange-tinged Las Vegas, Elvis Presley, Marilyn Monroe, and Frank Sinatra appear as holograms—as glitchy simulations of what once was real. The presence of these twentieth-century pop culture icons carries with it a nostalgic longing for the past they represent. Invested as it is in the idea of a family legacy, the sequel thus creates a backward-looking, almost reactionary, science fiction story in which the future recedes into the distance so that the past can continue forever. The movie resonates with the current political and cultural climate in the United States that is marked by debates about climate change action, women's reproductive rights, and a diversity of lifestyles, value systems, and experiences. *Blade Runner 2049*'s response is conservative, "calling for," as Rangwala puts it, "a return to an imagined past of whiteness and traditional gender norms."[101] This makes the sequel a fascinating cultural artifact for studying cultural repetition and continuation, for probing the persistence and malleability of dominant themes and ideologies and the recurrent urge to process them in familiar scenarios.

Meanwhile, discussions about another *Blade Runner* sequel have shifted: Amazon Studios is currently developing the live-action series *Blade Runner 2099* as a follow-up to *Blade Runner 2049*. Ridley Scott, who is involved as an executive producer and might direct the series, first announced that a pilot had been written in November 2021 and plans were confirmed in February 2022.[102] Scott is also developing an *Alien* television series for FX with *Fargo* showrunner Noah Hawley. At the Television Critics Association press tour in 2022, FX chief John Landgraf described the new show as an "extension and reinvention of the franchise" without familiar characters that will take place on Earth and "think forward about the future of the planet in terms of the environment."[103] There is also a new standalone *Alien* movie in the works, to be directed by Fede Alvarez.[104] It is set in the same shared universe as the other *Alien* movies and the television series that is underway. Furthermore, Amazon Studios released the prequel series *The Lord of the Rings: Rings of Power* on Prime Video in September 2022. The move to television and streaming platforms has become a popular strategy when working with recognizable properties and franchise material: to manage financial risks, but also because it allows more time for worldbuilding, character development, and slow-paced storytelling than big-budget blockbusters.

Disney, too, already adapted its shared universe approach after *Solo: A Star Wars Story* (Ron Howard, 2018), the second movie of the anthology series that had started with *Rogue One* (Gareth Edward, 2016) and was supposed to be released in the gaps between the sequel trilogy, disappointed at the box office. The company shelved its other planned standalone movie projects in order to contain an onset of franchise fatigue and focused on the production of spin-off television series set around the time of the original trilogy for the streaming platform Disney+ instead. In May

2022, Lucasfilm president Kathleen Kennedy laid out a "roadmap" for the *Star Wars* franchise that contains a growing list of live-action spin-off series on Disney+, including *The Mandalorian, The Book of Boba Fett, Obi-Wan Kenobi, Andor,* and *Ahsoka,* built around "different places on the timeline to look at, because there is this persistent story of *Star Wars,*" and movies that push the franchise further beyond "the sequel era" into the future.[105] Kennedy stressed that with the kind of persistent storytelling Lucasfilm is now pursuing, *Star Wars* "could go on forever, to be perfectly honest. If we have good storytellers, it will go on forever."[106]

The combination of shared universe and persistent (if modular) storytelling along a consistent timeline is where Hollywood remaking seems to be heading. If the strategy takes Hollywood's slowly changing representational regimes of race and gender into account, it promises to be decidedly less risky for studios with an eye on the bottom line than film remakes and reboots. These might alienate viewers, especially in the case of long-running franchises that have spun their stories over many decades and whose characters audiences have come to know and love. In contrast to film remakes that generally update, revise, and reinterpret older movies or reboots that restart dormant, creatively exhausted, or failed franchises with radically redesigned characters and storylines and a promise of narrative, aesthetic, and technological novelty, the current approach to sustaining long-running franchises favors *continuity* as it builds on cultural memory, nostalgic longings, and the role movies and other media play for processes of generational identity formations and for maintaining a coherent sense of self across different life stages. The franchise past remains relevant and adhering to it—through intertextual memory, narrative and aesthetic codes, the return of legacy characters and actors, and a persistent timeline that all foreground a pervasive sense of continuity—not only ensures the future of the franchise but also speaks to a growing need for stable memories and meanings that is increasingly emphasized in the practice of Hollywood remaking. Forever franchises, it seems, will always also be nostalgia franchises that revel in the past and mobilize emotional bonds. But will the futures such franchises envision be endlessly repetitive futures? If nostalgia franchises depend on maintaining narrative continuity in order to offer intertextual pleasures, to facilitate the immersion in an ongoing, already familiar story and fictional world, to fully exhaust the possibilities of serial one-upmanship, and to appeal to multiple generations of viewers, the question remains whether the need to preserve memories and sentimental attachments leaves enough room to process social, cultural, and political change and to meaningfully negotiate progressive and conservative ideologies.

Conclusion

REBOOTING THE PAST

Film remakes, series, sequels, prequels, crossovers, and spin-offs all belong to the practice of Hollywood remaking. They are based on movies that are already there, movies that they repeat, continue, revise and expand to generate new economic and cultural value, new meanings, and new memories. In the process, they present opportunities for rereading the older movies and for understanding them not as the self-contained texts they once were (or: pretended to be), but as forming part of larger, *ongoing* narratives about recurrent characters and their fictional worlds as well as about culture and the nation at large. By reactivating the past in this manner, Hollywood remaking always produces *serial* texts. With regard to film remakes, the importance of the past and past renditions of the same story is foregrounded through repetition and may seem more obvious than their serial existence, which is largely (but, as I have shown, surely not exclusively) constituted at one remove from the narrative and can best be understood in terms of second-order serialization. Here, continuation happens first and foremost outside of the filmic texts and their diegetic worlds. As film remakes present a variation on the same old plot and theme, they maintain the cultural currency of popular stories, while differences distinctly mark each iteration as a product of its own time and consequently highlight the social, economic, technological, and aesthetic transformations the United States and Hollywood cinema have undergone from one version to the next. For series and sequels, in contrast, future-oriented seriality may seem a more obvious characteristic than their investment in the past. They generally rely on serial memory, of course, requiring audiences to recall narrative events and returning characters or to recognize James Bond as James Bond regardless of the actor who portrays the serial figure. Yet rebooting the past has become part and parcel of these more explicitly serialized remaking formats, too. Think of the recent comebacks of *Star Wars*, *Rocky*, *Terminator*, and *Jurassic Park* with belated sequels that are firmly grounded in the franchise past and invested in an idea of legacy that extends that past into the present and makes it productive for the future.

Strictly speaking, Hollywood remaking always reboots the past, as it displays the difference between then and now. As explored in chapter 3, this was already the case with the talker remakes of the 1930s that helped construct the silent era against the talkies' sound film present. And it is still true for the forever franchise in the new millennium that I discussed in chapter 6. Here, rebooting the past specifically describes how franchises summon their own past and employ nostalgia as a method of renewal. Early definitions understood the reboot as a new critical category that is distinct from the remake, series, and sequel. According to William Proctor, *Batman Begins* (Christopher Nolan, 2005) and *Casino Royale* (Martin Campbell, 2006) were exemplary of the reboot that "wipes the slate clean" as it "'restarts' a series of films that seek to disavow and render inert its predecessor's validity."[1] I argue that the reboot and the idea of rebooting have already lost this specificity in industrial and critical discourses (and maybe never had it in the first place). The notion of the "reboot" contradicts the imperative of "industrial intertextuality" (a term Daniel Herbert introduced to describe how media franchises today are strategically designed to build ever-deeper referential connections to previously existing cultural texts)[2] and, consequently, has changed course to capitalize on nostalgically recalling the past and on sustaining linear narrative progression. The more recent "reboots," in short, operate quite differently from the movies that Proctor describes. *Star Wars: The Force Awakens* (J. J. Abrams, 2015), *Terminator: Genisys* (Alan Taylor, 2015), *Creed* (Ryan Coogler, 2015), and *Jurassic World* (Colin Trevorrow, 2015), for instance, still qualify as reboots in commercial and cultural terms because they attempt to re-instill interest in an already existing property and launch a string of new movies based on that property. However, they are not exactly "striv[ing] to disconnect [themselves], in a spatio-temporal sense, from the earlier incarnation in a quest for autonomy," nor do they want "to begin a franchise anew from the ashes of an old or failed property."[3] On the contrary, these nostalgia-driven reboots preserve and showcase their connections to the franchise past through calculated repetitions and sequelization strategies that maintain long-term continuity and build on the familiarity of characters and storyworlds. They are designed to mobilize memories and sentimental attachments that are not confined to the movies but reach beyond their borders to include memories of particular moments in time that become associated with the movies, media technologies, and the viewers' biographical circumstances. Mobilizing this whole array of memories bestows value on the new releases and simultaneously produces their transgenerational appeal. For these kinds of reboots, to put it in a nutshell, *the past matters* and they are eager to bring it back into the present, to make the old contemporaneous with the new.

This raises interesting issues, many of which I have tackled in this book. In this conclusion, I want to return to the question of how Hollywood remaking operates with regard to the past and how rebooting the past plays out in contemporary cinema. First, I will situate the current trend to reboot the past within the larger history of Hollywood remaking to emphasize once more that this is a dynamic practice of cultural reproduction. Hollywood remaking continues to evolve, seemingly at an ever-quicker pace that is in step with the acceleration of technological, social, cultural, economic, and political change that defines our times. Yet the basic principles of repetition and variation always remain the same. Amidst a conceptual crisis of the film remake proper and Hollywood's growing preference for other remaking formats like the crossover, spin-off, and prequel in the new millennium, "rebooting" initially emerges as a fancy term for "remaking." I argue that "reboot" is, in fact, not a new remaking category but should rather be considered as a *discursive intervention* seeking to distinguish new movies from earlier renditions by emphasizing *novelty* over repetition or continuation. However, once memory and nostalgia enter the "reboot" equation, the concept itself begins to change: the reboot preserves and upholds the past instead of overwriting and reconfiguring it.

PLUS ÇA CHANGE: REMAKING TRENDS IN THE NEW MILLENNIUM

Around the turn of the millennium, a reorientation of Hollywood remaking began to take foothold in the US film industry. A number of circumstances favored new storytelling approaches, including the unprecedented global success and profitability of carefully crafted multipart franchises like *Lord of the Rings* and *Harry Potter* and the burgeoning superhero trend with the *X-Men* and *Spider-Man* movies. At the same time, the bubbling discontent with the film remake as a tried-and-proven way of bringing old material back onto the big screen reached the boiling point when Gus Van Sant's shot-by-shot remake of Alfred Hitchcock's genre-defining horror movie *Psycho* (1960) was released in 1998. As I discussed in chapter 1, Van Sant's remake was met with frustration and outrage. *Psycho* turned into an object lesson of what could or could not be done with the cinematic past and its supposedly timeless classics, raising theoretical questions about the shifting temporalities of cinema and spectatorship and ultimately the meanings and cultural functions of the film remake in times when old movies form part of the cultural imagination and are readily available for (repeat) viewing. Why remake them at all? A few years later, in 2001, Tim Burton's failed "re-imagining" of the iconic *Planet of the Apes* (Franklin Schaffner, 1968) exacerbated the crisis of the film remake, whose production dropped to an all-time low in the new millennium.

Between 2000 and 2021, film remakes make up only 2 percent on average of total US film production, as compared to an average of 11 percent in the 1930s, and they constitute only 32 percent of all remaking formats in that time period (sequels: 51%), as compared to an average of 71 percent in the 1930s.[4] Instead of the film remake, other remaking formats have started to thrive in Hollywood: crossovers, spin-offs, and prequels. These movies creatively engage with an already existing franchise in ways that are clearly distinct from either the repetition-based update of the remake or the forward-moving continuation that drives the sequel. Even though crossovers, spin-offs, and prequels still rely on repetition and variation (like all remaking formats), they derive their novelty from expanding diegetic time and space or from providing new perspectives on familiar characters and events. Certainly, the numbers for movies falling within

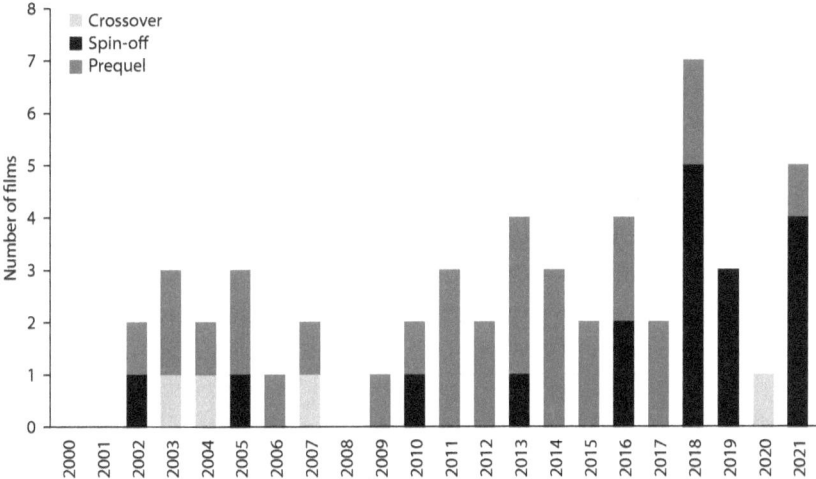

Figure 24. Production of crossovers, spin-offs, and prequels, 1998–2021. *Source*: Hollywood Remaking dataset.

these categories were remarkably low during the period from 1998 to 2021 (figure 24). Overall, film remakes still surpass the combined total of crossovers, spin-offs, and prequels combined, with the exception of 2018, which saw an equal number of releases (seven movies) on both fronts. Ultimately, the new remaking formats never account for more than 1 percent of US film production during these years, but there are significantly more crossovers, spin-offs, and prequels than at any other time in the history of Hollywood remaking.

In the past, one could find the occasional crossover with monsters from Universal's horror movies, such as *Frankenstein Meets the Wolfman* (Roy William Neill, 1943) and a series of Abbot and Costello crossover movies from the late 1940s and early 1950s, in which the comedy duo meet Frankenstein, the Invisible Man, and the Mummy, as well as other creatures from the studio's stable.[5] Or one would come across the genre-bending low-budget western horror movies *Billy the Kid Versus Dracula* (William Beaudine, 1966) and *Jesse James Meets Frankenstein's Daughter* (William Beaudine, 1966), which were released as a double-feature in 1966. Spin-offs were almost nonexistent in the past, with *Supergirl* (Jeannot Szwarc, 1984), about Superman's super-powered cousin, being an early example of this remaking format in Hollywood cinema. In comparison, prequels were more frequent: *Another Day in the Forest* (Michael Gordon, 1948), based on Lillian Hellman's Broadway play of the same title, was released after the adaptation of Hellman's play *Three Little Foxes* (William Wyler, 1941) but is concerned with the early years of the dysfunctional Southern Hubbard family around which both movies revolve; the sports drama *Go Man Go* (James Wong Howe, 1954) serves as a prequel of sorts to *The Harlem Globetrotters* (Phil Brown/Will Jason, 1954) about the all-Black American basketball team; and *Nevada Smith* (Henry Hathaway, 1966) as well as *Butch and Sundance: The Early Days* (Richard Lester, 1979) are westerns that provide the background for characters in *The Carpetbaggers* (Edward Dmytryk, 1964) and *Butch Cassidy and the Sundance Kid* (George Roy Hill, 1969), respectively.

In the new millennium, there are already more movies that qualify as crossovers, spin-offs, and prequels than in the entire twentieth century. Prequels emerge as the most regular of these remaking formats: a total of thirty-two such movies were released between 1998 and 2021 and they are relatively evenly distributed over the entire time period. Spin-offs take second place with eighteen movies, with a sharp increase since 2016. Fourteen of the eighteen spin-off movies were released between 2016 and 2021 alone. Crossovers come in last with only four movies. As indicated above, the *crossover* merges different, already-existing fictional worlds so that characters from separate franchises meet in a new context. For example, *Alien vs. Predator* (Paul W. S. Anderson, 2004) pits two extraterrestrial species—the Xenomorphs of the *Alien* franchise and the Yautja of the *Predator* series—against each other in a shared cinematic universe, and *Jason vs. Freddy* (Ronny Yu, 2003) does the same with serial killers Jason Vorhees of the *Friday the 13th* franchise and *Nightmare on Elm Street*'s Freddy Krueger. Both crossovers received mostly negative reviews, but they were box-office successes: *Alien vs. Predator* is the highest-grossing of six *Predator* films and ranks third in the *Alien* franchise behind *Prometheus* (Ridley Scott, 2012) and *Aliens* (James Cameron, 1986), whereas *Freddy vs. Jason* ranks highest among both the twelve *Friday the 13th* and the nine *Elm Street* movies released to date.[6] By establishing connections between two standalone franchises, these crossovers follow an expansive logic and partake in larger worldbuilding projects that, while still delivering more of the same, are designed to enhance the viewing experience through the fabrication of coherent, meaningfully shared fictional worlds that extend beyond the boundaries of each single franchise.

Crossovers have proven to be successful and spawned their own sequels, but the trend away from the film remake in the new millennium mainly manifests in an uptick in prequels and, more recently, spin-offs. Both formats present alternatives to the film remake and the sequel in that they detach well-known characters from familiar plots and thus offer new creative possibilities to explore these characters and their storyworlds within the constraints of an already-established larger narrative framework. In doing so, spin-off movies and prequels are also concerned with worldbuilding and with the creation of persistent shared cinematic universes. The *spin-off* shifts the focus to a supporting character or a main character from a larger ensemble. It stays within the same fictional world (if not the exact same setting or diegetic time) and does not interfere with the progression of a franchise's main, ongoing narrative. The spin-off supports worldbuilding efforts because it presents complementary settings, perspectives, and adventures that encourage audiences to imagine these fictions as existing in a coherent fictional world that maintains its consistence through time. *Beauty Shop* (Bille Woodruff, 2005), for instance, stars Queen Latifah, whose character Gina first appeared in a sequel of the popular *Barbershop* franchise about a barbershop on the South Side of Chicago. In the spin-off, hairstylist Gina moves from Chicago to Atlanta and opens her own salon. *Fast & Furious Presents: Hobbs & Shaw* (David Leitch, 2019) has Luke Hobbs (Dwayne Johnson) and Deckard Shaw (Jason Statham) team up for their own adventure in the *Fast & Furious* franchise that usually features a larger cast of recurring characters. And *Solo: A Star Wars Story* (Ron Howard, 2018) tells Han Solo's backstory and thus functions as both a spin-off and prequel to the Skywalker Saga.

The *prequel* extends diegetic time toward the past as it is concerned with events that happened before the events that have already taken place in the franchise and explores why and how characters have become the characters audiences know. The prequel is invested in retrospectively exploring origins and beginnings. Since the 2000s, this has been the case in a number of horror movies, including *Dominion: Prequel to the Exorcist* (Paul Schrader, 2005),[7] *Texas Chainsaw Massacre: The Beginning*

(Jonathan Liebesman, 2006), and *Hannibal Rising* (Peter Webber, 2007), which explain the origins of evil and motivations for becoming monstrous serial killers (Leatherface and Hannibal Lecter). The added backstories in horror film prequels often reference childhood trauma, abuse, and dysfunctional families as reasons for the abnormal behavior of the mass murderers (Leatherface is bullied as a child because he suffers from a facial disfigurement and young Hannibal witnesses how his sister is cannibalized by Nazi collaborators during World War II). They reconfigure fear and horror because suffering provides causality for the monsters' violent actions and humanizes them against all odds. Audiences are compelled to understand (and even sympathize) with Lecter, "an otherwise incomprehensible icon of evil, as the product of his environment,"[8] for instance, and to contextualize the unmasked Leatherface.

While contemporary horror has a predilection for prequels that extrapolate backstories, explain evil, and reveal previously masked faces in the name of franchise renewal, narrative strategies that shift the focus from repetition (remake) and continuation (sequel) to an exploration of the past have also been employed to engage with timeless classics in the present. *Rise of the Planet of the Apes* (Rupert Wyatt, 2011), *The Thing* (Matthijs van Heijningen Jr., 2011), and *Oz the Great and Powerful* (Sam Raimi, 2013), for example, deliver stories that ostensibly flaunt their ties to the classic *Planet of the Apes*, *The Thing* (John Carpenter, 1982), and *The Wizard of Oz* (Victor Fleming, 1939), but simultaneously dispel any intentions of replacing these movies with modern versions. By moving into the past with their own stories, to a narrative moment that precedes their respective classics, they do not disrupt established timelines but enhance the viewers' knowledge about existing characters, fictional worlds, and stories. As a matter of fact, the circumvention of explicit repetition and linear serial progression we find in crossovers, spin-offs, and prequels nonetheless affects older movies and main storylines because the new movies still reactivate the past and produce new layers of meanings and memories. The treatments of the material may not explicitly interfere with older versions, yet they still challenge the viewers' understanding of the ape's rule on Earth, the alien attack of the research station in Antarctica, or the wizard and witches that Dorothy meets in the Land of Oz. Ultimately, trying to maintain the singularity of some "untouchable original" is an illusion because Hollywood remaking—regardless of the remaking format—always introduces change and generates "multiplicities."[9]

REMAKING BY ANY OTHER NAME

The boundaries between the remaking formats that have gained prominence in the new millennium are fluid: crossovers can also be read as remakes, spin-offs can be prequels, and crossovers, spin-offs, and prequels can all spawn sequels, which still operate as crossovers, spin-offs, and prequels with regard to an older movie. To complicate matters, prequels like *Rise of the Planet of the Apes* have also been labeled reboots. After Burton's much-maligned 2001 remake, *Rise* re-instilled economic and cultural interest in the *Apes* property and relaunched it as an aesthetically, narratively, and technically reinvented franchise with two more sequels. This is the text-book definition of the "reboot." *Reboot* is a computer term that serves as a metaphor for restarting a film franchise. It was first used in comic book culture, where rebooting counts as "an approach towards clearing a narrative space for future iterations of already serialized texts."[10] The adoption of the term *reboot* in film criticism and scholarship echoes the seizing of the term *film remake* from the movie industry,[11] but it is also a result of the crisis of the film remake proper following the release of Van Sant's *Psycho* and Tim Burton's *Planet of the Apes* that I have discussed above. To be clear, the reboot is not a new remaking format and rebooting not a new industrial practice, even if they are commonly framed in this manner. Like *franchise* and *franchising*, the terms simply offer new ways of thinking about repetition and variation, serial proliferation, and intertextual relationships, of imagining where cultural reproduction is headed in the twenty-first century. To call a movie a "reboot," rather than a "remake," "sequel," or "prequel," then, is above all a *discursive choice* that is intricately linked to franchise logics and the industrial imperative to exploit intellectual properties and ensure their long-term profitability. The very notion of "reboot" flaunts the fact that Hollywood films, which are derived from existing material, are also always discursively constructed. Hollywood remaking turns movies into battlegrounds, where meanings and cultural power are fiercely disputed and fought over. The term *reboot* entered the lexicon with a promise of renewal that turned its back onto the past. It was remaking by any other name—a synonym, yes, and a label that discursively severed the old industry practice from failures and fatigue.

William Proctor insists that "reboots forget and disconnect," that they "delete established memory in order to begin again."[12] While this is certainly true for movies like *Batman Begins, Casino Royale, Star Trek* (J. J. Abrams, 2009), and *The Amazing Spider-Man* (Marc Webb, 2012), franchise logics are quickly evolving in the new millennium, so that pinning down exact definitions (even using *reboot* as a critical category) seems to be a doomed undertaking. In a piece titled "What Is a Reboot, Revival, Remake and Sequel?," one film critic recently explained not only the difference between the labels but also "Why These Terms Are Starting to No Longer Matter."[13] He suggested that "in a day and age wherein Hollywood has become desperate to dust off and either continue or reimagine older stories for the sake of making money, finding meaning in these terms and defining what films or TV shows have been rebooted, revived, remade, or continued is quickly becoming a fruitless effort."[14] This statement expresses frustration with the uncertainty and historical variability of labels. Yet, as Frank Kelleter and I have suggested, such distinctions are not fruitless efforts if we understand their communicative function and analyze how they shape the movie industry and culture more broadly.[15]

The reboot has already proven to be an incredibly malleable concept, seemingly impossible to pin down. Daniel Herbert and Constantine Verevis have recently proposed a broader, operative understanding of the reboot to address this impasse. They think of the reboot as a more versatile strategy to "recalibrate a franchise" (with the objective to reactivate and sustain its profitability), as can be observed, for instance, "in the effort invested by *Batman Begins* in wiping a narrative space clean, in *Star Trek* using time travel to re-do without re-writing, in *Prometheus* (2012) returning to the *Alien* universe most 'authentically' under the direction of Ridley Scott and in *The Force Awakens* ([J. J.] Abrams, 2015) aiming to reawaken excitement in *Star Wars* properties."[16] Since 2015, I argue, the kind of franchise recalibration associated with the reboot often involves reveling in the past (rather than renouncing it) and favors continuity over the radical reset. As discussed in chapter 2 on Hollywood's usable past, what is sometimes called a "soft reboot" purposefully disregards and erases aspects of previous movies that might be deemed problematic today (sexist and racist stereotypes, misogynistic behavior, an exclusive focus on the white male hero, and an overall lack of diverse characters), in order to be able to hold on to the rest of the franchise past and revitalize its memory, meanings, and identificatory power. As a result, nostalgia and the notion of legacy have now become the selling point when failed, creatively depleted, and—most importantly—dormant franchises are being reactivated in the present. Yet despite any necessary recalibrations, these kinds of reboots (which also qualify as requels or legacyquels)[17] still affirm the franchise past and tend to develop their stories within already existing narrative frameworks. Such constraints, however, often limit the progressive potential that the term *reboot* itself once seemed to promise. Rebooting the past in this way is always also a *commitment* to the past that comes with a stabilizing effect: for the profit-oriented film industry, for cultural memory but also values and ideologies that are inscribed in the movies, and for the viewers' generational identification and trajectories of the self. There are many such continuities that Hollywood remaking constructs and sustains over time; they deserve critical attention and make Hollywood remaking indeed a multifaceted object of study.

It is maybe not surprising that the concept of the reboot has evolved according to franchise logics. In contemporary Hollywood cinema those dictate long-term worldbuilding projects across time and space, with a reverence for extending and expanding already existing cinematic universes as well as the objective to generate enthusiasm among successive generations of viewers by delivering more of the same rather than causing feelings of alienation through gestures of disavowal. Rebooting the past—rather than revising or circumventing it—in order to continue decades-old stories in the present depends on cultural memory, the audiences' intertextual proficiency, and generational nostalgia. As the reliable catalyst for cultural reproduction it has always been, from talker remakes to the forever franchise, Hollywood remaking will continue to change and adapt according to industrial, cultural, social, and political developments and rely on usable pasts, just as it creates new ones through the serial dynamic of repetition and variation.

Notes

INTRODUCTION

1. Hannah Ewens, "Why Hollywood's Obsession with Remakes and Sequels Needs to Die," *VICE*, March 18, 2016, https://www.vice.com/en_us/article/qbxq77/end-the-hollywood-sequel-franchise-beetlejuice-indiana-jones.
2. Ewens.
3. Ewens.
4. Justin Chang, "The Summer of Our Discontent: When Franchise Overload Killed Movie Originality," *Los Angeles Times*, August 30, 2016, http://www.latimes.com/entertainment/movies/la-et-mn-looking-back-on-summer-2016-20160826-snap-story.html.
5. Mark Harris, "The Day the Movies Died," *GQ*, February 2011, http://www.gq.com/entertainment/movies-and-tv/201102/the-day-the-movies-died-mark-harris.
6. Harris.
7. Ewens, "Hollywood's Obsession."
8. Ewens.
9. Constantine Verevis, *Film Remakes* (Edinburgh: Edinburgh University Press, 2006), 58.
10. Rita Felski, *Uses of Literature* (Malden, MA: Blackwell 2008).
11. See also Frank Kelleter and Kathleen Loock, "Hollywood Remaking as Second-Order Serialization," in *Media of Serial Narrative*, ed. Frank Kelleter

(Columbus: Ohio State University Press, 2017), 125–47; Kathleen Loock, "Retro-Remaking: The 1980s Film Cycle in Contemporary Hollywood Cinema," in *Cycles, Sequels, Spin-Offs, Remakes, and Reboots: Multiplicities in Film and Television*, eds. Amanda Ann Klein and R. Barton Palmer (Austin: University of Texas Press, 2016), 277–98; Kathleen Loock, "'The past is never really past': Serial Storytelling from *Psycho* to *Bates Motel*," in *LWU: Literatur in Wissenschaft und Unterricht* 47, nos. 1–2 (2014): 81–95; Kathleen Loock and Constantine Verevis, eds., *Film Remakes, Adaptations and Fan Productions: Remake/Remodel* (Basingstoke, UK: Palgrave Macmillan, 2012).

12. Since the late 1990s, remake scholarship has focused on Hollywood remakes of European, especially French, films, for example, Carolyn A. Durham, *Double Takes: Culture and Gender in French Films and Their American Remakes* (Hanover, NH: University Press of New England, 1998); Lucy Mazdon, *Encore Hollywood: Remaking French Cinema* (London: BFI, 2000); Eduard Cuelenaere, Gertjan Willems, and Stijn Joye, eds., *European Film Remakes* (Edinburgh: Edinburgh University Press, 2021). Research also focuses on non-European, East Asian, and Bollywood films, for example, Kenneth Chan, *Remade in Hollywood: The Global Chinese Presence in Transnational Cinemas* (Hong Kong: Hong Kong University Press, 2009); Yiman Wang, *Remaking Chinese Cinema: Through the Prism of Shanghai, Hong Kong, and Hollywood* (Honolulu: University of Hawai'i Press, 2013); Valerie Wee, *Japanese Horror Films and Their American Remakes: Translating Fear, Adapting Culture* (New York: Routledge, 2014). On remake production that takes place outside of Hollywood, see Iain Robert Smith, *The Hollywood Meme: Transnational Adaptations in World Cinema* (Edinburgh: Edinburgh University Press, 2017).

13. See Kathleen Loock, "Remaking Winnetou, Reconfiguring German Fantasies of *Indianer* and the Wild West in the Post-Reunification Era," *Communications: The European Journal of Communication Research* 44, no. 3 (2019): 323–41.

14. Benedict Anderson, *Imagined Communities: Reflections on the Origins and Spread of Nationalism* (London: Verso, 1991 [1983]).

15. Marita Sturken, *Tangled Memories: The Vietnam War, the AIDS Epidemic, and the Politics of Remembering* (Berkeley: University of California Press, 1997), 1–2, 13.

16. Ulf Hedetoft, "Contemporary Cinema: Between Cultural Globalisation and National Interpretation," in *Cinema and Nation*, ed. Mette Hjort and Scott Mackenzie (London: Routledge, 2000), 281.

17. See also Andrew Higson, "The Concept of National Cinema," *Screen* 30, no. 4 (1989): 36–45; Andrew Higson, "The Limiting Imagination of National Cinema," in *Cinema and Nation*, ed. Mette Hjort and Scott Mackenzie (London: Routledge, 2000), 63–74; Stephen Crofts, "Reconceptualizing National Cinemas," *Quarterly Review of Film and Video* 14, no. 3 (1993): 49–67; Mette Hjort and Scott Mackenzie, eds., *Cinema and Nation* (London: Routledge, 2000).

18. Arjun Appadurai, *Modernity at Large: Cultural Dimensions of Globalization* (Minneapolis: Minnesota University Press, 1996), 3.
19. Appadurai, 3.
20. Building on the theory outlined in this book, my current project "Hollywood Memories: Cinematic Remaking and the Construction of Global Movie Generations" (2020–2026) conducts audience research in Germany, Mexico, the United States, and China to examine how Hollywood remaking operates as a global practice and how it is biographically and media-technologically embedded in viewers' lives. This project is funded by the German Research Foundation (DFG) in the Emmy Noether funding line (https://hollywood-memories.com/en/).
21. Iain Robert Smith and Constantine Verevis, "Introduction: Transnational Film Remakes," in *Transnational Film Remakes*, ed. Iain Robert Smith and Constantine Verevis (Edinburgh: Edinburgh University Press, 2017), 3.
22. Michael B. Druxman, *Make It Again, Sam: A Survey of Movie Remakes* (Cranbury, NJ: A. S. Barnes, 1975), 9.
23. The following book-length studies and edited collections engage (almost exclusively) with Hollywood films based on Hollywood films. On the film remake, see Verevis, *Film Remakes*; Anat Zanger, *Film Remakes as Ritual and Disguise: From Carmen to Ripley* (Amsterdam: Amsterdam University Press, 2006); Katrin Oltmann, *Remake | Premake: Hollywoods romantische Komödien und ihre Gender-Diskurse, 1930–1960* (Bielefeld, Germany: Transcript Verlag, 2008); Daniel Varndell, *Hollywood Remakes, Deleuze and the Grandfather Paradox* (Basingstoke, UK: Palgrave Macmillan, 2014); Daniel Herbert, *Film Remakes and Franchises* (New Brunswick, NJ: Rutgers University Press, 2017); and Lauren Rosewarne, *Sex and Sexuality in Modern Screen Remakes* (Cham, Switzerland: Palgrave Macmillan, 2019). Specifically on horror film remakes, see James Francis Jr., *Remaking Horror: Hollywood's New Reliance on Scares of Old* (Jefferson, NC: McFarland, 2013); David Roche, *Making and Remaking Horror in the 1970s and 2000s: Why Don't They Do It Like They Used To?* (Jackson: University Press of Mississippi, 2014); Christian Knöppler, *The Monster Always Returns: American Horror Films and Their Remakes* (Bielefeld, Germany: Transcript Verlag, 2017); and Laura Mee, *Reanimated: The Contemporary American Horror Remake* (Edinburgh: Edinburgh University Press, 2020). On the film sequel, see Carolyn Jess-Cooke, *Film Sequels: Theory and Practice from Hollywood to Bollywood* (Edinburgh: Edinburgh University Press, 2009); Carolyn Jess-Cooke and Constantine Verevis, eds., *Second Takes: Critical Approaches to the Film Sequel* (Albany: State University of New York Press, 2010); and Stuart Henderson, *The Hollywood Sequel: History and Form, 1911–2010* (London: BFI, 2014). On the film series, film trilogy, film reboot, and overall broader conceptualizations of remaking, see Jennifer Forrest, ed., *The Legend Returns and Dies Harder Another Day: Essays on Film Series* (Jefferson, NC: McFarland, 2008); Loock and Verevis, eds., *Film Remakes, Adaptations, and Fan Productions*;

Claire Perkins and Constantine Verevis, eds., *Film Trilogies: New Critical Approaches* (Basingstoke, UK: Palgrave Macmillan, 2012); Amanda Ann Klein and R. Barton Palmer, eds., *Cycles, Sequels, Spin-Offs, Remakes, and Reboots: Multiplicities in Film and Television* (Austin: University of Texas Press, 2016); and Daniel Herbert and Constantine Verevis, eds., *Film Reboots* (Edinburgh: Edinburgh University Press, 2020).

24. Frank Kelleter, "Five Ways of Looking at Popular Seriality," in *Media of Serial Narrative*, ed. Frank Kelleter (Columbus: Ohio State University Press, 2017), 10, emphasis in original.

25. Amanda Ann Klein and R. Barton Palmer, "Introduction," in *Cycles, Sequels, Spin-Offs, Remakes, and Reboots: Multiplicities in Film and Television*, ed. Amanda Ann Klein and R. Barton Palmer (Austin: University of Texas Press, 2016), 1–21.

26. Umberto Eco, "Innovation and Repetition: Between Modern and Post-Modern Aesthetics," *Daedalus* 114, no. 4 (Fall 1985): 161–84.

27. Cf. Kelleter and Loock, "Hollywood Remaking," 129.

28. On the integration of serial narratives into quotidian routines, see Christine Hämmerling and Mirjam Nast, "Popular Seriality in Everyday Practice: *Perry Rhodan* and *Tatort*," in *Media of Serial Narrative*, ed. Frank Kelleter (Columbus, OH: The Ohio State University Press, 2017), 248–60.

29. Kelleter and Loock, "Hollywood Remaking," 134; emphasis in original.

30. Kelleter and Loock, 134.

31. My understanding of Hollywood remaking through the lens of seriality studies is inspired by the conceptual framework of the Popular Seriality Research Unit (PSRU) that defines popular culture as "a set of social and aesthetic practices that first surfaced in the mid-nineteenth century, closely tangled up with the logic of industrial reproduction" and that today "constitute a large-scale system of commercial storytelling best described as popular seriality—an ever more self-aware and increasingly expansive field of narrative that has been causing significant shifts in the relationship of cultural domains and the technological affordances of new mass media." Kelleter, "Five Ways," 9. The PSRU, funded by the German Research Foundation (DFG), brought together researchers from the fields of American Studies, German Philology, Cultural Anthropology/European Ethnology, Empirical Cultural Studies, and Media Studies to research popular seriality. During its two funding periods (2010–2013 and 2013–2016), altogether thirteen projects explored the forms, dynamic processes, and functions of serial narration in popular culture. Many of the ideas developed here stem from a shared project with Frank Kelleter on cinematic remaking and retrospective serialization.

32. Kelleter and Loock, "Hollywood Remaking," 134.

33. Kelleter, "Five Ways," 26.

34. To study serial narratives that are "inevitably multiauthored, produced and consumed in many-layered systems of responsibility and performance,

and always dependent on both the material demands of their media and the constraints of their cultural environments," Kelleter combines Bruno Latour's Actor-Network-Theory (ANT) with a systems-theoretical approach, drawing on Niklas Luhmann and his notions of self-description and hetero-description. Kelleter, "Five Ways," 25–26.

35. Kelleter, "Five Ways," 26.
36. Kelleter and Loock, "Hollywood Remaking," 134.
37. Kelleter, "Five Ways," 29.
38. Kelleter and Loock, "Hollywood Remaking," 144.
39. Kelleter, "Five Ways," 14.
40. Astrid Erll, "Literature, Film, and the Mediality of Cultural Memory," in *Cultural Memory Studies: An International and Interdisciplinary Handbook*, eds. Astrid Erll and Ansgar Nünning (Berlin: de Gruyter, 2008), 389–98.
41. Cf. Paul Grainge, "Introduction: Memory and Popular Film," in *Memory and Popular Culture*, ed. Paul Grainge (Manchester, UK: Manchester University Press, 2003), 12.
42. Kelleter and Loock, "Hollywood Remaking," 132.
43. Sources for the Hollywood Remaking dataset are reference guides: James L. Limbacher, *Haven't I Seen You Somewhere Before? Remakes, Sequels, and Series in Motion Pictures, Videos, and Television, 1896–1990* (Ann Arbor: Pierian Press, 1991); Druxman, *Make It Again, Sam*; Manfred Hobsch, *Mach's noch einmal! Das große Buch der Remakes* (Berlin: Schwarzkopf & Schwarzkopf, 2002); Kim R. Holston and Tom Winchester, *Science Fiction, Fantasy, and Horror Film Sequels, Series and Remakes: An Illustrated Filmography, with Plot Synopses and Critical Commentary* (Jefferson, NC: McFarland, 1997); Ronald Schwartz, *Noir, Now and Then: Film Noir Originals and Remakes (1944–1999)* (Westport, CT: Greenwood Press, 2001); and Doris Milberg, *Repeat Performances: A Guide to Hollywood Movie Remakes* (Shelter Island, NY: Broadway, 1990). All entries derived from the books were checked and complemented by referring to: the sequel/series dataset in Henderson, *The Hollywood Sequel*; the collections of the MHDL; privately compiled datasets by fellow film scholars; and online databases (AFI catalog, IMDb, Silent Era website, Wikipedia). I manually curated the dataset with the help of Sarah Hönig (2013–2016) and Alissa Lienhard (2021–2023). Since 2018, data scientist Vitaly Belik has been working with me to analyze the data.
44. Thomas Schatz, "The New Hollywood," in *Movie Blockbusters*, ed. Julian Stringer (London: Routledge, 2003), 16.
45. Karl Mannheim, "The Problem of Generations," in *Collected Works*, vol. 5, *Essays on the Sociology of Knowledge*, ed. Paul Kecskemeti (London: Routledge/Kegan Paul, 1952), 276–320.
46. Joe Tompkins, "'Re-imagining' the Canon: Examining the Discourse of Contemporary Horror Film Reboots." *New Review of Film and Television Studies* 12, no. 4 (December 2014): 382.

1. MAKING SENSE OF REPETITION

1. Leo Braudy, "Afterword: Rethinking Remakes," in *Play It Again, Sam: Retakes on Remakes*, ed. Andrew Horton and Stuart Y. McDougal (Berkeley: University of California Press, 1998), 327.
2. Cf. Constantine Verevis, *Film Remakes* (Edinburgh: Edinburgh University Press, 2006), 67.
3. Thomas Leitch, "101 Ways to Tell Hitchcock's *Psycho* from Gus Van Sant's," *Literature/Film Quarterly* 28, no. 4 (2000): 269–72; see also Frank Kelleter, "Das Remake als Fetischkunst: Gus Van Sants *Psycho* und die absonderlichen Serialitäten des Hollywood-Kinos," *Pop: Kultur und Kritik* 7 (2015): 152–73.
4. Kelleter, "Das Remake," 162; Kathleen Loock, "'The past is never really past': Serial Storytelling from *Psycho* to *Bates Motel*," *LWU: Literatur in Wissenschaft und Unterricht* 47, no. 1–2 (2014): 84–85.
5. Loock, "The Past," 85.
6. Kathleen Loock, "Remaking *Funny Games*: Michael Haneke's Cross-Cultural Experiment," in *Transnational Film Remakes*, eds. Iain Robert Smith and Constantine Verevis (Edinburgh: Edinburgh University Press, 2017), 190.
7. Kelleter, "Das Remake," 163; my translation. "Hitchcocks Film [führte] ein merkwürdiges Doppelleben in zwei getrennten Erzähluniversen, die auf den ersten Blick unterschiedlicher kaum sein könnten: auf der einen Seite das Reich der Filmkunst, wo *Psycho* rasch als singuläres Werk kanonisiert wurde, und auf der anderen Seite die sehr viel weniger übersichtlichen Gefilde populär-serieller Wucherung."
8. Constantine Verevis, "For Ever Hitchcock: *Psycho* and Its Remakes," in *After Hitchcock: Influence, Imitation, and Intertextuality*, eds. David Boyd and R. Barton Palmer (Austin: University of Texas Press, 2006), 26; Verevis, *Film Remakes*, 73.
9. Loock, "The Past," 85.
10. Loock, 89; Kelleter, "Das Remake," 170.
11. Megan Carrigy, "Re-staging the Cinema: *Psycho*, Film Spectatorship and the Redundant New Remake," *Screening the Past* 34 (2012), http://www.screeningthepast.com/2012/08/re-staging-the-cinema-psycho-film-spectatorship-and-the-redundant-new-remake/.
12. Cf. Christian Knöppler, *The Monster Always Returns: American Horror Films and Their Remakes* (Bielefeld, Germany: Transcript Verlag, 2017), 46.
13. Braudy, "Rethinking Remakes," 327.
14. Cf. Andrew Horton and Stuart Y. McDougal, "Introduction," in *Play It Again, Sam: Retakes on Remakes*, ed. Andrew Horton and Stuart Y. McDougal (Berkeley: University of California Press, 1998), 3; Knöppler, *The Monster*, 48–49; Katrin Oltmann, *Remake | Premake: Hollywoods romantische Komödien und ihre Gender-Diskurse, 1930–1960* (Bielefeld, Germany: Transcript Verlag, 2008), 32–33; Verevis, *Film Remakes* 18–20.

15. Thomas Leitch, "Twice-Told Tales: The Rhetoric of the Remake," *Literature/Film Quarterly* 18, no. 3 (1990): 138.

16. "*Psycho*: Behind the Scenes," *Psycho: Official Website*, Universal Studios, last modified 1998, Internet Archive, https://web.archive.org/web/19990222064016/http://www.psychomovie.com/production/productionwhy.html.

17. Gus Van Sant quoted in "*Psycho*: Behind the Scenes."

18. James Naremore, "Remaking *Psycho*," *Hitchcock Annual* (1999–2000): 6.

19. See also Constantine Santas, "The Remake of *Psycho* (Gus Van Sant, 1998): Creativity or Cinematic Blasphemy?" *Senses of Cinema* 10 (November 2000), http://sensesofcinema.com/2000/feature-articles/psycho-2/.

20. "*Psycho*: Behind the Scenes."

21. Carrigy, "Re-staging."

22. Steven Jay Schneider, "A Tale of Two *Psychos* (Prelude to a Future Reassessment)," *Senses of Cinema* 10 (November 2000), http://sensesofcinema.com/2000/feature-articles/psychos/.

23. Naremore, "Remaking *Psycho*," 11.

24. Gérard Genette, *Palimpsests: Literature in the Second Degree*, trans. Channa Newman and Claude Doubinsky (Lincoln: University of Nebraska Press, 1997), 1–5.

25. Roger Ebert quoted in Schneider, "A Tale of Two *Psychos*."

26. Jonathan Rosenbaum quoted in Schneider.

27. Santas, "The Remake of *Psycho*."

28. Shannon Donaldson-McHugh and Don Moore, "Film Adaptation, Co-Authorship, and Hauntology: Gus Van Sant's *Psycho* (1998)," *The Journal of Popular Culture* 39, no. 2 (2006): 228.

29. Thomas Leitch, "Hitchcock without Hitchcock," *Literature Film Quarterly* 31, no. 4 (2003): 255.

30. Jonathan Romney, "Without a Hitch," *The Guardian*, January 8, 1999, https://www.theguardian.com/film/News_Story/Critic_Review/Guardian/0,,36035,00.html.

31. John Ellis, *Visible Fictions: Cinema, Television, Video* (1982; London: Routledge, 1992).

32. Robert Eberwein, "Remakes and Cultural Studies," in *Play It Again, Sam: Retakes on Remakes*, ed. Andrew Horton and Stuart Y. McDougal (Berkeley: University of California Press, 1998), 15–33.

33. Michael B. Druxman, *Make It Again, Sam: A Survey of Movie Remakes* (Cranbury, NJ: A. S. Barnes, 1975), 13–15.

34. Harvey Roy Greenberg, "Raiders of the Lost Text: Remaking as Contested Homage in *Always*," *Journal of Popular Film and Television* 18, no. 4 (Winter 1991): 170.

35. Druxman, *Make It Again*, 13. On the practice of retitling films, see also chapter 3.

36. Eberwein, "Remakes," 28–31.

37. Leitch, "Twice-Told Tales," 139.
38. Leitch, 142.
39. Leitch, 142–46.
40. Leitch, 47.
41. Carrigy, "Re-staging."
42. Leitch, "Hitchcock," 249.
43. Leitch, 250; emphasis in original.
44. On the use of genre theory's semantic/syntactic approach for taxonomies of remakes, see Verevis, *Film Remakes*, 84–86. See also Rick Altman, "A Semantic/Syntactic Approach to Film Genre," *Cinema Journal* 23, no. 3 (Spring 1984): 6–18.
45. Kelleter, "Das Remake," 170.
46. Verevis, *Film Remakes*, 23.
47. Verevis, 2.
48. Verevis, 2.
49. Verevis, 2.
50. Verevis, 2.
51. Daniel Herbert, *Film Remakes and Franchises* (New Brunswick, NJ: Rutgers University Press, 2017), 5.
52. Jason Mittell, *Genre and Television: From Cop Shows to Cartoons in American Culture* (New York: Routledge, 2004), xii.
53. Horton and McDougal, "Introduction," 2.
54. Eberwein, "Remakes," 15.
55. Eberwein, 15.
56. Eberwein, 16.
57. Stuart Hall, "Cultural Identity and Cinematic Representation," *Framework: The Journal of Cinema and Media* 36 (1989): 69.
58. Hall, 70.
59. Jennifer Forrest and Leonard R. Koos, "Reviewing Remakes: An Introduction," in *Dead Ringers: The Remake in Theory and Practice*, ed. Jennifer Forrest and Leonard R. Koos (Albany: State University of New York Press, 2002), 3.
60. Forrest and Koos, 4–5.
61. Jennifer Forrest, "The 'Personal' Touch: The Original, the Remake, and the Dupe in Early Cinema," in *Dead Ringers: The Remake in Theory and Practice*, ed. Jennifer Forrest and Leonard R. Koos (Albany: State University of New York Press, 2002), 89–126.
62. Naremore, "Remaking *Psycho*," 3.
63. Catherine Constable, "Reflections on the Surface: Remaking the Postmodern with Van Sant's *Psycho*," in *Adaptation in Contemporary Culture: Textual Infidelities*, ed. Rachel Carroll (London: Continuum, 2009), 25.
64. Adrian Martin, "Shot-by-Shot Follies," *Hitchcock Annual* 10 (2001–2002): 133.

65. Martin, 134.
66. Cf. Constable, "Remaking the Postmodern," 25–26.
67. Leitch, "Hitchcock," 251.
68. Leitch, 249.
69. Naremore, "Remaking *Psycho*," 6.
70. Carrigy, "Re-staging."
71. Carrigy.
72. Martin, "Shot-by-Shot," 134.
73. Carrigy, "Re-staging," emphasis added.
74. Cf. Carrigy.
75. Naremore, "Remaking *Psycho*," 12.
76. Martin, "Shot-by-Shot," 134.
77. Steve Neale, *Genre and Hollywood* (London: Routledge, 2000), 88–89.
78. Isabel Cristina Pinedo, *Recreational Terror: Women and the Pleasures of Horror Film Viewing* (Albany: State University of New York Press, 1997), 14–15; Andrew Tudor, "From Paranoia to Postmodernism? The Horror Movie in Late Modern Society," in *Genre and Contemporary Hollywood*, ed. Steve Neale (London: BFI, 2002), 114.
79. Pinedo, *Recreational Terror*, 5, 18.
80. Tudor, "From Paranoia," 109.
81. Tudor, 109.
82. Tudor, 106–7.
83. Tudor, 107.
84. See Vera Dika, *Games of Terror: "Halloween," "Friday the 13th," and the Films of the Stalker Cycle* (Rutherford, NJ: Fairleigh Dickinson University Press, 1990).
85. Steven Jay Schneider, "Kevin Williamson and the Rise of the Neo-Stalker," *Post Script: Essays in Film and the Humanities* 19, no. 2 (2000).
86. Naremore, "Remaking *Psycho*," 6.
87. Naremore, 5.
88. Each successive film plays out against the formulas and conventions audiences typically associate with (1) the horror film, (2) the sequel, (3) and the trilogy, as references to well-known horror movies occur alongside references to *Scream* itself and to *Scream*'s own film-within-a-film: the *Stab* franchise.
89. *Wes Craven's New Nightmare* is a film about filmmaking, in which director Wes Craven, actors, and New Line Cinema executives play themselves. In this seventh installment of the *Elm Street* franchise, Freddy Krueger enters the real world and attacks the cast and crew.
90. Verevis, *Film Remakes*, 105–25.
91. Verevis, 58.
92. Oltmann, *Remake | Premake*, 31.

93. Mieke Bal, *Quoting Caravaggio: Contemporary Art, Preposterous History* (Chicago: University of Chicago Press, 1999), 7. See Oltmann, *Remake | Premake*, 31–34.

94. Oltmann, *Remake | Premake*, 36.

95. Oltmann, 27; Loock, "'The Past,'" 83.

96. Oltmann, *Remake | Premake*, 28. Freud developed the concept in his psychoanalytical work on trauma and hysteria, in Sigmund Freud, "Entwurf einer Psychologie," in *Gesammelte Werke*, vol. 19, ed. Angela Richards (Frankfurt/M.: Fischer, 1999), 375–486; and in his study of the "Wolf Man": Sigmund Freud, "Aus der Geschichte einer infantilen Neurose [Der Wolfsmann]," in *Studienausgabe*, vol. 8, eds. Alexander Mitscherlich et al. (Frankfurt/M.: Fischer, 2000) 126–232.

97. Oltmann, *Remake | Premake*, 28; Michael A. Arnzen, "The Same and the New: *Cape Fear* and the Hollywood Remake as Metanarrative Discourse," *Narrative* 4, no. 2 (May 1996): 178, 187–89.

98. Schneider, "A Tale of."

99. Arnzen, "The Same and the New," 191.

100. Arnzen, 189; Oltmann, *Remake | Premake*, 28.

101. Cf. Oltmann, *Remake | Premake*, 32.

102. Stephen Greenblatt, *Shakespearean Negotiations: The Circulation of Social Energy in Renaissance England* (Oxford: Clarendon, 1988), vii.

103. Greenblatt, 5–6.

104. Cf. Amanda Klein and R. Barton Palmer, "Introduction," in *Cycles, Sequels, Spin-Offs, Remakes, and Reboots: Multiplicities in Film and Television*, ed. Amanda Ann Klein and R. Barton Palmer (Austin: University of Texas Press, 2016), 12.

105. Leonardo Quaresima, "Loving Texts Two at a Time: The Film Remake," *Cinémas* 12, no. 3 (2002): 75.

106. Quaresima, 78.

107. Frank Kelleter and Kathleen Loock, "Hollywood Remaking as Second-Order Serialization," in *Media of Serial Narrative*, ed. Frank Kelleter (Columbus: Ohio State University Press, 2017), 125.

108. Vera Dika, *Recycled Culture in Contemporary Art and Film: The Uses of Nostalgia* (Cambridge: Cambridge University Press, 2003), 205.

109. Dika, 206.

110. Forrest, "The 'Personal' Touch," 96.

111. Forrest, "The 'Personal' Touch," 91; cf. Oltmann, *Remake | Premake*, 59.

112. Leitch, "Twice-Told Tales," 139.

113. Barbara Klinger, *Beyond the Multiplex: Cinema, New Technologies, and the Home* (Berkeley: University of California Press, 2006), 72.

114. Verevis, *Film Remakes*, 18.

115. Quaresima, "Loving Texts," 80.

116. See Kelleter and Loock, "Hollywood Remaking," 131–34.

117. This discussion is based on Loock, "The Return."

118. Annette Insdorf, "Seeing Doubles," *Moving Image Source*, Museum of the Moving Image, June 26, 2008. http://www.movingimagesource.us/articles/seeing-doubles-20080626.

119. Barry Keith Grant, *Invasion of the Body Snatchers* (London: BFI/Palgrave Macmillan, 2010), 93.

120. Verevis, *Film Remakes*, 16; Leitch, "Twice-Told Tales," 139.

121. Verevis, *Film Remakes*, 17; emphasis in original.

122. Verevis, 17.

123. Klinger, *Beyond the Multiplex*, 82.

124. Gray, Jonathan Gray, *Show Sold Separately: Promos, Spoilers and Other Media Paratexts* (New York: New York University Press, 2010), 89.

125. Klinger, *Beyond the Multiplex*, 72.

126. Kelleter and Loock, "Hollywood Remaking," 137.

127. Kelleter and Loock, 139.

128. I borrow the term from Robert Stam, "Beyond Fidelity: The Dialogics of Adaptation," in *Film Adaptation*, ed. James Naremore (New Brunswick, NJ: Rutgers University Press, 2000), 66.

129. Kelleter and Loock, "Hollywood Remaking," 139.

130. Kelleter and Loock, 138.

131. Jason Mittell, "Serial Boxes," *Just TV* (blog), January 20, 2010, https://justtv.wordpress.com/2010/01/20/ serial-boxes/; see also Kelleter and Loock, "Hollywood Remaking," 138.

132. Gray, *Show Sold Separately*, 35.

133. Kelleter and Loock, "Hollywood Remaking," 139.

134. Kelleter and Loock, 139.

135. Kelleter and Loock, 138.

136. Kelleter and Loock, 138.

137. Kelleter and Loock, 138.

138. Klinger, *Beyond the Multiplex*, 72.

139. Jason Mittell, "Forensic Fandom and the Drillable Text," in *Spreadable Media: Creating Value and Meaning in a Networked Culture*, ed. Henry Jenkins, Sam Ford and Joshua Green (New York: New York University Press, 2013), https://spreadablemedia.org/essays/mittell/.

140. Richard Natale, "Classics on Video Get Jolt from Hot Remakes," *Variety*, December 9, 1991: 3, Newspaper Clippings (Remakes 1990–1994), AMPAS.

141. Cf. Natale, "Classics on Video," 3; Anne Thompson, "They're Back!" *Variety*, June 13, 1990: 42, 44, Newspaper Clippings, NYPL.

142. Thompson, "They're Back," 42; see also Kathleen Loock, "The Sequel Paradox: Repetition, Innovation, and Hollywood's Hit Film Formula," in *Film Studies* 17, no. 1 (Autumn 2017): 97–98.

143. Dika, *Recycled Culture*, 205.
144. Kelleter and Loock, "Hollywood Remaking," 130.

2. HOLLYWOOD'S USABLE PAST

1. Van Wyck Brooks, "On Creating a Usable Past," *The Dial*, April 11, 1918, 337.
2. Jeffrey K. Olick, "From Usable Pasts to the Return of the Repressed," *The Hedgehog Review* (Summer 2007): 19, emphasis mine.
3. Olick, 20; emphasis in original.
4. Raymond Williams, *Marxism and Literature* (New York: Oxford University Press, 1977), 132.
5. Frank Kelleter and Kathleen Loock, "Hollywood Remaking as Second-Order Serialization," in *Media of Serial Narrative*, ed. Frank Kelleter (Columbus: Ohio State University Press, 2017), 144. Also see introduction.
6. Frank Kelleter, "Five Ways of Looking at Popular Seriality," in *Media of Serial Narrative*, ed. Frank Kelleter (Columbus: Ohio State University Press, 2017), 29; emphasis in original.
7. Kelleter, 30.
8. Kelleter, 30.
9. Frank Kelleter, "'Toto, I Think We're in Oz Again' (and Again and Again): Remakes and Popular Seriality," in *Film Remakes, Adaptations and Fan Productions: Remake | Remodel*, ed. Kathleen Loock and Constantine Verevis (London: Palgrave Macmillan, 2012), 38.
10. Barbara Klinger, *Beyond the Multiplex: Cinema, New Technologies, and the Home* (Berkeley: University of California Press, 2006), 100–101.
11. Barbara Klinger, *Immortal Films: Casablanca and the Afterlife of a Historical Classic* (Berkeley: University of California Press, 2022).
12. Samuel Goldwyn Jr., quoted in Stella (1990) Production Notes, 11. PA 449203, LOC.
13. John Erman, quoted in Stella (1990) Production Notes, 12.
14. Ron Graham, "Stella, Reborn as an Unmarried Mother: Stella for the 80's," *New York Times*, July 16, 1989, H15–H16, ProQuest Historical Newspapers.
15. Bril., "Stella," *Variety*, February 7, 1990, 30, Review Clippings, NYPL.
16. Frank S. Nugent, "*Stella Dallas*," *New York Times*, August 6, 1937, 21, Review Clippings, NYPL.
17. Nugent, 21.
18. Janet Maslin, "Bette Midler as a Selfless Mother in Tear-Inducing *Stella*," *New York Times*, February 2, 1990, C10, Review Files, LOC.
19. Maslin, C10.
20. Georgia Brown, [Review], *The Village Voice*, February 13, 1990, 10, Review Clippings, NYPL.

21. David Denby, "Start Making Sense: . . . *Stella Dallas* Was Compromised by Its Worship of Wealth and Good Breeding," *New York*, February 12, 1990, 64, Review Clippings, NYPL.

22. Denby, 64.

23. Roger Ebert, "Same Old Farts Who Hate Rock and Roll," RogerEbert.com, uploaded October 12, 2011, https://www.rogerebert.com/reviews/footloose-2011.

24. Steven Zeitchik and Amy Kaufman, "Has *Footloose* Been Given a Conservative Makeover?" *Los Angeles Times*, October 14, 2011, https://latimesblogs.latimes.com/movies/2011/10/footloose-reviews-showtimes-movie-wormald-hough-bacon-theaters.html.

25. Zeitchik and Kaufman.

26. Craig Brewer, quoted in Zeitchik and Amy Kaufman.

27. Zeitchik and Kaufman, "Has *Footloose*."

28. Sesali Bowen, "*Jumanji: Welcome to The Jungle* Is Corny, But I'm Into It," *Refinery29*, December 21, 2017, https://www.refinery29.com/en-us/2017/12/186086/jumanji-cast-diversity-movie-review.

29. Bowen.

30. Kate Ryrie, "*Jumanji: Welcome to the Jungle*—It's Not All Fun and Games," blogpost, January 18, 2018, https://kateryrie.wordpress.com/2018/01/18/jumanji-welcome-to-the-jungle-its-not-all-fun-and-games/.

31. Rosalind Gill, "Postfeminist Media Culture: Elements of a Sensibility," *European Journal of Cultural Studies* 10, no. 2 (2007): 152.

32. Gill, 159.

33. Daniel Herbert, *Film Remakes and Franchises* (New Brunswick, NJ: Rutgers University Press, 2017), 114.

34. Herbert, 116.

35. Sarah Banet-Weiser, *Empowered: Popular Feminism and Popular Misogyny* (Durham, NC: Duke University Press, 2018), 22.

36. Banet-Weiser, 23; see also Herman Gray, "Subject(ed) to Recognition," *American Quarterly* 65, no. 4 (2013): 771–98.

37. See Sarah Nilsen and Sarah E. Turner, eds., *The Myth of the Colorblindness: Race and Ethnicity in American Cinema* (New York: Palgrave Macmillan, 2019); Kristen J. Warner, *The Cultural Politics of Colorblind TV Casting* (New York: Routledge, 2015).

38. Ashley "Woody" Doane, "Shades of Colorblindness: Rethinking Racial Ideology in the United States," in *The Colorblind Screen: Television in Post-Racial America*, ed. Sarah Nilsen and Sarah E. Turner (New York: New York University Press, 2014), 15.

39. For discussions of how popular culture co-opts progressive politics, see Banet-Weiser, *Empowered*; Maria Sulimma, *Gender and Seriality: Practices and Politics of Contemporary US Television* (Edinburgh: Edinburgh University Press, 2021).

40. Barry Keith Grant, *Invasion of the Body Snatchers* (London: BFI/Palgrave Macmillan, 2010), 100.

41. Grant, 102–3.

42. Kathleen Loock, "The Return of the Pod People: Remaking Cultural Anxieties in *Invasion of the Body Snatchers*," in *Film Remakes, Adaptations and Fan Productions: Remake/Remodel*, ed. Kathleen Loock and Constantine Verevis (Basingstoke, UK: Palgrave Macmillan, 2012), 139–40.

43. Angela McRobbie, "Post-feminism and Popular Culture," *Feminist Media Studies* 4, no. 3 (2004): 255.

44. Grant, *Invasion*, 101.

45. Cf. Banet-Weiser, *Empowered*.

46. Simran Hans, "*The Hustle* Review: Sugar Daddy Scam," *Guardian*, May 12, 2019, https://www.theguardian.com/film/2019/may/12/the-hustle-review-anne-hathaway-rebel-wilson#maincontent.

47. Amanda Hess, "The Trouble with Hollywood's Gender Flips," *New York Times*, June 12, 2018, https://www.nytimes.com/2018/06/12/movies/oceans-8-gender-swap.html.

48. Hess.

49. Hess.

50. The following discussion is based on Kathleen Loock, "Making Movie Generations: On the Cultural Work of Hollywood Remaking," in *What Film Is Good For: The Ethics of Spectatorship*, ed. Julian Hanich and Martin P. Rossouw (Berkeley: University of California Press, 2023), 249–60.

51. Marita Sturken, *Tangled Memories: The Vietnam War, the AIDS Epidemic, and the Politics of Remembering* (Berkeley: University of California Press, 1997), 1.

52. Cf. Jan Assmann, "Communicative and Cultural Memory," in *Cultural Memory Studies: An International and Interdisciplinary Handbook*, ed. Astrid Erll and Ansgar Nünning (Berlin: de Gruyter, 2008), 110–11.

53. Susannah Radstone and Katherine Hodgkin, eds., *Memory Cultures: Memory, Subjectivity and Recognition* (New Brunswick, NJ: Transaction, 2006).

54. José van Dijck, *Mediated Memories in the Digital Age* (Stanford, CA: Stanford University Press, 2007), 21; emphasis in original.

55. Alison Landsberg, *Prosthetic Memory: The Transformation of American Remembrance in the Age of Mass Culture* (New York: Columbia University Press, 2004), 20.

56. Landsberg, 20; emphasis in original.

57. Landsberg, 21.

58. In her study of "second-generation" Holocaust literature and art, Hirsch speaks of "postmemory" that prompts a shared sense of generationality among the children of parents who experienced the trauma (the "postgeneration"). Marianne Hirsch, *The Generation of Postmemory: Writing and Visual Culture after*

the Holocaust (New York: Columbia University Press, 2012). Erll adds: "'Postmemory' as a structure of mediation is . . . potentially producible by and available to members of very different generational locations." Astrid Erll, "Generation in Literary History: Three Constellations of Generationality, Genealogy, and Memory," *New Literary History* 45 (2014): 400.

59. Karl Mannheim, "The Problem of Generations," in *Collected Works*, vol. 5: *Essays on the Sociology of Knowledge*, ed. Paul Kecskemeti (London: Routledge/ Kegan Paul, 1952), 307.

60. My cultural approach to movie generations is closer to sociologist Bolin's concept of *media generations* than Lizardi's *nostalgic generations* or Johnson's transgenerational perspective. Bolin also builds on Mannheim's generation theory to examine the role of media (radio, television, cell phones) in the formation of generational experience, whereas Lizardi uses marketing categories, and Johnson is interested in the relationship between adulthood and childhood. Göran Bolin, *Media Generations: Experience, Identity and Mediatised Social Change* (London: Routledge, 2017); Ryan Lizardi, *Nostalgic Generations and Media: Perception of Time and Available Meaning* (Lanham, MD: Lexington Books, 2017); Derek Johnson, *Transgenerational Media Industries: Adults, Children, and the Reproduction of Culture* (Ann Arbor: University of Michigan Press, 2019).

61. Mannheim, "The Problem," 305.

62. Cf. Erll, "Generation," 388–96.

63. Cf. Andra Siibak, Nicoletta Vittadini, and Galit Nimrod, "Generations as Media Audiences: An Introduction," *Participations: Journal of Audience & Reception Studies* 11, no. 2 (2014): 101; Bolin, *Media Generations*.

64. Mannheim, "The Problem," 305.

65. Erll, "Generation," 396.

66. Erll, 396.

67. Mannheim, "The Problem," 293; cf. Bolin, *Media Generations*, 10–11.

68. Mannheim, "The Problem," 293.

69. Thomas Leitch, "Twice-Told Tales: The Rhetoric of the Remake," *Literature/Film Quarterly* 18, no. 3 (1990): 139.

70. Constantine Verevis, *Film Remakes* (Edinburgh: Edinburgh University Press, 2006), 17.

71. Hannah Ewens, "Why Hollywood's Obsession with Remakes and Sequels Needs to Die," *VICE*, March 18, 2016, https://www.vice.com/en_us/article/qbxq77/end-the-hollywood-sequel-franchise-beetlejuice-indiana-jones.

72. The following discussion is based on Kathleen Loock, "Retro-Remaking: The 1980s Film Cycle in Contemporary Hollywood Cinema," in *Cycles, Sequels, Spin-Offs, Remakes, and Reboots: Multiplicities in Film and Television*, ed. Amanda Ann Klein and R. Barton Palmer (Austin: University of Texas Press, 2016), 277–98.

73. Guy Adams, "Hollywood Ate My Childhood: Why Film Remakes Are Desecrating Our Most Precious Memories," *Independent*, July 22, 2010, http://www.independent.co.uk/arts-entertainment/films/features/hollywood-ate-my-childhood-why-film-remakes-are-desecrating-our-most-precious-memories-2032073.html.

74. Adams.

75. Adams.

76. Complaints centered around the character Jar Jar Binks and what longtime *Star Wars* fans considered poor acting and storytelling.

77. Metapolitical strategies use the affective power of emotions to propagate white supremacist and misogynistic alt-right ideologies through historical counternarratives and the redefinition of terms like "resistance," "oppression," "freedom of speech." Simon Strick, *Rechte Gefühle: Affekte und Strategien des digitalen Faschismus* (Bielefeld, Germany: Transcript Verlag, 2022), 74–81.

78. Derek Johnson, "From the Ruins: Neomasculinity, Media Franchising, and Struggles over Industrial Reproduction of Culture," *Communication Culture & Critique*, no. 11 (2018): 87.

79. Johnson, 87.

80. Mike Sampson, "*Ghostbusters* Remake the Most Disliked Trailer of All Time," *ScreenCrush.com*, April 29, 2016, https://screencrush.com/ghostbusters-trailer-most-disliked-movie-trailer-in-history/.

81. Ben Child, "Twitter Attacks on Ghostbusters' Leslie Jones a Symptom of Fan Entitlement," *Guardian*, July 19, 2016, https://www.theguardian.com/film/filmblog/2016/jul/19/twitter-attacks-on-ghostbusters-leslie-jones.

82. Mike Isaac, "Twitter Bars Milo Yiannopoulos in Wake of Leslie Jones's Reports of Abuse," *New York Times*, July 20, 2016, https://www.nytimes.com/2016/07/20/technology/twitter-bars-milo-yiannopoulos-in-crackdown-on-abusive-comments.html.

83. Amy O'Connor, "Some Men Are Really Angry about the All-Female Ghostbusters Remake," *Daily Edge*, January 28, 2015, www.dailyedge.ie/all-female-ghostbusters-reaction-1907535-Jan2015/.

84. Kayleigh Donaldson, "'You Ruined My Childhood': The Fetishizing of Nostalgia," *Bibliodaze.com*, May 1, 2016, https://web.archive.org/web/20160505114256/http://bibliodaze.com/2016/05/you-ruined-my-childhood-the-fetishizing-of-nostalgia/.

85. Derek Johnson, "Fan-tagonism: Factions, Institutions, and Constitutive Hegemonies of Fandom," in *Fandom: Identities and Communities in Mediated Culture*, ed. Jonathan Gray, C. Lee Harrington, and Cornel Sandvoss (New York: New York University Press, 2007), 287.

86. The "Great Replacement" theory is a far-right, white nationalist conspiracy theory that posits that white populations in Europe and North America are being systematically replaced through non-white immigration, abortion,

and violence against white people. French philosopher, novelist, and white nationalist Renaud Camus coined the term in his book *Le Grand Remplacement* (Nueilly-sur-Seine: David Reinharc, 2012). For academic discussions, see Eric Kaufmann, *Whiteshift: Populism, Immigration, and the Future of White Majorities* (New York: Penguin, 2019); Michael Feola, "You Will Not Replace Us": The Melancholic Nationalism of Whiteness," *Political Theory* 49, no. 4, 528–53; Strick, *Rechte Gefühle*, esp. 137–45.

87. William Proctor, "'Bitches Ain't Gonna Hunt No Ghosts': Totemic Nostalgia, Toxic Fandom and the *Ghostbusters* Platonic," *Palabra Clave* 20, no. 4 (2017): 1117.

88. Matt Hills, "Psychoanalysis and Digital Fandom: Theorizing Spoilers and Fans' Self-Narratives," in *Produsing Theory in a Digital World: The Intersection of Audiences and Production in Contemporary Theory*, ed. Rebecca Ann Lind (New York: Peter Lang, 2012), 113. On Giddens's concept of "ontological security" in the context of the 2016 *Ghostbusters*, see Matt Hills, "Always-On Fandom, Waiting and Bingeing: Psychoanalysis as an Engagement with Fans' 'Infra-Ordinary' Experiences," in *The Routledge Companion to Media Fandom*, ed. Melissa Click and Suzanne Scott (New York: Routledge, 2018), 21; and Proctor, "'Bitches'" 114–23.

89. Hills, "Always-On Fandom," 21.

90. Cf. Hills, "Psychoanalysis," 114–15.

91. Cf. Anthony Giddens, *Modernity and Self-Identity: Self and Society in the Late Modern Age* (Cambridge: Polity Press, 1991).

92. Cf. Banet-Weiser, *Empowered*, 2–3.

93. Derek Johnson, "Fantagonism, Franchising, and Industry Management of Fan Privilege," in *The Routledge Companion to Media Fandom*, ed. Suzanne Scott and Melissa Click (New York: Routledge, 2018), 399–400.

94. Quoted in Anthony Breznican, "*Ghostbusters* Resurrected: Jason Reitman Will Direct a New Film Set in the Original Universe," *Entertainment Weekly*, January 15, 2019, https://ew.com/movies/2019/01/15/new-ghostbusters-movie-jason-reitman/.

95. Breznican.

96. Breznican.

97. "Bill Rambles with Director Jason Reitman," *Monday Morning Podcast*, February 18, 2019, https://billburr.com/monday-morning-podcast-2-18-19/.

98. Ivan Reitman, quoted in Breznican, "*Ghostbusters* Resurrected."

99. There is footage from the first *Ghostbusters* and voiceover with a line from Bill Murray's Peter Venkman: "Call it fate, call it luck, call it karma. I believe everything happens for a reason." Played over a suspenseful montage of images and sounds, the words are repurposed in the trailer.

100. Frederic Jameson, *Postmodernism; or, The Cultural Logic of Late Capitalism* (Durham, NC: Duke University Press, 1991), 19.

101. Cherise Huntingford, "To Err Is Human, to Forget . . . Sublime," in *Stranger Things and Philosophy: Thus Spake the Demogorgon*, ed. Jeffrey A. Ewing and Andrew M. Winters (Chicago: Open Court, 2019), 102; emphasis in original.

102. Fernando Gabriel Pagnoni Berns, Diego Foronda, and Mariana Zárate, "Abnormal Is the New Normal," in *Stranger Things and Philosophy: Thus Spake the Demogorgon*, ed. Jeffrey A. Ewing and Andrew M. Winters (Chicago: Open Court, 2019), 183; emphasis in original.

103. Paul Monaco, *Ribbons in Time: Movies and Society since 1945* (Bloomington: Indiana University Press, 1987), 100. See also Jonathan Gray, "'Always Two There Are': Repetition, Originality, and *The Force Awakens*," in *Disney's Star Wars: Forces of Production, Promotion, and Reception*, ed. William Proctor and Richard McCulloch (Iowa City: University of Iowa Press, 2019), 162–65.

104. Jameson, *Postmodernism*, 20–21.

105. Philip Drake, "'Mortgaged to Music': New Retro Movies in 1990s Hollywood Cinema," in *Memory and Popular Film*, ed. Paul Grainge (Manchester: Manchester University Press, 2003), 189; emphasis in original.

106. Jeremy Gordon, "*Ghostbusters* Is the Future of the Culture Wars," *The Outline*, December 9, 2019, https://theoutline.com/post/8409/ghostbusters-reboot-trailer-stranger-things-paul-rudd-finn-wolfhard?zd=2&zi=znkj5pok.

107. Gordon.

108. Ronald Brownstein, "Trump's Rhetoric of White Nostalgia," *The Atlantic*, June 2, 2016, https://www.theatlantic.com/politics/archive/2016/06/trumps-rhetoric-of-white-nostalgia/485192/.

109. See also Kathleen Loock, "Reboot, Requel, Legacyquel: *Jurassic World* and the Nostalgia Franchise," in *Film Reboots*, ed. Daniel Herbert and Constantine Verevis (Edinburgh: Edinburgh University Press, 2020), 173–88.

110. Svetlana Boym, "Nostalgia and Its Discontents," *The Hedgehog Review* (Summer 2007): 10.

111. Shane Denson and Ruth Mayer, "Spectral Seriality: The Sights and Sounds of Count Dracula," in *Media of Serial Narrative*, ed. Frank Kelleter (Columbus: Ohio State University Press, 2017), 110.

112. Kathleen Loock, "'Whatever Happened to Predictability?': *Fuller House*, (Post)Feminism, and the Revival of Family-Friendly Viewing," *Television & New Media* 19, no. 4 (2018): 367.

113. Olick, "From Usable Pasts," 19.

3. CINEMATIC PASTS AND PRESENTS

1. Jennifer Forrest, "The 'Personal' Touch: The Original, the Remake, and the Dupe in Early Cinema," in *Dead Ringers: The Remake in Theory and Practice*, ed. Jennifer Forrest and Leonard R. Koos (Albany: State University of New York Press, 2002), 90.

2. Forrest stresses that "although Americans may have been the most enthusiastic remakers on the international scene . . . the remake was hardly a peculiar American phenomenon" (89–90). See also Jane M. Gaines, "Early Cinema's Heyday of Copying: The Too Many Copies of L'Arroseur arrosé (The Waterer Watered)," *Cultural Studies* 20, nos. 2–3 (March–May 2006): 227–44.

3. Tom Gunning, "The Cinema of Attractions: Early Film, Its Spectator and the Avant-Garde," *Wide Angle* 8, nos. 3–4 (1986): 64–66. Cf. Forrest, "The 'Personal,'" 89–90.

4. Charles Musser, *The Emergence of Cinema: The American Screen to 1917* (Berkeley: University of California Press, 1994), 2.

5. Musser, 2.

6. Forrest, "The 'Personal,'" 96.

7. Forrest, 98.

8. Miriam Hansen, *Babel and Babylon: Spectatorship in American Silent Film* (Cambridge, MA: Harvard University Press, 1991), 25.

9. Forrest, "The 'Personal,'" 91.

10. Hansen, *Babel*, 25.

11. Hansen, 25.

12. Hansen, 26.

13. Hansen, 28.

14. Frank Kelleter and Kathleen Loock, "Hollywood Remaking as Second-Order Serialization," in *Media of Serial Narrative*, ed. Frank Kelleter (Columbus: Ohio State University Press, 2017), 134.

15. See Eric Hoyt, *Hollywood Vault: Film Libraries before Home Video* (Berkeley: University of California Press, 2014); and Forrest, "The 'Personal.'"

16. Martin Martin, "Chatter from Hollywood," *Screenland* (October 1928): 68, MHDL. The discussion in this chapter is based on Kathleen Loock, "Sound Memories: 'Talker Remakes,' Paratexts, and the Cinematic Past," in *The Politics of Ephemeral Digital Media: Permanence and Obsolescence in Paratexts*, ed. Sara Pesce and Paolo Noto (New York, Routledge, 2016), 123–37.

17 Martin, 70.

18. "Old Silent Hits Offering a Solution for Shortage of Good Sound Material," *Motion Picture News*, January 25, 1930, 33, MHDL.

19. Hoyt, *Hollywood Vault*, 80.

20. Philip K. Scheuer, "Old Successes Being Revived," *Los Angeles Times*, May 11, 1930, Newspaper Clipping (EH).

21. Scheuer.

22. Donald Crafton, *The Talkies: American Cinema's Transition to Sound, 1926–1931* (New York: Charles Scribner's Sons, 1997), 6.

23. Crafton, 6.

24. For a transcript of such a Vitaphone trailer from 1928, and a detailed discussion, see Crafton, 121–26.

25. Crafton, 295.

26. Land, "Anna Christie." *Variety*, March 19, 1930: 34, MHDL.
27. Land, 34.
28. Land, 34; emphasis added.
29. Land, 34.
30. Peter Vischer, "Miss Garbo's Voice," *Exhibitor's Herald-World*, March 29, 1930, 18, MHDL.
31. "Screen Reviews: *Anna Christie*," *Talking Screen* (May 1930): 57, MHDL.
32. "Screen Reviews: *Anna Christie*," 57.
33. Dorothy Cartwright, "Who's the Best Talkie Bet?" *Talking Screen* (January 1930): 70, MHDL.
34. Cartwright, 70.
35. Cartwright, 70.
36. Cartwright, 92.
37. Cartwright, 71.
38. Crafton, *The Talkies*, 480.
39. Crafton, 480, 482.
40. Crafton, 485.
41. Crafton, 15.
42. "A Gift from Ramon Novarro," *Screenland* (September 1930): 61, MHDL. At the time, Novarro had already appeared in three talkies: *The Flying Fleet* (George Hill, 1929), *The Pagan* (W. S. van Dyke, 1929), and *Devil-May-Care* (Sidney Franklin, 1929).
43. "A Gift from Ramon Novarro."
44. Crafton, *Talkies*, 482.
45. "Between You and Me," *Modern Screen* (October 1932): 80, MHDL; emphasis added.
46. Jack Kleinman, "Remakes," *New Movie Magazine* (July 1933): 70, MHDL.
47. Kleinman, 70.
48. Mrs. Effie Myers, "Remakes in Sound," *New Movie Magazine* (January 1934): 68, MHDL.
49. "Critic Suggests Remakes," *Film Daily*, July 24, 1934, 6, MHDL.
50. Crafton, *Talkies*, 262.
51. Crafton, 262.
52. John Belton, *American Cinema/American Culture* (New York: McGraw-Hill, 1994), 3.
53. Vinzenz Hediger, "'You Haven't Seen It until You Have Seen It at Least Twice': Film Spectatorship and the Discipline of Repeat Viewing," *Cinéma & Cie* 5 (2004): 26.
54. Hediger, 26.
55. Tino Balio, "Feeding the Maw of Exhibition," in *Grand Design: Hollywood as a Modern Business Enterprise, 1930–1939*, ed. Tino Balio (Berkeley: University of California Press, 1995), 99.

56. Hoyt, *Hollywood Vault*, 80.
57. Hoyt, 80.
58. "Sound Bringing Remakes into B. O.?" *Motion Picture News*, January 25, 1930, 33, MHDL.
59. Robert E. Sherwood, "Silent Successes Adaptable for Talkies," *Film Daily*, October 2, 1930, 4, MHDL.
60. Sherwood, 4.
61. "Producers Find Talkie Material in Old Films," *Motion Picture News*, February 16, 1929, 486, 491, MHDL.
62. "Hits to Be Made Again as Dialogue Pictures," *Film Daily*, April 10, 1929, 6, MHDL.
63. "U Digging into Files for Sound Remakes of Silents," *Motion Picture News*, January 15, 1930, 33, MHDL.
64. Phil M. Daly, "Along the Rialto," *Film Daily*, October 31, 1935, 3, MHDL.
65. "Old Silent Hits Offering a Solution for Shortage of Good Sound Material," *Motion Picture News*, January 25, 1930, 33, MHDL.
66. Hoyt, *Hollywood Vault*, 12.
67. "Only 17 Remakes Scheduled for New Year," *Film Daily*, September 1, 1931, 1, MHDL.
68. "Nine Remakes Listed for 1932–33," *Film Daily*, August 31, 1932, 1, MHDL.
69. "Remake Question Still Puzzling Studio Chiefs," *Motion Picture News*, November 22, 1930, 47, MHDL.
70. "Remake Question," 47.
71. "Editorial: Inside Stuff—Pictures," *Variety* (WV), September 24, 1930, 56, MHDL.
72. "Picking Own Stars and Retitling Now Part of Routine for Exhibs." *Variety* (WV) December 24, 1930, 29, MHDL.
73. "Picking Own Stars," 29.
74. "Editorial: Inside Stuff," 56.
75. Phil M. Daly, "Along the Rialto," *Film Daily*, November 21, 1935, 6, MHDL.
76. Don Carle Gillette, "Viewing the Passing Parade," *Film Daily*, June 9, 1936, 1, MHDL.
77. Gillette, 1.
78. Chester B. Bahn, "New Themes . . . and Old Essentials," *Film Daily*, February 16, 1939, 1, MHDL.
79. Chester B. Bahn, "Great Stories . . . and Pix Remakes." *Film Daily*, December 6, 1939, 1, MHDL.
80. Harold Heffernan, "Fans Grow Irate When Old Films Turn Up Again," *Baltimore Sun*, July 2, 1939, MS6, ProQuest Historical Newspapers.
81. Heffernan, MS6.
82. Heffernan, MS6.
83. Heffernan, MS6.

84. Heffernan, MS6.
85. Heffernan, MS6.
86. Heffernan, MS6.
87. Heffernan, MS6.
88. Ted Taylor, "Studios on the Remake," *Variety* (WV), January 21, 1931, 11, MHDL.
89. "Remakes Headaches," *Variety* (DV), October 21, 1935, 2, MHDL.
90. "Remakes Headaches," 2.
91. Red Kann, "Insider's Outlook," *Motion Picture Daily*, May 12, 1937, 2, MHDL.
92. Kann, 2.
93. Kann, 2.
94. Mrs. Frank Kurlick, Letter, *Photoplay* (May 1941): 23, MHDL.
95. Mrs. Frank Kurlick, 23.
96. Sue Anna, "A Boo for an Encore," *Photoplay* (Dec. 1941): 6, MHDL.
97. Sue Anna, 6.
98. Llewellyn Miller, "Important Pictures," *Hollywood* (July 1941): 16, MHDL.
99. Miller, 17.
100. *"Beau Geste," The Movies . . . and the People Who Make Them* (Theatre Patrons, 1939), 159, MHDL.
101. *"Beau Geste," The Movies, 159.*
102. "Para's *Beau Geste* below Expectations," *Box Office Digest*, July 24, 1939, 10, MHDL.
103. Scheuer, "Old Successes."
104. "Remarks on Remakes." *Motion Picture Herald*, April 10, 1937, 35, MHDL.
105. "Remarks on Remakes," 35.
106. Clarence Thornbey, Letter, *Photoplay* (May 1942): 74.
107. Paul Grainge, "Introduction: Ephemeral Media," in *Ephemeral Media: Transitory Screen Culture from Television to YouTube*, ed. Paul Grainge (London: BFI, 2011), 5.
108. Hediger, "You Haven't," 27.
109. Hediger, 26.
110. Hoyt, *Hollywood Vault*, 86–87, 101.
111. "Editorial: Inside Stuff," 56.
112. Editorial: Inside Stuff," 56.
113. Editorial: Inside Stuff," 56.
114. Taylor, "Studios on the Remake," 26.
115. Daly, "Along the Rialto," 6.
116. Quoted in Bahn, "Great Stories," 1.
117. Bahn, "Great Stories," 1.
118. Bahn, "Great Stories," 1.
119. "Remakes Headaches," 2.
120. Gillette, "Viewing," 1.

121. Don Carle Gillette, "Screen Classics . . . A Permanent Repertory," *Film Daily*, July 9, 1934, 1, MHDL.
122. Gillette, 1.
123. Gillette, 1.
124. Gillette, 1.
125. Gillette, 1.
126. Gillette, 1.
127. Gillette, 1.
128. Crafton, *The Talkies*, 21.
129. Crafton, 21.
130. Crafton, 482.
131. "Yesterday–Today," *Modern Screen* (February 1936): 44, AMPAS.
132. "Yesterday–Today," 45.
133. "Yesterday–Today," 44.
134. Cf. Hoyt, *Hollywood Vault*, 100–105.
135. "Match Them If You Can," *Photoplay* (November 1938): 42, MHDL.
136. "Return of Stella Dallas," *Screenland* (August 1937), MHDL.
137. "Return of Stella Dallas."
138. "Return of Stella Dallas."
139. "Return of Stella Dallas."
140. Jennifer Parchesky, "Adapting *Stella Dallas*: Class Boundaries, Consumerism, and Hierarchies of Taste," *Legacy* 23, no. 2 (2006): 189; emphasis in original.
141. A. J. P. quoted in Parchesky, 188.
142. Parchesky, 188.
143. Parchesky, 188.
144. Parchesky, 188–89.
145. Parchesky, 187–88.
146. Jennifer Forrest and Leonard R. Koos, "Reviewing Remakes: An Introduction," in *Dead Ringers: The Remake in Theory and Practice*, ed. Jennifer Forrest and Leonard R. Koos (Albany: State University of New York Press, 2002), 3–4.
147. Cf. Kelleter and Loock, "Hollywood Remaking," 131.

4. THE REMAKE AS ARCHIVE

1. Jonathan Gray, *Show Sold Separately: Promos, Spoilers and Other Media Paratexts* (New York: New York University Press, 2010), 35.
2. For a detailed discussion, see chapter 3.
3. Katrina Mann, "'You're Next!': Postwar Hegemony Besieged in *Invasion of the Body Snatchers*," *Cinema Journal* 44, no. 1 (2004): 49.
4. Cf. Marlene Manoff, "Theories of the Archive from across the Disciplines," *Portal: Libraries and the Academy* 4, no. 1 (January 2004): 10; Diana Taylor,

The Archive and the Repertoire: Performing Cultural Memory in the Americas (Durham, NC: Duke University Press, 2003), 19.

5. Eivind Røssaak, "The Archive in Motion: An Introduction," in *The Archive in Motion: New Conceptions of the Archive in Contemporary Thought and New Media Practices*, ed. Eivind Røssaak (Oslo: Novus P, 2010), 11.

6. Jussi Parikka, *What Is Media Archaeology?* (Cambridge: Polity Press, 2012), 15.

7. Parikka, 15.

8. Michel Foucault, *The Archaeology of Knowledge*, trans. A. M. Sheridan Smith (1969; London: Routledge, 2007), 129.

9. Jacques Derrida, "Archive Fever: A Freudian Impression," trans. Eric Prenowitz, *Diacritics* 25, no. 2 (Summer 1995): 17; emphasis in original.

10. Manoff, "Theories of the Archive," 10.

11. Cf. Pierre Nora, "Between Memory and History: *Les Lieux de Mémoire*," *Representations* 26 (Spring 1989): 14.

12. Nora, 13.

13. Nora distinguishes between *lieux* and *milieux de mémoire*; ibid., 7. Taylor explains, "the milieux de mémoire constitute the primordial, unmediated, and spontaneous sites of 'true memory,' and the lieux de mémoire—the archival memory—are their antithesis, modern, fictional and highly mediated." Taylor, *The Archive*, 22.

14. Etienne François and Hagen Schulze, "Einleitung," in *Deutsche Erinnerungsorte*, vol. 1, ed. Etienne François and Hagen Schulze, 2001 (Munich: Beck, 2009), 18, my translation; "langlebige, Generationen überdauernde Kristallisationspunkte kollektiver Erinnerung und Identität."

15. Todd S. Purdum, "The Long Hollywood History of *A Star Is Born*," *Atlantic*, October 7, 2018. https://www.theatlantic.com/entertainment/archive/2018/10/star-born-endures-leads-like-barbra-streisand-and-lady-gaga/572374/.

16. Eric Hoyt, *Hollywood Vault: Film Libraries before Home Video* (Berkeley: University of California Press, 2014), 78.

17. The term is borrowed from Robert Stam, "Beyond Fidelity: The Dialogics of Adaptation," in *Film Adaptation*, ed. James Naremore (New Brunswick, NJ: Rutgers, 2000), 166; see also chapter 1.

18. Barry Keith Grant, *Invasion of the Body Snatchers* (London: BFI/Palgrave Macmillan, 2010), 8–9.

19. Grant, 7; Kathleen Loock, "The Return of the Pod People: Remaking Cultural Anxieties in *Invasion of the Body Snatchers*," in *Film Remakes, Adaptations and Fan Productions: Remake/Remodel*, ed. Kathleen Loock and Constantine Verevis (Basingstoke, UK: Palgrave Macmillan, 2012), 123.

20. Aja Romano, "*A Star Is Born* Has a Problem with Consent," *Vox.com*, October 11, 2018. https://www.vox.com/culture/2018/10/11/17949016/a-star-is-born-gender-consent-criticism-sexism.

21. Romano.

22. Except in the 2017 remake, in which Kong never leaves Skull Island and ultimately protects the humans against giant Skullcrawlers thus paving the way for follow-up movies set in the *MonsterVerse*.

23. David Crow, "Why King Kong Can Never Escape His Past," *Den of Geek*, March 2, 2018, https://www.denofgeek.com/culture/why-king-kong-can-never-escape-his-past/.

24. Fredric Jameson, *Postmodernism; or, The Cultural Logic of Late Capitalism* (Durham, NC: Duke University Press, 1991), 19.

25. Michael Millner, "The Ends of Identity Politics and the Case of *King Kong*," *Arizona Quarterly: A Journal of American Literature, Culture, and Theory* 69, no. 4 (Winter 2013): 126–27.

26. Millner, 127.

27. Jameson, *Postmodernism*, 21.

28. Jameson, 20–21.

29. Jameson, 18.

30. Paul Grainge, *Monochrome Memories: Nostalgia and Style in Retro America* (Westport, CT: Praeger, 2002), 30.

31. Valerie Frazier, "King Kong's Reign Continues: *King Kong* as a Sign of Shifting Racial Politics," *CLA Journal* 51, no. 2 (December 2007): 199.

32. Frazier, 198.

33. Frazier.

34. Frazier.

35. The following discussion is based on Loock, "The Return."

36. Stuart Samuels, "The Age of Conspiracy and Conformity: *Invasion of the Body Snatchers* (1956)," in *Hollywood's America: Twentieth-Century America Through Film*, ed. Steven Mintz and Randy W. Roberts (Malden, MA: Wiley-Blackwell, 2010), 200.

37. Annette Insdorf, "Seeing Doubles," *Moving Image Source*, Museum of the Moving Image, June 26, 2008, http://www.movingimagesource.us/articles/seeing-doubles-20080626.

38. Grant, *Invasion*, 98.

39. Barbara Klinger, *Beyond the Multiplex: Cinema, New Technologies, and the Home* (Berkeley: University of California Press, 2006), 11–14.

40. Frederick James Smith, "Reviews," *New Movie Magazine* (August 1931): 74, MHDL.

41. Jake Kring-Schreifels, "4 Stars, 4 Distinct Eras: Which Version of *A Star Is Born* Does It Best?," *New York Times*, October 4, 2018, https://www.nytimes.com/2018/10/04/watching/4-stars-4-distinct-eras-which-version-of-a-star-is-born-does-it-best.html.

42. Geoffrey Macnab, "*A Star Is Born* Review: An Unnecessary Remake," *Independent*, October 4, 2018, https://www.independent.co.uk/arts-entertainment/films/reviews/star-born-review-cast-lady-gaga-bradley-cooper-songs-shallow-a8513311.html.

43. Peter Travers, "*A Star Is Born* Review: Cooper, Lady Gaga Hit All the Right Notes," *Rolling Stone*, October 1, 2018, https://www.rollingstone.com/movies/movie-reviews/a-star-is-born-movie-review-lady-gaga-729475/.

44. Mark Kermode, "*A Star Is Born* Review: A Double Act to Leave You Star-Struck," *Guardian*, October 7, 2018, https://www.theguardian.com/film/2018/oct/07/a-star-is-born-review-bradley-cooper-lady-gaga.

45. Jason Mittell, "Forensic Fandom and the Drillable Text," in *Spreadable Media: Creating Value and Meaning in a Networked Culture*, ed. Henry Jenkins, Sam Ford, and Joshua Green (New York: New York University Press, 2013), https://spreadablemedia.org/essays/mittell/.

5. CINEMATIC SERIALITIES FROM "B" TO "A"

1. John Horn, "Franchi$e Fever," *Newsweek*, April 22, 2002, 58. *Academic OneFile* (accessed August 18, 2022). https://link.gale.com/apps/doc/A84838307/AONE?u=fub&sid=bookmark-AONE&xid=7b7888d5.

2. Horn, 58.

3. Horn, 58.

4. Derek Johnson, *Media Franchising: Creative License and Collaboration in the Culture Industries* (New York: New York University Press, 2013), 6.

5. Johnson, 34.

6. Johnson, 35.

7. Johnson, 41.

8. Johnson, 42.

9. Johnson, 41; emphasis in original.

10. Peter Bart, "Are All Films Created Sequel?" *Variety*, July 28, 2002, 7, Newspaper Clippings (Sequels), NYPL.

11. Bart, 5.

12. Bart, 7.

13. Bart, 7.

14. Stuart Henderson, *The Hollywood Sequel: History and Form, 1911–2010* (London: BFI, 2014), 86–87.

15. See chapter 3.

16. Ilka Brasch, *Film Serials and the American Cinema, 1910–1940: Operational Detection* (Amsterdam: Amsterdam University Press, 2018), 9–11.

17. Brasch, 12.

18. Brasch, *Film Serials*, 15–16.

19. Cf. Brasch, 14–23.

20. Jared Gardner, *Projections: Comics and the History of Twenty-First-Century Storytelling* (Stanford, CA: Stanford University Press, 2012), 22.

21. Brasch, *Film Serials*, 16.

22. Henderson, *The Hollywood Sequel*, 12.

23. Gene Gauntier, "Blazing the Trail," *Woman's Home Companion* (November 1928): 170, https://wfpp.columbia.edu/wp-content/uploads/2011/11/Womans-home-companion_Blazing-the-Trail_2.pdf.

24. Cf. Henderson, *The Hollywood Sequel*, 12.

25. Henderson, 11–12.

26. Henderson, 12.

27. Tino Balio, "Feeding the Maw of Exhibition," in *Grand Design: Hollywood as a Modern Business Enterprise, 1930–1939*, ed. Tino Balio (Berkeley: University of California Press, 1995), 101.

28. Henderson, *The Hollywood Sequel*, 35.

29. Frank Krutnik, "Chiller-Dillers for the Shiver-and-Shudder Set: The *Whistler* Film Series," *Film Studies* 17 (Autumn 2017): 52.

30. Krutnik, 51.

31. Krutnik, 52.

32. Thomas Schatz, *The Genius of the System: Hollywood Filmmaking in the Studio Era* (London: Simon & Schuster, 1989), 257.

33. Henderson, *The Hollywood Sequel*, 38.

34. Henderson, 40.

35. Henderson, 32.

36. Shane Denson and Ruth Mayer, "Spectral Seriality: The Sights and Sounds of Count Dracula," in *Media of Serial Narrative*, ed. Frank Kelleter (Columbus: Ohio State University Press, 2017), 110.

37. Henderson, *The Hollywood Sequel*, 33.

38. Henderson, 33; Denson and Mayer, "Spectral Seriality," 111.

39. Staiger in David Bordwell, Janet Staiger, and Kristin Thompson, *The Classical Hollywood Cinema: Film Style and Mode of Production to 1960* (London: Routledge, 1985), 332.

40. See also Henderson, *The Hollywood Sequel*, 55.

41. Christian Junklewitz and Tanja Weber, "Die Cineserie: Geschichte und Erfolg von Filmserien im postklassischen Kino," in *Serielle Formen: Von den frühen Film-Serials zu aktuellen Quality-TV- und Online-Serien*, ed. Robert Blanchet et al. (Marburg, Germany: Schüren, 2011), 340.

42. Henderson, *The Hollywood Sequel*, 57.

43. Joel W. Finler, *The Hollywood Story* (1988; London: Wallflower Press, 2003), 378.

44. Elaine Tyler May, *Homeward Bound: American Families in the Cold War Era* (New York: Basic Books, 1988), 16.

45. Henderson, *The Hollywood Sequel*, 58–59.

46. Henderson, 53.

47. Henderson, 53.

48. Sheldon Hall, "Tall Revenue Features: The Genealogy of the Modern Blockbuster," in *Genre and Contemporary Hollywood*, ed. Steve Neale (London: BFI, 2002), 11.

49. Tino Balio, "Introduction to Part 1," in *Hollywood in the Age of Television*, ed. Tino Balio (Boston, MA: Unwin Hyman, 1990), 23.

50. Steve Neale, "Hollywood Blockbusters: Historical Dimensions," in *Movie Blockbusters*, ed. Julian Stringer (London: Routledge, 2003), 50–51.

51. Henderson, *The Hollywood Sequel*, 62.

52. Henderson, 62.

53. Henderson, 62.

54. Hall, "Tall Revenue," 15.

55. Hall, 15.

56. Cf. Henderson, *The Hollywood Sequel*, 62; Junklewitz and Weber, "Die Cineserie," 340.

57. Hall, "Tall Revenue," 16.

58. Hall, 19.

59. Henderson, *The Hollywood Sequel*, 60.

60. Henderson, 65.

61. Henderson, 65–66.

62. David A. Cook, *Lost Illusions: American Cinema in the Shadow of Watergate and Vietnam* (New York: Charles Scribner's Sons, 2000), 194.

63. Cook, 193.

64. Cook, 283.

65. Henderson, *The Hollywood Sequel*, 69.

66. Jennifer Forrest, "The Poetics of Film Series," in *The Legend Returns and Dies Harder Another Day: Essays on Film Series*, ed. Jennifer Forrest (Jefferson, NC: McFarland, 2008), 22.

67. Forrest.

68. Umberto Eco, "The Myth of Superman," *Diacritics* 2, no. 1 (Spring 1972): 17.

69. Jennifer Forrest, "Introduction," in *The Legend Returns and Dies Harder Another Day: Essays on Film Series*, ed. Jennifer Forrest (Jefferson, NC: McFarland, 2008), 7.

70. Ben Child, "Time's Up for James Bond: Is 007 too Toxic for the #MeToo Era?" *Guardian*, 30 January 2018, https://www.theguardian.com/film/2018/jan/30/times-up-for-james-bond-is-007-too-brutish-for-the-me-too-era.

71. Alyssa Rosenberg, "'No Time to Die' Is a Radical End to Daniel Craig's Run as James Bond," *Washington Post*, 11 October 2021, https://www.washingtonpost.com/opinions/2021/10/11/no-time-die-is-radical-end-daniel-craigs-run-james-bond/.

72. Denson and Mayer, "Spectral Seriality," 111.

73. Henderson, *The Hollywood Sequel*, 70.

74. Henderson.

75. Brian Pendreigh, *Planet of the Apes: Or How Hollywood Turned Darwin Upside Down* (London: Boxtree, 2001), 2.

76. Eric Greene, *Planet of the Apes as American Myth: Race and Politics in the Films and Television Series* (Jefferson, NC: McFarland, 1996), 179.

77. Greene, 2–3.
78. Dale Winogura, "Dialogues on Apes, Apes, and More Apes," *Cinefantastique* (Summer 1972): 27.
79. At the time of preparing this book manuscript for publication (September 2023), a direct sequel, *Kingdom of the Planet of the Apes*, is in postproduction and scheduled for release in May 2024. Stephen Barker, "New Planet of the Apes Movie Finally Completes Matt Reeves' Reboot Vision 7 Years Later," *Screen Rant*, August 20, 2023, https://screenrant.com/planet-of-the-apes-matt-reeves-vision-villain-kingdom-story/.
80. Constantine Verevis, *Film Remakes* (Edinburgh: Edinburgh University Press, 2006), 96.
81. Verevis, 96.
82. Frank Kelleter and Kathleen Loock, "Hollywood Remaking as Second-Order Serialization," in *Media of Serial Narrative*, ed. Frank Kelleter (Columbus: Ohio State University Press, 2017), 142.
83. See also the discussion in chapter 4.
84. Cf. Henderson, *The Hollywood Sequel*, 72.
85. Cf. Henderson, 72; Hall, "Tall Revenue," 23.
86. Henderson, *The Hollywood Sequel*, 71.
87. Henderson, 71.
88. Cf. Pendreigh, *Planet*, 155.
89. Scott Higgins, "Saturday Afternoon Blockbuster: James Bond's Serial Heritage," *Film Studies* 17 (Autumn 2017): 86–87.
90. Henderson, *The Hollywood Sequel*, 6.

6. FROM SEQUELITIS TO THE FOREVER FRANCHISE

1. Ben Child, "A Third *Blade Runner* Movie Is as Inevitable as the Robot Revolution," *Guardian*, January 30, 2020, https://www.theguardian.com/film/filmblog/2020/jan/30/third-blade-runner-movie-denis-villeneuve.
2. Child.
3. Scott quoted in Megan Davies and Rosie Fletcher, "Ridley Scott Has Plans for another *Blade Runner* Sequel," *Digital Spy*, January 6, 2018, https://www.digitalspy.com/movies/a846834/ridley-scott-has-plans-another-blade-runner-sequel/.
4. Villeneuve quoted in Ben Travis, "Denis Villeneuve Wants to 'Revisit' the World of *Blade Runner*: Exclusive," *Empire*, January 23, 2020, https://www.empireonline.com/movies/news/denis-villeneuve-wants-to-revisit-the-world-of-blade-runner-exclusive/.
5. Travis.
6. "Spielberg Spanks Sequels as 'Cheap Carnival Trick,'" *Variety*, October 29, 1975, 30, Newspaper Clippings (Sequels), NYPL.

7. Manohla Dargis, "A Word with: Steven Spielberg," *New York Times*, May 15, 2016, https://www.nytimes.com/2016/05/17/movies/a-word-with-steven-spielberg.html; Anita Busch, "Steven Spielberg on Amblin Partners, What Happens to DreamWorks and Whether He'll Redo *Jaws*," *Deadline*, December 16, 2015, https://deadline.com/2015/12/steven-spielberg-dreamworks-plan-amblin-partners-jeff-skoll-remakes-1201668401/.

8. "Spielberg Spanks," 30.

9. Stuart Henderson, *The Hollywood Sequel: History and Form, 1911–2010* (London: BFI, 2014), 89.

10. Ryan Lambie, "Ridley Scott Interview: *Blade Runner 2049*, *Alien* and More," *Den of Geek*, October 1, 2017, https://www.denofgeek.com/movies/ridley-scott-interview-blade-runner-2049-alien-and-more/.

11. Kathleen Loock, "The Sequel Paradox: Repetition, Innovation and Hollywood's Hit Film Formula," *Film Studies* 17 (Autumn 2017): 94.

12. This discussion is based on Loock, "The Sequel Paradox."

13. Sheldon Hall, "Tall Revenue Features: The Genealogy of the Modern Blockbuster," in *Genre and Contemporary Hollywood*, ed. Steve Neale (London: BFI, 2002), 20.

14. Cf. Charles Fleming, "Hollywood Seeks Secret to Sequel Success," *Variety*, August 10, 1992, 73, Newspaper Clippings (Sequels), NYPL.

15. David A. Cook, *Lost Illusions: American Cinema in the Shadow of Watergate and Vietnam* (New York: Charles Scribner's Sons, 2000), 16.

16. Quoted in Aljean Harmetz, "The Sequel Becomes the New Bankable Film Star," *New York Times*, July 8, 1985, C15, Newspaper Clippings (Sequels), NYPL.

17. Cf. Fleming, "Hollywood Seeks," 73.

18. William Goldman, *Adventures in the Screen Trade* (New York: Warner Books, 1983).

19. Cf. Katie Allen, "Discovered at Last: The Formula for a Hit Film Sequel," *The Observer*, November 8, 2009, 18, 19, Newspaper Clippings (Sequels), NYPL.

20. Thorsten Hennig-Thurau, Mark B. Houston, and Torsten Heitjans, "Conceptualizing and Measuring the Monetary Value of Brand Extensions: The Case of Motion Pictures," *Journal of Marketing* 73 (November 2009): 167–83.

21. Thorsten Hennig-Thurau and Mark B. Houston, *Entertainment Science: Data Analytics and Practical Theory for Movies, Games, Books, and Music* (Cham, Switzerland: Springer, 2019).

22. Quoted in Andrea King, "The Sequel: If at First You Do Succeed, Try, Try Again," *Hollywood Reporter*, September 1988, 74, Newspaper Clippings (Sequels), NYPL.

23. Quoted in Alan Mirabella, "Once Is Not Enough: 'Sequel and Ye Shall Reap' Is Hollywood's Summer Credo," *New York Daily News*, June 11, 1989, 19, Newspaper Clippings (Sequels), NYPL.

24. Hall, "Tall Revenue," 22.

25. Tom Schatz, "The Studio System and Conglomerate Hollywood," in *The Contemporary Hollywood Film Industry*, ed. Paul McDonald and Janet Wasko (Malden, MA: Wiley-Blackwell, 2008), 21.

26. Leslie Wayne, "Hollywood Sequels Are Just the Ticket," *New York Times*, July 18, 1982, Sect. 3, 17, Newspaper Clippings (Sequels), NYPL.

27. Anne Thompson, "They're Back!," *Variety*, June 13, 1990, 42, Newspaper Clippings (Sequels), NYPL.

28. Quoted in Thompson.

29. Roger Hagedorn, "Doubtless to Be Continued," in *To Be Continued . . .: Soap Operas Around the World*, ed. Robert Clyde Allen (London: Routledge, 1995), 28–29.

30. See Andreas Jahn-Sudmann and Frank Kelleter, "Die Dynamik serieller Überbietung: Amerikanische Fernsehserien und das Konzept des Quality TV," in *Populäre Serialität: Narration—Evolution—Distinktion. Zum seriellen Erzählen seit dem 19. Jahrhundert*, ed. Frank Kelleter (Bielefeld, Germany: Transcript, 2012), 205–24.

31. Henderson, *The Hollywood Sequel*, 145. See also Todd Berliner, "The Pleasures of Disappointment: Sequels and *The Godfather Part II*," *Journal of Film and Video* 53, nos. 2–3 (2001): 109.

32. Quoted in Wayne, "Hollywood Sequels," 17.

33. Fleming, "Hollywood Seeks," 1.

34. Dave Kehr, "Once Is Never Enough: Titles, Not Actors, Are the Stars of the Eighties," *Chicago Magazine* (Sept. 1983): 138, Newspaper Clippings (Sequels), NYPL.

35. Kehr, 138.

36. Max Horkheimer and Theodor W. Adorno, "Kulturindustrie, Aufklärung als Massenbetrug," in *Dialektik der Aufklärung: Philosophische Fragmente* (1944; Frankfurt/Main: Fischer, 1988), 128–76.

37. Horkheimer and Adorno, 128–76.

38. Rainer, "Sequelmania: Is It Throttling Hollywood?," *Los Angeles Herald-Examiner*, July 8, 1983, D7, Newspaper Clippings (Sequels –1987), AMPAS. See also Aljean Harmetz, "Boom Summer for Film Sequels," *New York Times*, May 3, 1989, C19, Newspaper Clippings (Sequels), NYPL; and Harmetz, "The Sequel Becomes," C15.

39. Caryn James, "Twice-Told Tales Can Cast a Spell," *New York Times*, August 6, 1989, 28, Newspaper Clippings (Sequels 1985–1989), AMPAS.

40. Leonard Klady, "Sequel Season Has Studios Sweating," *Variety*, March 28, 1994, 82, Newspaper Clippings (Sequels), NYPL.

41. James, "Twice-Told Tales," 28.

42. Gregg Kilday, "Sequels: Will It Play again in Peoria?" *Los Angeles Herald-Examiner*, June 4, 1982, 6, Newspaper Clippings (Sequels –1987), AMPAS.

43. James, "Twice-Told Tales," 1, 28.

44. Mark Stuart Gill, "When a Movie Needs a (Very) Familiar Face," *New York Times*, July 11, 1993, 16, 19, Newspaper Clippings (Sequels), NYPL.
45. Quoted in Gill, 19.
46. Terry Castle, *Masquerade and Civilization: The Carnivalesque in Eighteenth-Century English Literature and Fiction* (Stanford, CA: Stanford University Press, 1986), 134.
47. Castle, 134.
48. Berliner, "The Pleasures of Disappointment," 109.
49. Berliner, 109.
50. Berliner, 108.
51. Cf. Umberto Eco, "Innovation and Repetition: Between Modern and Post-Modern Aesthetics," *Daedalus* 114, no. 4 (Fall 1985): 161–84; Jennifer Hayward, *Consuming Pleasures: Active Audiences and Serial Fictions from Dickens to Soap Opera* (Lexington: University of Kentucky Press, 1997); Kathleen Loock, "Introduction: Serial Narratives," *LWU: Literatur in Wissenschaft und Unterricht* 47, nos. 1–2 (2014): 5–9.
52. Frank Kelleter and Kathleen Loock, "Hollywood Remaking as Second-Order Serialization," in *Media of Serial Narrative*, ed. Frank Kelleter (Columbus: Ohio State University Press, 2017), 127.
53. Rainer, "Sequelmania," D7.
54. Rainer, D7.
55. Henderson, *The Hollywood Sequel*, 154.
56. Henderson, 155.
57. Quoted in Mirabella, "Once Is Not Enough," 19.
58. See Henderson, *The Hollywood Sequel*, 105–28.
59. I borrow this term from Ursula Ganz-Blättler, "DSDS als Reality-Serie: Kumulatives Storytelling 'on the go,'" in *Populäre Serialität: Narration—Evolution—Distinktion. Zum seriellen Erzählen seit dem 19. Jahrhundert*, ed. Frank Kelleter (Bielefeld, Germany: Transcript, 2012), 123–41.
60. Harvey O'Brian, *Action Movies: The Cinema of Striking Back* (New York: Columbia University Press, 2012), 54.
61. Cf. Hank Gallo, "Hollywood's Instant Replays," *New York Daily News*, January 20, 1991, 15, Newspaper Clippings (Sequels), NYPL.
62. Quoted in Jeff Melvoin, "Capping the Teeth of *Jaws II*," *Women's Wear Daily*, January 6, 1978, 13, Newspaper Clippings (Sequels), NYPL.
63. Lianne McLarty, "'I'll Be Back': Hollywood, Sequelization, and History," in *Part Two: Reflections on the Sequel*, ed. Paul Budra and Betty A. Schellenberg (Toronto: University of Toronto Press, 1998), 200.
64. McLarty, 202.
65. Cf. McLarty, 202; Henderson, *The Hollywood Sequel*, 132.
66. Frank Kelleter, "Five Ways of Looking at Popular Seriality," in *Media of Serial Narrative*, ed. Frank Kelleter (Columbus: Ohio State University Press, 2017), 18.

67. Todd McCarthy, "Smart Pix Just the Cure for Sequelitis," *Variety*, June 28, 2004, 5, Newspaper Clippings (Sequels), NYPL.

68. McCarthy, "Smart Pix," 5.

69. John Horn, "Franchi$e Fever," *Newsweek*, April 22, 2002, 58. *Academic OneFile*, go.galegroup.com/ps/i.do?p=AONE&sw=w&u=fub&v=2.1&id=GALE%7CA84838307&it=r&asid=c6324537b7943ff894bd20f03fb80212. Accessed November 2, 2017.

70. Horn.

71. Ryan Brown, "How Franchises Changed Hollywood," *UWIRE*, November 30, 2015, 1. *Academic OneFile*, go.galegroup.com/ps/i.do?p=AONE&sw=w&u=fub&v=2.1&id=GALE%7CA436253503&it=r&asid=d12e9a4b6bd5135a469a9b709e43fc3d. Accessed November 2, 2017.

72. Felix Brinker, *Superhero Blockbusters: Seriality and Politics* (Edinburgh: Edinburgh University Press, 2022), 100–101.

73. Daniel Herbert, *Film Remakes and Franchises* (New Brunswick, NJ: Rutgers University Press, 2017), 13.

74. Brown, "How Franchises."

75. Adam Rogers, "Star Wars and the Quest for the Forever Franchise," *Wired*, December 2015, https://www.wired.com/2015/11/building-the-star-wars-universe/.

76. Rogers.

77. Rogers.

78. See Kathleen Loock, "On the Realist Aesthetics of Digital De-Aging in Contemporary Hollywood Cinema," *Orbis Litterarum* 76 (2021): 214–25. https://doi.org/10.1111/oli.12302.

79. Ruth Mayer, *Serial Fu Manchu* (Philadelphia: Temple University Press, 2013), 10, 11. See also Shane Denson and Ruth Mayer, "Spectral Seriality: The Sights and Sounds of Count Dracula," in *Media of Serial Narrative*, ed. Frank Kelleter (Columbus: Ohio State University Press, 2017); Brinker, *Superhero Blockbusters*, 23–24.

80. Rogers, "Star Wars."

81. Hills similarly argues that the TV series revival *Twin Peaks: The Return* (Showtime, 2017) "collapses together the extra-diegetic and diegetic passage of time since its original 1990s incarnation." Matt Hills, "Cult TV Revival: Generational Seriality, Recap Culture, and the 'Brand Gap' of *Twin Peaks: The Return*," *Television & New Media* 19, no. 4 (May 2018): 311.

82. Henderson, *The Hollywood Sequel*, 166.

83. See also chapter 2 on the nostalgia franchise.

84. Ryan Lizardi, *Nostalgic Generations and Media: Perception of Time and Available Meaning* (Lanham, MD: Lexington Books), 2017.

85. Svetlana Boym, *The Future of Nostalgia* (New York: Basic Books, 2001); Fred Davis, *Yearning for Yesterday: A Sociology of Nostalgia* (New York: The Free Press, 1979); Katharina Niemeyer, ed., *Media and Nostalgia: Yearning*

for the Past, the Present and the Future (London: Palgrave Macmillan, 2014); Janelle L. Wilson, *Nostalgia: Sanctuary of Meaning* (Lewisburg, PA: Bucknell University Press, 2005).

86. Robert Buerkle, "Playset Nostalgia: *LEGO Star Wars: The Video Game* and the Transgenerational Appeal of the LEGO Video Game Franchise," in *LEGO Studies: Examining the Building Blocks of a Transmedial Phenomenon*, ed. Mark J. P. Wolf (New York: Routledge, 2014), 128.

87. Benjamin J. Robertson, "'It Is Just Us Now': Nostalgia and *Star Wars Episode VII: The Force Awakens*," *Science Fiction Film and Television* 9, no. 3 (2016): 482.

88. Tasha Robinson, "*Star Wars: The Force Awakens* Shows the Joys—and Limits—of Fulfilled Nostalgia." *Verge*, Vox Media, Inc., December 18, 2015, Accessed March 19, 2018.

89 ˢ See Loock, "On the Realist Aesthetics."

90. Lee Edelman, *No Future: Queer Theory and the Death Drive* (Durham, NC: Duke University Press, 2004).

91. Matt Singer, "Welcome to the Age of the Legacyquel," *ScreenCrush*, November 23, 2015, http://screencrush.com/the-age-of-legacyquels/.

92. Tom Boellstorff, "When Marriage Falls: Queer Coincidences in Straight Time." *GLQ: Journal of Lesbian and Gay Studies* 13, nos. 2–3 (2007): 227–48.

93. Elizabeth Freeman, *Time Binds: Queer Temporalities, Queer Histories* (Durham, NC: Duke University Press, 2010).

94. The following discussion draws on my video essay on *Blade Runner 2049*. Kathleen Loock, "Reproductive Futurism and the Politics of the Sequel," *[in]Transition: Journal of Videographic Film & Moving Image Studies* 6, no. 3 (2019): mediacommons.org/intransition/reproductive-futurism-and-politics-sequel.

95. Edelman, *No Future*.

96. Christian Stewen, "Ceding/Succeeding Images: Reproduktive und queere Zeitverhältnisse des Animationsfilms," in *Im Wandel . . . Metamorphosen der Animation*, ed. Julia Eckel, Erwin Feyersinger, and Meike Uhrig (Wiesbaden, Germany: Springer, 2018), 85–86. My translation.

97. Rebekah Sheldon, *The Child to Come: Life after the Human Catastrophe* (Minneapolis: University of Minnesota Press, 2016), 36.

98. Loock, "On the Realist Aesthetics," 219.

99. Shama Rangwala, "*Blade Runner 2049*: No Future," *Pyriscence*, November 3, 2017, https://www.pyriscence.ca/home/2017/11/3/blade-runner-2049-no-future.

100. Sheldon, *The Child*, 6.

101. Rangwala, "*Blade Runner 2049*."

102. Peter White and Nellie Andreeva, "*Blade Runner 2099* Live-Action Sequel Series from Ridley Scott, Silka Luisa & Alcon in Works at Amazon Studios," *Deadline*, February 11, 2022, Accessed August 6, 2022, https://deadline.com/2022/02/blade-runner-2099-sequel-series-ridley-scott-amazon-1234931521/.

103. James Hibberd, "FX Gives New Details on *Alien* TV Series, Teases 'Big Surprises,'" *Hollywood Reporter,* February 17, 2022, Accessed August 6, 2022, https://www.hollywoodreporter.com/tv/tv-news/fx-alien-tv-series-1235095576/.

104. Borys Kit, "New *Alien* Movie in the Works with *Don't Breathe* Filmmaker Fede Alvarez (Exclusive)," *Hollywood Reporter,* March 4, 2022, Accessed August 6, 2022, https://www.hollywoodreporter.com/movies/movie-news/alien-movie-fede-alvarez-20th-century-studios-1235037155/.

105. Anthony Lund, "Star Wars Could 'Go On Forever,' Lucasfilm President Says." *Movieweb.com,* May 27, 2022, Accessed August 1, 2022, https://movieweb.com/star-wars-could-go-on-forever-says-lucasfilm-president/.

106. Lund.

CONCLUSION: REBOOTING THE PAST

1. William Proctor, "Regeneration & Rebirth: An Anatomy of the Franchise Reboot," *Scope: An Online Journal of Film and Television Studies* 22 (February 2012): 4–5.

2. Daniel Herbert, *Film Remakes and Franchises* (New Brunswick, NJ: Rutgers University Press, 2017), 8–9.

3. Herbert, 4–5.

4. See also figure 16 in chapter 4.

5. The crossover series includes the horror comedies *Abbot and Costello Meet Frankenstein* (Charles Barton, 1948), *Abbot and Costello Meet the Killer, Boris Karloff* (Charles, Barton, 1949), *Abbot and Costello Meet the Invisible Man* (Charles Lamont, 1951), *Abbott and Costello Meet Dr. Jekyll and Mr. Hyde* (Charles Lamont, 1953), and *Abbott and Costello Meet the Mummy* (Charles Lamont, 1955).

6. See boxofficemojo.com.

7. There are two prequels to *The Exorcist*: Schrader was the first to shoot *The Exorcist: The Beginning,* but the studio replaced him with Renny Harlin as director. Harlin's completely reshot version was released in 2004 and Schrader's version in 2005.

8. Philip L. Simpson, "Whither the Serial Killer Movie?," in *American Horror Film: The Genre at the Turn of the Millennium,* ed. Steffen Hantke (Jackson: University Press of Mississippi, 2010), 132–33.

9. On the concept of "multiplicities," see Amanda Ann Klein and R. Barton Palmer, "Introduction," in *Cycles, Sequels, Spin-Offs, Remakes, and Reboots: Multiplicities in Film and Television,* ed. Amanda Ann Klein and R. Barton Palmer (Austin: University of Texas Press, 2016), 1–21.

10. Daniel Herbert and Constantine Verevis, "Introduction: Film Reboots," in *Film Reboots,* ed. Daniel Herbert and Constantine Verevis (Edinburgh: University of Edinburgh Press, 2020), 7; Proctor, "Regeneration," 5–7.

11. Leo Braudy, "Afterword: Rethinking Remakes," in *Play It Again, Sam: Retakes on Remakes*, ed. Andrew Horton and Stuart Y. McDougal (Berkeley: University of California Press, 1998), 327. See also chapter 1.

12. William Proctor, "Reboots and Retroactive Continuity," in *The Routledge Companion to Imaginary Worlds*, ed. Mark J. P. Wolf (New York: Routledge, 2017), 230.

13. Daniel Dimanna, "What Is a Reboot, Revival, Remake and Sequel? Differences Explained," *Screen Rant*, January 1, 2022, https://screenrant.com/reboot-revival-remake-sequel-definitions-differences-examples-explained/.

14. Dimanna.

15. Frank Kelleter and Kathleen Loock, "Hollywood Remaking as Second-Order Serialization," in *Media of Serial Narrative*, ed. Frank Kelleter (Columbus: Ohio State University Press, 2017), 130.

16. Herbert and Verevis, "Introduction," 9.

17. See chapter 2; and Kathleen Loock, "Reboot, Requel, Legacyquel: *Jurassic World* and the Nostalgia Franchise," in *Film Reboots*, ed. Daniel Herbert and Constantine Verevis (Edinburgh: Edinburgh University Press, 2020), 173–88.

Selected Bibliography

ARCHIVAL COLLECTIONS

Library of Congress, Moving Image Section, Washington, D.C.
Margaret Herrick Library, Academy of Motion Picture Arts and Sciences, Los Angeles
New York Public Library for the Performing Arts, New York

FILM INDUSTRY TRADE PAPERS

Box Office Digest
Deadline
Exhibitor's Herald-World
Film Daily
Hollywood Reporter
Motion Picture Daily
Motion Picture Herald
Motion Picture News
The Movies . . . and the People Who Make Them
Variety

FAN MAGAZINES

Hollywood
Modern Screen
New Movie Magazine
Photoplay
Screenland
Talking Screen

NEWSPAPERS, MAGAZINES, WEBSITES, BLOGS, AND PODCASTS

Atlantic
Bibliodaze
Chicago Magazine
Daily Edge
Den of Geek
Empire (UK)
Entertainment Weekly
GQ
Guardian (UK)
Independent (UK)
Kateryrie.wordpress.com
Los Angeles Herald-Examiner
Los Angeles Times
Monday Morning Podcast
Movieweb.com
Newsweek
New York
New York Daily News
New York Times
Observer (UK)
Outline
Pyriscence (CA)
Refinery29
RogerEbert.com
Rolling Stone
ScreenCrush
Screen Rant
Sun (Baltimore)
Telegraph (UK)

UWIRE
Vice
Village Voice
Vox
Washington Post
WIRED
Women's Home Companion
Women's Wear Daily

BOOKS, CHAPTERS, AND JOURNAL ARTICLES

Altman, Rick. "A Semantic/Syntactic Approach to Film Genre." *Cinema Journal* 23, no. 3 (Spring 1984): 6–18.

Anderson, Benedict. *Imagined Communities: Reflections on the Origins and Spread of Nationalism*. 1983. London: Verso, 1991.

Appadurai, Arjun. *Modernity at Large: Cultural Dimensions of Globalization*. Minneapolis: Minnesota University Press, 1996.

Arnzen, Michael A. "The Same and the New: *Cape Fear* and the Hollywood Remake as Metanarrative Discourse." *Narrative* 4, no. 2 (May 1996): 175–94.

Assmann, Jan. "Communicative and Cultural Memory." In *Cultural Memory Studies: An International and Interdisciplinary Handbook*, edited by Astrid Erll and Ansgar Nünning, 109–18. Berlin: de Gruyter, 2008.

Bal, Mieke. *Quoting Caravaggio: Contemporary Art, Preposterous History*. Chicago: University of Chicago Press, 1999.

Balio, Tino. "Feeding the Maw of Exhibition." In *Grand Design: Hollywood as a Modern Business Enterprise, 1930–1939*, edited by Tino Balio, 73–105. Berkeley: University of California Press, 1995.

———. "Introduction to Part 1." In *Hollywood in the Age of Television*, edited by Tino Balio, 3–38. Boston, MA: Unwin Hyman, 1990.

Banet-Weiser, Sarah. *Empowered: Popular Feminism and Popular Misogyny*. Durham, NC: Duke University Press, 2018.

Belton, John. *American Cinema/American Culture*. New York: McGraw-Hill, 1994.

Berliner, Todd. "The Pleasures of Disappointment: Sequels and *The Godfather Part II*." *Journal of Film and Video* 53, nos. 2–3 (2001): 107–23.

Boellstorff, Tom. "When Marriage Falls: Queer Coincidences in Straight Time." *GLQ: Journal of Lesbian and Gay Studies* 13, nos. 2–3 (2007): 227–48.

Bolin, Göran. *Media Generations: Experience, Identity and Mediatised Social Change*. London: Routledge, 2017.

Bordwell, David, Janet Staiger, and Kristin Thompson. *The Classical Hollywood Cinema: Film Style and Mode of Production to 1960*. London: Routledge, 1985.
Boym, Svetlana. "Nostalgia and Its Discontents." *The Hedgehog Review* (Summer 2007): 7–18.
———. *The Future of Nostalgia*. New York: Basic Books, 2001.
Brasch, Ilka. *Film Serials and the American Cinema, 1910–1940: Operational Detection*. Amsterdam: Amsterdam University Press, 2018.
Braudy, Leo. "Afterword: Rethinking Remakes." In *Play It Again, Sam: Retakes on Remakes*, edited by Andrew Horton and Stuart Y. McDougal, 327–34. Berkeley: University of California Press, 1998.
Brinker, Felix. *Superhero Blockbusters: Seriality and Politics*. Edinburgh: Edinburgh University Press, 2022.
Brooks, Van Wyck. "On Creating a Usable Past." *The Dial*, April 11, 1918, 337–41.
Buerkle, Robert. "Playset Nostalgia: *LEGO Star Wars: The Video Game* and the Transgenerational Appeal of the LEGO Video Game Franchise." In *LEGO Studies: Examining the Building Blocks of a Transmedial Phenomenon*, edited by Mark J. P. Wolf, 118–52. New York: Routledge, 2014.
Carrigy, Megan. "Re-staging the Cinema: *Psycho*, Film Spectatorship and the Redundant New Remake." *Screening the Past* 34 (2012), http://www.screeningthepast.com/issue-34-untimely-cinema/re-staging-the-cinema-psycho-film-spectatorship-and-the-redundant-new-remake/.
Castle, Terry. *Masquerade and Civilization: The Carnivalesque in Eighteenth-Century English Literature and Fiction*. Stanford, CA: Stanford University Press, 1986.
Chan, Kenneth. *Remade in Hollywood: The Global Chinese Presence in Transnational Cinemas*. Hong Kong: Hong Kong University Press, 2009.
Constable, Catherine. "Reflections on the Surface: Remaking the Postmodern with Van Sant's *Psycho*." In *Adaptation in Contemporary Culture: Textual Infidelities*, edited by Rachel Carroll, 24–33. London: Continuum, 2009.
Cook, David A. *Lost Illusions: American Cinema in the Shadow of Watergate and Vietnam*. New York: Charles Scribner's Sons, 2000.
Crafton, Donald. *The Talkies: American Cinema's Transition to Sound, 1926–1931*. New York: Charles Scribner's Sons, 1997.
Crofts, Stephen. "Reconceptualizing National Cinemas." *Quarterly Review of Film and Video* 14, no. 3 (1993): 49–67.
Cuelenaere, Eduard, Gertjan Willems, and Stijn Joye, eds. *European Film Remakes*. Edinburgh: Edinburgh University Press, 2021.
Davis, Fred. *Yearning for Yesterday: A Sociology of Nostalgia*. New York: The Free Press, 1979.
Denson, Shane, and Ruth Mayer. "Spectral Seriality: The Sights and Sounds of Count Dracula." In *Media of Serial Narrative*, edited by Frank Kelleter, 108–24. Columbus: Ohio State University Press, 2017.

Derrida, Jacques. "Archive Fever: A Freudian Impression." Translated by Eric Prenowitz, *Diacritics* 25, no. 2 (Summer 1995): 9–63.
Dika, Vera. *Games of Terror: "Halloween," "Friday the 13th," and the Films of the Stalker Cycle*. Rutherford, NJ: Fairleigh Dickinson University Press, 1990.
———. *Recycled Culture in Contemporary Art and Film: The Uses of Nostalgia*. Cambridge: Cambridge University Press, 2003.
Doane, Ashley "Woody." "Shades of Colorblindness: Rethinking Racial Ideology in the United States." In *The Colorblind Screen: Television in Post-Racial America*, edited by Sarah Nilsen and Sarah E. Turner, 15–38. New York: New York University Press, 2014.
Donaldson-McHugh, Shannon, and Don Moore. "Film Adaptation, Co-Authorship, and Hauntology: Gus Van Sant's *Psycho* (1998)." *The Journal of Popular Culture* 39, no. 2 (2006): 225–33.
Drake, Philip. "'Mortgaged to Music': New Retro Movies in 1990s Hollywood Cinema." In *Memory and Popular Film*, edited by Paul Grainge, 183–201. Manchester: Manchester UP, 2003.
Druxman, Michael B. *Make It Again, Sam: A Survey of Movie Remakes*. Cranbury, NJ: A. S. Barnes, 1975.
Durham, Carolyn A. *Double Takes: Culture and Gender in French Films and Their American Remakes*. Hanover, NH: University Press of New England, 1998.
Eberwein, Robert. "Remakes and Cultural Studies." In *Play It Again, Sam: Retakes on Remakes*, edited by Andrew Horton and Stuart Y. McDougal, 15–33. Berkeley: University of California Press, 1998.
Eco, Umberto. "Innovation and Repetition: Between Modern and Post-Modern Aesthetics." *Daedalus* 114, no. 4 (Fall 1985): 161–84.
———. "The Myth of Superman." *Diacritics* 2, no. 1 (Spring 1972): 14–22.
Edelman, Lee. *No Future: Queer Theory and the Death Drive*. Durham, NC: Duke University Press, 2004.
Ellis, John. *Visible Fictions: Cinema, Television, Video*. 1982. London: Routledge, 1992.
Erll, Astrid. "Generation in Literary History: Three Constellations of Generationality, Genealogy, and Memory." *New Literary History* 45 (2014): 385–409.
———. "Literature, Film, and the Mediality of Cultural Memory." In *Cultural Memory Studies: An International and Interdisciplinary Handbook*, edited by Astrid Erll and Ansgar Nünning, 389–98. Berlin: de Gruyter, 2008.
Felski, Rita. *Uses of Literature*. Malden, MA: Blackwell 2008.
Feola, Michael. "'You Will Not Replace Us': The Melancholic Nationalism of Whiteness." *Political Theory* 49, no. 4 (2021): 528–53. https://doi.org/10.1177/0090591720972745.

Finler, Joel W. *The Hollywood Story*. 1988. Reprint, London: Wallflower Press, 2003.
Forrest, Jennifer. "Introduction." In *The Legend Returns and Dies Harder Another Day: Essays on Film Series*, edited by Jennifer Forrest, 1–19. Jefferson, NC: McFarland, 2008.
———, ed. *The Legend Returns and Dies Harder Another Day: Essays on Film Series*. Jefferson, NC: McFarland, 2008.
———. "The 'Personal' Touch: The Original, the Remake, and the Dupe in Early Cinema." In *Dead Ringers: The Remake in Theory and Practice*, edited by Jennifer Forrest and Leonard R. Koos, 89–126. Albany: State University of New York Press, 2002.
———. "The Poetics of Film Series." In *The Legend Returns and Dies Harder Another Day: Essays on Film Series*, edited by Jennifer Forrest, 21–38. Jefferson, NC: McFarland, 2008.
Forrest, Jennifer, and Leonard R. Koos. "Reviewing Remakes: An Introduction." In *Dead Ringers: The Remake in Theory and Practice*, edited by Jennifer Forrest and Leonard R. Koos, 1–36. Albany: State University of New York Press, 2002.
Foucault, Michel. *The Archaeology of Knowledge*, translated by A. M. Sheridan Smith. 1969; London: Routledge, 2007.
Francis, James. *Remaking Horror: Hollywood's New Reliance on Scares of Old*. Jefferson, NC: McFarland, 2013.
François, Etienne, and Hagen Schulze. "Einleitung." In *Deutsche Erinnerungsorte*, vol. 1, edited by Etienne François and Hagen Schulze, 9–24. 2001. München: Beck, 2009.
Frazier, Valerie. "King Kong's Reign Continues: *King Kong* as a Sign of Shifting Racial Politics." *CLA Journal* 51, no. 2 (December 2007): 186–205.
Freud, Sigmund. "Aus der Geschichte einer infantilen Neurose [Der Wolfsmann]." In *Studienausgabe*, vol. 8, edited by Alexander Mitscherlich et al., 126–232. Frankfurt/M.: Fischer, 2000.
———. "Entwurf einer Psychologie." In *Gesammelte Werke*, vol. 19, edited by Angela Richards, 375–486. Frankfurt/M.: Fischer, 1999.
Freeman, Elizabeth. *Time Binds: Queer Temporalities, Queer Histories*. Durham, NC: Duke University Press, 2010.
Gaines, Jane M. "Early Cinema's Heyday of Copying: The Too Many Copies of *L'Arroseur arrosé* (The Waterer Watered)." *Cultural Studies* 20, nos. 2–3 (March/May 2006): 227–44.
Ganz-Blättler, Ursula. "DSDS als Reality-Serie: Kumulatives Storytelling 'on the go.'" In *Populäre Serialität: Narration—Evolution—Distinktion. Zum seriellen Erzählen seit dem 19. Jahrhundert*, edited by Frank Kelleter, 123–41. Bielefeld, Germany: Transcript Verlag, 2012.
Gardner, Jared. *Projections: Comics and the History of Twenty-First-Century Storytelling*. Stanford, CA: Stanford University Press, 2012.

Genette, Gérard. *Palimpsests: Literature in the Second Degree*. Translated by Channa Newman and Claude Doubinsky. Lincoln: University of Nebraska Press, 1997.
Giddens, Anthony. *Modernity and Self-Identity: Self and Society in the Late Modern Age*. Cambridge: Polity Press, 1991.
Gill, Rosalind. "Postfeminist Media Culture: Elements of a Sensibility." *European Journal of Cultural Studies* 10, no. 2 (2007): 147–66.
Goldman, William. *Adventures in the Screen Trade*. New York: Warner Books, 1983.
Grainge, Paul. "Introduction: Ephemeral Media." In *Ephemeral Media: Transitory Screen Culture from Television to YouTube*, edited by Paul Grainge, 1–19, London: BFI, 2011.
———. "Introduction: Memory and Popular Film." In *Memory and Popular Culture*, edited by Paul Grainge, 1–20. Manchester, UK: Manchester University Press, 2003.
———. *Monochrome Memories: Nostalgia and Style in Retro America*. Westport, CT: Praeger, 2002.
Grant, Barry Keith. *Invasion of the Body Snatchers*. London: BFI/Palgrave Macmillan, 2010.
Gray, Herman. "Subject(ed) to Recognition." *American Quarterly* 65, no. 4 (2013): 771–98.
Gray, Jonathan. "'Always Two There Are': Repetition, Originality, and *The Force Awakens*." In *Disney's Star Wars: Forces of Production, Promotion, and Reception*, edited by William Proctor and Richard McCulloch, 153–65. Iowa City: University of Iowa Press, 2019.
———. *Show Sold Separately: Promos, Spoilers and Other Media Paratexts*. New York: New York University Press, 2010.
Greenberg, Harvey Roy. "Raiders of the Lost Text: Remaking as Contested Homage in *Always*." *Journal of Popular Film and Television* 18, no. 4 (Winter 1991): 164–71.
Greenblatt, Stephen. *Shakespearean Negotiations: The Circulation of Social Energy in Renaissance England*. Oxford: Clarendon, 1988.
Greene, Eric. *Planet of the Apes as American Myth: Race and Politics in the Films and Television Series*. Jefferson, NC: McFarland, 1996.
Gunning, Tom. "The Cinema of Attractions: Early Film, Its Spectator and the Avant-Garde." *Wide Angle* 8, no. 3-4 (1986): 63–70.
Hagedorn, Roger. "Doubtless to Be Continued." In *To Be Continued . . . : Soap Operas around the World*, edited by Robert Clyde Allen, 27–48. London: Routledge, 1995.
Hall, Sheldon. "Tall Revenue Features: The Genealogy of the Modern Blockbuster." In *Genre and Contemporary Hollywood*, edited by Steve Neale, 11–26. London: BFI, 2002.

Hall, Stuart. "Cultural Identity and Cinematic Representation." *Framework: The Journal of Cinema and Media* 36 (1989): 68–81.
Hämmerling, Christine, and Mirjam Nast. "Popular Seriality in Everyday Practice: *Perry Rhodan* and *Tatort*." In *Media of Serial Narrative*, edited by Frank Kelleter, 248–60. Columbus: Ohio State University Press, 2017.
Hansen, Miriam. *Babel and Babylon: Spectatorship in American Silent Film*. Cambridge, MA: Harvard University Press, 1991.
Hayward, Jennifer. *Consuming Pleasures: Active Audiences and Serial Fictions from Dickens to Soap Opera*. Lexington: University of Kentucky Press, 1997.
Hedetoft, Ulf. "Contemporary Cinema: Between Cultural Globalisation and National Interpretation." In *Cinema and Nation*, edited by Mette Hjort and Scott Mackenzie, 278–97. London: Routledge, 2000.
Hediger, Vinzenz. "'You Haven't Seen It Until You Have Seen It at Least Twice': Film Spectatorship and the Discipline of Repeat Viewing." *Cinéma & Cie* 5 (2004): 24–42.
Henderson, Stuart. *The Hollywood Sequel: History and Form, 1911–2010*. London: BFI, 2014.
Hennig-Thurau, Thorsten, and Mark B. Houston. *Entertainment Science: Data Analytics and Practical Theory for Movies, Games, Books, and Music*. Cham, Switzerland: Springer, 2019.
Hennig-Thurau, Thorsten, Mark B. Houston, and Torsten Heitjans. "Conceptualizing and Measuring the Monetary Value of Brand Extensions: The Case of Motion Pictures." *Journal of Marketing* 73 (November 2009): 167–83.
Herbert, Daniel. *Film Remakes and Franchises*. New Brunswick, NJ: Rutgers University Press, 2017.
Herbert, Daniel, and Constantine Verevis, eds. *Film Reboots*. Edinburgh: Edinburgh University Press, 2020.
——. "Introduction: Film Reboots." In *Film Reboots*, edited by Daniel Herbert and Constantine Verevis, 1–16. Edinburgh: Edinburgh University Press, 2020.
Higgins, Scott. "Saturday Afternoon Blockbuster: James Bond's Serial Heritage." *Film Studies* 17 (Autumn 2017): 73–93.
Higson, Andrew. "The Concept of National Cinema." *Screen* 30, no. 4 (1989): 36–45.
——. "The Limiting Imagination of National Cinema." In *Cinema and Nation*, edited by Mette Hjort and Scott Mackenzie, 63–74. London: Routledge, 2000.
Hills, Matt. "Always-On Fandom, Waiting and Bingeing: Psychoanalysis as an Engagement with Fans' 'Infra-Ordinary' Experiences." In *The Routledge Companion to Media Fandom*, edited by Melissa Click and Suzanne Scott, 18–26. New York: Routledge, 2018.

———. "Cult TV Revival: Generational Seriality, Recap Culture, and the 'Brand Gap' of *Twin Peaks: The Return*." *Television & New Media* 19, no. 4 (May 2018): 310–27.

———. "Psychoanalysis and Digital Fandom: Theorizing Spoilers and Fans' Self-Narratives." In *Produsing Theory in a Digital World: The Intersection of Audiences and Production in Contemporary Theory*, edited by Rebecca Ann Lind, 105–22. New York: Peter Lang, 2012.

Hirsch, Marianne. *The Generation of Postmemory: Writing and Visual Culture after the Holocaust*. New York: Columbia University Press, 2012.

Hjort, Mette, and Scott Mackenzie, eds. *Cinema and Nation*. London: Routledge, 2000.

Hobsch, Manfred. *Mach's noch einmal! Das große Buch der Remakes*. Berlin: Schwarzkopf & Schwarzkopf, 2002.

Holston, Kim R., and Tom Winchester. *Science Fiction, Fantasy, and Horror Film Sequels, Series and Remakes: An Illustrated Filmography, with Plot Synopses and Critical Commentary*. Jefferson, NC: McFarland, 1997.

Horkheimer, Max, and Theodor W. Adorno. "Kulturindustrie, Aufklärung als Massenbetrug." In *Dialektik der Aufklärung: Philosophische Fragmente*, 128–76. 1944. Frankfurt/M.: Fischer, 1988.

Horton, Andrew, and Stuart Y. McDougal. "Introduction." In *Play It Again, Sam: Retakes on Remakes*, edited by Andrew Horton and Stuart Y. McDougal, 1–11. Berkeley: University of California Press, 1998.

Hoyt, Eric. *Hollywood Vault: Film Libraries before Home Video*. Berkeley: University of California Press, 2014.

Huntingford, Cherise. "To Err Is Human, to Forget . . . Sublime." In *Stranger Things and Philosophy: Thus Spake the Demogorgon*, edited by Jeffrey A. Ewing and Andrew M. Winters, 101–16. Chicago: Open Court, 2019.

Insdorf, Annette. "Seeing Doubles." *Moving Image Source*. Museum of the Moving Image, June 26, 2008. http://www.movingimagesource.us/articles/seeing-doubles-20080626.

Jahn-Sudmann, Andreas, and Frank Kelleter. "Die Dynamik serieller Überbietung: Amerikanische Fernsehserien und das Konzept des Quality TV." In *Populäre Serialität: Narration—Evolution—Distinktion. Zum seriellen Erzählen seit dem 19. Jahrhundert*, edited by Frank Kelleter, 205–24. Bielefeld, Germany: transcript Verlag, 2012.

Jameson, Fredric. *Postmodernism; or, The Cultural Logic of Late Capitalism*. Durham, NC: Duke University Press, 1991.

Jess-Cooke, Carolyn. *Film Sequels: Theory and Practice from Hollywood to Bollywood*. Edinburgh: Edinburgh University Press, 2009.

Jess-Cooke, Carolyn, and Constantine Verevis, eds. *Second Takes: Critical Approaches to the Film Sequel*. Albany: State University of New York Press, 2010.

Johnson, Derek. "Fan-tagonism: Factions, Institutions, and Constitutive Hegemonies of Fandom." In *Fandom: Identities and Communities in Mediated Culture*, edited by Jonathan Gray, C. Lee Harrington, and Cornel Sandvoss, 285–300. New York: New York University Press, 2007.

———. "Fantagonism, Franchising, and Industry Management of Fan Privilege." In *The Routledge Companion to Media Fandom*, edited by Suzanne Scott and Melissa Click, 395–405. New York: Routledge, 2018.

———. "From the Ruins: Neomasculinity, Media Franchising, and Struggles over Industrial Reproduction of Culture," *Communication Culture & Critique* 11 (2018): 85–99.

———. *Media Franchising: Creative License and Collaboration in the Culture Industries*. New York: New York University Press, 2013.

———. *Transgenerational Media Industries: Adults, Children, and the Reproduction of Culture*. Ann Arbor: University of Michigan Press, 2019.

Junklewitz, Christian, and Tanja Weber. "Die Cineserie: Geschichte und Erfolg von Filmserien im postklassischen Kino." In *Serielle Formen: Von den frühen Film-Serials zu aktuellen Quality-TV- und Online-Serien*, edited by Robert Blanchet et al., 337–56. Marburg, Germany: Schüren, 2011.

Kaufmann, Eric. *Whiteshift: Populism, Immigration, and the Future of White Majorities*. New York: Penguin, 2019.

Kelleter, Frank. "Das Remake als Fetischkunst: Gus Van Sants *Psycho* und die absonderlichen Serialitäten des Hollywood-Kinos." *Pop: Kultur und Kritik* 7 (2015): 152–73.

———. "Five Ways of Looking at Popular Seriality." In *Media of Serial Narrative*, edited by Frank Kelleter, 7–34. Columbus: Ohio State University Press, 2017.

———. "'Toto, I Think We're in Oz Again' (and Again and Again): Remakes and Popular Seriality." In *Film Remakes, Adaptations and Fan Productions: Remake | Remodel*, edited by Kathleen Loock and Constantine Verevis, 19–44. Basingstoke, UK: Palgrave Macmillan, 2012.

Kelleter, Frank, and Kathleen Loock. "Hollywood Remaking as Second-Order Serialization." In *Media of Serial Narrative*, edited by Frank Kelleter, 125–47. Columbus: Ohio State University Press, 2017.

Klein, Amanda Ann, and R. Barton Palmer, eds. *Cycles, Sequels, Spin-Offs, Remakes, and Reboots: Multiplicities in Film and Television*. Austin: University of Texas Press, 2016.

———. "Introduction." In *Cycles, Sequels, Spin-Offs, Remakes, and Reboots: Multiplicities in Film and Television*, edited by Amanda Ann Klein and R. Barton Palmer, 1–21. Austin: University of Texas Press, 2016.

Klinger, Barbara. *Beyond the Multiplex: Cinema, New Technologies, and the Home*. Berkeley: University of California Press, 2006.

———. *Immortal Films: Casablanca and the Afterlife of a Historical Classic*. Berkeley: University of California Press, 2022.

Knöppler, Christian. *The Monster Always Returns: American Horror Films and Their Remakes*. Bielefeld, Germany: Transcript Verlag, 2017.
Krutnik, Frank. "Chiller-Dillers for the Shiver-and-Shudder Set: *The Whistler* Film Series," *Film Studies* 17 (Autumn 2017): 49–72.
Landsberg, Alison. *Prosthetic Memory: The Transformation of American Remembrance in the Age of Mass Culture*. New York: Columbia University Press, 2004.
Leitch, Thomas. "Hitchcock without Hitchcock." *Literature Film Quarterly* 31, no. 4 (2003): 248–59.
———. "101 Ways to Tell Hitchcock's *Psycho* from Gus Van Sant's." *Literature/Film Quarterly* 28, no. 4 (2000): 269–72.
———. "Twice-Told Tales: The Rhetoric of the Remake." *Literature/Film Quarterly* 18, no. 3 (1990): 138–49.
Limbacher, James L. *Haven't I Seen You Somewhere Before? Remakes, Sequels, and Series in Motion Pictures, Videos, and Television, 1896–1990*. Ann Arbor: Pierian Press, 1991.
Lizardi, Ryan. *Nostalgic Generations and Media: Perception of Time and Available Meaning*. Lanham, MD: Lexington Books, 2017.
Loock, Kathleen. "Introduction: Serial Narratives." *LWU: Literatur in Wissenschaft und Unterricht* 47, no. 1–2 (2014): 5–9.
———. "Making Movie Generations: On the Cultural Work of Hollywood Remaking." In *What Film Is Good For: The Ethics of Spectatorship*, edited by Julian Hanich and Martin P. Rossouw, 249–60. Berkeley: University of California Press, 2023.
———. "On the Realist Aesthetics of Digital De-Aging in Contemporary Hollywood Cinema." *Orbis Litterarum* 76 (2021): 214–25. https://doi.org/10.1111/oli.12302.
———. "'The Past Is Never Really Past': Serial Storytelling from *Psycho* to *Bates Motel* LWU: *Literatur in Wissenschaft und Unterricht* 47, nos. 1–2 (2014): 81–95.
———. "Reboot, Requel, Legacyquel: *Jurassic World* and the Nostalgia Franchise." In *Film Reboots*, edited by Daniel Herbert and Constantine Verevis, 173–88. Edinburgh: Edinburgh University Press, 2020.
———. "Remaking *Funny Games*: Michael Haneke's Cross-Cultural Experiment." In *Transnational Film Remakes*, edited by Iain Robert Smith and Constantine Verevis, 177–94. Edinburgh: Edinburgh University Press, 2017.
———. "Remaking Winnetou, Reconfiguring German Fantasies of *Indianer* and the Wild West in the Post-Reunification Era." *Communications: The European Journal of Communication Research* 44, no. 3 (2019): 323–41.
———. "Reproductive Futurism and the Politics of the Sequel," *[in]Transition: Journal of Videographic Film & Moving Image Studies* 6, no. 3 (2019): mediacommons.org/intransition/reproductive-futurism-and-politics-sequel.

———. "Retro-Remaking: The 1980s Film Cycle in Contemporary Hollywood Cinema." In *Cycles, Sequels, Spin-Offs, Remakes, and Reboots: Multiplicities in Film and Television*, edited by Amanda Ann Klein and R. Barton Palmer, 277–98. Austin: University of Texas Press, 2016.

———. "The Return of the Pod People: Remaking Cultural Anxieties in *Invasion of the Body Snatchers*." In *Film Remakes, Adaptations and Fan Productions: Remake/Remodel*, edited by Kathleen Loock and Constantine Verevis, 122–44. Basingstoke, UK: Palgrave Macmillan, 2012.

———. "The Sequel Paradox: Repetition, Innovation and Hollywood's Hit Film Formula." *Film Studies* 17 (Autumn 2017): 92–110.

———. "Sound Memories: 'Talker Remakes,' Paratexts, and the Cinematic Past." In *The Politics of Ephemeral Digital Media: Permanence and Obsolescence in Paratexts*, edited by Sara Pesce and Paolo Noto, 123–37. New York: Routledge, 2016.

———. "'Whatever Happened to Predictability?' *Fuller House*, (Post)Feminism, and the Revival of Family-Friendly Viewing." *Television & New Media* 19, no. 4 (2018): 361–78.

Loock, Kathleen, and Constantine Verevis, eds. *Film Remakes, Adaptations and Fan Productions: Remake/Remodel*. Basingstoke, UK: Palgrave Macmillan, 2012.

Mann, Katrina. "'You're Next!': Postwar Hegemony Besieged in *Invasion of the Body Snatchers*." *Cinema Journal* 44, no. 1 (2004): 49–68.

Mannheim, Karl. "The Problem of Generations." In *Collected Works*. Vol. 5: *Essays on the Sociology of Knowledge*, edited by Paul Kecskemeti, 276–320. London: Routledge/Kegan Paul, 1952.

Manoff, Marlene. "Theories of the Archive from across the Disciplines." *Portal: Libraries and the Academy* 4, no. 1 (January 2004): 9–25.

Martin, Adrian. "Shot-by-Shot Follies." *Hitchcock Annual* 10 (2001–2002): 133–39.

May, Elaine Tyler. *Homeward Bound: American Families in the Cold War Era*. New York: Basic Books, 1988.

Mayer, Ruth. *Serial Fu Manchu*. Philadelphia: Temple University Press, 2013.

Mazdon, Lucy. *Encore Hollywood: Remaking French Cinema*. London: BFI, 2000.

McLarty, Lianne. "'I'll Be Back': Hollywood, Sequelization, and History." In *Part Two: Reflections on the Sequel*, edited by Paul Budra and Betty A. Schellenberg, 200–217. Toronto: University of Toronto Press, 1998.

McRobbie, Angela. "Post-feminism and Popular Culture." *Feminist Media Studies* 4, no. 3 (2004): 255–64.

Mee, Laura. *Reanimated: The Contemporary American Horror Remake*. Edinburgh: Edinburgh University Press, 2020.

Milberg, Doris. *Repeat Performances: A Guide to Hollywood Movie Remakes*. Shelter Island, NY: Broadway, 1990.

Millner, Michael. "The Ends of Identity Politics and the Case of *King Kong*." *Arizona Quarterly: A Journal of American Literature, Culture, and Theory* 69, no. 4 (Winter 2013): 111–32.
Mittell, Jason. "Forensic Fandom and the Drillable Text." In *Spreadable Media: Creating Value and Meaning in a Networked Culture*, edited by Henry Jenkins, Sam Ford, and Joshua Green. New York: New York University Press, 2013. https://spreadablemedia.org/essays/mittell/.
———. *Genre and Television: From Cop Shows to Cartoons in American Culture*. New York: Routledge, 2004.
———. "Serial Boxes." *Just TV*, January 20, 2010. https://justtv.wordpress.com/2010/01/20/serial-boxes/.
Monaco, Paul. *Ribbons in Time: Movies and Society since 1945*. Bloomington: Indiana University Press, 1987.
Musser, Charles. *The Emergence of Cinema: The American Screen to 1917*. Berkeley: University of California Press, 1994.
Naremore, James. "Remaking *Psycho*." *Hitchcock Annual* (1999–2000): 3–12.
Neale, Steve. *Genre and Hollywood*. London: Routledge, 2000.
———. "Hollywood Blockbusters: Historical Dimensions." In *Movie Blockbusters*, edited by Julian Stringer, 47–60. London: Routledge, 2003.
Niemeyer, Katharina, ed. *Media and Nostalgia: Yearning for the Past, the Present and the Future*. London: Palgrave Macmillan, 2014.
Nilsen, Sarah, and Sarah E. Turner, eds. *The Myth of the Colorblindness: Race and Ethnicity in American Cinema*. New York: Palgrave Macmillan, 2019.
Nora, Pierre. "Between Memory and History: Les Lieux de Mémoire." *Representations* 26 (Spring 1989): 7–24.
O'Brian, Harvey. *Action Movies: The Cinema of Striking Back*. New York: Columbia University Press, 2012.
Olick, Jeffrey K. "From Usable Pasts to the Return of the Repressed." *The Hedgehog Review* (Summer 2007): 19–31.
Oltmann, Katrin. *Remake | Premake: Hollywoods romantische Komödien und ihre Gender-Diskurse, 1930–1960*. Bielefeld, Germany: Transcript Verlag, 2008.
Pagnoni Berns, Fernando Gabriel, Diego Foronda, and Mariana Zárate. "Abnormal Is the New Normal." In *Stranger Things and Philosophy: Thus Spake the Demogorgon*, edited by Jeffrey A. Ewing and Andrew M. Winters, 183–93. Chicago: Open Court, 2019.
Parchesky, Jennifer. "Adapting *Stella Dallas*: Class Boundaries, Consumerism, and Hierarchies of Taste." *Legacy* 23, no. 2 (2006): 178–98.
Parikka, Jussi. *What Is Media Archaeology?* Cambridge: Polity Press, 2012.
Pendreigh, Brian. *Planet of the Apes: Or How Hollywood Turned Darwin Upside Down*. London: Boxtree, 2001.
Perkins, Claire, and Constantine Verevis, eds. *Film Trilogies: New Critical Approaches*. Basingstoke, UK: Palgrave Macmillan, 2012.

Pinedo, Isabel Cristina. *Recreational Terror: Women and the Pleasures of Horror Film Viewing*. Albany: State University of New York Press, 1997.
Proctor, William. "'Bitches Ain't Gonna Hunt No Ghosts': Totemic Nostalgia, Toxic Fandom and the *Ghostbusters* Platonic." *Palabra Clave* 20, no. 4 (2017): 1105-41. https://doi.org/10.5294/pacla.2017.20.4.10.
———. "Reboots and Retroactive Continuity." In *The Routledge Companion to Imaginary Worlds*, edited by Mark J. P. Wolf, 224-35. New York: Routledge, 2017.
———. "Regeneration & Rebirth: An Anatomy of the Franchise Reboot." *Scope: An Online Journal of Film and Television Studies* 22 (February 2012). 1-19. https://www.nottingham.ac.uk/scope/documents/2012/february-2012/proctor.pdf.
Quaresima, Leonardo. "Loving Texts Two at a Time: The Film Remake." *Cinémas* 12, no. 3 (2002): 73-84.
Radstone, Susannah, and Katherine Hodgkin, eds. *Memory Cultures: Memory, Subjectivity and Recognition*. New Brunswick, NJ: Transaction, 2006.
Robertson, Benjamin J. "'It Is Just Us Now': Nostalgia and Star Wars Episode VII: The Force Awakens." *Science Fiction Film and Television* 9, no. 3 (2016): 479-88.
Roche, David. *Making and Remaking Horror in the 1970s and 2000s: Why Don't They Do It Like They Used to?* Jackson: University Press of Mississippi, 2014.
Rosewarne, Lauren. *Sex and Sexuality in Modern Screen Remakes*. Cham, Switzerland: Palgrave Macmillan, 2019.
Røssaak, Eivind. "The Archive in Motion: An Introduction." In *The Archive in Motion: New Conceptions of the Archive in Contemporary Thought and New Media Practices*, edited by Eivind Røssaak, 11-26. Oslo: Novus Press, 2010.
Samuels, Stuart. "The Age of Conspiracy and Conformity: *Invasion of the Body Snatchers* (1956)." In *Hollywood's America: Twentieth-Century America Through Film*, edited by Steven Mintz and Randy W. Roberts. Malden, MA: Wiley-Blackwell, 2010. 198-206.
Santas, Constantine. "The Remake of *Psycho* (Gus Van Sant, 1998): Creativity or Cinematic Blasphemy?" *Senses of Cinema* 10 (November 2000). http://sensesofcinema.com/2000/feature-articles/psycho-2/.
Schatz, Thomas. *The Genius of the System: Hollywood Filmmaking in the Studio Era*. London: Simon & Schuster, 1989.
———. "The New Hollywood." In *Movie Blockbusters*, edited by Julian Stringer, 15-44. London: Routledge, 2003.
———. "The Studio System and Conglomerate Hollywood." In *The Contemporary Hollywood Film Industry*, edited by Paul McDonald and Janet Wasko, 13-42. Malden, MA: Wiley-Blackwell, 2008.
Schneider, Steven Jay. "Kevin Williamson and the Rise of the Neo-Stalker." *Post Script: Essays in Film and the Humanities* 19, no. 2 (2000): 73-87.

———. "A Tale of Two *Psychos* (Prelude to a Future Reassessment)." *Senses of Cinema* 10 (November 2000). http://sensesofcinema.com/2000/feature-articles/psychos/.

Schwartz, Ronald. *Noir, Now and Then: Film Noir Originals and Remakes (1944–1999)*. Westport, CT: Greenwood Press, 2001.

Sheldon, Rebekah. *The Child to Come: Life after the Human Catastrophe*. Minneapolis: University of Minnesota Press, 2016.

Siibak, Andra, Nicoletta Vittadini, and Galit Nimrod. "Generations as Media Audiences: An Introduction." *Participations: Journal of Audience & Reception Studies* 11, no. 2 (2014): 100–107.

Simpson, Philip L. "Whither the Serial Killer Movie?" In *American Horror Film: The Genre at the Turn of the Millennium*, edited by Steffen Hantke, 119–41. Jackson: University Press of Mississippi, 2010.

Smith, Iain Robert. *The Hollywood Meme: Transnational Adaptations in World Cinema*. Edinburgh: Edinburgh University Press, 2017.

Smith, Iain Robert, and Constantine Verevis. "Introduction: Transnational Film Remakes." In *Transnational Film Remakes*, edited by Iain Robert Smith and Constantine Verevis, 1–18. Edinburgh: Edinburgh University Press, 2017.

Stam, Robert. "Beyond Fidelity: The Dialogics of Adaptation." In *Film Adaptation*, edited by James Naremore, 54–76. New Brunswick, NJ: Rutgers University Press, 2000.

Stewen, Christian. "Ceding/Succeeding Images: Reproduktive und queere Zeitverhältnisse des Animationsfilms." In *Im Wandel . . . Metamorphosen der Animation*, edited by Julia Eckel, Erwin Feyersinger and Meike Uhrig, 83–102. Wiesbaden, Gemany: Springer, 2018.

Strick, Simon. *Rechte Gefühle: Affekte und Strategien des digitalen Faschismus*. Bielefeld, Germany: Transcript Verlag, 2022.

Sturken, Marita. *Tangled Memories: The Vietnam War, the AIDS Epidemic, and the Politics of Remembering*. Berkeley: University of California Press, 1997.

Sulimma, Maria. *Gender and Seriality: Practices and Politics of Contemporary US Television*. Edinburgh: Edinburgh University Press, 2021.

Taylor, Diana. *The Archive and the Repertoire: Performing Cultural Memory in the Americas*. Durham, NC: Duke University Press, 2003.

Tompkins, Joe. "'Re-imagining the Canon: Examining the Discourse of Contemporary Horror Film Reboots." *New Review of Film and Television Studies* 12, no. 4 (December 2014): 380–99.

Tudor, Andrew. "From Paranoia to Postmodernism? The Horror Movie in Late Modern Society." In *Genre and Contemporary Hollywood*, edited by Steve Neale, 105–16. London: BFI, 2002.

van Dijck, José. *Mediated Memories in the Digital Age*. Stanford, CA: Stanford University Press, 2007.

Varndell, Daniel. *Hollywood Remakes, Deleuze and the Grandfather Paradox.* Basingstoke, UK: Palgrave Macmillan, 2014.
Verevis, Constantine. *Film Remakes.* Edinburgh: Edinburgh University Press, 2006.
———. "For Ever Hitchcock: *Psycho* and Its Remakes." In *After Hitchcock: Influence, Imitation, and Intertextuality*, edited by David Boyd and R. Barton Palmer, 15–29. Austin: University of Texas Press, 2006.
Wang, Yiman. *Remaking Chinese Cinema: Through the Prism of Shanghai, Hong Kong, and Hollywood.* Honolulu: University of Hawai'i Press, 2013.
Warner, Kristen J. *The Cultural Politics of Colorblind TV Casting.* New York: Routledge, 2015.
Wee, Valerie. *Japanese Horror Films and Their American Remakes: Translating Fear, Adapting Culture.* New York: Routledge, 2014.
Williams, Raymond. *Marxism and Literature.* New York: Oxford University Press, 1977.
Wilson, Janelle L. *Nostalgia: Sanctuary of Meaning.* Lewisburg, PA: Bucknell University Press, 2005.
Winogura, Dale. "Dialogues on Apes, Apes, and More Apes." *Cinefantastique* (Summer 1972): 16–31, 34–37.
Zanger, Anat. *Film Remakes as Ritual and Disguise.* Amsterdam: Amsterdam University Press, 2006.

Index

Abbott and Costello crossover movies, 225
aboutness, thematic, 7
academic scholarship. *See* remake scholarship
access, as archival function of remakes, 154–58
acknowledged close remake, 38
acknowledged transformed remake, 38
actor-networks, 12, 13, 63
actors: all-female reboots, 23, 67, 68, 73; long-term studio contracts, 168–69; nostalgia franchises and, 97; passage of time and aging actors, 207–11, 213; talker remakes and, 105, 106–12. *See also* specific film titles
Adams, Guy, 88, 89
adaptation: defined, 35
adventure genre: conventions of, 76; crossovers and spin-offs, 227; franchise films and, 206; sequels and audience expectations, 198, 202; series figures in, 171–72; in studio era, 165–67. *See also* specific film titles
Adventures of Kathlyn, The (Selig, 1913), 165
Adventures of Robin Hood, The (Michael Curtiz and William Keighley, 1938), 59
Alien (Ridley Scott, 1979), 47, 188, 230
Alien 3 (David Fincher, 1992), 188

Alien: Covenant (Ridley Scott, 2017), 188
Alien Resurrection (Jean-Pierre Jeunet, 1997), 188
Aliens (James Cameron, 1986), 188, 226
Alien vs. Predator (Paul W. S. Anderson, 2004), 226
All That Heaven Allows (Douglas Sirk, 1956), 39
Always (Steven Spielberg, 1989), 38
Amazing Spider-Man, The (Marc Webb, 2012), 230
American Graffiti (George Lucas, 1973), 14
American International Pictures (AIP), 177
A-movies, 168, 169, 170
Anderson, Benedict, 6
Andy Hardy films, 172
anecdotal storytelling, 165–66
Anna Christie (Clarence Brown, 1930), 24, 106–10, 108*fig*
Anna Christie (John Griffith Wray, 1923), 106
Anna Karenina (Clarence Brown, 1935), 126
Anna Lucasta (Arnold Laven, 1958), 38
Anna Lucasta (Irving Rapper, 1949), 38
Another 48 Hrs. (Walter Hill, 1990), 60
Another Day in the Forest (Michael Gordon, 1948), 226
antitrust litigation, 173

286 INDEX

Apocalypse Now (Francis Ford Coppola, 1979), 146
Appadurai, Arjun, 7
architextuality, defined, 36
archive, remake as, 135–40, 138*fig*; access as archival function, 154–58; classification function of remakes, 145–54; storage and preservation function of remakes, 143–45
archive, use of term, 138–40
Arnzen, Michael A., 50
Around the World in 80 Days (Michael Anderson, 1956), 175
Arrivée d'un train (1895), 101
art form, cinema as, 2
A-Team, The (Joe Carnahan, 2010), 88
audience appeal, 2; DVD collections and, 59; nostalgia and, 94–97, 209; remakes and audience prior knowledge, 40–41, 47; remakes with diverse casts and characters, 74, 74*fig*; ruined childhood trope and, 68, 88, 89–93; sequels and, 191, 196–200; seriality and, 10–11, 171
audience expectations: backlash against retitling of talker remakes, 117–19; backlash to gender and racial diversity in films, 79, 79*fig*, 81, 90–94, 96–98; blockbuster films and, 175; cultural studies approach to remakes, 41–51; film series in the studio era, 165–67; intertextually proficient viewers and remakes, 135–36; in *James Bond* series, 178–85; *Planet of the Apes* franchise and, 184; prequels and older film storylines, 227–29; remaking as a concept, 5; reproduction logics, linear time, and repetitive futures, 211–20, 215*fig*; ruined childhood trope, 68, 88, 89–93; sequels and, 188–89, 191, 203–4; serial figures and, 171; television's impact on film industry, 173–76; worldbuilding in crossovers and spin-offs, 226–27
auteur films, 32, 33, 37, 187–88
Avildsen, John, 201
Awful Truth, The (Leo McCarey, 1937), 48

Back to the Future Part II (Robert Zemeckis, 1989), 202–3, 203*fig*
Bahn, Chester B., 112, 117, 122
Bakhtin Mikhail, 35
Bal, Mieke, 49
Balio, Tino, 169
Baltimore Sun, 117
Banet-Weiser, Sarah, 77
Barbershop franchise, 227

Bart, Peter, 163
Barthes, Roland, 35
Bates Motel (A&E, 2013–2017), 59
Batman (Tim Burton, 1989), 64
Batman Begins (Christopher Nolan, 2005), 62, 188, 222, 230
Batman franchise, 62, 69, 188
Batman series (Columbia, 1943), 165
Battle for the Planet of the Apes (1973), 181, 182–83
Beach Party (William Asher, 1963), 177
beach party movies, 177
Beau Geste (William A. Wellman, 1939), 119–20
Beauty Shop (Bille Woodruff, 2005), 227
Bedtime Story (Ralph Levy, 1964), 80
Beneath the Planet of the Apes (1970), 181, 182
Ben-Hur (Fred Niblo, 1925), 38, 110
Ben-Hur (Sidney Olcott and Frank Oakes Rose, 1907), 38, 121
Ben-Hur (Timur Bekmambetov, 2016), 1, 3
Ben-Hur (William Wyler, 1959), 38, 175
Berliner, Todd, 198
B-films: repurposed for television, 174; series production model for, 167–72, 168*fig*
Big Five studios: B-film series production model, 168–72, 168*fig*; big picture approach in post-studio era, 173–76
Big Parade, The (King Vidor, 1925), 121
Bill of Divorcement, A (George Cukor, 1932), 119
Billy Jack (Tom Laughlin, 1971), 177
Billy the Kid Versus Dracula (William Beaudine, 1966), 225
Biograph, 101
Birth of a Nation, The (D. W. Griffith, 1915), 121
Black action films (Blaxploitation), 177
Black Diamond Express, The (1896), 101
Blade Runner (Ridley Scott, 1982), 186–90, 212–13
Blade Runner 2049 (Denis Villeneuve, 2017), 26, 186–90, 208; reproduction logics, linear time, and repetitive futures, 211–20, 215*fig*
blind-bidding, 168–69, 173
block-booking, 19, 168–69, 173
blockbuster films, 175–76, 178–85; saturation booking, 191
Blondie series (1938–1949, Columbia), 171–72
Bloom, Harold, 146
Blow Out (Brian De Palma, 1981), 33
Body Double (Brian De Palma, 1984), 33

INDEX   287

Body Heat (Lawrence Kasdan, 1981), 48
Brasch, Ilka, 165–66
Braudy, Leo, 31
Bride of Frankenstein (James Whale, 1935), 172
Bridge on the River Kwai, The (David Lean, 1957), 175
Brinker, Felix, 206
Broadway Melody (1935–1940, MGM), 170–71
Broadway musicals, film adaptations, 106, 175, 226
Brooks, Van Wyck, 66
Brown, David, 202
Brown, Georgia, 72
Burton, Tim, 1. *See also Batman* (Tim Burton, 1989); *Planet of the Apes* (Tim Burton, 2001)
Butch and Sundance: The Early Days (Richard Lester, 1979), 226
Butch Cassidy and the Sundance Kid (George Roy Hill, 1969), 226

Camille (George Cukor, 1937), 128
Camille (Ray C. Smallwood, 1921), 128
Cape Fear (J. Lee Thompson, 1962), 59
Cape Fear (Martin Scorsese, 1991), 59
Captain Blood (David Smith, 1924), 127
Captain Blood (Michael Curtiz, 1935), 127
Carolco Pictures, 192
Carpetbaggers, The (Edward Dmytryk, 1964), 226
Carrigy, Megan, 39
Casino Royale (Martin Campbell, 2006), 62, 178, 222, 230
Chang, Justin, 1–2, 4
Charcuterie mécanique (1895), 101
Child, Ben, 186
Child's Play (Tom Holland, 1988), 47
Chinatown (Roman Polanski, 1974), 59
chrononormativity, 212
cinema as an art form, 2
cinematic past, 67–68, 81–98. *See also* movie generations
cinematic self-historicization, 11, 103–4, 133; Hollywood takes "just one more look," *A Star Is Born*, 140–43
cinematic universe: Marvel Cinematic Universe (MCU), 189, 205–8; MonsterVerse, 146; reboots, 230–1; sequels and prequels, 186–7, 218–20, 226–7; shared universes, time, and nostalgia, 205–10;
Citizen Kane (Orson Welles, 1941), 43

Clark's Thread Mill (1896), 101
classification: as archival function of remakes, 145–54; processes of, 145
Cleopatra (Joseph L. Mankiewicz, 1963), 176
climate change fiction (cli-fi), 182, 218
Cold War, 137, 174, 180, 181–82
colorblindness, 77–78
Columbia Studio: B-film series production model, 168–72
comedy: horror genre, evolution of, 47
communities of knowledge and belonging, 14
comparative mode of viewing, 56
Complete Collections, DVDs, 56–59
complexification: serialization and, 51–63
conceptual series, 170–71
Conquest of the Planet of the Apes (1972), 181, 182, 183
conservatism. *See* politics of representation
content differentiation, 162
contextual model of film remakes, 48
continuity: cultural continuity, 69, 221–22; film industry reliance on, 164, 221–22; film series in the studio era, 165–72, 168*fig*; importance of, 61–62, 221–22; *James Bond* franchise, 178–81; *Planet of the Apes* franchise, 181–85; remaking, timeliness, and the politics of representation, 68–81; reproduction logics, linear time, and repetitive futures, 211–20, 215*fig*; sequels and, 187, 188–89, 199, 201–3; serial figures and, 171; series with continuity, 171–72; in *Star Wars* franchise, 207–11; worldbuilding in crossovers and spin-offs, 226–27. *See also* movie generations
Cook, David A., 178
copyright, 52; history of film, transition to sound and, 104–6
Cotton Comes to Harlem (Ossie Davis, 1970), 177
Countryman's First Sight of the Animated Pictures, The (Robert W. Paul, 1901), 102–3
country rube genre, 102–3
Crafton, Donald, 106, 109, 112, 124–25
Creed (Ryan Coogler, 2015), 62, 96–98, 208, 222–23
Crime School (Lewis Seiler, 1938), 38
critical category, contextual model of remakes, 48
crossovers: Black action films, 177; defined, 62, 226; Hollywood historical production trends, 15–20, 16*fig*, 17*fig*, 18*fig*; Marvel Cinematic Universe (MCU), 207;

crossovers (continued)
    remaking as a concept, 4–5, 26–27, 145, 221–23; remaking trends in the new millennium, 224–29, 225fig; use of term, 229–31
Crow, David, 148–49
cultural change: audience backlash to films, 79, 79fig, 81; *Blade Runner 2049* and, 214; James Bond franchise and, 179–81; reboots and preservation of the past, 223; remakes and regressive narratives, 148–49, 231; remakes as means to process change, 70–81
cultural continuity, 69, 221–22
cultural identity: extratextual memory and, 14, 84, 210; forever franchise, shared universes, time, and nostalgia, 205–11, 210fig; movie generations, 23, 68, 81–98; remakes as a means to process cultural change, 70–81; remake scholarship and, 41–51; remaking of films and self-understanding, 3–4; usable cinematic past and, 67–68
cultural memory, 64–68; archive, use of term, 138–40; cinematic self-historicization, 11, 142–43; defined, 82; extratextual memory and, 14, 84, 210; fictional stories and characters in, 6–7; intertextual referentiality, 40; movie generations, 81–98; *Planet of the Apes* franchise and, 183; reboots and, 26–27, 221–23; remakes as a cultural category, 41, 231; remaking as a concept, 4–5, 6, 8, 22–23; seriality and, 10–14; *Star Wars* franchise and, 207–11. *See also* archive, remake as
cultural objects, films as, 50–51
cultural studies: cultural memory studies and movie generations, 81–98; remake scholarship, cultural studies approach, 41–51
cultural translation, 6
culture: cultural value of remaking, 4–5; defined, 236n31
Curse of the Fly, The (Don Sharp, 1965), 58

Daly, Phil M., 116, 121–22
Dark Angel, The (George Fitzmaurice, 1925), 127
Dark Angel, The (Sidney Franklin, 1935), 127
Dark Knight, The (Christopher Nolan, 2008), 64
Davis, Mike, 156
Dawn of the Planet of the Apes (Matt Reeves, 2014), 57, 183

Dead Ringers: The Remake in Theory and Practice (Forrest and Koos, 2002), 42–43
Deep Throat (Gerard Damiano, 1972), 177
degree of transformation, 38
Dehn, Paul, 182, 183, 185
Denby, David, 72
Denson, Shane, 171
Departed, The (Martin Scorsese, 2006), 6
Derrida, Jacques, 139
de Souza, Steven E., 198
detective genre: Black action films, 177; B-movies, 170; buddy cop films, 202; detective *noir*, 189, 213; series figures in, 171–72; in studio era, 165–66; television production of, 174. *See also* specific film titles
diachronic remaking, 6
Diamonds Are Forever (Guy Hamilton, 1971), 180
Dick Tracy series (Republic, 1937), 165
Die Hard 2 (Harlin, 1990), 203
Dika, Vera, 52
direct remake, 38
Dirty Rotten Scoundrels (Frank Oz, 1988), 80
discursive opportunity, 26–27
disguised remakes, 38, 116–24
diversity in film: *Blade Runner 2049* (Denis Villeneuve, 2017), 218; *Jumanji: Welcome to the Jungle* (Jake Kasdan, 2017), 74–78, 74fig; men's rights activists and alt-right backlash, 89–90, 93, 96–98; nostalgia franchises and, 97–98; *Stranger Things*, 94–95
Doane, Ashley ("Woody"), 77
Dominion: Prequel to the Exorcist (Paul Schrader, 2005), 227–28
Don Q, Son of Zorro (Donald Crisp, 1925), 172
Dracula's Daughter (Lambert Hillyer, 1936), 172
Dr. Dolittle (Richard Fleischer, 1967), 176
Dressed to Kill (Brian De Palma, 1980), 33
drillable text, 59
Dr. Kildare (1938–1941, MGM), 171, 172, 174
Dr. No (Terence Young, 1963), 179
Druxman, Michael B., 8, 37–38
Dr. Zhivago (David Lean, 1965), 175
Durango Kid, The series (1940–1952, Columbia), 169
DVDs, 52–53; access, archival function of remakes, 154–58; Complete Collections, 56–59; paratexts on, 156–58; titles released under Double Take: Original and Remake label, 55–56, 55tab

INDEX 289

Ebert, Roger, 72
Eberwein, Robert, 37–38, 42
Eco, Umberto, 9, 179
economic value, remaking as a concept, 4–5. *See also* film industry
Edelman, Lee, 211, 213
Edison, Thomas, 101
Emmanuelle (Just Jaeckin, 1974), 178
Empire State Express (1896), 101
entryway paratexts, 135
Erll, Astrid, 86
Escape from the Planet of the Apes (1971), 181, 182
Even Cowgirls Get the Blues (1993), 50
Ewens, Hannah, 1, 2, 4
exhibitors: big picture approach in post-studio era, 174–76; four-walling, 178; *Paramount Decree*, antitrust litigation, 173; saturation booking, 178, 191; studio era block-booking, 168–69; studio-owned theater chains, 169, 173
Exhibitors Herald-World, 107
Exorcist II: The Heretic, The (John Boorman, 1977), 194
expandable text, 59
exploitation films, 177–78
Exploits of Elaine, The (Pathé, 1915), 165
extratextual memory, 14, 84, 210

family series, 171–73
fan magazines, 11–12; coverage of talker remakes, 24, 104, 107–12, 110*fig*, 125–34, 126*fig*, 130*fig*; remakes, introduction of term, 128. *See also* specific publication names.
fantagonism, 90
Far from Heaven (Todd Haynes, 2002), 39
Fast & Furious franchise, 227
Fast & Furious Presents: Hobbs & Shaw (David Leitch, 2019), 227
Father of the Bride (Charles Shyer, 1991), 59
Father of the Bride (Vincente Minnelli, 1950), 59
Felski, Rita, 3
feminism: *Blade Runner 2049* and cultural change, 214; *Ghostbusters: Answer the Call* (Paul Feig, 2016), 79, 79*fig*, 80, 90–94, 96–98; *The Invasion* (Oliver Hirschbiegel, 2007), 78–79, 154; *James Bond* franchise and cultural change, 179–81; *Jumanji: Welcome to the Jungle* (Jake Kasdan, 2017), 75–77; men's rights activists and alt-right backlash, 89–90, 93, 96–98; *Ocean's Eight* (Gary Ross, 2018), 79, 80; *A Star Is Born* remakes and regressive narratives, 148; *Stella Dallas* remakes and, 72, 132–33; tropes in *Jumanji: Welcome to the Jungle* (Jake Kasdan, 2017), 74–76
film canons, 146–47
film critics: as cultural gatekeepers, 12; *James Bond* franchise in MeToo movement, 180–81; as opponents of remakes, 87–88; paratexts as means to access cinematic past, 155–56; on *Psycho* (Gus Van Sant, 1998), 36–37; on sequelitis, 195–200, 205; suggestions for talker remakes by, 112. *See also* specific critic names; specific film names
Film Daily, 11–12, 104, 114–15, 116, 117, 121–22
film industry: actor contracts, 168–69; B-film series expansion in, 167–72; Big Five studios, 168; big picture approach in post-studio era, 173–76; blind-bidding, 168–69, 173; block-booking, 168–69, 173; blockbuster films, economics of, 175–76; changing corporate structure in 1970s, 176; economic viability of remakes, 87; evolution of remakes in, 52–53; exploitation films, 177–78; fan magazines and promotion of talker remakes, 24, 104, 107–12, 110*fig*, 125–34, 126*fig*, 130*fig*; fantagonism, response to, 90–94; film canons, 146–47; film series in the studio era, 165–73, 168*fig*; four-walling, 178; franchises, types of, 61–63; franchising as a business strategy, 161–65, 230–31; global media entertainment market, 6–7; history of remakes, overview, 101–4; Little Three studios, 168; mergers and acquisitions, 162; *Paramount Decree*, antitrust litigation, 173; remakes, production data by year, 15–20, 16*fig*, 17*fig*, 18*fig*, 114–16, 115*fig*, 137–38, 138*fig*, 167–68, 168*fig*, 193–94, 194*fig*; remaking trends in the new millennium, 224–29, 225*fig*; run-zone-clearance system, 168–69; saturation booking, 178, 191; self-historicization and, 11, 103–4, 133, 140–43; sequel production in 1970s and 1980s, 190–95, 194*fig*; sequels, monetary value of, 191–93, 204–5; seriality, 9–14; serial logic of one-upmanship for sequels, 193–94; studio system, 19, 25, 168–69; talker remakes, recycling strategies to meet demand, 112–16, 115*fig*; talker remakes, stars and fans, 106–12, 108*fig*, 110*fig*;

film industry (*continued*)
    talker remakes, titles, audience memory, and timing, 116–24; talkies, from silent past to sound film present, 124–34, 126*fig*, 130*fig*; television advertising, use of, 178; television's impact on, 173–76; transition to sound, remaking boom during, 104–6; trends in, 2; usable cinematic past, 67–68. *See also* archive, remake as
film noir, 48
film remake, defined, 62. *See also* remakes
Film Remakes (Verevis, 2006), 48
film serials: big picture approach in post-studio era, 173–76; complexification and, 51–63; film franchises as business strategy, 161–65; film series in the studio era, 165–73, 168*fig*; history of early film, 105; Hollywood historical production trends, 15–20, 16*fig*, 17*fig*, 18*fig*; Hollywood remaking and, 9–14, 221–23; managing continuity and change, 68–81; narrative continuity, importance of, 61–62; narrative in *Invasion of the Body Snatchers* (1956, 1978, 1993, 2007), 54; nostalgia franchises, 68, 96–98, 205–11, 210*fig*, 222–23; Popular Seriality Research Unit (PSRU), 236n31; in the post-studio era, 176–85; regime of continuation, 69–70; remaking as a concept, 4–5; remaking trends in the new millennium, 224–29, 225*fig*; retrospective serialization, 53; second-order seriality, 13, 69, 164–65, 221; serial figure, 171; television and home media technologies, impact of, 60–61, 173–76; use of terms, 229–31. *See also* archive, remake as
film series: conceptual series, 170–71; as distinct from sequels, 164–65; series film proper, 171; series with continuity, 171–72
Fly, The (David Cronenberg, 1986), 58
Fly, The (Kurt Neumann, 1958), 58
Fly, The: Ultimate Collector's Edition, 58
Fly II, The (Chris Walas, 1989), 58
Footloose (Craig Brewer, 2011), 72–73, 88
Footloose (Herbert Ross, 1984), 72–73
Force Awakens, The (J. J. Abrams, 2015), 96–98, 222–23, 230
forever franchises, 205–11, 218–19
Forrest, Jennifer, 42–43, 179
48 Hrs. (Walter Hill, 1982), 59
Foucault, Michel, 139
Four Daughters (Michael Curtiz, 1938), 172
Four Mothers (William Keighley, 1941), 172
four-walling, 178
Four Wives (Michael Curtiz, 1939), 172
franchises, film: crossovers between, 226–27; decline of cinema as art form and, 2; defined, 62; forever franchise, shared universes, time, and nostalgia, 205–11, 210*fig*, 230–31; franchising as a business strategy, 161–65; nostalgia franchise, 68, 96–98, 205–11, 210*fig*, 222–23; remaking as a concept, 4–5; remaking trends in the new millennium, 224–29, 225*fig*; reproduction logics, linear time, and repetitive futures, 211–20, 215*fig*; sequels and, 188–89; series and sequels in the post-studio era, 176–85; use of term, 229–31. *See also* archive, remake as
Francois, Etienne, 139
Frankenstein (James Whale, 1931), 38
Frankenstein Meets the Wolfman (Roy William Neill, 1943), 225
Frazier, Valerie, 149–50
Freeman, Elizabeth, 212
fresh contact, 86–87
Friday the 13th (Marcus Nispel, 2009), 88
Friday the 13th (Sean S. Cunningham, 1980), 47
Friday the 13th crossovers, 226
Friedman, Rob, 193
Front Page, The (Lewis Milestone, 1931), 38, 48

Garbo, Greta, 106–10, 108*fig*, 126, 127
Gardner, Jared, 166
Gauntier, Gene, 166
gender: all-female reboots, 23, 67, 68, 73; cultural studies approach to remakes, 43; *Ghostbusters: Answer the Call* (Paul Feig, 2016), 79, 79*fig*, 80, 90–94, 96–98; *The Invasion* (Oliver Hirschbiegel, 2007), 78–79; *James Bond* franchise and cultural change, 179–81; Katrin Oltmann on pre-make and remake, 48–50; men's rights activists and alt-right backlash, 89–90, 93, 96–98; *Ocean's Eight* (Gary Ross, 2018), 79, 80; remakes and cultural attitudes, 22–23, 73–81; *A Star Is Born* remakes and regressive narratives, 148; tropes in *Jumanji: Welcome to the Jungle* (Jake Kasdan, 2017), 74–76; waning interest in female moviegoers, 174
genealogy, 86
generational canons, 89
generational communities, 89

generational identification: access, archival function of remakes, 156–58; archive as place of stored memory, 138–40; forever franchise, shared universes, time, and nostalgia, 205–11, 210*fig*; media generations, 247n60; movie generations, 23; *Planet of the Apes* franchise, 184; postmemory and, 246–47n58; remaking as a concept, 6; seriality and, 10–11; *Star Wars* franchise and, 207–11; talker remakes and, 127–28; transgenerational audiences, sequels and, 193
generationality, 86
Genette, Gérard, 35, 36
genre: country rube genre, 102–3; crossovers and spin-offs, 225–26; film series in studio era, 171–72; horror genre, evolution of, 44–48; remakes and genre choice, 43; remakes and genre theory, 40–41; serial figures in, 171–72. *See also* adventure genre; detective genre; horror genre; western genre
Ghostbusters (Ivan Reitman, 1984), 90, 93, 95
Ghostbusters II (Ivan Reitman, 1989), 90, 93, 95
Ghostbusters: Afterlife (Jason Reitman, 2021), 68, 92–97, 208
Ghostbusters: Answer the Call (Paul Feig, 2016), 2, 3, 23, 68, 73, 76–77, 79, 79*fig*, 80, 90–94, 96–98
Giddens, Anthony, 91
Gidget (Paul Wendkos, 1959), 177
Gidget Goes Hawaiian (Paul Wendkos, 1961), 177
Gidget Goes to Rome (Paul Wendkos, 1963), 177
Gill, Rosalind, 75
Gillette, Don Carle, 116–17, 122–24
Girl Spy series (Kalem), 166, 167
Girl with the Dragon Tattoo, The (David Fincher, 2011), 6
global media entertainment market, 6–7
Godfather Part II, The (Francis Ford Coppola, 1974), 61, 198–99
Godzilla (Roland Emmerich, 1998), 163
Godzilla, films about, 146
Gold Diggers (1933–1938, Warner Bros.), 170–71
GoldenEye (Martin Campbell, 1995), 180
Goldfinger (Guy Hamilton, 1964), 179
Goldman, William, 192
Goldwyn, Sam, 129, 133
Goldwyn, Samuel, Jr., 71

Go Man Go (James Wong Howe, 1954), 226
Gordon, Jeremy, 96
Grant, Barry Keith, 152
Grease 2 (Patricia Birch, 1982), 194
Great Depression: B-film production in, 167–72
"Great Replacement" theory, 90, 248–49n86
Greenberg, Harvey Roy, 38
Greenblatt, Stephen, 50
Greene, Eric, 182
Greene Murder Case, The (S. S. Van Dine, 1929), 118
Gremlins (Joe Dante, 1984), 59, 193
Gremlins 2: The New Batch (Joe Dante, 1990), 60, 193
Griffith, D. W., 166
Gunning, Tom, 101–2

Hagedorn, Roger, 193
Hall, Sheldon, 175–76, 192–93
Hall, Stuart, 42
Halloween (John Carpenter, 1978), 33, 46, 47
Hamlet (Laurence Olivier, 1948), 35–36
Hamlet (Tony Richardson, 1969), 39
Hannibal Rising (Peter Webber, 2007), 228
Hansen, Miriam, 102–3
Hardy family series (1937–1958, MGM), 171
Harlem Globetrotters, The (Phil Brown and Will Jason, 1954), 226
Harry Potter franchise, 224
Hays Code, 177
Heart of Darkness (Conrad, 1899), 145–46
Heaven Can Wait (Warren Beatty and Buck Henry, 1978), 38
Hedetoft, Ulf, 7
Hediger, Vinzenz, 113, 121
Heffernan, Harold, 117, 118
Hellman, Lillian, 226
Hell's Kitchen (Lewis Seiler, 1939), 38
Henderson, Stuart, 163–64, 167, 169, 170–71, 174, 176–77, 181, 185
Hennig-Thurau, Thorsten, 192, 195
Henry Aldrich series (1939–1944, Paramount), 172
Herbert, Daniel, 41, 76–77, 222, 230
Hess, Amanda, 80
Higgins, Scott, 185
Hills, Matt, 91
His Girl Friday (Howard Hawks, 1940), 38, 48
historical experiences: cultural objects, films as, 50–51; cultural studies approach to remakes, 41–51; remakes and the passage

historical experiences (*continued*)
of time, 147–48. *See also* archive, remake as; cultural change; timekeeping
Hitchcock, Alfred, as auteur, 32, 33, 37. *See also Psycho*
Hjort, Mette, 7
Hodgkin, Katharine, 82–83
Hoffman, Peter, 192
Holiday (Edward H. Griffith, 1930), 128
Holiday (George Cukor, 1938), 128
Hollywood: *A Star Is Born* remakes as self-assessment of Hollywood, 142–43. *See also* film industry
Hollywood (fan magazine), 119
Hollywood Remaking dataset, 15–19, 16*fig*, 17*fig*, 18*fig*, 23, 114–15, 115*fig*, 137, 138*fig*, 167–68, 168*fig*, 194, 194*fig*, 224–25, 225*fig* homage, 39
home film cultures, 154
home media technologies: access, archival function of remakes, 154–58; impact of, 60; online streaming, 19, 20, 52–3, 60, 155, 218–9; sequels, profits of, 193; VHS, 19, 20, 52–3, 155, 193. *See also* DVDs
Hop-Along Cassidy series (1935–1948, Paramount/United Artists), 169
Horn, John, 161, 163, 205
horror genre: crossover films, 225; evolution of, 44–48; prequels and, 227–28; series figures in, 171–72. *See also* specific film titles
Horton, Andrew, 41–42
Houston, Mark B., 192
Hoyt, Eric, 113
Huntingford, Cherise, 94
Hustle, The (Chris Addison, 2019), 23, 73, 76–77, 80
hypertextuality, defined, 36
hypertext, 36, 37
hypotexts, 36, 145

identity formation, extratextual memory and, 14, 84, 210. *See* cultural identity
If I Were King (Frank Lloyd, 1938), 128
If I Were King (J. Gordon Edwards, 1920), 128
Incredible Hulk, The (Louis Leterrier, 2008), 205
Independence Day: Resurgence (Roland Emmerich, 2016), 1, 3
industrial category, contextual model of remakes, 48
industrial intertextuality, 222
industry trends. *See* film industry

Infernal Affairs (Andrew Lau and Alan Mak, 2002), 6
intellectual property: franchising as a business strategy, 162–65, 229; sequels as an investment, 193–94, 194*fig*
intertextuality: classification and archival functions of remakes, 145–54; defined, 36; humor in horror remakes, 47; industrial intertextuality, 222; Katrin Oltmann on premakes and remakes, 48; managing continuity and change, 69; passage of time in forever franchises, 210; proficient viewers and film remakes, 135–36; referentiality, 40; in remakes of *Invasion of the Body Snatchers*, 54; remake strategies and, 53; serial texts, 69; titles released under Double Take: Original and Remake label, 55–56
intertextual memory, 14, 84
intertextual models, remake scholarship and, 34–41
Invasion, The (Oliver Hirschbiegel, 2007), 23, 53–54, 73, 76, 78–79, 147, 152–54, 156
Invasion of the Body Snatchers (1956, 1978, 1993, 2007), 24–25, 53–54, 54*fig*, 69, 136, 144–45, 147, 150–54, 156
Invasion of the Body Snatchers (Abel Ferrara, 1993), 53–54, 147, 152
Invasion of the Body Snatchers (Don Siegel, 1956), 53–54, 54*fig*, 147, 151
Invasion of the Body Snatchers (Philip Kaufman, 1978), 53–54, 54*fig*, 147, 151–52
Iron Man (Jon Favreaux, 2008), 205
It's a Mad, Mad, Mad, Mad World (Stanley Kramer, 1963), 175

Jackson, Peter, 157
James, Caryn, 196–97, 202
James Bond franchise, 25–26, 62, 178–85, 180*fig*
Jameson, Fredric, 95, 149
Jason vs. Freddy (Ronny Yu, 2003), 226
Jaws (Steven Spielberg, 1975), 58, 187, 191, 202
Jaws 2 (Jeannot Szwarc, 1978), 58
Jaws 3-D (Joe Alves, 1983), 58
Jaws Quadrilogy, 58
Jaws sequels, 69
Jaws: The Revenge (Joseph Sargent, 1987), 58, 202
Jesse James Meets Frankenstein's Daughter (William Beaudine, 1966), 225
Johnson, Derek, 90, 92, 161–62
Jones, Leslie, 90

Jones series (Biograph), 166, 167
Jumanji (Joe Johnston, 1995), 73–78, 74*fig*
Jumanji: Welcome to the Jungle (Jake Kasdan, 2017), 23, 73–78, 74*fig*
Jurassic World (Colin Trevorrow, 2015), 96–98, 208, 222–23

Kajganich, David, 156
Kann, Red, 118
Karate Kid, The (Harald Zwart, 2010), 88
Karate Kid Part II, The (John Avildsen, 1986), 192, 201
Karate Kid Part III, The (John Avildsen, 1989), 201
Kaufman, Amy, 73
Kehr, Dave, 195–96
Kelleter, Frank, 11–12, 13, 33, 40, 51–52, 53, 59, 69, 103, 204, 230
Kennedy, Kathleen, 219
Kilday, Gregg, 197
King Kong (1933, 1976, 2005, 2017), 24–25, 136, 144–45; classification and archival functions of remakes, 145–50
King Kong (Peter Jackson, 2005), 144–50, 156–57
Klein, Amanda Ann, 9
Kleinman, Jack, 111–12
Klinger, Barbara, 53, 56, 154
Kong: Skull Island (Jordan Vogt-Roberts, 2017), 145–46
Koos, Leonard R., 42–43
Kristeva, Julia, 35
Krutnik, Frank, 170

Laemmle, Carl Jr., 113–14
La femme Nikita (Luc Besson, 1990), 38
Landgraf, John, 218
Landsberg, Alison, 83
La sortie des usines (1895), 101
Last Picture Show, The (Peter Bogdanovich, 1971), 14
legacyquel, 62, 95–96, 211, 231
Legendary Pictures, 146
Leitch, Thomas, 32, 35, 37, 44, 87; remake taxonomy of, 38–39
Lethal Weapon (Richard Donner, 1987), 202
Lethal Weapon 2 (Richard Donner, 1989), 192, 203
Lethal Weapon 2, 3, and *4* (Richard Donner, 1989, 1992, 1998), 202
LGBTQ+ community: men's rights activists and alt-right backlash, 89–90, 93, 96–98; queer sexuality in film, 50; tropes in

Jumanji: Welcome to the Jungle (Jake Kasdan, 2017), 74–76
Little Three studios, 168
Lord of the Rings, The (Peter Jackson), 187–88
Lord of the Rings franchise, 224
Lost World, The (Harry O. Hoyt, 1925), 111
Love (Edmund Goulding, 1927), 126
Lucas, George, 185

Ma and Pa Kettle series (Universal), 173
Maisie (1939–1947, MGM), 172
Mala Noche (1985), 50
Mannheim, Karl, 85, 86
Man som hatar kvinnor (Michael Nyqvist, 2009), 6
Mark of Zorro, The (Fred Niblo, 1920), 172
Martin, Martin, 105
Marvel Cinematic Universe (MCU), 189, 205–8
Maslin, Janet, 72
May, Elaine Tyler, 174
Mayer, Ruth, 171
Mayor of Hell, The (Archie Mayo, 1933), 38
Maytime (Louis Gasnier, 1923), 128
Maytime (Robert Z. Leonard, 1937), 128
McCarthy, Todd, 205
McDougal, Stuart, 41–42
meaning-making process: crossovers, spin-offs, and prequels, effects of, 227–29; intertextually proficient viewers and remakes, 135–36; remaking, scholarship on, 31–34
media generations, defined, 247n60. *See* movie generations
mediated memories, 83
Memento (Christopher Nolan, 2014), 14
memory: archives, purposes of, 138–40; extra-textual memory, 14, 84, 210; forever franchise, shared universes, time, and nostalgia, 205–11, 210*fig*; intertextual memory, 14, 84; mediated memory, 83; movie generations, 81–98; of narrative events and recurring characters, 222; postmemory, 246–47n58; prosthetic memories, 83; technologies of memory, 82–83; usable past, 66–67. *See also* archive, remake as; cultural memory
memory-making fictions, 14
merchandise, revenue from, 178, 185; brands, establishment of, 190; sequels and, 193
metatextuality, defined, 36
MeToo movement, 180–81, 214

INDEX

MGM Studio: B-film series production model, 168–72; Greta Garbo and talker remakes, 106–10, 108*fig*; talker remakes, recycling strategies to meet demand, 112–16, 115*fig*
Miami Vice (Michael Mann, 2006), 88
Miller, Llewellyn, 119
Millner, Michael, 149
Mittell, Jason, 41, 58, 59
mnemonic communities, 65, 84–85
Modern Screen (fan magazine), 11–12, 104, 111, 125–27, 126*fig*, 127, 128–29
modes of transformation, 38
Monaco, Paul, 94
MonsterVerse, 146, 189
More American Graffiti (Bill L. Norton, 1979), 194
Motion Picture Association of America: Production Code, 32; rating system, 177
Motion Picture Daily, 118
Motion Picture Herald, 120
Motion Picture News, 104, 105, 107, 108*fig*, 113, 115
movie generations, 23, 67–68; access, archival function of remakes, 156–58; defined, 84–85; media generations, 247n60; memory, nostalgia, and generational identities, 81–98; *Planet of the Apes* franchise and, 184; *Star Wars* franchise and, 207–11; transgenerational audiences, sequels and, 193
musical genre, blockbusters and, 175–76
Musser, Charles, 102
Myers, Effie, 112
My Own Private Idaho (1991), 50

Naremore, James, 35, 45, 47
narrative continuity: cultural continuity and, 69, 221–22; film industry reliance on, 164, 221–22; film series in the studio era, 165–72, 168*fig*; importance of, 61–62, 221–22; *James Bond* franchise, 178–81; *Planet of the Apes* franchise, 181–85; remaking, timeliness, and the politics of representation, 68–81; reproduction logics, linear time, and repetitive futures, 211–20, 215*fig*; sequels and, 187, 188–89, 199, 201–3; serial figures and, 171; series with continuity, 171–72; in *Star Wars* franchise, 207–11; worldbuilding in crossovers and spin-offs, 226–27
national identity formation, extratextual memory and, 14, 84, 210

Neale, Steve, 46
Neighbors (Nicholas Stoller, 2014), 64–65, 65*fig*
neo-noir, 48
Nevada Smith (Henry Hathaway, 1966), 226
New Line Cinema, 192
New Movie Magazine (fan magazine), 111–12, 155
New Queer Cinema, 50
Nightmare on Elm Street, A (Wes Craven, 1984), 46, 47
Nightmare on Elm Street crossovers, 226
Nightmare on Elm Street sequels (New Line Cinema), 192
Night of Mystery (E. A. Dupont, 1937), 118
Night of the Living Dead (George A. Romero, 1968), 46
non-remake, 38
Nora, Pierre, 139
nostalgia: movie generations, 81–98; nostalgia-driven reboots, 222–23; *Planet of the Apes* franchise, 184; postmodern waning of historicity, 149; by proxy, 209; sequels, appeal of, 198–200; *Star Wars* franchise and, 207–11
nostalgia franchise, 68, 96–98, 205–11, 210*fig*, 222–23
No Time to Die (Cary Joji Fukunaga, 2021), 178
Novarro, Ramon, 109–11, 110*fig*
Nugent, Frank S., 71–72

Ocean's Eight (Gary Ross, 2018), 23, 73, 76–77, 79–80
Oklahoma! (Fred Zinneman, 1955), 175
Olcott, Sidney, 166
Oltmann, Katrin, 48–50
"On Creating a Usable Past" (Brooks, 1918), 66
One Way Passage (Tay Garnett, 1932), 118–19
ongoing narratives, 95
online streaming platforms, 52–53, 60; access, archival function of remakes, 154–58
open-endedness, sequels and, 199–200
original/remake binary, 48–50
Oz the Great and Powerful (Sam Raimi, 2013), 228

package-unit system, 173
Palmer, R. Barton, 9
Paramount Decree, 173
Paramount Studios: B-film series production model, 168–72; talker remakes, recycling strategies to meet demand, 112–16, 115*fig*

"paranoid" horror films (1960-present), 46
paratexts, 11–12; access, archival function of remakes, 154–58; DVD bonus features as, 156–58; entryway paratexts, 135
paratextuality, defined, 36
Parchesky, Jennifer, 131
Parikka, Jussi, 139
Perkins, Anthony, 33
Phantom of the Opera, The (Rupert Julian, 1925), 121
Photoplay (fan magazine), 11–12, 104, 109, 111, 118–19, 120, 128, 129
Pinedo, Isabel, 46
Planet of the Apes (Franklin J. Schaffner, 1968), 178, 224
Planet of the Apes (Tim Burton, 2001), 26, 57, 183, 224
Planet of the Apes franchise, 25–26, 57, 61, 181–85
Play It Again, Sam: Retakes on Remakes (Horton and McDougal, 1998), 41–42
Point of No Return (John Badham, 1933), 38
politics of representation: 23, 25, 67; *James Bond* franchise in MeToo movement, 180–81; managing continuity and change, 68–81; men's rights activists and alt-right backlash, 89–94, 96–98; *Planet of the Apes* franchise and, 184; remakes and regressive narratives, 148–49; remakes as a means to process cultural change, 70–81; reproductive futurism, 213–14; waning interest in female moviegoers, 174; visibility and, 77, 79, 81
popular culture, defined, 236n31
popular culture texts, 2
Popular Seriality Research Unit (PSRU), 236n31
pornographic films (Sexploitation), 177–78
posters, 11–12
Postman Always Rings Twice, The (Bob Rafelson, 1981), 39, 48
Postman Always Rings Twice, The (Tay Garnett, 1946), 39
postmemory, 246–47n58
postmodern films: cultural studies on, 41–42; horror genre, evolution of, 46–48; nostalgia and waning of historicity, 149–50; repetition and intertextual references in, 60; self-awareness of, 203–4
postwar United States, 52, 137, 151, 161–2, 173–4
premake, 48–50
preposterous reading of versions, 49

prequels: category definitions and, 61; defined, 62, 227; Hollywood historical production trends, 15–20, 16*fig*, 17*fig*, 18*fig*, 225*fig*; *Planet of the Apes* franchise, 183–84; reboot, use of term, 27; remaking as a concept, 4–5, 221–23; remaking trends in the new millennium, 224–29, 225*fig*; timekeeping and, 227–29; use of term, 229–31
press kits, 11–12
Price, Frank, 191
Prisoner of Zenda (Johns Cromwell, 1937), 128
Prisoner of Zenda (Rex Ingram, 1922), 128
Prisoner of Zenda, The (Rex Ingram, 1922), 110
Problem of Generations, The (Mannheim, 1928), 85
processes of classification, 145
Proctor, William, 90–91, 222, 230
Production Code, Motion Picture Association of America, 32
progressivism. *See* politics of representation
Prometheus (Ridley Scott, 2012), 188, 226, 230
promotional materials, 11–12
prosthetic memories, 83
Psycho (Alfred Hitchcock, 1960), 21, 43, 58–59, 224; remakes of, scholarship on, 31–33. *See also Bates Motel* (A&E, 2013–2017)
Psycho (Gus Van Sant, 1998), 21, 26, 31–33, 35–36, 45*fig*; critical reception of, 36–37, 224; cultural studies approach to, 43–48, 45*fig*; queer sexuality in, 50; remake taxonomy for, 39–41
Psycho Collection I–IV, 58–59
Psycho II (Richard Franklin, 1983), 58–59
Psycho III (Anthony Perkins, 1986), 58–59
Psycho IV: The Beginning (Mick Garris, 1990), 58–59, 61
publicity campaigns, 191
Pulp Fiction (Quentin Tarantino, 1993), 14
Purdum, Todd S., 142

Quantum of Solace (Mark Foster, 2008), 178
Quaresima, Leonardo, 51, 53
queer sexuality, 50

race: Black action films (Blaxploitation), 177; colorblindness, 77–78; *King Kong* films, racial undertones in, 146, 150; men's rights activists and alt-right backlash, 89–90, 93, 96–98; remakes, managing continuity and social change, 73–81;

race (*continued*)
    tropes in *Jumanji: Welcome to the Jungle* (Jake Kasdan, 2017), 74–76
Radstone, Susannah, 82–83
Raiders of the Lost Ark (Steven Spielberg, 1981), 14
Rangwala, Shama, 216, 218
rating systems, 177
readaptation, 39
reboots, 26–27; all-female reboots, 23, 67, 68, 73; defined, 62; as a mode of timekeeping, 70; rebooting the past, 222–31, 225*fig*; soft reboot, 230–31; use of term, 27, 222–23, 229–31. *See also* archive, remake as
reciprocity between film versions, 55–56
recontextualization, serial texts and, 69
regime of continuation, 69
Reitman, Ivan, 93
Reitman, Jason, 92–93
Remake | Premake: Hollywood's romantische Komödien und ihre Gender-Diskurse, 1930–1960 (Oltmann, 2008), 48–50
remakes: B-films repurposed for television, 174; critical category, contextual model of remakes, 48; as a cultural category, 41; defined, 62; DVD box sets, 55–60, 55*tab*; evolution of, 51–63; fan magazines introduction of term, 128; franchises, types of, 61–63; Hannah Ewens on, 1, 2, 4; Justin Chang on, 1–2, 4; managing continuity and change, 68–81; original/remake binary, 48–50; production data by year, 15–20, 16*fig*, 17*fig*, 18*fig*, 114–16, 115*fig*, 137–38, 138*fig*, 167–68, 168*fig*, 193–94, 194*fig*, 224–25, 225*fig*; reboot, use of term, 27, 62; remaking as a concept, 4–5, 221–23; titles released under Double Take: Original and Remake label, 55–56, 55*tab*; of foreign films, 5–6; trends in the new millennium, 224–29, 225*fig*; use of term, 31, 34–35, 229–31 (*See also* remake scholarship). *See also* archive, remake as
remake scholarship, 21–22, 31–34; on appeal of sequels, 198–200; complexification and serialization, 51–63; cultural studies approach, 41–51; intertextual models and taxonomies, 34–41; original/remake binary, 48–50
remaking: as a commercial practice, 9; as a concept, 4–5; diachronic remaking, 6; seriality and, 9–14; synchronic remaking, 6

repetition: complexification and serialization, 51–63; film industry reliance on, 164; history of early film, 102, 105; sequels, appeal of, 196–200; in sequels, 47–48
reproductive futurism, 211, 213–14
requels, 62, 231
retitling of silent films, 116–24
retrospective serialization, 53
Return of the Fly, The (Edward Bernds, 1959), 58
Ring, The (2002, Gore Verbinsky), 6
Ringu (Hideo Nakata, 1998), 6
Rise of the Planet of the Apes (Rupert Wyatt, 2011), 57, 183, 228
RKO Studios: B-film series production model, 168–72; talker remakes, recycling strategies to meet demand, 112–16, 115*fig*
roadshow mode of exhibition, 175–76
Robin Hood (Allan Dwan, 1923), 128
Robin Hood (Michael Curtiz, 1938), 128
Robin Hood: Prince of Thieves (Kevin Reynolds, 1991), 59
RoboCop (Jose Padilha, 2014), 88
Rocky (John Avildsen, 1976), 193
Rocky II (Sylvester Stallone, 1979), 193
Rocky III (Sylvester Stallone, 1982), 192
Rogers, Adam, 206–7
Rogue One (Gareth Edward, 2016), 218
Romano, Aja, 148
Rose-Marie (Lucien Hubbard, 1928), 127
Rose-Marie (W. S. Van Dyke, 1936), 127
Rosenbaum, Jonathan, 37
Rosenberg, Alyssa, 181
Roundhouse, Ruby, 75–76
ruined childhood trope, 68, 88, 89–93
run-zone-clearance system, 168–69

Sally, Irene and Mary (Edmund Goulding, 1925), 128
Sally, Irene and Mary (William A. Seiter, 1938), 128
Santas, Constantine, 37
saturation booking, 178
Sausage Machine, The (1897), 101
Saving Private Ryan (Steven Spielberg, 1998), 14
Scaramouche (Rex Ingram, 1924), 110
Scheuer, Philip, 106, 120
scholarship. *See* remake scholarship
Schulze, Hagen, 139
Scott, Ridley, 188, 218
Scream (Wes Craven, 1996), 33, 47

Screenland (fan magazine), 104, 105, 109, 110–11, 110*fig*, 129, 130*fig*
Sebald, W. G., 85
second-order seriality, 13, 69, 164–65, 221
"secure" horror films (1931-1960), 46
self-historicization, 11, 103–4, 133; Hollywood takes "just one more look," *A Star Is Born*, 140–43
self-referential cinematic moments, 203–4
Selma (Ava DuVernay, 2014), 14
sequels, 26; *Blade Runner 2049* (Denis Villeneuve, 2017), 186–90; directors attitudes about, 186–88; as distinct from series, 164–65; Hollywood historical production trends, 15–20, 16*fig*, 17*fig*, 18*fig*; horror genre, evolution of, 47; legacyquel, 95–96, 211; managing continuity and change, 68–81; as a mode of timekeeping, 70; monetary value of, 191–93; original storytelling and, 186–90; *Planet of the Apes*, continuity in, 181–85; in the post-studio era, 176–85; as precursor to franchise films, 164; production of in 1970s and 1980s, 190–95, 194*fig*; reboot, use of term, 27; remaking as a concept, 4–5, 221–23; remaking trends in the new millennium, 224–29, 225*fig*; reproduction logics, linear time, and repetitive futures, 211–20, 215*fig*; self-reflexive sequels, 200–205, 203*fig*; sequelitis, 26, 187, 189, 196–200, 205; serial logic of one-upmanship, 193–94; uncanny success of formulaic fare, 195–200; use of term, 229–31. *See also* archive, remake as
serial aesthetic, 199
serial figure, 97, 171, 207, 222; *James Bond* series, 178–85
serial texts, 69
serials. *See* film serials.
series. *See* film series.
series film proper, 171
series with continuity, 171
sexuality: audience expectations and, 75, 81; in *Psycho* (Gus Van Sant, 1998), 32, 50; reproductive futurism, 213–14, 217; tropes in *Jumanji: Welcome to the Jungle* (Jake Kasdan, 2017), 74–76, 77
Shaft (Gordon Parks, 1971), 177
Sheik, The (George Melford, 1921), 172
Sheldon, Rebekah, 213–14
Sherwood, Robert E., 114
silent era films, 23, 24; film series in the studio era, 165, 166; talker remakes, fan magazine promotion of, 24, 104, 107–12, 110*fig*, 125–34, 126*fig*, 130*fig*; talker remakes, titles, audience memory, and timing, 116–24. *See also* film serials
Singer, Matt, 211
Singin' in the Rain (Stanley Donen and Gene Kelly, 1952), 14
Skyfall (Sam Mendes, 2012), 178
Smith, Frederick James, 155
Smith, Iain Robert, 7–8
soft reboot, 230–31
Solo: A Star Wars Story (Ron Howard, 2018), 218, 227
Son of Dracula (Robert Siodmak, 1943), 172
Son of Frankenstein (Rowland V. Lee, 1939), 172
Son of the Sheik, The (George Fitzmaurice, 1926), 172
sound, transition to, 104–12, 125–34
Sound of Music, The (Robert Wise, 1965), 175, 176
South Pacific (Joshua Logan, 1958), 175
Spectre (Sam Mendes, 2015), 178
Speed (Jan de Bont, 1994), 163
Speed 2: Speed Control (Jan de Bont, 1997)
Spider Man films, 188, 224
Spielberg, Steven, 187
spin-offs: defined, 62; Hollywood historical production trends, 15–20, 16*fig*, 17*fig*, 18*fig*; remaking as a concept, 4–5, 221–23; remaking trends in the new millennium, 224–29, 225*fig*; use of term, 229–31
Spoorloos (George Sluizer, 1988), 6
Squaw Man, The (Cecil B. DeMille, 1912), 155
Squaw Man, The (Cecil B. DeMille, 1918), 172
Squaw Man, The (Cecil B. DeMille, 1931), 155, 172
Squaw Man's Son, The (E. J. Le Saint, 1917), 172
Staiger, Janet, 173
Star! (Robert Wise, 1968), 176
Star Is Born, A (1932, 1937, 1954, 1976, 2019), 24–25, 38, 136, 140–42, 142*fig*, 144, 148, 155–56
Star Is Born, A (Bradley Cooper, 2018), 140–43, 142*fig*, 148, 155–56
Star Is Born, A (William A. Wellman, 1937), 141
Star Trek (J. J. Abrams, 2009), 230
Star Wars (George Lucas, 1977), 14
Star Wars: Episode IV—A New Hope (George Lucas, 1977), 206

Star Wars: Episode VII—The Force Awakens (J. J. Abrams, 2015), 206, 209–11, 210*fig*
Star Wars: Episode VI—Return of the Jedi (Richard Marquand, 1983), 206
Star Wars franchise, 189, 206–11, 210*fig*, 230; angry fan response to prequel trilogy (1999-2005), 89; Disney reboot of, 26; Disney television spin-off series, 219; flexible storytelling in, 61–62; multiracial, multiethnic, and multinational casts, 73
Star Wars: The Force Awakens (J. J. Abrams, 2015), 62, 76–77
Stella (John Erman, 1990), 23, 38, 71–72, 136
Stella Dallas (Henry King, 1925), 71–72, 128, 136
Stella Dallas (King Vidor, 1937), 24, 71–72, 128, 129–33, 130*fig*, 136
storytelling: anecdotal storytelling, 165–66; cultural memory and, 83–84; film series in the studio era, 165–72, 168*fig*; flexible storytelling, *Star Wars* franchise and, 61–62; forever franchises and generational renewal, 211; in *James Bond* series, 178–85; narrative continuity, importance of, 61–62; repetition, film industry reliance on, 164; seriality and, 10, 69–70; talker remakes, recycling strategies to meet demand, 113; technological progress and, 23–25; usable cinematic past, 67–68; worldbuilding in crossovers and spin-offs, 226–27
Stranger Things (2016–), 93, 94–96
Student Prince, The (Ernst Lubitsch, 1928), 110
studio-owned theater chains, 169, 173
studio system, Hollywood, 19, 25; B-film series production model, 168–72, 168*fig*; Big Five studios, 168; echoes in modern franchise production, 184–85; Little Three studios, 168
Sturken, Marita, 6, 82
Super Fly (Gordon Parks, 1972), 177
Supergirl (Jeannot Szwarc, 1984), 225
Superman series (Columbia, 1948), 165
Supreme Court: *Paramount Decree*, 173
Sweet Bird of Youth (Nicholas Roeg, 1989), 38
Sweet Bird of Youth (Richard Brooks, 1962), 38
synchronic remaking, 6
synergy, 190

A Tale of Two Cities (1917), 127
talker remakes, 103–6; fan magazine promotion of, 24, 104, 107–12, 110*fig*, 125–34, 126*fig*, 130*fig*; recycling strategies to meet demand, 112–16, 115*fig*; stars and fans, 106–12, 108*fig*, 110*fig*; titles, audience memory, and timing, 116–24
Talking Screen (fan magazine), 107–9
Tarzan series (1932–1942, MGM), 170, 171, 172
taxonomies: Harvey Roy Greenberg, 38; Michael B. Druxman, 37–38; remake scholarship and, 34–41; Robert Eberwein, 37–38; Thomas Leitch, 38–39
technology: access, archival function of remakes, 154–58; attitudes toward old movie, evolution of, 52–53; blockbuster films, 175–76; comparative mode of viewing, 56; DVD bonus content about, 156–57; history of remakes, overview, 101–4; *Planet of the Apes* franchise and, 184; *Psycho* (Gus Van Sant, 1998) remake and evolution of horror genre, 44–48; remakes as a mode of timekeeping, 70, 136–37; talkies, from silent past to sound film present, 124–34, 126*fig*, 130*fig*; technological progress, as seen in remakes, 11, 23–25, 136–37; technologies of memory, 82–83; television, impact on film industry, 173–76. *See also* archive, remake as
teen movie cycle, 177
television, 60; big picture approach in post-studio era, 173–76; changing audience expectations and, 196–97; film advertising on, 178; film remakes of television series, 88; forever franchise programming on, 218; *Planet of the Apes* series on, 183; sequels, profits of, 193
temporality. *See* timekeeping
Ten Commandments, The (Cecil B. DeMille, 1923), 121
Ten Commandments, The (Cecil B. DeMille, 1956), 175
Terminator: Genisys (Alan Taylor, 2015), 62, 96–98, 208, 222–23
Texas Chainsaw Massacre, The (Tobe Hooper, 1974), 46
Texas Chainsaw Massacre: The Beginning (Jonathan Liebesman, 2006), 227–28
textual category, contextual model of remakes, 48
theaters: big picture approach in post-studio era, 174–76; four-walling, 178; *Paramount Decree*, antitrust litigation, 173; saturation booking, 178, 191; studio era block-booking, 168–69; studio-owned, 169, 173

thematic aboutness, 7
Thing, The (John Carpenter, 1982), 228
Thing, The (Matthijs van Heijningen Jr., 2011), 228
Thin Man series (1934–1947, MGM), 170, 171, 172, 174
Thornbey, Clarence, 120
Three Little Foxes (William Wyler, 1941), 226
Three Men and a Baby (Leonard Nimoy, 1987), 6
Three Mesquiteers, The series (1936–1942, Republic), 169
Three Musketeers, The (Fred Niblo, 1921), 127
Three Musketeers, The (Rowland V. Lee, 1935), 127
Thunderball (Terence Young, 1965), 180
'Til We Meet Again (Edmund Goulding, 1949), 119
timekeeping: chrononormativity, 212; cultural studies approach to remakes, 41–51; forever franchise, shared universes, time, and nostalgia, 205–11, 210*fig*; home viewing and the coexistence of multiple versions, 52–53; James Bond series, 179; in Marvel Cinematic Universe (MCU), 207–8; memory, nostalgia, and generational identities, 81–98; premake-remake model, Oltmann, 49–50; prequels and, 227–29; remakes as a mode of timekeeping, 70, 136–37, 147–48; remaking as a concept, 6; remaking as a time machine, 84–85; reproduction logics, linear time, and repetitive futures, 211–20, 215*fig*; second-order seriality, 13; in *Star Wars* franchise, 207–11; usable past, 66–67; worldbuilding in crossovers and spin-offs, 226–27. *See also* archive, remake as
timeliness, managing continuity and change, 68–81
titles of remakes: talker remakes, audience memory, and timing, 116–24
Tompkins, Joe, 27
Tom Sawyer (Norman Taurog, 1938), 128
Tom Sawyer (William D. Taylor, 1917), 128
trade papers, 11–12; talker remakes and, 104, 107–12, 110*fig*, 125–34, 126*fig*, 130*fig*. *See also* specific publication names
trailers, 11–12
transformative process, 36; cultural identity and, 42; remake taxonomies and, 38
transgenerational audiences, 193
transnational remakes, remaking as a concept, 5–8

transtextuality, defined, 36
Trois hommes et un couffin (Coline Serreau, 1985), 6
true remake, 39
Tudor, Andrew, 46, 47
20th Century Fox Studios: B-film series production model, 168–72; talker remakes, recycling strategies to meet demand, 112–16, 115*fig*
21 Jump Street (Phil Lord and Chris Miller, 2012), 88
Two Jakes, The (Jack Nicholson, 1990), 60

unacknowledged disguised remake, 38
Uncle Josh at the Moving Picture Show (Edwin S. Porter, 1902), 102, 133, 135
United Artists Studio: B-film series production model, 168–72
Universal Studio: B-film series production model, 168–72; horror movies, 225
update (remake taxonomies), 39
usable past, 26, 66–67, 72, 98, 230–31

van Dijck, José, 83
Vanishing, The (George Sluizer, 1993), 6
Variety, 11–12, 104, 107, 116, 118, 121, 122, 163, 205
Verevis, Constantine, 7–8, 40–41, 48, 55, 183, 230
VHS tapes, 52–53; access, archival function of remakes, 154–58
viewing, comparative mode of, 56
Villeneuve, Denis, 186–90
violent vigilante films, 177
Vischer, Peter, 107
Vitascope, 101
Volga Boatman, The (Cecil B. De Mille, 1926), 111

Walking Tall (Phil Karlson, 1973), 177
War for the Planet of the Apes (Matt Reeves, 2017), 57, 183
Warner Bros. Studio, 193; B-film series production model, 168–72; talker remakes, recycling strategies to meet demand, 112–16, 115*fig*
Warner Brothers, 105
War of the Worlds (George Pal, 1953), 56
War of the Worlds (Steven Spielberg, 2005), 56
Washington Post, 181
Weigel, Sigrid, 86
Weinstein, Harvey, 180, 214
Wes Craven's New Nightmare (1994), 47

western genre: crossovers with horror genre, 225; prequels, 226; series figures in, 171–72; in studio era, 169; television productions, 174. *See also* specific film titles

West Side Story (Robert Wise/Jerome Robbins, 1961), 175

What Happened to Mary (Edison, 1912), 165

What Price Hollywood? (George Cukor, 1932), 141, 156

White Christmas (Michael Curtiz, 1954), 48

white nationalism, 89–90, 96–98, 248–49n86

white nostalgia, 96–97

"Why Hollywood's Obsession with Remakes and Sequels Needs to Die," 1

William Shakespeare's Romeo + Juliet (Baz Luhrmann, 1996), 39

Wizard of Oz, The (Victor Fleming, 1939), 228

women: all-female reboots, 23, 67, 68, 73; *Blade Runner 2049* and cultural change, 214; *Ghostbusters: Answer the Call* (Paul Feig, 2016), 79, 79*fig*, 80, 90–94, 96–98; *The Invasion* (Oliver Hirschbiegel, 2007), 78–79; *James Bond* franchise and cultural change, 179–81; men's rights activists and alt-right backlash, 89–90, 93, 96–98; *Ocean's Eight* (Gary Ross, 2018), 79, 80; *A Star Is Born* remakes and regressive narratives, 148; tropes in *Jumanji: Welcome to the Jungle* (Jake Kasdan, 2017), 74–76; waning interest in female moviegoers, 174

World War I, 83, 85–86

World War II, 14, 228

Wood, Sam, 122

work-bound aesthetic, 199

worldbuilding, crossovers and spin-offs, 226–27

X-Men films, 188, 224

Yiannopoulos, Milo, 90

Young Frankenstein (Mel Brooks, 1974), 38

Zanuck, Richard D., 202

Zeitchik, Steven, 73

zeitgeist, 70, 137, 143

Zeitheimat (home in time), 85

Founded in 1893,
UNIVERSITY OF CALIFORNIA PRESS
publishes bold, progressive books and journals
on topics in the arts, humanities, social sciences,
and natural sciences—with a focus on social
justice issues—that inspire thought and action
among readers worldwide.

The UC PRESS FOUNDATION
raises funds to uphold the press's vital role
as an independent, nonprofit publisher, and
receives philanthropic support from a wide
range of individuals and institutions—and from
committed readers like you. To learn more, visit
ucpress.edu/supportus.

www.ingramcontent.com/pod-product-compliance
Lightning Source LLC
Chambersburg PA
CBHW021338230426
43666CB00006B/328